THE CULTURAL
APPROACH TO HISTORY

THE CULTURAL APPROACH TO HISTORY

Edited for the

American Historical Association

By CAROLINE F. WARE

KENNIKAT PRESS, INC./PORT WASHINGTON, N. Y.

THE CULTURAL APPROACH TO HISTORY

This edition published by Kennikat Press by
arrangement with Columbia University Press

Library of Congress Catalog Card No: 64-24473

Manufactured in the United States of America

Indexed in ESSAY AND GENERAL LITERATURE INDEX
under main entry "American Historical Association"

CONTENTS

Introduction, by CAROLINE F. WARE 3

PART ONE: TECHNIQUES OF CULTURAL ANALYSIS

Introductory Note 19

Society as Viewed by the Anthropologist, by GEOFFREY GORER 20

Clio and Psyche: Some Interrelations of Psychology and History, by GOODWIN WATSON 34

Psychology and the Interpretation of Historical Events, by FRANZ ALEXANDER 48

PART TWO: CULTURAL GROUPS

Introductory Note 61

Cultural Groups in the United States, by CAROLINE F. WARE 62

Approaches to the Study of Nationality Groups in the United States 74

The Cultural "Syncretism" of Nationality Groups, by MAURICE R. DAVIE 74

Cultural Contribution versus Cultural Assimilation, by RAY ALLEN BILLINGTON 78

The Transitional Character of Nationality Group Culture, by CARLTON C. QUALEY 82

European Backgrounds and American Rivalries, by OSCAR OSBURN WINTHER 84

Summary of the Discussion, by JOSEPH S. ROUCEK, CAROLINE F. WARE, and M. W. ROYSE 86

PART THREE: CULTURAL INSTITUTIONS

Introductory Note 93

CONTENTS

The Peasant Family: The Zadruga, or Communal Joint-Family in the Balkans, and Its Recent Evolution, by PHILIP E. MOSELY 95

The Peasant Family: The Chinese Large-Family, Its Role and Recent Trends, by KNIGHT BIGGERSTAFF 109

The Peasant Household under the Mir and the Kolkhoz in Modern Russian History, by LAZAR VOLIN 125

The Emergence of the First Industrial City: Manchester, 1780–1850, by LEON S. MARSHALL 140

The Corporation: An Institutional Factor in Modern History, by STEPHEN RAUSHENBUSH 162

The Social History of the Corporation in the United States, by THOMAS C. COCHRAN 168

The German Army of the Second Reich as a Cultural Institution, by ALFRED VAGTS 182

PART FOUR: THE CULTURAL ROLE OF IDEAS

Introductory Note 199

Medieval Intellectual History: Ecclesiastical or Secular? by GRAY C. BOYCE 202

The Historical Position of Liberalism, by GEORGE H. SABINE 212

PART FIVE: THE DYNAMICS OF CULTURAL CHANGE

Introductory Note 225

The Industrial City: Center of Cultural Change, by RALPH E. TURNER 228

The Modernization of China and Japan: A Comparative Study in Cultural Conflict, by HU SHIH 243

The Flowering of New England, edited by RALPH H. GABRIEL 252

Economic Ferment, by EDWARD C. KIRKLAND 252

Basic Cultural Unity, by ARTHUR E. BESTOR 254

CONTENTS

The Social and Economic Characteristics of the Leaders, by MERLE CURTI 259

Boston's Puritan Heritage and Its "Flowering" in Literature and Theology, by RICHARD H. SHRYOCK 264

Connecticut's "Flowering" in Science and Reform, by C. R. KELLER 267

PART SIX: SOURCES AND MATERIALS FOR THE STUDY OF CULTURAL HISTORY

Introductory Note 273

The Value of Local History, by CONSTANCE McLAUGHLIN GREEN 275

The Use of Population Data 287

The Historical Context of Population Study, by FRANK LORIMER 287

Medieval Demography, by JOSIAH C. RUSSELL 291

The New South, 1880–1936: A Study in Population Movements, by RUPERT B. VANCE 294

Local Historical Studies and Population Problems, by JAMES C. MALIN 300

Folklore as a Neglected Source of Social History, by B. A. BOTKIN 308

Folk Music as a Source of Social History, by CHARLES SEEGER 316

Documentary Photographs, by ROY E. STRYKER and PAUL H. JOHNSTONE 324
With nine photographs

Dialect Areas, Settlement Areas, and Culture Areas in the United States, by HANS KURATH 331
With eight charts

Latin Literature as a Source for the Study of Medieval Culture, by CORNELIA C. COULTER 346

Index 353

PREFACE

FIRST credit for this volume belongs to Eugene N. Anderson, who, as chairman of the Program Committee for the American Historical Association meetings in December, 1939, was mainly responsible for planning the sessions at which the papers constituting this volume were presented. In addition to Mr. Anderson, the following members of the Program Committee and others outside of the Committee were responsible for arranging the particular sessions at which the papers here included were given: Merle Curti, Psychology and History; Carlton C. Qualey, Nationality Groups in the United States; Philip E. Mosely, The Peasant Family; Ralph E. Turner, The Industrial City; Paul Lewinson, The Corporation—an Institutional Factor in Modern History; Wayne Grover, Land Power and Sea Power; Walter F. Dorn, Liberalism; Edgar N. Johnson, Medieval Culture, Ecclesiastical or Secular?; Viola F. Barnes and Ralph H. Gabriel, How Explain the "Flowering of New England"?; Louis C. Hunter, Local History, and Population Studies and History; Ben A. Botkin, Some Neglected Sources of Social History; Cyrus H. Peake, The Modernization of China and Japan. In the editing of the volume, Ralph E. Turner furnished editorial advice and assistance and Miriam Camp assumed responsibility for checking.

C. F. W.

Washington, D.C.
September, 1940

INTRODUCTION

selves as "economic" or "social" historians. It first took the form, conspicuously represented by Charles A. Beard's *Economic Interpretation of the Constitution,* of insistence that the political "facts" habitually included within the historian's purview told only part of the story and were themselves not to be fully understood in the absence of certain economic "facts." The addition of economic data was only a beginning. "Social" histories, and histories of "everyday life," followed close on the heels of "economic" histories. All sorts of data relating to manners and customs, to artists, inventions, and even women's fashions began to compete with dates of battles and figures on shipping tonnage for a place in historical books. The first answer to the question "Which facts?" was an extensive answer. It led the historian into highways and byways, where he dug out material on private and public lives, on issues and places great and small; but it provided no basis for attaching particular significance to one or another body of data.

The wider the range of facts covered, however, the more pressing the problem of selection and integration. Which facts should be used? How should those facts be interrelated and interpreted? What conceptual tools could the historian bring to the search for and arrangement of his data? However much he might aim to let the facts speak for themselves, they remained eloquently silent until some terms in which to express them were employed.

Earlier historians, such as Gibbon and Macaulay, had faced no difficulty here. They had brought to their task the assumptions and prejudices of the educated, politically minded Englishmen of their respective times. Their categories of "good things" and "bad things" were frankly part of their social outlook; the terms of controversy were set by the climate of opinion of their worlds.

The "scientific" historians acknowledged no such basis of selection and interpretation, but the terms in which they shaped their questions and presented their data were still largely determined by their own social outlook. They were members of the academic fraternity, which implied a certain position in society, certain social experience, social values, and contacts with certain social groups. As professionals, they enjoyed a measure of prestige and security, they moved across class lines with an ease denied to other social groups; they associated, directly or indirectly, with those who wielded political power, but themselves rarely shouldered the responsibilities of active political life; they trained the elite that was to exercise power in the future. This position provided the windows through which they looked on the past as well as on the present. The intellectual concepts with which they supplemented their own social outlook were largely drawn from philosophy and logic, law and political theory; their methods and approach were derived from the natural sciences.

Furthermore, the scientific historians necessarily depended for selection and emphasis largely on the availability of material. If the facts were to speak for themselves, they must be discoverable; where but in formal records were they to be found? They must be sufficiently well substantiated to provide a basis for more than merely a shrewd guess. The burden of documentation led scientific historians inevitably to focus their attention on these events of which written records had survived. Although the literate parts of the population were always in the minority, these were necessarily regarded as the "people," since it was they concerning whom the historians had direct evidence. Those aspects of living that had been deemed suitable for comment or that had been a matter of institutional record held the center of the stage. Moreover, those matters which were of national concern and which left their trace on national documents preserved in national archives, libraries, or museums were exploited largely because of the ease of access. The chance that local records had been preserved was always poor; the physical problem of going about from place to place presented almost insuperable obstacles; and the general interest in events which were attached to local figures was much less than in those attaching to persons of national prominence.

These conditioning factors impinged upon the scientific historians of all schools. However much historical writers might differ in their general philosophy of history—whether they subscribed to the "great man" theory, or believed in the "hand of God," or accepted economic determinism, or the mystical power of ideas—they shared the same limitation of sources in respect to the facts observed and employed the same basic intellectual tools with which to apprehend those facts.

In recent decades, several things have happened to change this situation. The sight of historians becoming propagandists in war time cast doubt not only on the individual historians but on the possibility of real objectivity. The scientific approach no longer inspired the confidence that it had commanded in the period when the scientific method was introduced into the historical field, for science had obviously failed to bring the social gains which it had appeared to promise. At the same time, the development of the various social sciences brought new understandings of man and society. The findings of social psychology and sociology, on one level, and, on another level, the democratization of literate culture, brought new social groups into view. And, finally, the crisis of Western civilization, whose values had provided the main basis for the historical writing of the nineteenth century, raised anew broad questions of historical interpretation, such as those which had preoccupied Gibbon and Macaulay. Spengler's *Decline of the West,* Pareto's *Mind and Society,* Marx's dialectical materialism could not fail to disturb the intellectual ease of the most detached student.

The first impact of these developments upon the writing of history was to make historians recognize their biases and their unconscious major premises and attempt to make these biases articulate. They recognized, as Charles Beard pointed out in his 1933 presidential address to the American Historical Association, that "any selection and arrangement of facts pertaining to any large area of history . . . is controlled inexorably by the frame of reference in the mind of the selecter and arranger." [2] In so doing, they were aware primarily of national prejudices, of schools of thought, and of intellectual limitations growing out of schooling received, books read, and intellectual contacts made. They were less aware of the bias which reflected the class position, the fact of literacy, and the place in the total culture occupied by the historical profession; few, moreover, were aware of the limitations of outlook inherent in Western culture itself.

The second impact was that reflected in the so-called "new history," with its insistence that the historian, in order to interpret the past, must be equipped with all the newly developed intellectual tools used to interpret the present. Before he could be a sound historian, this argument ran, he must be a good psychologist,

[2] "Written History as an Act of Faith," *American Historical Review,* XXXIX (1934), 227.

anthropologist, economist, sociologist, geographer, political scientist, biologist—in short, a specialist in every field whose work was throwing light on the nature of man and society. Challenging though this call to intellectual adventure might be, its very comprehensiveness left scholars and students aghast. It was a life's work to become an expert in any one of these fields. Was a historian a creature with nine lives, who could spend the first eight mastering the tools, and reserve till the ninth the writing of history? If not, when and how could he acquire all this equipment?

Perhaps just because the scope of the new history was so vast, it had only limited reflection in either the writing or the study of history. No student of history could crowd into his graduate study—or his undergraduate study either—sufficient work in all these fields to make him their master. Since a little knowledge might be a danger rather than an advantage, it appeared better that the historian should stick to his last and learn to use his own critical tools. Few programs of graduate study in history left room for significant work in other fields.

Moreover, the new history was suspect on the ground that it tempted facile generalization without sufficient documentation. The so-called "psychological" biographies which appeared in such profusion in the 1920's were looked upon by many as awful examples of what hypothesis without fact might bring in the field of history. Scientific historians had long protested against this very practice and they were loath to see it return in a new form.

But the new currents of thought were not to be stemmed or sidestepped. World events undermined all patterns of thought and belief that rested on the outlook and faith of the nineteenth century. The "West" showed many symptoms of "decline"; new "elites" were emerging; the Russian experiment, however it might be interpreted, was none the less real. It took a man of great faith, indeed, to face the years between the outbreak of the First and Second World Wars with unshaken confidence in the rationalism, scientific attitude, and assurance of progress in which the nineteenth century had believed. Historians who stuck to their last found students searching for other tools and other materials, in their effort to understand the modern world. Social-science departments grew, often as offshoots from departments of history, and in many places history was classed with the humanities rather than with those academic disciplines more systematically directed toward an undertanding of the social order.

Finally, both the course of events and the findings of the various social sciences made increasingly clear the inadequacy of all treatments of the past which dealt only with the articulate groups. As economists examined social situations by reference to statistical series which reflected mass behavior; as sociologists undertook to probe the experience of inarticulate social groups; as psychologists revealed something of the nature of man in his social relationships; and as the new techniques of mass expression and communication sucked all parts of the society within their orbit, historians were inevitably forced to face the question of how the masses had lived and thought and reacted in the past. They began to realize that whereas they had considerable information about rulers and how they had exercised their power, they had little or none about the ruled and how they had responded. They knew something of the literary and artistic high lights, but little of the mass culture from which these high lights stood out. However little they knew about Shakespeare, they knew less about his audiences. Least of all did they know the manner of living and the processes of change which affected the multitude. They had, on the whole, assumed that the texture of social life in any time and place was more or less of a piece—that the experience, attitudes, thoughts, and values which found record were representative of those which went unrecorded. The possibility that within any society there had been groups whose values, attitudes, and experience were at variance with those of the dominant, articulate group had received little recognition.

But no contemporary observer can fail to recognize to what a limited extent present society is reflected in the lives and utterances of its intellectual and political "leaders"—even though the growth of mass literacy has narrowed the historic gulf between the literate few and the nonliterate many. He cannot overlook the evidence indicating that many cultural processes continue to operate in spite of the neglect or even the opposition of the so-called leaders, or ignore the existence of processes by which the inarticulate and semiarticulate masses influence the elite who write the record. Nor can he fail to realize, in the face of a world in which old institutions are failing to cope with new situations, how obscure, how deeply imbedded in the ways of the society, and yet how drastic and revolutionary are the forces of social change. As he observes the present struggle to subject the machine to social ends, and to make an urban society yield meaning to those who come to it with an agrarian tradition, he cannot be content to interpret past change only from the evidence of official records and pronouncements.

In the face of such a situation, the historian who despairs of mastering all the disciplines which the new history would require cannot simply turn his back and ignore those disciplines; nor can he rest upon the prescription of the scientific historians to let the facts speak and to be guided wherever the material may lead; nor can he be content merely to acknowledge his intellectual predilections. He must direct his thought and attention toward questions that are pressing but as yet largely unexplored; he must find materials that will give him factual evidence to illumine the lives and activities, not alone of dominant groups, but of people of all ranks in society; and, if he is to understand and interpret his findings, he must learn to use new tools in addition to those more traditionally considered his own.

There is an urgency, moreover, which impels him to seek such understanding. No intellectual group can stand by while the society of which it is a part experiences drastic change, without being impelled to seek perspective on that change, an understanding of the basic forces at work, and the ability to distinguish between the superficial and the fundamental characteristics of the social order. Urban birth rates far below the level of replacement; mass unemployment; the erosion of land and men; the degradation of totalitarian war—these are the realities of today which provide the historian's milieu and inevitably shape the terms in which he will study the past.

Against this background, the intellectual tools which historians must bring to the writing of history in the present age must have certain characteristics, some of which were recognized by older historians, others not. These tools must permit the ordering of vast and varied quantities and types of data and provide a basis for classification and selection; they must use, and not do violence to, the new understandings of man and society which study in other fields has brought; they must be applicable to the basic, structural aspects of society, not merely the unique events, and to the processes as well as the results of change; they must be able to deal with society as a whole and to find meaning in the specific detail in terms of the whole; they must take cognizance of nondominant as well as dominant groups, and of factors which cut across national lines. The historian of today, no longer secure within the framework of nineteenth-century Western European assumptions, needs new intellectual tools with which to view his own society, in order that he may achieve a sound and penetrating view of the past.

In turning to other disciplines for tools which will serve this purpose, historians have found various techniques of greater or less usefulness. Neither economics nor political science yields more than partially useful instruments. Economics has made "laws" on the basis of those assumptions about human nature and cultural values which are most distinctive of nineteenth-century Western culture. The thinking of political scientists has been largely dominated by considerations which reflect a preindustrial society and has been confined to the study of the state, in disregard of political relationships in many other areas such as those within the corporation.

One discipline which has necessarily freed itself from the frame of reference of Western culture is anthropology. The study of primitive societies, wholly apart from the "civilized" world, forced anthropologists to make a conscious effort not only to acknowledge, but to abandon, their preconceptions and to attempt to view primitive societies in terms of the culture of those societies. Moreover, the fact that they stood outside of these societies and came to them without the ability to take anything for granted forced the anthropologists to view the whole culture, in order to apprehend any part or any event. The smallness of the group—be it tribe, island, or other unit—and the relative simplicity of its social structure made an understanding of the whole seem feasible. So anthropologists developed the concept of "culture" and applied it to an understanding of the patterns of societies, the groups, institutions, and ideologies that characterized these societies, the personality types which these patterns tended to develop, and the processes by which modification and change were taking place.

The concept of culture implies that any given society is an integral—though not necessarily a completely integrated—whole, in which basic processes of living and characteristic social relationships constitute a pattern of social behavior. The pattern of culture conditions individuals, providing their basic assumptions and their tools of observation and thought, and setting the frame of reference for their living. It determines the forms of institutions, the types of personality which will be developed, and the types of conduct which will be sanctioned. In no society are all human capacities and abilities utilized. Every culture acts selectively upon the individuals who grow up within it, stressing some characteristics, discarding others, and molding a culturally acceptable personality.

Applying this concept to some of the familiar subjects of historical study, the historian finds his attention focused upon the place of the subject studied in the total structure of the society. If he is especially interested in the history of ideas, he will not be concerned with problems of intrinsic merit, but with the cultural role of the ideas and their relationship to other social phenomena. His inquiry into the Nominalist-Realist quarrel, for example, will not apply abstract concepts of right and wrong to each side in the argument, but will note the way these arguments were used to serve social purposes. If, on the other hand, his special interest lies in technological developments and if he is concentrating his attention on eighteenth-century English agriculture, he will be similarly concerned with functional relationships, not with facts for their own sakes. Facts concerning experiments, new methods, new machines are relevant, but they have only antiquarian value unless the changes that occurred in agricultural technology are seen in relation to the changes that occurred in the total structure of English society.

The cultural approach has much to offer to the modern historian. It deals with whole societies and all aspects of life; it recognizes the uniqueness of a particular group in time and place; it provides new terms in which to approach the problem of change. It corresponds, moreover, to the findings of students in a number of fields. In each area of social inquiry, intensive study reveals almost endless interrelationships among social functions not ordinarily considered akin. The observations of sociologists and anthropologists indicate that certain types of social functions appear to be common to all societies or cultures to which they have been applied, and that in any given society the form in which one such social function is performed is somehow related to the form in which other functions are performed. Psychologists, especially those of the Gestalt school, have verified the fact that a process of patterning goes on in the individual mind.

Adoption of a cultural approach by historians may, indeed, be regarded as a cultural phenomenon in itself. It is the obvious product of a society with an increasingly collectivist base, in which specialization of function, with its fragmentation of experience, has been carried to the point where there can be no illusion that the experience of the individual constitutes a microcosm of the whole. The integration of an assembly line, a corporation, and, most conspicuously, of totalitarian nations engaged in totalitarian war forces an awareness of total organization, total patterning, and the impossibility of appraising the significance of any part or any aspect without relation to the whole.

In the hands of the sophisticated historian, the concept of culture makes possible an awareness of assumptions that are deeper than the biases which the older historian has learned to acknowledge. It allows him to recognize and state his assumptions in terms of the basic values of his society, and not simply in terms of the disagreements arising within the frame of reference provided by that society. It forces recognition that human motivations are culturally conditioned and that, within the limits of universal human nature as revealed by biology and psychology, the historian must allow for the possibility of a pattern of motivation alien to that of his own culture. It helps the historian, too, to recognize his own identification with groups in the past. The historian today is usually the bearer of the cultural tradition which triumphed in the past, rather than of that which went down to defeat. If his own society looks good to him, identification with the successful elements and those which produced change is likely to characterize his thought; if he is dissatisfied with his own world, the defeated patterns of the past gain a nostalgic attractiveness. Identification with the virtues of the medieval economy has been a common reflection of disjunctures in the economic structure of modern capitalist society.

The concept of culture helps the historian to ask significant questions of the period to which he addresses himself. Since it implies that certain social processes are common to all societies, with variations in their manifestation culturally determined, it allows him to inquire into corresponding phenomena in all times and places. He may, in any society, view the technological basis and the social relationships imposed by that technology; the bases of group association—the categories of "we" and "they"—and the social structure which governs the interrelationships among and within these groups; the value structure which sets the terms in which the society accords prestige and imposes taboos; the relation between sanctioned behavior and pressures toward and away from such behavior. It thus provides a basis for the comparative study of societies. Comparative historical study is fraught with grave danger so long as phenomena, superficially similar or dissimilar, are compared outside of their respective cultural contexts. Comparison among the parliamentary systems of England, France, Italy, and Germany, for example, has little meaning if confined to purely parliamentary comparisons. Comparative study which uses the concept of culture to keep relationships in view, on the other hand, has great possibilities for throwing light on aspects of particular cultures and on those cultures as a whole.

This concept, too, gives a tool with which to study change. If it is applied merely as a static frame into which to fit a still-life picture, the concept of culture has little more value to the historian than any other static frame. But the position of any element or group in the cultural pattern can be adequately described only in terms which reveal the dynamics of the process of change implicit in that culture. Though implying that all parts of a society are functionally interrelated, the concept of culture does not imply a necessary harmony, either among aspects of the society or among the cultural patterns of the several social groups of which the society is composed. Disharmony among aspects or groups or the introduction of a new element into the culture from outside or from invention within provide a condition ripe for cultural change; impetus for such change may be found in the cultural drive of a nondominant group, in a particular development of one aspect of the culture which changes its role in the whole, or in the form of infiltrations into the culture from outside.

The cultural approach develops beyond, and differs fundamentally from, that of the new history, although it is directed toward many of the same ends. The new history proliferated diverse approaches and multiplied materials and ideas, all of which had equal relevance and significance. It provided neither a basis for selection nor principles for organization. The cultural approach provides a basis for selection, organization, and interpretation by its assumption that every society has a structure of institutions, of values, of ideologies and by assuming that no part is to be understood without reference to its place in the whole. The new history drove off many historians by the apparent impossibility of the intellectual program which it offered and by its tendency to disperse still further the already scattered efforts of historical students. The cultural approach allows for the building of a framework, in terms of which specific pieces of investigation can fit together, and for determining some of the more significant questions calling for investigation and some of the larger gaps which need to be filled. It invites historians to direct their specialized efforts always in terms of their knowledge of the cultural whole, and so to build continuously toward a fuller understanding to which all students of history may contribute.

The process of applying new intellectual tools, as they are developed, to any area of knowledge and understanding is a slow one. From small, isolated, or sporadic beginnings, new concepts spread through wider areas as more people seek more appropriate intellectual instruments with which to satisfy new curiosities. It then becomes timely to take stock of the new tools, to examine the range of their usefulness, and to make them available to the general student.

The cultural approach to history is now in the stage where a few excursions by individual writers have revealed its possibilities. Partly consciously, and partly as the work of certain cultural anthropologists has affected the climate of opinion, some historians have begun to use these concepts and therewith to explore new materials and to reorganize old. Many, however, are still doubtful of the possibility of such an approach and somewhat at a loss as to how to find and use the necessary tools. The present volume is designed to usher in the next stage by making available to scholars, teachers, and students a discussion of the tools, together with such illustrations of their use as will reveal their possibilities to other historians. The types of topics and materials which make up the content of the book suggest the sorts of focus and emphasis which this approach implies. The book lays no claim to completeness, either in its analysis of the conceptual tools or in its demonstration of their applicability. Nor does it undertake either to discuss or to demonstrate the limitations of the approach. Its sole purpose is to make explicit, in terms which students of history may find useful, the meaning of "culture" and the manner in which this concept may be employed by historians; to furnish a variety of examples of such use; and to consider new types of materials which may yield rich results when approached in this way.

The contents of this volume were determined by the circumstances in which the individual papers were prepared, namely for presentation at the December, 1939, meetings of the American Historical Association. Had the book grown out of other circumstances, other subjects than those here included might have been chosen for illustration, treatment of the several subjects might have been differently proportioned, and other aspects of the cultural approach to history might have been stressed.

In planning these meetings, the Program Committee, under the chairmanship of Eugene N. Anderson, felt that the time was ripe for a discussion of the cultural approach and for an attempt to try it out in different fields. The Committee, therefore, planned a series of sessions which would present an analysis and application of the cultural approach to history. It considered a number of aspects and emphases, including such applications of the cultural approach as the analysis of a culture as a whole, the comparative study of cultures, the role of geography, the relation between biological and cultural factors, technology in relation to cultural change, factors affecting the development of personality types. From among the many possible emphases it selected three major ones for the principal papers. The Committee's statement, appearing in the program of the meetings, reads:

> This meeting of the American Historical Association is devoted to evaluating accepted historical interpretations, to calling attention to phases of the past of special significance to our age, and to discussing problems of technique for handling both new and old matters and arriving at syntheses. Emphasis is being put on the study of history from the standpoint of the total culture, and three main topics are being treated: the technique of cultural analysis and synthesis, the cultural role of ideas, and cultural conflict and nationality groups.

The program aims to bring together scholars from various fields of history with those from the other social sciences and humanities in such a way as to permit them to test their different frames of reference and methods on a common body of material. The intention is not to strive for definitive answers but to explore frontier areas and to suggest lines of work for the future.

Although the results were inevitably uneven, and coverage was far from complete, these papers constituted the best body of material demonstrating the cultural approach in the historical field which has yet appeared. Since the approach is beginning to receive wide recognition, it has seemed appropriate to make the material available in this volume. Selection was made from among the papers, and a number of them were reworked to fit in as chapters of the book. The resultant volume is more than a mere collection of essays; it is an integral whole, with a framework provided in the introductory chapter and introductory notes.

The book contains a demonstration, rather than a mere prescription of method. The chapters which make up the body of the book, Parts Two to Five inclusive, are, with few exceptions, the work of historians. In Part One, devoted to techniques, an anthropologist, a social psychologist, and a psychoanalyst discuss concepts and method; in Part Six, devoted to materials, specialists from various fields analyze the usefulness for historians of local materials, population data, folk materials, documentary photographs, speech, and literature.

PART ONE: TECHNIQUES OF CULTURAL ANALYSIS

INTRODUCTORY NOTE

SOME MAJOR conceptual tools with which to apply the cultural approach to the field of history are considered in this section. The first chapter discusses the concept of culture as used by the anthropologist; the next two chapters discuss many of the same concepts from the point of view of the social psychologist.

Both viewpoints are essential; they supplement rather than compete with each other; they represent different points of focus in a totality in which, both would agree, no dividing line exists. The cultural anthropologist focuses on the society; the social psychologist focuses on the individual in that society. But both recognize that there can be no division between society on the one hand and the individual on the other. Society does not exist apart from the individuals who compose it; the individual is what he is by virtue of the society of which he is a part. Both cultural anthropologist and social psychologist are concerned with the process by which culture shapes individuals and is at the same time a product of their activity. The cultural anthropologist looks at the process in terms of the patterning of culture; the social psychologist views the same process in terms of the impact of the cultural processes on the individual and his reactions thereto. The two meet in the concept of "personality," the "individual-in-society."

SOCIETY AS VIEWED BY THE ANTHROPOLOGIST [1]

GEOFFREY GORER

SOCIAL anthropology is the study of human beings, living together in society, and of their culture.[2] I should like to emphasize the four concepts posited in this sentence. Anthropology is concerned with human beings—that is to say, with a certain type of animal. As an animal, man has certain biological needs and tendencies, which are imposed by his physiological make-up, and certain biological rhythms imposed by his physiological growth. Among the biological needs common to human animals can be listed the necessity for man to feed himself, to reproduce himself, to control the immediate environment, and to live in groups. Among the biological tendencies can be listed intercommunication through speech, dreaming, and an attempt to understand the immediate and remote environments.

Anthropology is concerned with people living together. Except from the point of view of methodology, anthropology is not concerned with the isolated individual per se. It is concerned with the relations between individuals and between groups. To understand the motives of interpersonal relations in a given society, it may be helpful to concentrate careful attention on the behavior of individuals, and also to understand at what points, or for what types of character, social pressure may become intolerable. Anthropology may also concentrate attention on individual deviants and maladjusted people. Fundamentally, however, anthropology is concerned with the behavior of groups.

Thirdly, anthropology is concerned with human beings living together in society. The unit with which anthropology is primarily concerned is the discrete society. Although I believe that every anthropologist would assent to this definition, nevertheless the con-

[1] I should like to thank very sincerely Professor George Peter Murdock for his assistance in the preparation of this paper.

[2] For the use of the concepts "society" and "culture" as here employed, see W. Sumner and A. G. Keller, *The Science of Society*, New Haven, 1927; R. Linton, *The Study of Man*, New York, 1936; J. Dollard, "Culture, Society, Impulse and Socialization," *American Journal of Sociology*, XLV (July, 1939), 50–63.

cept of society is one of the vaguest and the most unsatisfactory in the whole discipline. I shall revert to some of the questions raised by it later. Meanwhile, I would suggest that at least the following criteria are necessary for a group of people to qualify as a society:—the group must be able to maintain and reproduce itself over a period of more than one generation; its members must demonstrate types of behavior and attitudes common to all the members of the group and not shared in their entirety by the members of any other group. All the members of the society must have a common language or dialect. In highly developed states the political and societal groups (nations) are by no means always identical; one political unit may be made up of two or more societies, and a single society may be divided politically into two or more states. When such situations do occur, the society or portion of a society which is incorporated into the larger political group is inevitably influenced by this event, and the anthropologist should take this influence into account; but whereas for most modern historians the political state is the fundamental unit to be studied, for anthropologists the fundamental unit always is—or at least should be—the society.

Anthropology is, then, the study of human beings living together in society, these human beings having certain biological needs and tendencies. But, unlike other animals, the ways in which these needs are fulfilled are not conditioned entirely by genetic instinct and the impact of the environment. Different groups of people have evolved different approved ways of gratifying these needs for the individuals who make up the group and have made a selection in favor of some of these methods and against other alternatives. In every human society, therefore, there are the same basic biological needs and tendencies, and specific local methods of gratifying these needs.

The gratification of these needs can be regarded on two levels. There is the directly materialist level, at which level each society has its own methods of deriving food, shelter, and so forth from the environment by means of the technology at its command. This is usually called the material culture.

On a more abstract level these needs are given symbolic elaboration by means of ritual, mythology, and belief; and this symbolic elaboration is addressed not only to the gratification of the basic biological needs, but also to a great deal of other human behavior.

By "symbolic elaboration" is meant all the behavior, both nonverbal and verbal, which is commonly manifested by all members of a society on any given occasion, and which is in excess of the minimum necessary for the attainment of the goal they are pursuing. With this concept, it is possible to present all the knowledge and beliefs about the immediate and remote environments which are held in any society at a given time, and also the preferences and avoidances enjoined on the members of this society.

These preferences and avoidances of different types of conduct and of different methods of getting satisfaction are not biologically inherited. They are implanted by training both conscious and unconscious, but overwhelmingly unconscious; and this training takes place throughout the life of every individual who is born into the group, with special emphasis on the earlier and formative years. It is this nonbiological complex of preferences and avoidances, of formalization, interpretation, of symbolic elaboration, and of material equipment which is commonly referred to as a culture.

Culture, which was our fourth point, can be described as the nonbiological attitudes and the patterned norms of expected behavior which are statistically common to the members of a society. All the technical equipment, all the rules which regulate individual and group behavior—either formalized or unformalized—the economic systems erected for exchanges of goods and services, the legal system, the social organization of methods of government, the art and ritual, the religion and superstitions of the group, are all part of the culture of that group.

In the combinations and permutations of these different facets of life, each culture is unique; but because cultures are carried by human animals who vary very slightly all over the world, societies all have certain traits in common.

From the earliest time, and in the most primitive groups of which we have any record, there has always been a certain division of labor within the society. It would seem as though these divisions were originally biologically imposed, the primary differentiations being the differentiations between man and woman, and between the mature and the immature.

The relative immobility imposed on the mother through her pregnancies and through the necessity for caring for young infants seems to have established the immediate difference between the man as food gatherer and the woman as food preparer. In some of the most primitive societies this is still the fundamental differentiation in labor.

Concurrently with division of labor between the sexes, there has always been a division of labor between different age groups. The immature and the old have not the strength and skill necessary, in the greatest number of environments, to maintain themselves, and consequently the mature have always had to make some extra effort to support the immature and the feeble. It seems, also, that if and when societies come into close and hostile contact with neighboring societies, offensive and defensive fighting and plundering take place. On account of their biological strength, the fighting is mostly entrusted to young men, whereas women and older men have to look after the food and safety of the rest of the population. The fighting was done by one portion of the society for the benefit of the whole, and consequently the nonfighting portion of the society had to exert extra effort to maintain the fighters.

With the elaboration of culture, that is to say, with the increasing ability to control and modify the environment, certain skills were developed which, because of their difficulty or elaboration or time-consuming qualities, demanded the partial or complete withdrawal from the search for food of some members of the society, who became specialists. Although the majority of these specialized skills are founded on the elaboration of the material culture, not all of them are. The urge to understand and control the immediate and remote environments produces professional explainers, medicine men and priests. In this way occurred the third differentiation with the society—the differentiation based on skills.

Here there should be noted a situation which appears to be universal, but which has never been adequately explained. As soon as differences in occupation and skill are established, these occupations and skills are placed in an honorific hierarchy. Some occupations are deemed to be more worthy of deference than others. At the moment we have little evidence as to how this invidious distinction, to use Thorstein Veblen's phrase,[3] arises. Some argument might be made that those occupations which give the greatest narcissistic or libidinal satisfaction—those which demand the most conspicuous skill or give the most direct pleasure—are singled out for distinc-

[3] Thorstein Veblen, *The Theory of the Leisure Class*, New York, 1899.

tion. But this does not seem to be necessarily so on any overt level. Neither cow-milking nor water-carrying can be considered to provide any immediate psychological satisfaction; yet these are honorific occupations among the Toda [4] and the Hindu [5] respectively.

There do seem, however, to be two generalizations of fairly wide applicability: men's occupations are generally considered to be more honorific than women's, and historically old skills more honorific than new ones. The emphasis on men's skills can, I think, be connected with the fact that symbolic elaboration would appear to be predominantly a masculine trait: that man, with his biological leisure, and perhaps also with a fundamental jealousy of the life-giving functions of women, has a general tendency to attempt to establish his superiority by other criteria.

The greater social esteem of old skills as against new ones would seem to reside in human biological conservatism. It would seem as though, to the human animal, learning new habits is a painful process, only to be undertaken in the face of a dilemma, when abstention is threatened by punishment or loss. If such a sentiment is universal, it would appear that in any society those people who are in the less honorific positions, or else the maladjusted, are forced by social pressure to do the requisite new learning for the rest of the society. Consequently, the new skill, when it is first acquired, is acquired by a group in the society already qualified as less honorific, though the roles may be subsequently modified.

There are two possible methods of recruiting specialists. They may be chosen either through manifestations of potential ability or through hereditary training. In most of the known societies in which there are specializations demanding life-long application, the latter mode has been used. Where this has occurred, there has been established within the society a subgroup with habits and attitudes different from those of the majority of the population. With such hereditary specialization arise the germs of a class system.

The varying groups which make up a society have each their own role to play or function to fulfill in the total society of which they are members.

It is indeed possible and practical to view a culture as the sum

[4] W. H. R. Rivers, *The Todas,* London, 1906.

[5] J. A. Dubois and H. K. Beauchamp, *Hindu Manners, Customs and Ceremonies* 3d. ed., Oxford, 1906.

of the functions of its component groups, and this viewpoint, which is technically known as functionalism, has been very fully developed by Professors Radcliffe-Brown [6] and Malinowski.[7] Such a methodology is admirably fitted for the cross-section description of a given culture at a given time. I would suggest, however, that it is not by itself adequate to describe developments through time.

I have already said that all societies are divided into groups. The behavior, ideas, and aims of the different groups are always contrasted to a certain degree, and varying emphasis is given to the importance of each group. With the progressive elaboration of material and nonmaterial culture, more facets are added to the complex making up the culture, and the culture becomes the sum of the distinct and partly contradictory behavior, ideas, and aims of these contrasting groups. A useful term for the varied behavior, ideas, and aims of each group is the "ethos" of the group, which Sumner has defined as "the sum of the characteristic usages, ideas, standards and codes by which a group is differentiated and individualized in character from other groups." [8]

The ethos of the group supplies the secondary motivations and types of choice for biological actions and provides symbolic elaboration and rationalization for nonbiological actions and attitudes. Most interpersonal relations within the society, and the vastly greater part of the relations between societies are determined by the prevailing ethos within the different societies or groups. In any given moment in the course of existence, a culture can be described as the algebraic sum of its group ethoses.

These ethoses do not habitually carry equal weight. Most generally there is one predominating ethos, by and large a male ethos, to which the varying underlying ethoses are subordinated. It is theoretically possible, however, that two or more ethoses may be of equal importance in a society viewed internally. It is perhaps neces-

[6] A. R. Radcliffe-Brown, "Methods of Ethnology and Social Anthropology," *South African Journal of Science,* XX (1923); "On the Concept of Function in the Social Sciences," *American Anthropologist,* XXXVII (1935).

[7] B. Malinowski, "Culture," *Encyclopedia of the Social Sciences,* IV, 621–57; *Coral Gardens and Their Magic,* London, 1935; "The Group and the Individual in Functional Analysis," *The American Journal of Sociology,* XLIV (1939), 938–64.

[8] William Graham Sumner, *Folkways,* Boston, 1906, p. 36; compare the definition in Gregory Bateson, *Naven* (Cambridge, England, 1936), p. 118, of *ethos* as "a culturally standardised system of organization of the instincts and emotions of the individuals."

sary to state categorically that the predominating ethos is not necessarily the ethos of the statistically largest group. It is the ethos of that group receiving the greatest amount of deference within a society which is predominant, and it can quite conceivably be held by only a very small portion of the population. An obvious example of such a predominating ethos, which was almost certainly not shared by the majority of the population, would be the knightly ethos of medieval Europe.

In the most primitive societies it is usually legitimate to speak of the ethos of the predominating group as the ethos of the culture. But with successive elaboration there will inevitably arise an increasing number of subgroups whose ethoses will, to a greater or lesser extent, contradict the ethos of the predominating group.

Most contemporary anthropology consists inevitably in a cross-section description of a society over a relatively short period of time, since there are few occasions when either extant records or repeated field trips make it possible to trace the development of the different facets of a culture through a period of time. Such descriptive cross sections may be spoken of as a synchronic view of society, as opposed to a diachronic view, which would give a description of modification and alteration through time.

The contrast between these two approaches is relative and not absolute. Even in a synchronic view, a certain amount of attention is paid to the explanations given by informants of modifications from remembered or legendary earlier epochs; and even a diachronic account would have to start with a synchronic description. The difference between a diachronic view of society and history as it is normally written is a question of the type of concepts employed.

An anthropological study does, or at least should, have a more unbiased statistical approach than that used by historians. A normal historical view is overweighted in favor of those groups having influence and deference, and inevitably against those groups whose ethoses receive comparatively little symbolic elaboration and who do not have the same access to whatever media of communication the society has evolved.

Although, as has been said, the ethoses of such secondary underlying groups are liable to be neglected, since they usually receive comparatively little symbolic elaboration or publicity, they are nevertheless liable to have important repercussions on the society as a whole. By their existence these secondary ethoses modify and are modified by the prevailing ethos.

The number of socially effective groups within a given society can be discovered only by inspection. A striking example of the discovery of relevant social groups in a contemporary setting can be found in the study of Yankee City, by Warner and his associates.[9] The distinction between groups in any given society may vary from the most trifling modifications, as for example the very slight contrast in the roles of the sexes in such societies as the Arapesh [10] and the Lepcha,[11] to a contrast so great that only mutual integration in a common social structure prevents the two groups from being treated as separate cultures: for example, the Brahmins and the Untouchables in southern India; the Gaelic-speaking, Catholic, Irish peasant, and the English-speaking, Protestant landlord; the American Negro in the deep South and the aristocrat in Boston.

When the divergence between groups in a society reaches a certain point, it is common to speak of the underlying group or groups as a sub-society. But there are not as yet any satisfactory criteria to distinguish the sub-society from a divergent society. Usually some fairly overt characteristic is seized upon to define a sub-society—difference in physical appearance, in language, or in religion. But so far anthropology has dealt to such a great extent with primitive and internally relatively unelaborated societies that this problem of underlying groups, which is one of the most obvious when a complex society is investigated, has received little theoretical discussion or clarification.

The number of varying groups within a society is, within certain limits, correlated with the absolute size of the society. As societies increase in numbers, there is every probability that there will also be an increase in the number of groups with differing ethoses.

From the historical point of view, it would seem as though the most drastic change in the composition of societies and of their cultures takes place through conquest. These modifications may be of two sorts: either an invading people may conquer the territory of another people and take up residence there; or, alternatively, they

[9] W. L. Warner, *Yankee City*. In press, New Haven.

[10] Margaret Mead, *Sex and Temperament in Three Primitive Societies*, London, 1935.

[11] Geoffrey Gorer, *Himalayan Village*, London, 1938.

may take back a sufficient number of slaves and captives to their home country as laborers.

The most drastic step in the elaboration of a society would appear to occur when groups of originally disparate cultures inhabit the same area. Under such circumstances the culture of the conquered group is liable to become either disintegrated or submerged, since the underlying culture will have greatly decreased opportunities for self-validation and little or no access to the media of communication. Two well-known examples may be given.

In Athens, in the classical period, slaves of foreign origin were considerably more numerous than the free-born Athenians, and yet all our information about this society concerns the male portion of the predominant group, about whose ethos, attitudes, and speculations we have a great deal of evidence. Our knowledge of the statistically far more important underlying groups is nil.

The second example can be taken from the England of the twelfth century. After the Norman conquest was consolidated, the prevailing ethos which has come down to us is that of the relatively insignificant band of invaders, with their Christianity, with their concept of honor and personal dignity which had to be continually validated, and their competitive quest for material and nonmaterial advantage. Our knowledge of the underlying population, apparently chiefly pagan, relatively nonwarlike, and with a great degree of social coöperation and communal holding of land and animals, is so slight that only recently has it been carefully deduced from such scraps of evidence as can be gathered from charges, complaints, and lawsuits instigated by members of the predominating group.

A good example of the anthropological approach to history can be found in the works of Margaret Murray.[12] She has uncovered the beliefs, practices, and ethoses of important groups of the underlying population, which, because they were in contradiction to the predominant ethos of the societies of that period, were given little importance in nearly all historical works.

The diachronic view of a society would show variations in the ethoses of the different groups through time, as they interact on one another, and changes in deference and importance accorded to different groups at different periods. Such concepts have been em-

[12] *The God of the Witches,* London, n.d.; *The Witch Cult in Western Europe,* London, n.d.

ployed in the later history of Europe to a certain degree, but not consistently. Successful revolutions and attempts at revolution are usually described in terms of the struggle between differing economic class interests and ethoses. But by and large, it is only when there is an overt struggle for power that such concepts are utilized.

The processes by which the newborn animal is fitted into his culture and by which the culture is maintained seem to be twofold: these are character formation and social organization. The two are, of course, not contradictory; both devices are used in all cultures and the difference is one of emphasis.

As far as our present knowledge goes, there seems very little evidence for supposing that psychological and intellectual potentialities and different types of temperament are more or less common in any one human group than in any other. It is possible that the Australian aboriginals and some of the scattered pigmy groups do possess a genetic inferiority, as contrasted with other races. But all the evidence available suggests that apart from these insignificant exceptions, ability and temperament types are distributed in much the same proportion throughout the whole human race.

Although it seems that the genetic potentialities are much the same everywhere, evidence also shows that the actual development of potentialities and the statistically most common temperament types vary very considerably from society to society. It further seems that these variations in ability and favored character types are culturally produced.

Psychoanalysis and the allied disciplines have demonstrated to what a great extent the treatment received by individuals during infancy influences their adult character. In any society the type of treatment which infants receive is almost entirely decided by what is known as common sense and common tradition, but which may be more properly described as unformulated cultural habits and practices. Even in the most complex societies, it is only very recently that there has been any discussion as to the methods by which infants should be trained and reared. Anthropological evidence shows that in any given group or society there are relatively uniform methods of infant rearing, and from the same evidence it appears that from these relatively uniform methods there develop relatively uniform adult characters in the society or group.

Some psychoanalytic anthropologists, of whom Róheim [13] is the best known, have even gone so far as to speak of cultural traumata. This would mean that each culture, or at any rate most cultures, have, as it were, a constant psychological plot; that is to say that each culture chooses some special occasion to block drastically the tendencies to impulse-gratification of the infants born into that society, and that the type, time, and method by which these attempts at gratification are blocked are decisive for the formation of the common adult character and for the types of anxiety and stress manifested in adult life. It is possible that such a hypothesis could be usefully extended to explore the character variations in different castes and classes in complex societies.

The other device by which a society's culture is maintained is that technically known as social structure. It has already been pointed out that the most primitive types of social differentiation were those founded on age and sex. Different types of behavior are socially expected from people of different age and sex. Groups of people differentiated on biological grounds can be called, following Linton,[14] categories; the members of any one category will manifest relatively stable types of behavior in their relationship with other members of their category and with the members of other categories. To take a simple example, different types of behavior are expected from grandparents, parents, and children. As the individual changes in age, he will pass from one category to another, and, by aging, his rights, attitudes, and duties will also change. At any given moment a society will always include grandparents, parents, and children, behaving in approximately similar fashions; but the individuals who compose these categories constantly change.

When societies develop beyond the most primitive level, certain individuals are designated who perform certain functions for the groups as a whole, or for a portion of it, and these individuals have assigned to them certain rights and duties and are expected to manifest relatively stable behavior in their dealings with the different members of the community. Such socially designed positions Linton [15] has called "status." According to the society studied, there

[13] G. Róheim, *The Riddle of the Sphinx*, London, 1934.

[14] R. Linton, "Culture, Society and the Individual," *Journal of Abnormal and Social Psychology*, XXXIII (Oct., 1938), 425–36.

[15] R. Linton, *The Study of Man* (New York, 1936), p. 113.

are an indeterminate number of such social statuses: chiefs or presidents, cabinet ministers or elders, soldiers or braves, slaves or servants, policemen, priests—the list can be continued almost indefinitely. Each of these status positions demands certain fixed types of behavior from the person occupying the status; and it may be remarked that status usually gives less opportunity for choice in the types of behavior which may be manifested than does membership of a category.

Social structure can be described as the meshwork of culturally determined relationships between the members of a society. The proportion of the population to whom status is ascribed varies from society to society. There are some hierarchical societies, such as the Ba-Thonga,[16] or ancient Sparta, where almost every individual has social status, and consequently has relatively little choice in the type of behavior he may manifest. Other societies, such as the Eskimos [17] and the Lepchas,[18] have so rudimentary a social structure that their continuance depends almost entirely on developing and maintaining a suitable character structure in their members.

Social structure is one of the methods evolved for keeping individual rivalry, competition, and aggression within bounds, and most primitive societies which lack an elaborate social structure have developed as an alternative a noncompetitive and nonaggressive character structure. It is in those societies which have neither produced a nonaggressive character structure nor a sufficiently elaborate social structure that the greatest internal competitiveness and aggression can be found. Instances of such societies are the Ifugao [19] and the Mundugamor,[20] and probably Western European societies.

From the psychological point of view, the role of culture can be envisaged as a social device for keeping the destructive urges of individuals within tolerable bounds. All cultures have to place limitations on the extent to which the individual can gratify his urges to sexuality, aggression, and destruction, and also to offer patterns for gratification.

[16] Cf. H. A. Junod, *The Life of a South African Tribe,* 2 vols., London, 1927.

[17] Cf. E. Weyer, *The Eskimos,* New Haven, 1932.

[18] Cf. G. Gorer, *Himalayan Village,* London, 1938.

[19] Cf. R. Barton, *Ifugao Law,* "University of California Publications in Anthropology," XV (1919), 1–186, at p. 2.

[20] Cf. M. Mead, *Sex and Temperament in Three Primitive Societies,* London, 1935.

From the sociological point of view, the role of culture is to provide patterns for regulating the relationships between individuals, between groups, and between societies, and also the exchanges of goods and services, on which all but the simplest social life is based.

To sum up, I should like to mention for consideration some of the concepts employed in anthropology which might possibly be usefully applied to history. Of these, probably the most important is the concept of societies with their cultures as internally integrated units. Each society is made up of a number of groups with differing roles, composition, and ethoses, and a society may be described both in terms of the algebraic sum of the functions of each group in relation to the total society, and in terms of the algebraic sum of the group ethoses.

Complementary to these concepts is the concept of the diachronic development of society through the mutual interaction of its constituent groups. If the ethoses of the constituent groups and the relationships between them are adequately described, there should be available very considerable leads as to the probable development of that society.

Although anthropological evidence makes the concept of naïve economic determinism untenable, it suggests that if psychological as well as material factors are taken into account, a clearer understanding of the past and of the present might be obtained.

Finally, there are the concepts of character structure and social structure. To what extent does any society or group foster a statistically common type of character? And to what extent does such a society allow gratifications for the demands and relief from the anxieties which make up such a character? For example, if the society encourages aggressive or competitive characters, what provision does it make for successful aggression and competition? To what extent can stress in a society be accounted for by the fact that cultural conservatism produces a type of character which is not in accord with the changed social structure? Similarly, to what extent does the social structure provide adequate roles for the character structures which the culture fosters? To what extent, for individuals or for groups, is the social structure felt as a constraint or as a fulfillment? What groups does the formalized social structure include or exclude? To what extent is the social structure restrictive or permissive? To what extent do the character structure, the social structure, the material culture, and the group ethoses develop harmoniously and on parallel lines, and to what extent are the rates of development uneven, so that energy is used up in internal friction and stress?

I believe that a history which employed such concepts and was able to answer such questions would aid enormously our ability to understand the past, and thereby the present.

CLIO AND PSYCHE: SOME INTERRELATIONS OF PSYCHOLOGY AND HISTORY

GOODWIN WATSON

SOME pertinent criticism both of history and of psychology is implicit in their respective mythological symbols. Clio, daughter of Zeus and Mnemosyne, the goddess of memory, appears to have had deplorably little interest in the life of the average man, woman, and child. The laurel on her head, the trumpet in one hand, and the half-opened scroll of papyrus were all devoted to extolling the renowned and the glorious. Psyche, whose beauty aroused the jealousy of her sisters and of the gods, was reputedly unable to keep her curiosity within respectable bounds. As psychology ventures today to inquire into historiography, I remember with some trepidation that Psyche lost her perfect lover, and later almost lost her life, because she pried into matters with which she had been distinctly told not to meddle.

It is strange that there has been so little conscious collaboration between historians and psychologists. Both are engaged primarily in the observation and interpretation of human behavior. The difference between psychology and history seems to be mainly a matter of size of sample. All history which attempts more than narration involves generalizations about individual and social psychology. The psychologist in the clinic or the laboratory studies a smaller sample of history, more intensively, for a shorter time, and under conditions which he can in larger measure control. The historian works with the protocols from grand experiments in social psychology—experiments which he did not devise and which can never be repeated. Because the psychologist limits his study to a small bit of history, he has the advantage of opportunity to use more refined measures and statistical checks on reliability. Since psychological experiments can be set up to test controversial hypotheses, a science can be more readily developed. Yet the psychologist's fragment of history is too often abstracted from appropriate context. The historian's advantage is that he is more apt to see the whole Gestalt of circumstances which serves as a matrix for the ensuing behavior. The historian is more likely than the psychologist to be aware of the forest; the psychologist is fortunate if his twigs turn out to belong on the same tree.

The regrettable barriers which commonly separate our academic fields seem to me to have impoverished psychology more than they have hampered historians. If psychologists had been wiser, we might have discovered many significant truths about human nature by analysis of historical records of individual and social action. No doubt we would often have wished for data—especially on the experiences of infancy and early childhood—which the record fails to give us, but each such need would point a way toward more fruitful collaboration.

Historians have had some reason to be skeptical of contributions from academic psychology. We psychologists had to free ourselves from seriously limiting conceptions before we could work fruitfully with other scientists who were looking at real human beings in a real world. We had to dispel the naïve mysticism of preformed instincts and inherited traits before we were ready to pay serious attention to the life-experiences which are so potent in molding patterns of behavior. We had to abandon conditioned reflexes and fixed habits as our central units, recognizing that every unspoiled layman knew from common sense that human behavior is organized toward goals, not simply played upon like a typewriter keyboard. We had to redefine "mind" to include not only the higher intellectual processes, but action over the whole rich range of personality. We had to recognize that man's conscious picture of himself is a biased selection, which ignores or contradicts some of his important needs and characteristics. We had to discover, also, that the behavior of men in groups or social institutions is not simply an aggregate of the tendencies which the members may show as individuals in other situations.

Some of the errors we are trying to outgrow persist in common thought-habits and can be found also in the writing of history. Each culture seems to have a kind of Ptolemaic universe of morals, within which its own institutions are central and are viewed as the final and perfect flower of the will of God and the essential nature of man. Our wars are still mistakenly attributed to man's eternal pugnacious "instincts," our capitalism to competitive and acquisitive "instincts," our marriage mores to monogamous "instincts," our churches to religious "instincts," and our science to "instincts" of curiosity. Racial characteristics are too often regarded as expressions of innate biological determiners, despite the mounting evidence for striking transformation of these "traits" by changes in the social situation. Biographers have sometimes traced the family tree of a distinguished individual with care, but have begun his life story at age six or twelve, neglecting the formative impact of the cultural heritage during the vitally important first few years of family relationships.

Motivation, as presented in the perspective of history, is often too simple and straightforward, reflecting the psychology of the Age of Reason which culminated in the French Revolution. Contrast and contradiction in personality puzzle the biographer who has anticipated the consistent and rational. Psychology has come somewhat reluctantly to recognize the enormous weight of irrational and intimately personal impulses in conduct. In history, biography, and in autobiography, especially of public characters, the tendency is strong to present "good" reasons instead of "real" reasons.

The psychological satisfactions in one line of action may not be at all what they seem. We know from clinical experience that it is perilous to assign conventional motives to the acts of our clients. Boys sometimes steal to be able to give away their loot; sometimes quarrel with a mother to whom they are too strongly attached; sometimes fight without anger, compete from coöperative motives, or coöperate competitively; apparent altruism may be perniciously egocentric.

The psychological concept of "reaction formation" denotes the dialectic dynamic by which stinginess cloaks itself in generosity, or rabid pacifism arises from the attempt to repress strong aggressive impulses. Even when the conduct does not overtly contradict the impulse, there is likely to be a great deal of what the psychologist calls "ambivalence." Fear accompanies bravado; intolerance is followed by indulgence; love and hate mingle and alternate. Psychologically, it is comprehensible that at Arlington in 1869, while Union soldiers stood guard to prevent flowers being placed upon Confederate graves, an orator spokesman should have been pleading for reconciliation. It is not surprising that the generation of southern young men, who in the 1880's and 1890's were giving most of their life to importing new northern patterns of industrial society, should have been also the generation which idealized and romanticized the old plantation culture. "Show me a gentle person," writes Kenneth Burke, "and I'll show you one who, when balked or warped, will do the most thorough job of brutality." The demands of the meek often become intolerable.

It is probable, then, that if the historian could secure more detailed data about the psychological dynamics of the men and women involved in any critical event, the resulting picture would be strikingly different from the one which is based upon their public acts and statements. The purpose of the public aspects of life is often to conceal, even from the actor himself, his private and personal motives. History that is not psychologically critical seems likely to lend itself to the perpetuation of fallacious respectability. Perhaps, indeed, that is one reason why we revere historians.

Increased coöperation may be expected in the near future between a more mature psychology and a more analytical history. There are problems before our citizens in these days of internal and international crisis which seem so urgent that every resource of understanding is needed. We might choose one or two issues of profound present concern to illustrate ways in which historians and psychologists could work together. If this seems to put history into unwelcome utilitarian harness, I can answer in the words of Professor Charles A. Beard [1] that

> Historiography . . . furnishes such guides to grand public policy as are vouchsafed to the human mind. They may be frail guides, but what else have we?

Let us as historians and psychologists look first, in this war-wrecked world, at the problem of peace and conflict. Fighting seems to be universally interesting. A dogfight will stop traffic; prize fights will fill stadiums; laws won't stop cockfights; the clever reporter will give his news story the angle of controversy; so we can hardly wonder that historians have been much occupied with battles.

Wars seem to be periods of overt expression, with lethal

1 Charles A. Beard and Alfred Vagts, "Currents of Thought in Historiography," *American Historical Review*, XLII (April, 1937), 482.

weapons, of conflicts which are carried on at other times by other means. Quite possibly the tendency in historical writing has been to exaggerate the significance of this change of weapons. Wars are indeed impressive, but the discipline of research, both in psychology and in history, leads us to discount the dramatic. When psychologists are asked to help a boy who has tried to injure his small brother, we do not center our attention on the precipitating situation, the threats, the attack, or upon some single incident in their previous relationship. We have learned the futility of inquiring "Who started this fight?" We can be confident that we will find in the background of this outbreak persistent patterns of frustration. We know that peace can be restored in the family only when vital interests have found open channels to satisfaction. Is it not true in history also that wars are of significance, not so much in themselves, but as symptoms of a rising demand which has met opposition, thwarting, and so led to struggle, resentment, hostility, and aggression? As the psychologist views conflict, the study of war should be subordinated to the study of frustration and consequent aggression.

We shall want also to distinguish, more sharply than historians have sometimes done, the psychology of dominant, policy-making groups, the psychology of propagandists, the psychology of soldiers, and that of the women and children at home. Writing about large units of political history, such as the Roman Empire, the Confederacy, the British Commonwealth, or the Third Reich, tends to obscure inner divisions. Yet these inner divisions are of vital importance. There are plenty of satisfied groups within dissatisfied nations, and there are groups that "have not" even in the wealthiest of countries. Tensions and hostilities arising from constant struggle within a country may be projected upon an enemy without. It is common observation that an insecure power group sometimes welcomes a war, to relieve its anxiety by a temporary national unity. At the same time it is clear that for some of the groups within such a culture victory in their national war would mean only a continuance of their frustration.

The rank and file of an army have so little to gain in most wars that we may well be astounded that they ever fight at all. We know, of course, that propaganda helps them to identify their self-fulfillment with the success of their country's cause. But back of their response to propaganda is a reservoir of aggression which has been too little explored either by psychologists or by historians. Resentment commonly arises, for example, in children whose parents reject them or train them to satisfy primarily the parental egos; then the resulting grudge against the world may be augmented by petty tyrants seeking to impose irrelevant curricula in regimented schoolrooms, and the attitudes later may be made worse by autocratic domination of a foreman or boss. Whenever such experiences are widespread in a culture, we might expect that almost any pretext would serve to canalize aggressive impulses against some traditional foe or some minority race. Can one find, in the usual historical analyses of conditions leading up to war, the necessary facts for an understanding of the hostility generated by the everyday life of the competing cultures? Have we not, in recent days, overstressed the propaganda which directs the impulse against the enemy and understressed the chronic tensions which demanded some such outlet?

As we consider the present situation in Europe, we may apply some hypotheses drawn from our knowledge of both psychology and history. Clearly the present fighting, with or without declarations of war, is only a change of weapons in a chronic conflict, which has been, and is being, and will be steered by competing economic and power-seeking interests. Never has the distinction between war and peace meant less. So far as the people are concerned, long-continued frustration of everyday desires has accumulated in most European nations, and now the vague resentment of the masses is being directed by expert propaganda away from exploitation within their nation, against a scapegoat enemy without. Churches, journals, and scholars have rationalized and will continue to rationalize the aspirations of the power-groups in each society.

The people in every land today have been led to feel that their own welfare and their highest ideals are at stake. Hitler has wisely pointed out that if men are asked to fight only for their own economic advantage, they can too easily decide that the game is not worth the candle. When their cause is felt to be supported by God, by Nature, by social evolution and right and justice, men will endure all and accept no compromise.

In the present war situation we see once again how attitudes are "de-differentiated," blurring important distinctions, and reducing the situation to stark primitive contrasts. As self-righteousness is exalted in the we-group, evil impulses are projected on the enemy, and real human beings disappear in what purports to be an Armageddon between angels and devils. Hatred for the common foe unites each nation, and temporarily blots out vital differences in way of life, in privilege and aspiration, between the rulers and the ruled, but those inner conflicts remain to threaten any proposed stability.

We may expect that for psychological reasons rank-and-file soldiers will find reconciliation easier than will high officers or those who have been fighting mainly on the propaganda front, and that the victors will again forget and forgive more easily than the vanquished. We must anticipate that, after any probable peace, politicians, seeking their own advantage and the continued dominance of the class they represent, will endeavor to gloss over the strains and tensions within their nation by continuing the "patriotic" war appeal to fear and hate.

It is apparent that psychological conditions for peace and coöperation will not emerge from a truce of guns or from any change in the figures who remain only spokesmen for continuing and conflicting interests. The only hope for long-time peace requires reorganization of economic and cultural systems as well as governments, so as to permit the coöperative expansion of the energies of all people concerned. We can believe that the opposition to such a drastic way of peace will arise *within*, rather more than between, nations.

Two other areas for fruitful coöperation between psychology and history may be briefly suggested. One very promising problem for coöperative research is that of democratic versus authoritarian controls. The history of democracy still does not seem to me to have reached the heart of the problem. Professor Kurt Lewin [2] has guided a series of very stimulating experiments in the psychological approach to this issue. Boys under authoritarian leadership quickly developed attitudes of resigned submission or, in

[2] K. Lewin, R. Lippitt, and R. K. White, "Patterns of Aggressive Behavior in Experimentally Created Social Climates," *Journal of Social Psychology*, X (1939), 271–300. See also R. Lippitt, *An Experimental Study of Authoritarian and Democratic Group Atmospheres*. "University of Iowa Studies in Child Welfare," 1939.

some cases, of overt or disguised hostility. In one experiment, in which an adult leader made the plans for the boys and directed their club work in detail, the resulting frustration turned the boys to persecuting a member of their own group. The analogy to the Negro in Reconstruction days or to the treatment of racial minorities in certain contemporary dictatorships may be more than superficial. Another consequence of the autocratic control was found to be a corresponding increase in ego-assertion. In groups under democratic leadership, in which all members coöperated in planning each step of the work, the records of conversation show less animosity and more friendliness, less boasting and more praise of others, less subjectivity and more matter-of-fact comments. In the autocratic group there was significantly more use of the singular pronouns "I," "my," and "me," and less of "we," "us," and "our." A similar result has been observed by Professor H. H. Anderson,[3] in his studies of very young children. Dominating attitudes in one child are found to arouse counter-dominance or submission in a companion, but rarely lead to what Anderson calls "integrative" behavior. Hence the failure of coercion as an aid in building coöperative and democratic institutions.

Historians can testify that when men who have been held in subjection break their bonds, the promised freedom does not appear, and psychologists add that this is because the reaction of the dominated is themselves to dominate. Those who have learned helpless submission are better prepared to exercise tyranny than to coöperate in social integration. Can history help us to understand the conditions under which this vicious circle of dictatorships, succeeding one another, is broken, and genuinely democratic relationships are introduced? I do not refer to the paraphernalia of constitutions, parliaments, and elections, which may or may not bring democracy. If the psychologist is right, our attention should turn to the actual power relations, rather than to the political machinery. A major problem for American democracy today is that there are so few areas of our civilization in which democracy is, in fact, practiced.

It is our democratic theory that each should have a voice in the

[3] H. H. Anderson, "Domination and Integration in the Social Behavior of Young Children in an Experimental Play Situation," *Genetic Psychology Monographs*, XIX (1937), 341–408.

matters which most concern him, but illustrations of genuinely democratic practice within our homes, schools, community agencies, industry, finance, and national affairs are regrettably few. Although we readily give allegiance to democracy as a general ideal, we are apt to feel that in any particular case it would be more efficient to "get things done" by arbitrary methods. It may well be that the threat to democracy in our country today is not so much foreign invasion, or allegiance to totalitarian "isms," as it is lack of knowledge about the importance and possibility of democratic relationships in everyday life. Here is, it seems to me, a challenge to history. What is the still unwritten story of actual democracy in the life of human cultures? Today, as the area of private enterprise contracts and the area of public operation expands, the new patterns of control which are being set up remind one more of the tribal chief, the business executive, the political boss, and the army officer than of a town meeting. We act in such desperation to "get things done" that we do not trouble our heads very much about the extent of democratic participation of all those affected by public works, or work relief, or youth programs. It looks as though it would take the coöperative efforts of all the social sciences to prevent an unintentional, step-by-step repudiation of democracy, simply because we know only autocratic ways of getting things done efficiently.

The problem of democracy most widely studied by psychologists is that of the intelligence of the masses. The prevailing low level of political appeals raises an interesting issue. Are the masses inevitably morons on public policies, or have traditional campaign methods tended to make political audiences what they were assumed to be? One very influential political writer recently expressed amazement when we explained that the distribution of intelligence in the population followed the Gaussian curve of normal distribution, with no more morons than geniuses. He said he had always assumed, and he thought most other journalists did, that the distribution of intelligence was a kind of cone, with a few at the peak, and ever more numbers at each level down the scale, to a broad mass base of stupidity. Political speeches and newspaper articles tend to create the appetites they feed. Recent experimental investigations at the University of Iowa have emphasized again a truth which has been clear to all the scientific students of intellect since the early pronouncements of Binet and Thorndike, but which has been confused in popular thought about the I. Q. Test performance is always and inevitably a product both of native aptitude and of educational opportunity, and extreme differences in opportunity, especially during the years of childhood, will be reflected in higher or lower scores in intelligence tests. Even more important for the historian is the finding that when groups of individuals try to solve problems coöperatively, the joint result is distinctly superior to the average intelligence of the individuals and may surpass the performance of the best individual working unassisted.

A profound psychological problem for democracy is raised by Hitler's assertion that the psyche of the masses is feminine and yearns for a leader who asserts an aggressive, dominant, uncompromising will. The psychologist recognizes that dictatorship is not a one-way satisfaction; it is not imposed upon the unwilling to gratify solely the leader. History must take account of an evident desire to be ruled by strength and ability, which may be as natural as for children to have stern fathers and which may be prevalent even though the nation is nominally a democracy. Psychologists and anthropologists are saying that the acceptability of democracy depends upon the extent to which the culture has developed independence in children and youth. The roots of the need for "the strong man" are to be sought in our education, rather than in foreign traditions or in unalterable human nature. Do our homes and schools give more reward for acquiescence or for initiative? Do we prize submission more than participation on some basis of equal dignity? Does this reflect the fact that the number one institution of our society is not a political state resting upon the coöperative action of free and independent equals, but is a business system in which the man at the top expects subordinates to do as they are told? If our educational institutions are primarily concerned with the production of docile employees, that danger to democracy far outweighs any innate impulses toward submission and any danger that foreign ideologies will undermine our government. There are good reasons in psychology to believe that the absence of genuinely democratic relationships with youth is closely related to phases of American life which are widely deplored. Our disgraceful crime record; the irresponsibility of young people, about which the old complain; our egocentric boasting, which Europeans criticize; the ruthless disregard of others shown by the "climber" as he pushes his way to the top; and even chauvinistic patriotism all give expression to ego-assertion and give outlets for hostility. If democracy were more real, and liberty, equality, and fraternity characterized most of our facc-to-face relationships, we could expect less obnoxious assertion of personal and national egos.

Psychologist and historian face in common another problem of democracy, that of readiness for responsibility. In America, as in Europe, Africa, and Asia, in the North as well as in the South, equality of opportunity is delayed because of the idea that some races are naturally simple-minded, dependent, indolent, superstitious, thoughtless, and irresponsible. Autocracy in empires, autocracy in industry, autocracy in universities is frequently said to be necessary because the subjects are unable to govern themselves. Psychological experiments and historical records will agree, I think, in showing that no group held in subservience is likely to develop the attitudes, insights, and skills essential for independence. In Lewin's experiments, when clubs changed over from autocratic to freer methods of control the boys indulged in a reaction of rioting which might easily have led an observer to feel that they were quite incapable of running their own affairs. Yet in half a dozen sessions, a democratic, coöperative, and work-minded atmosphere had been set up, such that the leader might leave the room and work would go forward without interruption. Experiences in psychological clinics with adolescents who are sowing wild oats after a period of strict parental restraint and records in history of people who have suddenly been liberated from domination illustrate the same problem. Today as the movement which Ortega has called a "revolt of the masses" puts new powers in the hands of unprepared men, may we not derive encouragement from the agreement of psychology and history that man gradually rises up to but seldom much above his share in responsible authority?

We have presented possibilities for the collaboration of history and psychology in dealing with peace and war, and have mentioned some problems connected with the realization of democracy. A third most important area for coöperative study is that of the process of social change. The Society for the Psychological Study of Social Issues, which is a section of the American Psychological Association, is eager to enlist the coöperation of scholars from other social sciences in the preparation of an integrated volume on social change.

It may be possible with the help of historians to discover recurrent and significant patterns. We think, for example, of *The Anatomy of Revolution* [4] in which Professor Crane Brinton presents a comparison of common elements in four great revolutions. In each case, inefficiency of the old regime hampered growing business interests and cost the government the allegiance of some of its own privileged members as well as the support of a rising power group. Each revolution was precipitated by some successful illegal act which was not intended to lead to revolution; most people were surprised by these revolutions, having expected something of the sort for their children but not for themselves. Many of his generalizations seem to be supported by studies in social psychology as well as in history, but one basic question should be raised. All of Brinton's examples deal with a period in which the order of private enterprise was emerging and bursting bonds of feudal restraint.

Today our threat of revolution comes from those who oppose that capitalistic order and who hold that the class which then came to power has outlived its usefulness. Should not our changed social situation, with the present different distribution of economic and other interests, lead us to expect rather a different pattern of change? No longer does rising economic power, on one side, challenge entrenched political obstacles. Revolutionary movements now face a powerful coalition of economic and political interests which have learned how to mold public opinion. Furthermore, in our highly differentiated and interdependent society, are not men more insecure, and therefore more apprehensive lest something should upset the apple cart? Is there not some reason to fear that if the old economic order should have lost its vitality, then chronic depression, petty hostilities, and slow deterioration may be more likely than the revolutionary emergence of new and liberating social patterns?

Whether or not the days of revolution are past, we can be sure that there will be rapid important social changes. Historians and

[4] Crane Brinton, *The Anatomy of Revolution* (New York, 1938), p. 326.

psychologists together may help to interpret these movements. How do the strains in a culture, which lead to social change, commonly arise? Are they the result of technological advance, of cultural diffusion, or of social and intellectual innovations? What personal and social factors produce the leaders and martyrs who take up a cause long before the world is ready to listen? Why does it happen that hundreds of worthy reform movements never grow, but some few show that mysterious acceleration described by Le Conte when he wrote of the growth of public opinion for secession in the South? [5]

> Gradually a change came about—how, who can say? It was in the atmosphere; we breathed it in the air; it reverberated from heart to heart; it was like a spiritual contagion.

Then, is it true, that as every action in physics involves an equal and opposite reaction, and as every incoming tide creates its own undertow, so the very progress made by a social movement brings about a reaction of opposing forces? Does not every major social change, by its most encouraging advance, frighten and mobilize whatever interests are strongly in opposition?

Most basic of all questions about social change are those of direction and goal. I wonder whether historians, psychologists, and other social scientists cannot contribute more explicitly toward the definition of a good life and a good social order. I realize that this suggestion may be alarming, because it seems to introduce values other than the objective search for truth into the direction of the efforts of social scientists. It raises the question Professor Lynd discussed in his Stafford Little lectures at Princeton under the title, *Knowledge for What?* [6] I once asked several historians "In what land, and at what time, among all those that you know well, has there been the highest level of happiness among the common people?" The answers suggested as much about historians as about happiness. Is it not a part of our proper function to attempt to discover at what periods and in what kinds of cultures men have been most miserable, and what epochs have maximized joy in living? Cultural anthropologists have suggested that some types of civilization do produce more tension, anxiety, insecurity, and ha-

[5] Joseph Le Conte, *Autobiography*, pp. 179–81. Quoted by Paul H. Buck, *Road to Reunion* (Boston, 1937), p. 30.

[6] R. S. Lynd, *Knowledge for What?* Princeton, 1939.

tred, while others foster friendly content. It is reassuring to read Professor Beard's assertion.[7]

> Contemporary historiography finds nothing human alien to it. . . . All those realities of life connected with the biological and cultural relations of the sexes, families, the continuance, care and elevation of life come more and more clearly into the scope of historical concern.

May we look forward to a time when the most important historical sources will be, not the memoirs of statesmen, but observations revealing the relationship of social change to the intimate joys and sorrows of ordinary fathers and mothers and boys and girls?

[7] C. A. Beard and Alfred Vagts, "Currents of Thought in Historiography," *American Historical Review,* XLII (April, 1937), 482.

PSYCHOLOGY AND THE INTERPRETATION OF HISTORICAL EVENTS

Franz Alexander

THE question of the relation of psychology to history touches upon the fundamentals of both these disciplines. The actors of the drama of history are human beings; it is obvious that their nature must determine the course of historical events. On the other hand, fundamental human nature has not changed within historical times, and yet the scenes upon the stage of history offer us a view of confusing kaleidoscopic variety. It is just as obvious, therefore, that the psychological knowledge of man alone does not suffice to explain the causal sequence of historical events. The same type of people, with the same biological and psychological structure, lived at the same time in Athens as in the neighboring Sparta and yet created in many respects entirely opposing civilizations and modes of living. Common in the contemporary Spartan and Athenian were only the fundamental laws of human psychology. These cannot account for the vast differences in their attitude.

The common elements in human nature seem to offer an almost indefinite variety of possible configurations; which of these configurations will prevail in one or another historical period can obviously be understood only on the basis of the different forms of interaction between human beings, that is to say, the difference of cultural patterns. It is true that history is the creation of man, yet one may also reverse this statement by saying that man is the creation of his history and is constantly modified within the limits of his fundamental structure by social configurations. Thus it seems that psychology and history are inseparably linked. No individual can be understood without knowing the social scene in which he lives and which has molded his personality, but no historical event can be understood without knowing the fundamental principles of human motivation, which are the dynamic driving force behind the ever-shifting scenes of history.

As a physician who is concerned in the microscopic study of individual fates, I feel hesitant to apply the psychological knowledge of single persons to the fate of nations as they evolve in the wide perspective of history. I have witnessed only too often the methodological blunders which psychologists are apt to commit when they attempt to apply to group phenomena their knowledge of the psychology of the individual. It is only natural that they are tempted to consider nations as one magnified individual and to attribute to them psychological qualities similar to those of a single person. They explain wars between nations as if they were duels between persons. One often hears, as a psychological explanation of war, that a nation is humiliated and now seeks revenge. One might excuse such generalizations by saying that they refer to feelings which are common in the majority within a nation. It is obvious, however, that such explanations are not admissible.

A nation is a highly heterogeneous composite of individuals, who feel differently. The psychologist is apt to explain war as a manifestation of man's destructive instinct and as an expression of mass aggression. This is certainly an incorrect statement, based on an uncritical application of the psychology of the individual to group phenomena. It might be well said that a violent physical fight between two individuals is always the expression of their aggressive impulses. On the other hand, it is quite possible for an autocratically ruled country to engage in war without any emotional participation of the population.

A modern highly organized mechanical war, in which the opponents only very occasionally get into physical combat, but shoot at one another from a long distance by the manipulation of complicated mechanical instruments, a war which is started without the initiative of the combatants, can be waged without any hostile emotion in the actual belligerents. In fact, as an officer of the Hungarian army, during the World War, I had an opportunity to see on the Russian front a definitely friendly feeling between the Austro-Hungarian and Russian soldiers who were lying close together in opposing trenches. There were long periods in the war without activity. During these pauses, there was a tacit agreement in the opposing trenches not to shoot at the enemy. This allowed free movement behind the lines. The shooting started only when orders came from the commanding officers to take up activities again. During the quiet periods, the opposing soldiers became acquainted with each other by sight, and even by name, were calling to each other, and it even happened that cans of food were exchanged. Individual motivations and emotions played, indeed, a very subordinate role in that war.

With all this I wish only to emphasize the fact that the simple application of the psychology of an individual to a complex, highly organized social unit such as a nation is a serious methodological blunder, which is apt to make sociologists and historians skeptical as to what they can learn from the psychologist.

What, then, can modern dynamic psychology contribute to the better understanding of historical events? The topic is obviously a tremendous one and cannot be dealt with exhaustively in a brief essay. I wish to single out one important psychological fact which has a decisive bearing upon the correct interpretation of historical events. This psychological phenomenon, discovered by psychoanalysis, became popularly known under the name of rationalization. It touches on the central issue of modern dynamic psychology, on the fact that people do not know the deepest and strongest motives of their behavior. Clinical evidence is overwhelming that both normal and emotionally disturbed individuals have only very incomplete knowledge of the dynamic forces which account for their daily activities, both in important and in trivial matters.

The real meaning of the term rationalization is, however, widely misunderstood. In an erroneous way it is assumed that rationalization means necessarily the invention of nonexisting motives. The correct interpretation of this interesting phenomenon is based on the overdetermination of human behavior. Our actions are not determined by one single motive, but by a great complexity of motives. The student sits behind his book and tries to learn something because he wants to pass an examination, but also because he wishes to obtain praise and admiration, and also to out-do his schoolmates, and to secure a scholarship, and perhaps also because he is puzzled by the problem which he is studying.

Rationalization is, then, the arbitrary selection from a variety of existing motives, which all contribute to our actions, those pleasing ones which we like best, and the denial of those which we do not like to admit. Rationalization makes it possible for a person to explain his actions in a self-complacent way, saves him from the necessity of admitting to himself his objectionable motives.

The amateur psychologist who has read a few books of psychoanalysis often finds delight in exposing some hidden motives behind socially highly valued acts; he will triumphantly point out that the surgeon by amputating a patient's leg only gives vent to his cruel sadistic tendency, that he is really a latent sadist. He will overlook the surgeon's wish to help the sufferer. The modern up-to-date cynic, with an air of sophistication, will expose the soldier who fights for his country *only* to give vent to his murderous impulses; or the benefactor, who helps a young man *only* to dominate his protégé and to feel important. After man has indulged for centuries in a naïve and irritating self-adulation, seeing in his nature only what he wanted to see—the acceptable and self-flattering motivations—now the discovery of dynamic psychology is utilized by many to see nothing but the repressed and nonsocial forces in man.

Nothing is more discouraging to me than to see how even the scientific mind regularly becomes a victim to this primitive pattern of dialecticism. After the falsity of an accepted thesis has been proved, the dialectic mind necessarily falls into the opposite error. Only after these long detours of committing errors in both directions, can truth be found. That homo sapiens, the crown of creation, is fundamentally a fine, socially minded being, was the thesis for centuries. If he was not good, then in the Middle Ages he was considered obsessed by evil spirits, while in the biologically minded nineteenth century he was called constitutionally inferior, and even thought distinguishable, according to Lombroso, by the shape of his jaw or ears, forehead, or by other physical stigmata. In this way people in whom the universal nonsocial tendencies found franker expression than in others became sharply segregated from the rest of men, who thus could continue to indulge in the self-admiration of their social qualities and overlook their nonsocial nucleus. The discovery of the dynamic power of unconscious and nonsocial forces which exist in everyone led many to adopt the opposite view. As in the primitive, vaudeville drama, there must be a hero and a villain, so the students of human nature are inclined to see only these two extremes. "Man is a hero" was the older view, "man is a villain" the modern; that he might be both at the same time is a fact which still awaits recognition.

It is only natural that the writing of history did not escape the effects of the various fallacious conceptions of human nature. In our present era of enlightenment, few human endeavors have been exposed to as much criticism as the writing of history. It has been repeatedly stated that historians glorify the past, even if they have to falsify the facts; that they attribute imaginary motives to historical figures; that historiography deliberately misrepresents the past for ulterior, political motives; that it is a means to keep the subjugated classes under the sway of their rulers, by cloaking the brutal, power-seeking forces which alone make history.

Thus historiography, too, became the victim of the dialectic process. After a period during which history was nothing but a form of folklore, a heroic epic written in prose, we now observe the beginnings of a so-called critical era, in which the ulterior, nonsocial motives hidden behind the overt scenario of history are alone considered. We learn that the Crusades were not expressions of religious ardor, but were merely cunningly planned schemes to serve the imperialistic aims of the Pope; that in the French Revolution, Liberty, Fraternity, and Equality were only slogans to cover the real aims of the rising middle class to wrench the power from the feudal lords; that the League of Nations was nothing but a cynically constructed instrument of the Allies to perpetuate their domination of the world; that democracy is only a new means of mass exploitation.

The amusing part of this new popular application of the theory of the unconscious is that each party uses this theory for its own benefit, to demask the opponent's ulterior motives. Each party exposes its opponent's aggressive, power-seeking aspirations and at the same time makes a generous use of rationalization to defend its own point of view. Russia attacks Finland in self-defense, and the Allies pretend that they do not want to do anything like maintain rigidly a *status quo* advantageous to them, but that they fight only to uphold the sanctity of treaties and orderly coöperation between nations. Each nation violently denies its own imperialistic aspirations, but readily discovers those of its opponent.

The disquieting question arises: is it true that all major historical events are the expression of exclusively nonsocial, aggressive, power-seeking, and destructive impulses of individuals and groups in their eternal fight against each other? Was the carrying of the flag of Christ against the nonbelievers in the Middle Ages, the proclamation of the principles of Liberty, Fraternity, and Equality in the eighteenth century, the abolition of slavery in the Civil War, the present fight for decent international relationships—were they nothing but *ad hoc* invented motives which are nonexistent and are merely hypocritical pretenses to hide the only real driving force, the thirst for power? Was historiography, which glorified the past, nothing but a naïve acceptance of these high-sounding, pretended motives; were historians who tried to see progress in human development nothing but naïve fools, victims of their own wishful thinking? Is the modern critic of historiography right when he, with the help of dynamic psychology, claims the predatory instincts as the sole factors in the history of mankind?

Max Nordau, the author of the once-sensational book *The Conventional Lies of Civilized Mankind,* interpreting the meaning of history, writes:

> Not only up to the middle of the eighteenth century was history merely the biography of might, it has been so since, and is so this day, in spite of the chapters dealing with sociology and the development of moral ideas that historians nowadays amuse themselves by introducing into their works; not only for three centuries has it been an uninterrupted conspiracy against the truth, it has always been so, ever since the earliest chronicler sat him down to record the events within his knowledge, for the honor and glory of those whom he loved, reverenced, or feared, and the defamation of those whom he hated. . . . The stronger individuals caused the weaker to provide them with the favorable conditions of existence indispensable to them. Less effort was involved in robbing men of the fruits of their labour than in wresting from nature warmth, dryness, nourishment, and comfortable rest. Parasitism proved by experience to be the easiest form of adaptation. As far back as historical tradition goes the strong are found directing their efforts in this manner. This parasitism on the part of the strong is the object—the obvious or occult, direct or indirect—of almost all the institutions that have arisen in the course of centuries, and represent the framework, even the substance, of civilization. . . . Externally, then history is a melodrama on the theme of parasitism, characterized by scenes that are exciting or dull, as the case may be, and many a sudden stage-trick.[1]

It does not even require an argument to show that this interpretation of history is just as one-sided as was the naïve or willful glorification of the past. In this interpretation of history the power-seeking, selfish interest is attributed exclusively to the opponent.

[1] Max Nordau, *The Interpretation of History* (London, 1910), pp. 367, 359.

The capitalist becomes the villain and the proletariat a miraculous exception from the law—the unselfish hero of justice. If we eliminate from this theory this obvious, naïve inconsistency and apply to all classes the view of the universality of predatory instincts, the only logical conclusion is that the sole improvement of which man is capable is to become more sincere as to his real aims. He should then call his bluff and admit that social life is nothing but a crude, uncompromising battle for power. According to this view, this was always so and it will remain always so, unless one expects a miracle —that one day humanity will discard its destructive impulses and wake up with a really social mind.

As an exponent of modern dynamic psychology, I am the last to want to expose myself to the accusation of wishful thinking in regard to human nature. My clinical experience has made me aware of those motives in people which they do not like to admit even to themselves, motives which are of the same kind as those which Nordau and many modern critics of traditional historiography claim to be the only motivating forces in man's history. Yet the same clinical experiences have also taught me not to overlook the other side of the picture. The basic concept of our discipline is that of conflict. If there were only one force in operation, how could a conflict arise? Why do people repress their asocial motives, why do they rationalize—that is to say, try to explain their acts from acceptable, socially approved motivations? Why this desperate battle for self-vindication? Why has man developed elaborate codes of morals and religion? What gives dynamic power to these—let us call them—illusions? The tiger does not feel any need of justifying his aggressions.

All the critics of traditional historiography who expose man's true predatory nature fail to see that if man is a beast, he is one who has a peculiar need for denying even to himself his true nature. Nordau has also an answer for this.

Superior individuals always devoted their best efforts to the direct exploitation of those less highly gifted of the average people, and also to their education in habits of thought and feeling which would lead them not only to see no violence or injustice in the parasitism to which they were subjected, but even to feel themselves so distinguished by it that they worked with heart and soul for those that exploited them, and felt a moral glow, a sense of pride, in being permitted to sacrifice themselves.[2]

This is the same Marxian idea according to which religion and morals are nothing but mental drugs, invented by the rulers to keep the exploited masses content and to hide from them their real power-seeking motivations.

This theory, however, is fully contradicted by clinical observation. The trouble with this theory is that both ruler and ruled indulge in the same need for self-justification. It is a naïve mistake to assume that all social ideals were invented by the rulers with cool calculation, in order to keep the toiling masses in check. Both the rulers and the ruled repress their own self-seeking tendencies and wish to live up to some kind of moral standards. From a clinical point of view, the historical theory of a Nordau and a Marx, in spite of much truth, is equivalent to a paranoid delusion. Also the persecutory delusions of the insane contain a kernel of truth. As Freud has formulated it so succinctly, the paranoiac, who sees in everyone a persecutor, falsifies reality only insomuch as he sees in others nothing but the repressed unconscious hostility, which unfortunately all people, even friends, harbor against each other in their unconscious. He simply does not take into consideration the fact that this unconscious hostile impulse may be deeply buried and powerfully inhibited in the other person. Also these modern critics of historiography see only the instinctual skeleton, which is the same in everyone, but overlook the real living, dynamic covering. They make the same mistake as the paranoiac. After learning of the unconscious asocial nucleus of man, they see only these repressed, underground forces and forget the dynamically effective superstructure of social attitudes. Who can deny the dynamic power of these social adaptations, in view of the tremendous efforts which man is constantly making, though not very successfully, to become a social being, or at least to persuade himself that he is one?

The significant fact that people at least pretend to be social is a fact which, in view of the appalling manifestations of human destructiveness, cannot be overvalued.

Indeed historiography should apply a correct knowledge of man's

[2] *Ibid.*, p. 360.

motivations. Evidently for centuries it has not done so. It has naïvely overlooked the unconscious destructive forces in human nature and has taken the rationalizations of man at their face value. This does not mean, however, that it should now fall into the opposite error and disregard the dynamic power of the other side of conflictful human nature, those forces which create the urge for self-justification. One must distinguish between two types of self-justification. One is a conscious process and serves merely to convince another person of one's righteousness, even if one does not believe in it. There is nothing constructive in this. There is, however, another form of self-justification—an unconscious process, an attempt to justify oneself before one's own conscience. Certainly this, too, is not an admirable trend. It obviously requires more courage to recognize and admit one's own objectionable tendencies. This is a better preparation for improvement. The mere fact, however, that people have the urge to persuade themselves of their own righteousness and do this not to deceive others but to deceive themselves is a sign that one part of their personality does not approve of the asocial motives. This desperate need for self-justification is an irrefutable proof that man is not only asocial but that he is also at the same time a socially minded being.

The fact that it is consoling that man has to lie to himself about his motives may sound paradoxical, but it shows that at least one part of his ego must be fooled before it gives in to the powerful underground motives. Of course frank and regretful admission, followed by change in attitude, would mark the only real progress in human relationships. Since this seems to be utopian at present, we must be satisfied that instead of cynical admission and acceptance of the solely predatory aims, at least one part of the personality upholds social ideals and must be fooled or even compromised with.

It might be true that Pope Urban initiated his Crusade basically not for the liberation of the Holy Sepulchre, but in order to acquire more prestige and power for the church over the contemporary worldly rulers of Europe. He could, however, win for such an imperialistic maneuver the coöperation of a man like Godfrey of Bouillon and the support of the masses only by appealing to their pure and sincere religious fervor. It may also be true that the Civil War was fought primarily to decide whether the ideals and the economic and political interests of the industrial North or those of the feudal South should rule the country. Yet this war could be fought as a popular issue only as a war to save the Union and to free the slaves, a cause which appealed to the idealism of the masses. That this motive animated both leaders and masses not only as a thin rationalization but as a deep conviction can hardly be questioned. As was said before, human actions are overdetermined. The elemental dynamic force of such mass movements as the French Revolution or the Civil War is based on the fact that in these cases the unconscious, selfish motives required the same type of action as the conscious, altruistic, social motivations.

Historians may become discouraged and disillusioned in facing these self-deceptions which hide the real motive forces behind all great and small events of history. For the clinician the same phenomena are a source of hope. Historians for centuries saw nothing but the surface motivations; no wonder that they are disillusioned by witnessing the power of the hidden, destructive forces. The psychiatrist senses in these phenomena of self-deception the low but permanent and inescapable voice of human conscience. All these pretensions of higher aims are nothing but desperate efforts to win the approval of the conscience. If conscience were not a force to reckon with, man would indulge in his destructive aims cynically, without the need for any self-justification. He must, however, compromise with his conscience. One wonders when its low voice will become louder.

PART TWO: CULTURAL GROUPS

INTRODUCTORY NOTE

HISTORICAL writing during the past century has been largely in terms of national units. Divisions within states, unless they have reached the point of open conflict, have received far less attention than relations among states. In dealing with the national or political state as a whole, it is necessarily the dominant element in the state or nation which provides the basis for generalization. But the dominant element has never fully reflected the underlying divisions and groups within the society. At all times it has been a minority, separated by a wide gulf from both urban masses and rural multitudes.

The importance of understanding nondominant as well as dominant groups has become increasingly apparent as social psychology and sociology have called attention to mass phenomena, and political developments have reflected real divisions and often conflict between the cultures of dominant and nondominant elements. Where national minorities with language, cultural traditions, and group aspirations at variance with those of the dominant group have existed, the importance of understanding the component national groups is clear. Where varying national strains have combined to make a single society, as in the countries of mass colonization—North and South America, Siberia, Australia, South Africa—the group cultures within the culture of the whole society are less clearly defined, but may be none the less important. Differences among groups at different economic levels and between rural and urban areas may be as fundamental as between groups at the same economic level in different nations.

The two chapters in this section illustrate the problem of understanding nondominant groups by exploring the cultural groups of varied national origins that make up much of the population of the United States. They consider the relations of the group cultures of the nondominant ethnic groups with those which characterize nondominant economic groups and discuss some of the terms in which these nondominant cultural elements may be studied.

CULTURAL GROUPS IN THE UNITED STATES

CAROLINE F. WARE

IN AN earlier chapter of this volume, stress is laid on the fact that in a society composed of a number of cultural groups it is the dominant, literate group whose culture is accepted as that of the whole, while large but inarticulate groups may differ significantly from the dominant group, yet go unrecorded. American history, which has largely ignored the varied cultural groups which comprise the American population, well illustrates this tendency.

The present paper, and the discussion summary which follows, seek to redress the balance by attention to nondominant groups in the United States, suggesting something of the process by which group cultures have been shaped and the dominant pattern modified. This essay presents generalizations, not as assertions of fact, but as hypotheses with which to approach the study of American cultural groups, offering specific material as illustration to give concreteness to hypotheses rather than as documentation. It is confined to a discussion of groups of European and Latin American origin, though many of the points would apply with even greater force to groups set apart by color, e. g., Negro and oriental, and also, in some degree, to groups with an old-American heritage, e. g., the Mormons, who maintain a separate entity and a distinguishing cultural complex.

It must be obvious from the start that the relationship among the cultural groups in America has been very different from the relationship among these same groups in the places from which they came. They have met within a single political entity where no national political rivalries can draw upon cultural differences. More important—for minorities within political entities are an all-too-familiar European phenomenon—they are not rooted in the soil. Except for the Spanish in the Southwest, cultural differences in the United States are not associated with places to which a long past binds them. All have been transplanted within relatively recent times, and share a common rootlessness in the American scene. Such place associations as have grown up are local—the Pennsylvania Dutch country, small Finnish towns in New England or

Michigan, the Polish city of Hamtramck embedded in Detroit. For the most part, cultural groups have been scattered through new western lands, plunged into cosmopolitan urban areas, and swept into the stream of moving people hunting for better opportunity farther west or in another industrial city.

The significance of these groups for American life is none the less great, as they affect both the structure of American society and the changing patterns of American culture.

National self-consciousness, group identity, and much of the characteristic culture of American ethnic groups are the product of American conditions, not importations from abroad. Though the traditional American expectation that the melting pot would merge all peoples into one and obliterate cultural differences had enough foundation to give it credence and currency, the melting pot has not, in fact, performed the function expected of it, and the impact of American life has tended to accentuate, rather than to obliterate group consciousness. The mass of peasant immigrants did not bring with them a national consciousness, for nationalism, on the whole, has been a product of the middle class, while the peasant has known only his family and his village. By the process of education and the imposition of bourgeois attitudes in America, the basis for such consciousness has been laid where it did not exist before. Many an Italian immigrant has discovered in America that he is an Italian and not simply a "paesano" of a village or, at most, a province. The direct attempt to teach American patriotism and national consciousness has provided terms in which to think of national identifications and allegiances. The many occasions in which persons are made to identify themselves by their national origin—as in filling out forms for social agencies or employment applications—have served as a constant reminder. Finally, the quota immigration law has stamped the idea of nationality, especially on those groups whom the legislators sought to limit as "less desirable." There is significance in the statement, some years ago, of a strongly anti-Fascist Italian-American girl, who, in spite of her opposition to Mussolini and his program, declared, "But you've got to admit one thing: He has enabled four million Italians in America to hold up their heads, and that is something. If you had been branded as undesirable by a quota law, you would understand how much that means."

Group consciousness has grown in America, in spite of the fact that the pressures in the American community have been to "Americanize" individual members of immigrant groups. In fact, this very process of individual "Americanization" is partly responsible for group attitudes, intergroup relations, and the status of groups in the community. It has tended to draw off potential leaders, who become successful in American terms, and to merge them in the general American community. The leaders who remain within groups are thus often those who can exploit group consciousness for their own ends, or who are on the defensive vis-à-vis the broader American community. It has resulted, too, in perpetuating stereotypes with respect to cultural groups which reflect the continued low economic and social status of the group as a whole. The Polish-American doctor or business man is an "American"; the Polish-American worker remains a "Polack."

Relationships among groups, moreover, have been built up out of the American situation in which these groups have found themselves. Relations between Irish and Italian, Polish and Mexican, French-Canadian and Portuguese in American cities can obviously rest in no way upon the relationship among these national groups outside of America. The lines of cleavage that divide these groups coincide largely with class lines. Social hierarchies have grown out of the process whereby each new immigrant group has come in at the bottom of the economic and social pyramid, raising by its new presence the last group which occupied that position.

The story of the manner in which each new group has been characterized as inferior mentally, morally, and culturally, with a taste for the attributes of poverty, and poverty-producing habits of shiftlessness and irresponsibility, is too familiar to bear repeating. This was the picture of the Irish a hundred years ago. Then it was transferred to French Canadians, Italians, Poles. The Mexicans inherited it after the first World War. Today it has come down to the old-stock American migrants, hill-billies and drought refugees, who occupy the lowest economic position and experience the greatest insecurity and the deputy sheriff's blackjack or gun in the steel and auto cities of the East and in the pea fields of California. The result of this process has been a stratification of society, especially of urban society, into a series of economic-occupational-nationality groups.

These group relationships in some communities have been institutionalized as, for example, in a New England city where it is common knowledge that the Police Department belongs to the Knights of Columbus and the Fire Department belongs to the Masons; i. e., a person born into that community with an Irish background can look forward to a career on the force, whereas a German-American has prior access to the career of fireman. Everyone who has engaged in any civic enterprise will recognize the way in which group distinctions are woven into the institutional structure of American communities.

In this situation, it is the next to last group which "Americanizes" the latest comers, for it is they with whom contacts are most direct and through whom the operations of American society are most intimately to be seen. Irish and Germans have borne the brunt of "Americanizing" the people from southern and eastern Europe; more recently, it is the Poles of Chicago and Detroit who have been revealing American ways to the Mexicans, while old-American migrants from the southern highlands and the Dust Bowl are being inducted into the life of northern industrial cities by the Italians and Slavs who work beside them on the automobile assembly line.

The Greek organization, Ahepa (American Hellenic Educational Progressive Association), well illustrates the manner in which self-conscious group activity has been shaped by the situation it has had to meet. In the midst of the alien-baiting which followed the World War, Greek grocers and fruit dealers found it hard to maintain their business. In Atlanta, Georgia, where the Ku Klux Klan was active, a group of these men formed Ahepa for the specific purpose of establishing Greek prestige in the American community. Their program was to fete every distinguished person from Greece or of Greek origin, being sure to invite press and important persons to lend the maximum publicity and dignity. They organized expeditions of bachelors to Greece, saw that the expedition was pictured in the rotogravure section of the *New York Times,* that it was received and feted by the prime minister or king in Greece and reports thereof carried in the American press, and that those who brought back wives from Greece got their pictures in the papers when they returned home. The Ahepa made a policy of holding its affairs, wherever possible, in the best hotels; of giving banquets for outstanding political figures; of picking up and answering all references that tended to slur Greeks, as, for example, in the following letter from the president of the Richmond chapter of Ahepa to the editor of the Richmond *Times-Dispatch* (June 21, 1937):

A LEVEL REPLY

Editor of the Times-Dispatch:
Sir:—We have noticed with much distress and surprise, in your issue of The Times-Dispatch of last Tuesday, June 15, on page 10, that a paid advertisement coming from the Catholic Bureau of Information apparently, contains the rather strange analogy in these words: "In the little store below the street level, the Greek delicatessen dealer figures his profits on the basic principle that two and two make four. . . ." We quote the very words. . . . We have called at the Cathedral to take the matter up with proper authorities in a personal friendly manner, and they sent us to P.O. Box 269-A, so the association decided to write this letter to you, expressing our disapproval of such contemptuous and contemptible words appearing in a paid advertisement in the name of a great body of Christian people, using a name that denotes an illustrious race that has contributed much to our civilization and culture. Why not any other name, but "the Greek delicatessen dealer"? . . . We object to it because of the false analogy or comparison it demonstrates. There is not one Greek in this city that has a "delicatessen store below the street level." This is a self-evident fact. Why the contrast?

. . . We do feel that such a publicity does not invite sympathy and willingness to understand, but breeds contempt, and we believe that contempt invites contempt. And further, we feel that some correction must be made to promote fairness and Christian fellowship. This is the spirit of true Americanism and of our association.

Very truly yours,
The American Hellenic Educational Progressive Association, Richmond Chapter, No. 83
SPYROS LAMBIDIS, President
Richmond.

So far as national consciousness and a pattern of group relationships exist in America, it is thus largely American conditions which have produced them and which have determined their forms.

The determining American conditions have varied with time and place of settlement. Newcomers to America, from the time of earliest settlement, have been subjected to two major environmental influences: first, the influence of the wilderness frontier, and then the influence of the city.

In the initial stages of settlement, the frontier either stripped people of much of their cultural heritage or accentuated cultural values which could survive under frontier conditions only if rigorously maintained. On the one hand, we have the exaltation of physical prowess and contempt for the "effete and cultured" societies of the Old World and the East; on the other, the rigorous enforcement of social standards, such as characterized the New England settlement and its westward extension, or the Mennonite communities, or the valiant struggles of educational institutions in the frontier country to keep cultural traditions alive and intact.

As compared with other frontier countries, the American frontier has tended to strip rather than to accentuate cultural characteristics. The presence of a continuous stream of English-speaking immigrants mingling with those of foreign tongues; the absence of the policy of group settlement, such as characterized the settlement of certain parts of Canada; the assumption of a single culture with a common language, rather than the bicultural tradition of Quebec; the fact that in spite of rapid expansion frontier settlement quickly lost the isolation which has characterized some of the settlements of the South American states—all these factors combined to make the American frontier predominantly a stripper rather than a preserver of culture.

The great bulk of newcomers during the past one hundred years have found their way into cities, rather than to the land. Here, in spite of ghettos and Little Italies, they have been subjected to what is, in many ways, the most standardizing milieu which the world has known. The regimentation of industrial discipline and the routines of city life have inescapably molded people to a common manner of life and have narrowed the range of observable differences and of group distinction. Especially to the peasant peoples who constituted the overwhelming mass of citywards immigrants, the contrast between the experience of New World and of Old was so great as to mean for the immigrant almost two unrelated existences. His traditional institutions and his traditional lore have given him few terms in which to interpret life to his New World children. Of only one group has it been true that the greater number of members have come with an urban background—the Jewish group.

The very quality of the city impact upon newcomers has obscured the process by which cultural groups have been incorporated into American society. On the one hand, there is an external appearance of adjustment; on the other hand, immigrants have constituted a city "problem." The immigrant areas were the city slums; the immigrants and their children, the city's slum problem. Few people had any sense of the social organization, the process of adaptation, and the evolving new American culture bred in these areas—not even the schools and social agencies, certainly not the "other half" of the city, and least of all the people of traditional rural America.

Moreover, in order to understand the process of urban immigrant adaptation, it is necessary to recognize the ambivalent position which the city has occupied in American culture. On the one hand, the city has been the seat of wealth and "Culture" with a capital "C," the source of literate expression, the center from which innovation has spread, the locus of economic and—at times and in some respects—of political controls, and the mecca which has drawn rural people from America as well as from abroad so consistently that even while the immense acres of the West were drawing new settlers from home and abroad, cities were drawing more. In only one decade, 1840–50, since the first census in 1790 has the proportion of urban to rural population in America failed to increase.

Yet while the city occupied a strategic and dominant position, its way of life was suspect. The main stream of American tradition has been intensely rural, the approach to the values of city life largely negative. In the 1840's the popular play *Fashion* depicted the weakness and foolishness of city people, in contrast to the "independent farmer" and his fine country daughter, who represented true Americanism. In the 1890's, the settlement-house movement sought to introduce into the urban environment the relationships of the small-town neighborhood. Until very recently, and in many city schools even today, city children learn reading and spelling from books about cows, chickens, and the business of rural life.

Peasant immigrants, confronted with the task of developing an urban way of life, have received little help from American sources in adjusting themselves to their new experience, for Americans themselves have lacked a positive set of city values. In these circumstances, new Americans have had to develop attitudes and patterns of behavior on the basis of what they could observe of the realities of American urban life. It is well to consider some of the implications of this situation.

In any culture, centuries of accumulated habit and tradition produce a mass of contradictions which are given order by the categories into which certain pieces of behavior are made to fit. American culture is no exception. Those bred in the tradition have learned to believe in equality, in spite of the color line; to believe in freedom, in spite of traffic regulations; to distinguish advertising "puffing" from personal dishonesty; to classify schooling as a right and school lunches as charity. But those who come to it fresh lack this traditional basis for sorting out contradictory pieces of experience. A certain health center in New York has worked for years to teach Italian mothers to bring their babies to the clinic, instead of trying to doctor them themselves, and prides itself on the effect that this education has had on women of the first and second generations. But the family welfare agency complains that the families in this district are the most difficult to work with, because once they have been served they will never stand on their own feet but come back and back, exhibiting what the case worker enters on her record as a "begging tendency." To the Italian mother, the lady from the health center and the lady from the welfare agency both come into her life from the outside world and, for all that she can see, look just the same. Yet one blames her for being independent, the other for being dependent. Why? This same woman gets a bad reputation at the school which her children attend, because she has come to ask for shoes for the children when obviously she could afford to buy shoes herself. Yet her husband, who keeps a grocery store, has learned that he must take advantage of every opportunity if he is to become a good American business man. Must not she, then, take advantage of every opportunity, if she is to be a good American mother and raise up her children right?

A vivid example of the use of observation to discover the pattern of American society comes from a political club of young American-born Italians in an eastern city in 1935. The following letter, printed under the letterhead of the "East-Side Italiano Club" of the city in question, was sent, obviously without self-consciousness, to the voters of the district, including a college president.

November 2, 1935

Dear Voters:

The Italians must have recognition in this Ward, and we are making a campaign to get representation.

The Republican Leaders of this Ward have honored us by nominating one of our nationality for Alderman.

Alberto Cucinell is the candidate we must elect if we must get all of our friends jobs with the City, this can easily be done.

Alberto is a very fine type of young Italian and can well represent our people.

He has had three years of High School. We admit he has had no business experience, but he can get on to the way things are done, very quickly. He has promised to represent the Italian People if he is elected.

At present he is working as a laborer on a sewer job in the County, but the Republican Party has promised him a better job, if he is elected.

Yours very truly,

East Side Italiano Club

While these illustrations are drawn from the relatively recent history of a particular group in a particular part of the United States, the process which they reveal is equally characteristic of earlier periods, other groups, and other areas. It is a process by which peasant newcomers have built up a set of attitudes and a way of living out of their attempt to interpret American urban life as they are able to observe it.

The net effect of the efforts of new Americans to find for themselves a way of life within American cities has been substantially to modify the dominant pattern of traditional American culture. The dominant tradition has been Anglo-Saxon, Protestant, and bourgeois. In respect to each of these characteristics, it has been, and is being modified.

The Anglo-Saxon majority has been supplanted by an ever-increasing proportion of other stocks in the industrial Northeast in particular, but also in the German and Scandinavian sections of the Northwest, in the Spanish and Mexican Southwest, and on the Pacific coast. The mere substitution of German, Slavic, or Latin stocks for Anglo-Saxon in the population, however, does not necessarily mean a corresponding modification of Anglo-Saxon cultural traditions, for to some extent these traditions have been transmitted to others. The nearly universal use of the English language in the United States has been perhaps the strongest single factor in Anglicizing people of varied strains. You remember Mr. Dooley's immortal bit on the Anglo-Saxon "hurtage":

An Anglo-Saxon, Hinnissy, is a German that's forgot who was his parents. . . . I'm an Anglo-Saxon. . . . Th' name iv Dooley has been th' proudest Anglo-Saxon name in th' County Roscommon f'r many years. . . . Pether Bowbeen down be th' Frinch church is formin' th' Circle Francaize Anglo-Saxon club, an' me ol' frind Dominigo . . . will march at th' head iv th' Dago Anglo-Saxons whin th' time comes. There ar-re twinty thousan' Rooshian Jews at a quarther a vote in th' Sivinth Ward; an', ar-rmed with rag hooks, they'd be a tur-r-ble thing f'r anny inimy iv th' Anglo-Saxon 'lieance to face. Th' Bohemians an' Pole Anglo-Saxons may be a little slow in wakin' up to what th' pa-apers calls our common hurtage, but ye may be sure they'll be all r-right whin they're called on . . . I tell ye, whin th' Clan an' th' Sons iv Sweden an' th' Banana Club an' th' Circle Francaize an' th' Pollacky Benivolent Society an' th' Rooshian Sons of Dinnymite an' th' Benny Brith an' th' Coffee Clutch that Schwartzmeister r-runs an' th' Tur-rnd'yemind an' th' Holland society an' th' Afro-Americans an' th' other Anglo-Saxons begin f'r to raise their Anglo-Saxon battle-cry, it'll be all day with th' eight or nine people in th' wurruld that has th' misfortune iv not bein' brought up Anglo-Saxons.[1]

Whatever the content of the "Anglo-Saxon hurtage" may be, at least some attitudes and points of view at variance with those probably comprised within the Anglo-Saxon tradition have developed and are developing. The presence of alternative values is suggested by the comment of a group of second-generation New York City boys in discussing the relative merits of Lincoln Steffens' *Autobiography* and Samuel Ornitz's *Haunch, Paunch, and Jowl,* the story of the political rise of a New York East-Sider. Their comment was: "When we read Lincoln Steffens, we have to turn the page to find out his reaction to a situation, because we don't feel the way he does. But in *Haunch, Paunch, and Jowl,* we don't have to read the next page to find out what he does. We put ourselves in his place, and we just know."

In respect to its Protestantism, the dominant pattern of American culture has been even more subject to modification. While the main rural regions and the southern and western Bible belts have remained pretty solidly Protestant, the northern industrial cities have become overwhelmingly Catholic and Jewish.

[1] Finley P. Dunne, *Mr. Dooley in Peace and in War* (Boston, 1898), pp. 54–56.

The Catholic church has become one of the most powerful of American institutions, and the United States is rapidly becoming one of the great Catholic countries of the world. The church has been sufficiently affected by the impact of the American environment to elicit the Pope's recent admonition to American bishops to guard against American materialistic influences. The church, moreover, means something quite different to different immigrant groups: to the Irish and Poles it has been associated with a struggle for national identity; in contrast, to the Italians and Germans it has been merely a part of the *status quo*. Yet the channels of Catholic influence upon institutions which shape American life are widespread, including not only an extensive parochial school system, but the overwhelming predominance of Catholic schoolteachers in the public schools of northern cities, not to mention such bodies as the Legion of Decency. Through these and other channels, either dominant Protestant attitudes are being modified or a Catholic American culture is growing up by the side of the traditional Protestant one. A study of Burlington, Vermont,[2] showed that almost every activity and institution in the community was split on religious lines, with wealth still predominantly on the Protestant side, and numbers on the Catholic.

Finally, the bourgeois pattern of individual enterprise, accumulation, thrift, economic success is being subjected to modification in its turn. This is perhaps the toughest part of the dominant cultural tradition, the most deeply sanctioned, the most used by conscious power groups, and the most implicit in the viewpoint of the articulate, literate part of the society.

Yet ever since the beginning of the industrial revolution there has been evolving an industrial culture within the framework of bourgeois tradition. The ethnic groups drawn to industrial cities have been the people in terms of whose lives this industrial culture has been taking shape. They are the industrial workers. The issue of the status of cultural minorities is the issue of the status of workers. The emerging patterns of their lives, their attitudes, values, habits, are the patterns, attitudes, and habits of workers in an industrial society. Bourgeois tradition accords high prestige to work, but not to the worker—to the self-made man, not the man of the

[2] Elin L. Anderson, *We Americans; A Study of Cleavage in an American City*, Cambridge, Mass., 1937.

masses, and certainly not to the man who leads the masses. Under pressure of this dominant ideology, those who have written about the achievement of ethnic groups in America have written a series of success stories,—or they have dealt with "immigrant gifts to American life." But the great bulk of urban new Americans are and always have been the factory workers, miners, bridge builders, pick-and-shovel men, and, more lately, white-collar workers. They are the readers of the mass "pulp" magazines and the sport pages; they are the rank and file in the mass unions. It is here that one must look for the central aspects of the new, urban, industrial culture, developing in the hands of new Americans and old, peasant peoples and hill-billies.

As Louis Adamic has pointed out, it is to Ellis Island rather than to Plymouth Rock that a great part of the American people trace their history in America. More people have died in industrial accidents than in subduing the wilderness and fighting the Revolution. It is these people rather than the frontiersmen who constitute the real historical background and the heroic tradition of the mass of urban Americans.

The attempt to write American history from the bottom up started a generation ago with the study of the frontier; it has recently extended into the study of local communities and culturally homogeneous regions. In the still unexplored history of the non-dominant cultural groups of the industrial cities lies the story of an emerging industrial culture that represents the dynamic cultural frontier of modern America.

APPROACHES TO THE STUDY OF NATIONALITY GROUPS IN THE UNITED STATES

The Cultural "Syncretism" of Nationality Groups

MAURICE R. DAVIE

THE essential fact in immigration, from a sociological point of view, is movement from one social group to another. This transfer involves the crossing of not only a political boundary line, but in some instances a racial line and always a cultural line. The immigrants and the natives of the immigrant-receiving country belong to different social or cultural groups. This fact underlies the problem of adjustment of the newcomers, the conflict they may experience with the natives, and the whole question of assimilation or acculturation.

The immigrant brings with him his culture, which differs more or less markedly from that of America. As time goes on, it is modified toward the American type through the process of assimilation or, more specifically, Americanization. "In the United States, an immigrant is ordinarily considered assimilated as soon as he has acquired the language and the social ritual of the native community and can participate, without encountering prejudice, in the common life, economic and political."[1] The term assimilation stresses our point of view, the bringing of the immigrant's culture into conformity with the native American's. It tends to lead to the erroneous assumption that the change is all on the immigrant's side. Indeed some writers maintain that the process is one of complete abandonment by the immigrant of his cultural background and its replacement by the American pattern. The process, however, is not unilateral, even though the American pattern remains dominant. Anthropologists are coming to use the term acculturation—the adjustment of a subordinate group to a dominating culture group—which stresses the immigrant's point of view, the changes being effected in his culture through contact with the dom-

[1] R. E. Park, "Assimilation," in *Encyclopaedia of the Social Sciences*, I (New York, 1937), 281.

inant group. But again the concept usually implies that the change is all on one side.

We need a term which will describe the interaction that takes place when peoples of unlike cultural antecedents come into contact, and the culture of both is modified in consequence, even though the modification is greater in the case of one group than in that of another. Following a suggestion of Sumner,[2] I propose the term "syncretism" (if one can forget its philosophical and religious connotation), to denote the process whereby, in a composite society, culture is influenced by borrowing and selection. There is giving and taking among the component groups, though one of them takes precedence and sets the standards. The other groups or classes imitate the ways of the dominant group, and they and their children gradually cease to observe the traditions of their own ancestors. Thus there is a selection of the folkways, and some of them perish.

That immigrant groups have been affected by American culture is well known, and the process has been subjected to considerable investigation. That American culture has been influenced by immigrant groups is also commonly realized by historians as well as sociologists, but the extent of this reciprocal influence has never been adequately traced.

The full story of immigrant gifts to American life has never been told. Here is a significant field for research. It will involve, among other things, the history of inventions by immigrants, which have been adopted and have influenced American life. Also prominent in the story will be the role of sculptors, painters, musicians, leaders in business, writers, actors, scientists, and others. A rich source available for a study of this sort is the *Dictionary of American Biography*. For current information, publications such as *Who's Who in America* and *American Men of Science* come readily to mind. In this instance, the sociologist is interested not only in the individuals themselves and their specific contributions, but also in the comparison of foreign-born with native-born in the production of leaders, the differences, if any, in the fields in which the two groups have attained eminence, and the variations among the nationality groups in these respects.

[2] William G. Sumner uses the term in a closely related sense in his *Folkways* (Boston, 1907), pp. 115–17.

A second part of the story would be the introduction by immigrants of practices which have been taken over by the whole society or by those parts of it directly concerned. Thus the cotton-mill industry was introduced by the English, the iron industry by the English and Welsh, while the coöperative movement in agriculture in the United States is said to be largely of Danish origin, as are also certain developments in the dairy industry, including in particular the introduction of the cream separator, a Danish invention. Immigrants have also made notable contributions in the field of folk arts and crafts, of folk music and dances. They have undoubtedly affected our diet and cooking.

Less tangible but perhaps equally important has been the influence of immigrants and their children on American politics, education, religion, fine arts, industry and business, labor organization, sports and recreation.

It is probably true that syncretism takes place first and most readily in the case of elements of material culture and economic arrangements—form of dress, type of food, work techniques, manufactured objects, mode of transportation—since they are most readily communicable and demonstrable and are least imbued with moral or emotional values. Only later and more slowly is language modified and elements of nonmaterial culture affected. Finally come common ties of interest and sentiment, and mutual participation in political and social activities. The process is one extending over generations. The foreign-born are seldom if ever assimilated. The second generation clearly show that they are in a transitional stage. Usually they have changed far more than their parents, with resulting problems of contempt for the latter's foreign background, impairment of parental control, and weakening of family ties; on the other hand, they may not be able to participate fully in the common life, but may experience difficulty in getting jobs and in making other adjustments, and thus develop feelings of inferiority. The inevitable situation of conflict which ensues when different cultures come in contact finds perhaps its most acute expression in the case of individuals of the second generation, who are torn between the opposing ideas of Old World culture, represented by their parents, and the American culture, which they receive in school and through other associations.

All these points need checking and expansion through intimate studies of nationality groups and their role in American society. There is great need for more descriptive local histories with reference to immigrant settlements, the transformation of their institutions, and their role in the community or region. Intimate first-hand knowledge of immigrant communities, ability to surmount the language barrier, and familiarity with the cultural background or social heritage of the group are prerequisites to such studies.

The procedure entails a combination of the field-survey technique and the historical method. In addition to demographic facts concerning the nationality group, such as numbers, sex and age distribution, marital status, occupation, citizenship, and the like, material should be gathered concerning the organized community life, the formal institutions—societies, churches, newspapers—which serve the dual purpose of tending to perpetuate the cultural background of the group and of aiding in adjustment to American life.

The anthropological technique of using informants—persons who can speak for the group as to its history, experiences, manners and customs—should prove highly useful. It differs from the interview with schedule or questionnaire in that in the latter instance information concerning the person himself is requested, which, either in complete coverage or on a sampling basis, may provide statistical data on any topic. The use of informants is a way of getting at the generalized culture pattern and also at historical facts which are not recorded but exist only in the memory of living persons.

The technique of participant observation—whereby the investigator lives in the community and participates as far as possible in its life, or at least attends its society meetings, church services, and festivals, becomes acquainted with individuals, visits homes, and learns what he can by observation—is useful both in checking other data and in gaining additional information.

Life histories or intensive case studies of individuals are indicated in the instance of special topics where more intimate knowledge is required, such as delinquency or other maladjustment, conflict between the two generations or with native Americans, feelings of inferiority, the process of assimilation, and social attitudes. Biographies of outstanding people of the nationality group, in the degree to which their experiences are illustrative of the life of the group, are also valuable with reference to the process of acculturation and the role of the leader. Immigrant letters and diaries often contain a wealth of vitally significant material. Wherever possible, attention should be centered on the day-by-day life of the group, as indicative of its culture and the changes occurring. The method of the novelist might well be heeded in this respect. Frequently he has more insight into the role of culture, its meaning to the individual, conflict situations, and the process of cultural change than have many cultural historians and social scientists.

Instead of making the immigrant group the center of attention, another procedure would be to take the local community as the main object of study and examine the role of all constituent cultural groups in its life. By studying nationality groups as a part of local history, one may perceive interrelationships more clearly and obtain a more balanced treatment. If the community contains several nationality groups, it may be advantageous to compare the varying adjustments of different groups to relatively the same situation. It should also be noted that a cultural study, as outlined above, may well be applied to native American groups. They, too, are worthy of investigation, and I venture to say that our first-hand knowledge of American culture, strictly speaking, is more deficient than our knowledge of immigrant ways.

Cultural Contribution versus Cultural Assimilation

RAY ALLEN BILLINGTON

The approach to the study of nationality groups suggested in the preceding section sounds so plausible today that it is difficult to realize the newness of the study of the cultural contributions of the immigrant. Sociologists and historians of only a generation ago, blinded by their rigid use of political and economic materials, viewed the alien only as an untrained voter and a disturbing element in the industrial system, not as a medium for the transfer of civilization. Prescott F. Hall,[3] typical of his day, listed as the sole "Effects of Immigration": the sweating system, the padrone system, unemployment, illiteracy, crime, insanity, disease, pauperism, and congestion in cities. Twenty years later sound scholars such as Fair-

[3] *Immigration and Its Effect upon the United States,* New York, 1906.

child and Stephenson still dwelt upon the slums, the lower standard of living, the poverty that accompanied the immigrant invasion, yet wholly ignored America's cultural debt to the foreign-born. This emphasis was so strong that it dictated the procedure even of historians of particular nationality groups, whose natural tendency to glorify their subjects was limited to a scanty listing of artists, writers, inventors, and industrialists, without attempting to assess the effect of these figures on American culture as a whole. Such an excellent recent work as that of William F. Adams [4] on the Irish dismissed the contributions of this important strain in one sentence: "The Irish names in the history of American poetry, fiction, drama and music suggest that the race has done its share."

The attitude of historians toward immigration helped shape public opinion and was at the same time a reflection of that opinion. Through most of the nineteenth century, Americans were unwilling to recognize alien cultural contributions because they hated immigrants. Foreigners from the Catholic despotisms of Europe, they honestly believed, endangered both Protestantism and democracy. These fundamental institutions could be protected only if aliens became thoroughly conversant with the American way before naturalization; the programs of the Know-Nothing party and the American Protective Association merely exaggerated this popular belief. This attitude naturally discouraged any recognition of foreign contributions to this country's cultural patterns. Nor did the changed sentiment concerning the immigrant which accompanied the dawn of the twentieth century improve the situation. Now Americans worried lest the alien be not naturalized, whereas before they had feared that he would be. Their country, they knew, could absorb the hordes of aliens swarming upon its shores only if all European customs were immediately sloughed off and the immigrants turned, overnight, into thorough Americans. To encourage this process the concept of the melting pot was developed.

Probably no more unfortunate phrase to describe assimilation could be found. The melting pot implies a giant caldron in which foreigners are boiled down into a colorless mass—as insipid as any stew. I can remember with distaste a pageant staged by Henry Ford in Detroit some thirty years ago. A giant melting pot was erected

[4] *Ireland and Irish Emigration to the New World from 1815 to the Famine*, New Haven, 1932.

outside his factory, and into this marched a great line of immigrants, clad in their colorful native costumes, singing their folk songs, and stopping now and then to reconstruct their Old World dances. They emerged on the other side, scrubbed to a point of uncomfortable perfection, dressed alike in the approved American way, and all trying to stretch their vocal cords around the high notes of "The Star-Spangled Banner." Even then I regretted that the warm color of their Old World lives was being cast aside so suddenly. Yet that was the spirit of the day, and both historians and the public ignored the contributions of these foreigners, in the rush to convert them into standardized products worthy of the label: "Made in the United States of America."

A more accurate appraisal of the role of nationality groups in American life was begun a few years ago, with the rise of the modern school of social history. The assimilation process is viewed not in terms of a melting pot, but as the bringing together of numerous varicolored strands, each representing a nationality group, and each lending brilliance and strength to the fabric of America. Carl Wittke [5] makes the first general attempt to describe the cultural contributions of the foreign-born, a task accomplished even more thoroughly within a limited area by Thomas J. Wertenbaker.[6] Equally significant is a series of volumes being prepared by the Federal Writers' Project of the Works Progress Administration. These are written by workers familiar with the language of the group under investigation, who obtain information both by approved historical methods and by interviews and questionnaires. Studies such as these will enrich the whole story of America's development.

Yet I wonder whether the scholar of tomorrow will conclude, as we so glibly do today, that cultural interchange is hurried by the assimilation of foreign-born elements. Are there not two types of cultural contribution? One is the superficial or surface culture: the inventions, art, architecture, music, economic devices, and the like. These are based on Old World experiences, which can be transferred without the assimilation of the group bringing them to America. Rather it might be argued that failure to assimilate increases these contributions, by forcing immigrants to continue Eu-

[5] *We Who Built America: The Saga of the Immigrant,* New York, 1939.
[6] *The Founding of American Civilization: The Middle Colonies,* New York, 1938.

ropean customs which can then be observed and imitated by natives. Would the Palatine Germans of the eighteenth century, for example, have left the mark they did if they had been speedily absorbed into the native population? The isolation forced upon them by antagonistic Englishmen gave to America the Palatine barn, the vegetable garden, the Conestoga wagon, the central stove to replace the uneconomical fireplace, and significant musical and architectural innovations. A century later the forced segregation of a portion of a new German migratory stream enriched American life with musical societies, beer drinking, and the Continental Sabbath.

This line of argument leads to an unpleasant conclusion: The United States can wring the greatest cultural contribution from its foreign-born by preventing assimilation. Nativists thus assume a new importance; can it be said that the scoundrels joining the Know-Nothings, the American Protective Association, or the modern Ku Klux Klan contributed more to American culture than the disciples of the melting pot?

The second type of cultural contribution made by the immigrant is more intangible: the mode of thought, the manner of living, the intellectual and spiritual concepts. Such cultural traits are not transmitted by a mere mingling of two groups, or even by use; they become part of the life of the adopting people only when they have been reëvolved within the social structure of that people. Thus an alien is assimilated not when he has learned the language and customs of a country, but only when he is able to make those customs his own; similarly, alien culture is transplanted only after it has been accepted and reëvolved within the American social structure.

American conditions encourage immigrants to slough off their Old World habits before this slow reëvolution of cultural patterns takes place. Countless forces, in addition to the usual social pressure toward Americanization, operate in this direction. Changed living conditions is one, for the farmers of Europe become the city dwellers of the New World, and their old patterns of life are speedily forgotten. Another factor discouraging the perpetuation of European culture is the antagonism with which the average immigrant views his homeland. Bad conditions there drove him to America, and he often wants to disassociate himself entirely from an unpleasant past, even by changing his habits of life. Still another force preventing fundamental alien cultures from affecting our own has been the economic or racial gulf separating the immigrant from the native population.

It might be shown, then, that assimilation is ineffective in transferring the fundamental cultural traits of nationality groups to the inhabitants of this country, and that their tangible contributions can best be made by isolation rather than absorption. I hope that this is not the case. I would like to believe that the cultural richness of America, as well as its economic wealth, has been created by the merging of many nationalities. Research along the lines already suggested will alone provide a solution to these problems.

The Transitional Character of Nationality Group Culture

CARLTON C. QUALEY

Recent approaches to the study of immigrant groups have challenged not only the old manner of regarding immigrants as "problems," but the somewhat newer approach which looks for "contributions" to American life. Instead of viewing immigrant groups as "aliens" or "minorities" who brought "gifts"—some good, some bad—to "American civilization," we have begun to realize that the subject of nationality groups is a complex one, not easily adapted to facile generalizations.

It has been realized that we know relatively little about the family and group life of the respective nationalities; that much of what has been done on these groups has suffered from antiquarianism, amateurism, and what the late J. F. Jameson called "filiopietism." We have any number of lists of immigrant men and women who in a great variety of fields have contributed "gifts" to American life. A host of immigrant-American societies have been formed, some of them scarcely more than mutual admiration societies, whose scholarly contributions have been limited. In an occasional such society, thanks to the presence of some genuine scholar, notable work has been accomplished. An example is the work of Professor T. C. Blegen, in the Norwegian-American Historical Association. But in all too many of these societies, the valuable materials at their disposal have been neglected or misused. With the gradual infiltration of trained historians into these societies, it is to be hoped that more worth-while research work and publication will ultimately result. It is hoped also that the mass of ephemeral materials which constitute sources for the study of these groups will be captured before they are destroyed.

Largely because of the language factor, but also because of natural interest, the students of immigrant groups in the United States have come chiefly from the ranks of each group. I suppose no historian can completely emancipate himself from the psychological and cultural patterns that consciously or unconsciously shape his viewpoint. Certainly this emancipation is difficult to achieve in the case of students who are themselves either members of an immigrant group or descendants of older stocks. "In-group" and "out-group" viewpoints so easily interfere with objectivity of research and interpretation. A prerequisite for a student of nationality groups is a thoroughgoing self-analysis. I would suggest that the use of such "out-group" terms as "immigrant gifts" and "minorities" tends to obscure the reciprocal influences among immigrant groups and between these groups and older stocks.

The use of the term "group culture" as applied to immigrants in the United States is suggestive, but requires careful limitation and definition. To the degree to which an immigrant group retains in the New World the language, customs, institutions, and modes of thought of the Old Country community, to that extent can it be said to possess a "culture" distinct from the prevailing culture of the American community in which the immigrants settle. Essentially, the term should be applied only to the *transitional* stage in the transplanting of persons of a given nationality from an Old World community to one in the New World. The duration of this transitional stage varies with each nationality and is always in terms of each person's or each family's purpose, cultural equipment, and experiences in the new community. To study an immigrant group culture in isolation is largely meaningless. The group culture must be studied as part of the larger community culture in which the immigrant lives.

I should like to emphasize the interpretation of an immigrant-American group culture as being essentially transitional, by brief reference to that group with which I happen to be most familiar—the Norwegian-American. Thanks in large part to the work of the

Norwegian-American Historical Association, the nature of the Norwegian-American group culture is gradually becoming more apparent. It is becoming apparent that those habits, institutions, viewpoints, customs, and other aspects that combine to form the somewhat loosely defined thing called a "group culture," came into being in response to the genuine need of the Norwegian immigrant for social prestige, religious comfort, political effectiveness, economic security, and psychological strength or stability, during the period when he was no longer a "Norwegian" but was at the same time not yet an "American." Thanks to this "cushioning" culture, many Norwegian immigrants, especially those of the first generation but also those of the second, never had to make much of a transition. This was especially true in rural communities. But in later generations, thanks to American schools and opportunities and acceptance, the transition was completed. When, in a large number of families in any community, this transition is completed, their Norwegian-American group culture tends to disintegrate and merge with the prevailing community culture.

European Backgrounds and American Rivalries

OSCAR OSBURN WINTHER

It is interesting to observe that as far back as the eighteenth century Hector Saint-John de Crèvecœur called attention to the complicated character of American nationality. "What then is the American, this new man?" asked Crèvecœur. ". . . He is an American, who leaving behind him all his ancient prejudices and manners, receives new ones from the new mode of life he has embraced, the new government he obeys, and the new rank he holds." [7] Today the historian's understanding of the problem of American nationality is little better than that of Crèvecœur's a century and a half ago.

Speaking as one chiefly concerned with the Pacific region, I am of the opinion that a sharp distinction should be made between European immigrant groups in America and groups set apart by color, the Negroes, Chinese, Japanese, and Indians in this coun-

[7] J. Hector St. John de Crèvecœur, *Letters from an American Farmer*, Everyman's Library, New York (n.d.), p. 43.

try. It should be recognized, too, that situations of conflict are not always ones involving the ideas of Old World and New World cultures, but often ones, as the late Professor Larson indicated, involving different Old World cultures. Some years ago, as the son of Danish immigrant parents living in Nebraska, I found the cultural clash was not so much one between myself and the so-called American as it was between me and the Germans and the Irish.

Furthermore, it is of great importance to know the historical background of the subordinate groups which go to make up the America of the twentieth century. It is not enough to acquire first-hand knowledge of immigrant communities in this country. Rather, it is equally important to go to the land of origin of the particular subordinate group under consideration.

How, for example, can one begin to understand or interpret Danish-American interrelations without a knowledge, first of all, of the Danish language, of the history of the Danish coöperative system, the development of varieties of Danish Lutheranism, the growth of representative government in Denmark, and, most important of all, a profound understanding of the Danish ways of life? Only with a thorough grounding in Danish economic history can one explain why and how the Danes have contributed to the progress of the coöperative movement in the United States and why they invented the cream separator. And why on the other hand some Danes, and particularly those from Copenhagen where the profit system is still esteemed, would denounce the coöperative as highly undesirable and un-American. Consumers' coöperatives in Denmark are as much social as they are economic institutions—an aspect that cannot be fully appreciated without an intimate knowledge of the European background. And only with a thorough understanding of the religious history of the old country can one begin to realize why, in many instances, synodical factionalism makes for syncretism rather than resistance to said process. Oftentimes, for example, have hard-shell Danish Intermission Lutherans—faced with the choice of belonging either to a Danish Grundvig Lutheran church or to some liberal American church—cast their lot with the latter in order to escape the heretical tendencies of the former.

It is therefore fallacious to generalize on the background of even the smallest of immigrant groups; and so when writers fail to distinguish between Swedes, Danes, Norwegians, and Icelanders, and simply call them Scandinavians—and most writers do—it is high time that more scholarly attention be paid to the European background of immigrant groups.

Moreover, the fact must be recognized that the land of origin may well have a culture fully as dynamic as that of America. In view of this, it is incumbent upon both the sociologist and the historian studying nationalities to recognize the relative difference between, shall we say, the background of the immigrant Germans of the eighteenth century, the forty-eighters, and, finally, those of the post-war era.

Summary of the Discussion

JOSEPH S. ROUCEK, CAROLINE F. WARE, AND M. W. ROYSE

The suggestions for the study of nationality groups contained in these four papers raise questions of method which challenge students in this field.

1. Is it sound to study nationality groups by focusing attention upon the leaders or outstanding representatives of the group? Do *Who's Who* and the *Dictionary of American Biography*, as suggested by Mr. Davie, reveal significant data relating to the groups from which outstanding individuals have come? These persons are often accorded honor by the country of their origin and made to occupy a position of prestige out of proportion to the activity which has brought them their distinction. On the other hand, those who achieve "success" often do so by sloughing off their traditional culture; their success is evidence of their adaptation to American conditions; the very characteristics which account for their presence in *Who's Who* distinguish them from their fellows and make them poor sources for a study of their group. Moreover, the majority of every group is made up of workers, farmers, and others of lower social and economic status whose culture is very imperfectly revealed in that of the rare "outstanding" individual.

2. Is it sound to look for "contributions" of groups to "American life"? Does the search for immigrant "gifts," as suggested by Mr. Davie and Mr. Billington (whether these gifts be material or

nonmaterial), lead to fruitful results? The concept of immigrant "contributions" implies that the culture of old-American groups constitutes "American civilization" and that bits of immigrant culture are added to it. The experience of the directors of the Federal Writers Project casts doubts on this approach. In setting up a series of social-ethnic studies, they first attempted to use the "contributions" approach. After trying it out for several months in different places, they abandoned it. In their study of North Dakota, for example, they found it quite inapplicable, for all the people in North Dakota were recent immigrants from somewhere —Europe or the eastern United States.

The idea of "contributions" of immigrants in North Dakota raised the question of "contributions to what?" The same difficulty arose in eastern communities in which the great majority of the population belongs to recent immigrant groups. Immigrants and the children of immigrants *are* the American people. Their culture *is* American culture, not merely a contributor to American culture. The Federal Writers Project consequently abandoned the "contribution" approach and focused its attention on "participation" in various aspects of the life of the communities in which ethnic groups are living.

The tendency to assume that American culture is the culture of the old-American, Anglo-Saxon group is perpetuated by the fact that historical studies and history textbooks continue to be written primarily from the standpoint of the Anglo-Saxon myth. While we abuse the Germans for overemphasizing the Nazi myth, we continue to employ a historical myth of our own. The growing number of studies showing that other than Anglo-Saxons have influenced the course of our history has not been reflected in the steady output of textbooks which preserve the myth. Nor has the work of Bolton and others, showing that Spanish and other cultures are at the base of the history of various regions in the West and South, broken down the habit of writing American history from the "Plymouth Rock" view. If we would follow a cultural approach to American history, we must find ways by which the available information on the role played by "new" immigrants can seep into the textbooks which are mostly still rehashing "old viewpoints in American history."

3. Is the process upon which students of nationality groups should

focus attention that of "transition," as suggested by Mr. Qualey and his illustration from the Norwegian-American group?

Just what is in transit, and what constitutes "American culture" in the meantime? Should we think of Norwegian culture as one entity, American culture as a second entity, and a temporary, transitional, Norwegian-American culture which drops off as members of the group make the transition into American culture?

Thomas and Znaniecki pointed out with respect to the Polish group that

> The fundamental process which has been going on during this period is the *formation of a new Polish-American society* out of those fragments separated from Polish society and embedded in American society.
>
> [This society] in structure and prevalent attitudes is neither Polish nor American but constitutes a specific new product whose raw materials have been partly drawn from Polish traditions, partly from the new conditions in which the immigrants live and from American social values as the immigrant sees and interprets them.[8]

A large proportion of the people in American communities are Polish-American, Norwegian-American, Italian-American of the first, second, or third generation. These Polish-American, Italian-American, Norwegian-American societies are integral parts of the American cultural whole. In the opinion of Thomas and Znaniecki, the significant process is that by which Polish-American culture *as a whole* is changing toward greater similarity with the culture of other parts of American society, rather than a process by which members of the group become "American" and the Polish-American group culture falls away.

Moreover, the culture of the American people at any time is a composite of the cultures of these groups. American culture is not something in the future, when "transitional" states have been passed. Neither is it a constant pattern which absorbs successive increments from alien groups, nor yet a separate stream with a cultural momentum of its own. At any point in time, American culture has been the culture of these people. Today, New England culture is not Plymouth Rock culture, with transitional French, Portuguese, Polish, Italian, Greek, Syrian, Irish, and other group cultures held, as it were, in suspension within it. New England

[8] W. I. Thomas and F. Znaniecki, *The Polish Peasant in Europe and America* (Chicago, 1920), V, ix.

today *is* French, Portuguese, Polish, Italian, Greek, Syrian, Irish-American. These *are* the New England people—who vote in elections, work in mills and offices, pay taxes, support churches, listen to radios, drive over the highways, stage Fourth of July carnivals, St. Patrick's day parades and Our Lady of Mt. Carmel celebrations, and bring up the next generation of Americans. They *are* the American people. Their culture *is* contemporary American culture as truly as is the culture of Iowa-American farmers or Appalachian-American hill-billies.

Understanding of both new Americans and old suffers from failure to recognize the position which the several groups occupy in American society. The assumption on the part of old Americans that they are *the* Americans obscures a realistic examination of American cultural trends. It has been aptly said that in many communities, particularly in New England, the old Americans live in a "Yankee ghetto," as cultural islands in the broader American community.

Perhaps the most important reminder in using any of the suggested approaches to the study of nationality groups is the closing statement in Mr. Davie's paper: "I venture to say that our first-hand knowledge of American culture is more deficient than our knowledge of immigrant ways."

PART THREE: CULTURAL INSTITUTIONS

INTRODUCTORY NOTE

THE CULTURAL historian must almost certainly turn to the institutions of the society which he studies as a first approach to an understanding of its culture. They are the repetitive relationships, whether formally or informally organized, in terms of which life is led. They provide the channels through which persistent human drives find their outlet and are shaped. The four institutions considered in this section are major elements in the basic framework of the cultures in which they are found.

In virtually all agrarian cultures, the most basic institution is the family. Three family types belonging to nonindustrial societies are analyzed here; in each case they are seen in a situation where the impact of industrial culture is bringing certain modifications. The communal joint-family, the zadruga, of the Balkans is seen adjusting itself to various westernizing influences, particularly the changing status of women with respect to the holding of land; the Chinese large-family system, the basic political and economic as well as social unit of Chinese culture, is examined under conditions in which modernization and land pressure are combining to individualize members of the group; the Russian peasant family is viewed under two forms of collective organization, the traditional mir and the modern collective farm, or kolkhoz, which represents a transition to industrial forms of agricultural production.

While the family has provided the basis of organization in most agrarian societies, the industrial city has become the basic institution of modern industrial society, taking over many of the functions of the rural family, and supplanting it as the central unit of social organization. Urban life is not new. The city has been the center of control and of innovation in the Western world since ancient times. But the pre-industrial city was essentially a service unit for a basically agrarian society. It tied together the threads of that society through trade and through political administration; it serviced that society by developing the professions, leaving to the hinterland the major task of supplying the bases of livelihood and providing self-support for the masses of the population. The industrial revolution has so changed the economic basis of society as to alter fundamentally the role of the city. The industrial city has come to provide the organized social relationships and the milieu within which the life of increasing proportions of the population is passed.

The characteristics of the industrial city as a cultural institution may be seen in the developmental period of the first industrial city, Manchester, England, which is here described.

The modern corporation is one of the major new institutional forms which has emerged in recent years. It has received relatively little consideration as an institution, partly because it exists in the economic sphere, in which behavior has customarily been analyzed not in institutional terms but in terms of calculations of advantage and disadvantage and the processes of exchange; partly because political scientists, most obviously equipped to analyze the power relationships which play so large a part in corporate organization have been preoccupied with one single institution, the state. In modern society, the corporation is not merely a legal form or an economic unit but an institution within which and through which power relationships are expressed, decisions affecting vast numbers of people are arrived at, and the basis for many social relationships are established. In terms of scope and power, the modern corporation stands beside the modern state; the interrelations of corporate and political institutions provide the major institutional tensions of the industrial age.

The two essays on the corporation treat the emergence of the modern corporation and its relationship to the modern state, and the internal structure of the corporation, viewed as a social institution.

It is an ironic fact that the military organization of many societies not only reflects the major relations and values which characterize the whole society, but represent these relations and values in their most highly developed form. The best ingenuity, the most effective organization, the greatest prestige appears in the military institutions of such a society. The German army of the Second Reich was much more than a war machine. It was an institution of economic and social organization which epitomized the organizational techniques, the class structure, and the cultural drives of the society. It is here analyzed in those terms.

THE PEASANT FAMILY: THE ZADRUGA, OR COMMUNAL JOINT-FAMILY IN THE BALKANS, AND ITS RECENT EVOLUTION

PHILIP E. MOSELY

WHILE historians have devoted much attention to the turbulent politics and intricate diplomacy of the Balkans, relatively little study has been made of the social development of the Balkan peoples. Yet during the last 50 to 150 years these peoples have undergone numerous and radical changes, including the destruction of serfdom and of a long-established caste system; the emergence of a preponderantly land-owning peasantry; an intense process of internal colonization; the growth of emigration to foreign countries; the development of modern systems of communication and transportation; the growing penetration of a money economy and the relative decline of a natural economy; the destruction of the old regional equilibrium between town and village; the development of national states, of national bureaucracies, and of national intelligentsias; the growth of professional life and of factory production; the extension of state services, of public education, of compulsory military service; the spread of literacy; the growing impact of statute law on customary law; and so forth.

The investigation of Balkan social development may be approached through several avenues. One of them is the study of an outstanding institution of peasant life in the Balkans, the "zadruga," or communal joint-family. Although no single definition embraces all varieties of the zadruga, it may be considered, tentatively, as a household composed of two or more biological or small-families, closely related by blood or adoption, owning its means of production communally, producing and consuming the means of its livelihood jointly, and regulating the control of its property, labor, and livelihood communally.

Studies of the zadruga have been chiefly historical and ethnographical in their approach. Historical literature has dealt mainly with the problem of the national or "racial" character and origin of the zadruga. At first historical controversy hinged largely on the question of whether the zadruga was a peculiarly Slav institution, expressive of some innate Slav tendency toward family communism, or whether it was found among non-Slav peoples. As a result of this discussion, traces of the zadruga have been found among widely scattered peoples, both Slav and non-Slav. A second aspect of the controversy has run parallel with the dispute over the origins of the Great Russian "mir," or distributional land commune. Some students of the zadruga have held that it was very old, probably of prehistoric origin, others that it arose as a product of the fiscal and legal systems of the Byzantine and Ottoman empires. The entire documentation on which the controversy is based consists of a few much-disputed statutes; probably the most that one can assert is that while Byzantine and Ottoman legislation seems to have favored the continued existence of the zadruga, it could hardly have penetrated so deeply into the life of the village as by itself to have created the zadrugal way of life.

The abundant ethnographical literature on the zadruga has, unfortunately, little value for the study of social history. The ethnographers have collected numerous examples of the zadruga, but without presenting a full analysis of the individual zadrugas with respect to their internal structures and their village and regional settings.[1] An undifferentiated approach to the study of the zadruga unconsciously assumes a uniform background for all Balkan zadrugas; in this part of the world, with its sharp regional variations, such an assumption is very misleading. There are, however, several valuable monographs which present full and detailed accounts of single zadrugas in Bosnia and Croatia.[2]

[1] The most important ethnographical studies are those of Valtazar Bogišić, *Pravni običaja u slovena; privatno pravo*, Zagreb, 1867, and *Zbornik sadašnjih pravnih običaja u južnih slovena; gragja u odgovorima iz različnih krajeva slovenskoga juga*, Zagreb, 1874; S. S. Bobchev, "Bulgarskata cheliadna zadruga v segashno i minalo vreme; istoriko-yuridicheski studii," *Sbornik za narodni umotvoreniya, nauka i knizhnina*, XII–XIII (Sofia, 1906–7), 1–207; Vasilj Popović, *Zadruga; istorijska rasprava*, Sarajevo, 1921; J. Cvijić, *La péninsule balkanique*, Paris, 1918; and numerous volumes of his *Naselja*.

[2] Milan Karanović, "Nekolike velike porodične zadruge u Bosni i Hercegovini," *Glasnik zemaljskog muzeja u Bosni i Hercegovini*, XLI (Sarajevo, 1929), 63–80; *ibid.*, XLII (1930), 133–56; Držislav Švob and Franko Petrić, "Zadruga Domladovac," *Zbornik za narodni život i običaje južnih slavena*, XXVII (Zagreb, 1929), 92–110. The best juridical studies are those of V. Krišković, *Hrvatsko pravo kućnih zadruga; historijskodogmatski nacrt*, Zagreb, 1925; M. Utiešenović, *Die Hauskommunion der Südslaven*, Vienna, 1859, and same, *Die Militärgränze und die Verfassung*, Vienna, 1861.

One purpose in making a fresh study of the zadruga is, by applying a uniform method of case-study investigation, to define the various regional types of zadruga found in the Balkans, to place the regional types in relation to their geographical and social environment, and to discover, as far as possible, the main lines in the evolution of the Balkan zadruga over the last hundred years or so.[3] This investigation was based on the method of sampling, by picking typical villages or hamlets in each region, rather than by applying statistical methods over a broader area. The statistical material now available does not lend itself to refined treatment. In one village, for example, a family which had been divided into seven smaller families for nearly thirty years was listed in the official records as a joint-family, chiefly because the separate families had continued to inhabit a single courtyard.[4] In another village a former zadruga was listed as completely divided into individual small-families, although three of the small-families had, after the general division of the zadrugal property, recombined at once to form a new zadruga with twenty-three members.[5] In the beginning of the study it became obvious that the statistical method, if applied accurately and with significant results, would require several years of work in each separate region. It seemed preferable to leave the statistical approach to later workers in the field, and to devote the limited time available to a comparative study of regional types of the zadruga and of regional patterns in its evolution.

Further stimulus to make this study, if such was needed, was supplied by the deep interest of the Balkan peoples themselves in the zadruga. Whole schools of scholars, poets, and politicians regard the zadruga as one of the poles of Balkan life, its peasant pole, in contrast with the "charshia," or market place. For many decades economists and jurists as well as political leaders have debated whether or not the zadruga has outlived its usefulness and whether

---

Several recent studies of social geography have thrown valuable light on the zadruga, especially those of G. Gunchev, "Vakarel, antropogeografski prouchvanya," *Godishnik na sofiiskiya universitet,* XXIX (Sofia, 1933), 1–188; Herbert Wilhelmy, *Hochbulgarien. I. Die ländlichen Siedlungen und die bäuerliche Wirtschaft,* Kiel, 1935; Richard Busch-Zantner, *Agrarverfassung, Gesellschaft und Siedlung in Südosteuropa, unter besonderer Berücksichtigung der Türkenzeit,* Leipzig, 1938.

[3] This investigation was made possible by a Grant-in-Aid of the Social Science Research Council in 1938.

[4] Recorded Sept. 9, 1938, village of Korovo, district of Peshtera, Bulgaria.

[5] Recorded Aug. 20–21, 1938, village of Lazina, district of Karlovac, Croatia.

it should be encouraged or attacked. Of late the controversy has been especially sharp in Croatia.[6] Even in Rumania there has been a certain agitation in favor of promoting the zadruga as one possible means of combating the extreme subdivision of peasant holdings and the growing proletarianization of the village. Such a proposal seems highly utopian, but that it is being seriously discussed in a country which is almost entirely without a zadrugal tradition is in itself significant.

Before one or two of the conclusions reached in this new study of the zadruga can be presented, the procedure followed should be explained, at least in bare outline. With the assistance of local teachers, priests, or civic leaders, a "typical" village was chosen in each region to be studied, chiefly by eliminating those which showed deviations from the normal status of villages in the area. The next step was to go to the village and establish a friendly relationship with the leading villagers, usually with the elders of one or more zadrugas.

The following step, the first in the actual study, was to draw up a genealogy of the family; sometimes this reached back only 50 or 60 years, but not infrequently it covered a period of 100 or 150 years. The composition of the family now and in earlier periods could then be analyzed, together with the transmission of the leadership of the family from one head or elder to his successor. By inquiring about each woman who had married into or out of the zadruga, it was possible to ascertain the dowry received or given, or the bride-price paid or received, and to record significant changes in the sphere of marriage and dowry custom. A further step involved the recording of the division of labor within the zadruga among age groups, sex groups, and skill groups.

Another desirable step was to draw up a budget for the family; in some instances this was impossible, either because the peasant, who is very ready to narrate in great detail the history of his family, is reluctant to part with budgetary information, or because a high degree of natural economy resulted in wide yearly fluctuations in income and outlay. In these cases the study of the budget had to

[6] The zadruga has been championed by Milan Ivšić, *Les Problèmes agraires en Yougoslavie*, Paris, 1926; *Temelji seljačkoga zakonika*, Zagreb, 1933; *Seljačka politika*, Zagreb, 1937–38; and by Milovan Gavazzi, *Seljačka zadružna obitelj kao činjenica i kao problem*, Sarajevo, 1934. It has been attacked by Rudolf Bićanić, *Kako živi narod*, Zagreb, 1936.

be replaced by two rough criteria of the balance between natural and money economy: one, the listing of commodities bought and sold during the preceding year, with approximate quantities and prices; the other, the listing of labor services sold by the family through local wage labor or through migration in search of work, and of labor services bought by the family through the hiring of local laborers and artisans.

A further line of inquiry entailed listing all the landed property held or rented by the zadruga, its time and method of acquisition, together with an inventory of its livestock and equipment. It was also important to determine the boundaries of communal and individual property within the zadruga by listing and checking every possible kind of property and income. The analysis of the communal rights exercised by the zadruga in village or clan property, such as forests, pastures, and fisheries, and of the role of these rights in the zadrugal economy was very significant. A further line of inquiry dealt with the division of the zadruga, its causes, the methods by which it was carried out, and the problems of readjustment which it raised. General conversations with the individual members of the zadruga helped to draw out their attitudes toward the zadruga, the village, and the state, and to discover changes which had occurred within their memory. Other information was secured through direct observation of life in the zadruga and of the unspoken attitudes of its members, and through photographing the members of the zadruga, their possessions, and their activities.

One of the first surprises in studying the zadruga was to discover that it was not usually regarded by the peasants as an institution distinct from the individual, or small-family. In Croatia, to be sure, the term "zadruga" had long been popularized in the villages by the special legal status which it received in the codes of the former Military Border of Austria and in that of Civil Croatia; elsewhere the peasants do not use this term in describing what scholars call the zadruga—not even in pre-1912 Serbia, where the term is also used in the law code. Outside of Croatia, the zadruga is more commonly referred to as "a large house" or "a large household," "a lot of people," sometimes as "an undivided house." In Serbia proper "to live in zadruga" means "to live in concord" or "in harmony," not "to live in *a* zadruga." In brief, except in certain regions where the law codes have given a special status to the zadruga, and not always there, the peasants themselves make no distinction between the joint-family and the small or biological-family household, except to indicate the greater size of the former. Both the multiple family and the small-family are part of one social environment. When the social atmosphere, that is, the customary rules and attitudes, remains favorable to the communal family, the zadruga persists with much vitality; when new rules arise, hostile to the spirit of the zadruga, the communal joint-family disappears.

In regions where the zadruga spirit is strong among the peasants, any small-family may, through biological expansion, become a zadruga. In many parts of Bosnia and Herzegovina, the zadruga is strong today, even though its existence is ignored by the law. On the other hand, in the former Military Border of Croatia-Slavonia the separate zadrugal status of a substantial part of peasant land has been maintained by the law code, but the peasant family has been steadily approaching the non-zadrugal or small-family way of life. In that area, although a large part of peasant property is still zadrugal in legal status, the peasants usually treat it, or try to treat it, as individual, or Roman-law property. The important factor in the persistence or decline of the zadruga is the persistence or decline of traditional communal attitudes toward the family, toward ownership of land, and toward customs of dowry and inheritance, rather than the positive provisions of the written law.

One of the customary rules on which the zadrugal way of life rests is that, as long as there are male heirs to carry on the communal family, women inherit no share in the zadrugal land. In the zadruga of Simo Bašić, in the village of Dobrinje, in the district of Banjaluka, northern Bosnia, the custom is for the bride to bring to her husband's household a large hope chest or even two, filled with her own handiwork; this is called the "sprema" or "oprema." In return the bridegroom's family makes a compensating but less valuable payment called the "gage of friendship" or "ujma prijateljstva." The third transaction involved in the marriage is the "dar," or "gift," of the bride's father to the bride, made a year after the marriage, and consisting of livestock, usually a cow, or a cow and two sheep. The daughter, once married out of the zadruga, has no claim to a share of the inheritance in land, which passes to her brother. A daughter still unmarried at her father's death can claim from her brothers only the customary marriage outfit and the "gift."

If a peasant family in this district has no son to carry on the household, one of the sons-in-law, usually the husband of the youngest daughter, becomes a member of his wife's household, in some cases even taking his wife's family name. By exclusion of women from the inheritance of real property and of agricultural equipment, the zadruga gives consistency to the large household. Wherever the zadruga is well preserved today, the rule of male inheritance is dominant. Significantly, in the same district, northern Bosnia, the custom of exclusive male inheritance also prevails among the small-families.[7] Both the joint-family and the small-family exist in the same social atmosphere, in this case, an atmosphere favorable to the persistence of the joint-family.

An entirely different picture is presented by the German village of Neudorf, or Novo Selo, near Vinkovci, Slavonia. This community, although settled by Swabian colonists in the eighteenth century, formed a part of and was subject to the laws of the former Military Border of Croatia-Slavonia. While all the land except the common lands was originally held by zadrugas, the communal families have divided rapidly during the last sixty years, until today it is rare to find one with as many as ten members. By a new law of the 1870's, exclusive male inheritance of land was abolished; according to the new rules of inheritance, zadrugal land could be divided among the daughters when there was no son, and in any division of a zadruga a woman member acquired the right to a share equal to one-half that of a man. A further factor which contributed to breaking down the zadruga was the adoption of the "Zweikindersystem," or "two-child-family," instead of the larger families of earlier days; the restriction of births increased the number of families without sons, and hence the number of women who received land from their fathers as dowry or inheritance. For example, Jakob Jakober had no sons and four daughters; his thirty-two Joch of zadrugal land, or "Kommunionsland," were divided equally among his daughters and became their full individual property, or "Eigentum." In turn, a wife who had received land as dowry or heritage could now bequeath it as she wished to her own daughters and sons, or dispose of it in any way she might choose. By this process much former communal, or zadrugal land has been transformed into full individual property.

[7] Recorded Aug. 18–19, 1938.

In Neudorf there have been many conflicts over applying the rules for the division of the zadruga and its property. In the case of the zadruga of Georg Hupbauer, which divided in 1921 for the first time in about 130 years, much bitterness was aroused in some members of the zadruga because, contrary to the unwritten custom, but in accord with written law, the head of the household took a full share of the communal property for himself, in order to add it to the holding of his favorite son, Ludwig, with whom he then went to live. Another common complaint was that the head of the zadruga had bought private land, or "Eigentum," from the common earnings of the zadruga, and had then disposed of it as his individual property instead of treating it according to the rules customary for communal land.

One further trait which showed how far Neudorf had moved from the old communal-family way of life was the new custom of reserving a yearly support for life, or "Aussenhalt," for the former head of the zadruga, after its division. When Philipp Teiber divided his land among his three sons in 1888, he reserved ten Joch of land for his own support; as long as he lived his three sons worked this share of land, paid the taxes on it, and turned over the product to him. Another and now commoner type of "Aussenhalt" is illustrated in the case of Jakob's second son, Heinrich Teiber, who divided all his land among his three sons in 1926; by a written contract each son obligated himself to furnish the father with a fixed amount of wheat, corn, wine, firewood, eggs, poultry, and milk; Heinrich and his wife also had a separate room and kitchen, and kept house for themselves.[8] Nothing could be more remote than this from the life of a genuine zadruga, with its close family cooperation and common housekeeping. Although Neudorf still has a large part of its land in zadrugal status, the individualistic way of life has made such headway that the peasants try in every way to evade the restrictions inherent in the zadrugal property status, and as far as possible they treat all their property as full individual property of the Roman-law type.

A similar picture of the evolution away from the zadrugal way of life is to be found in Rokovci, a Croatian village in the same district, and, like Neudorf, a community of former "Grenzer," or soldiers of the Military Border. With the granting of rights of inheritance

[8] Recorded Aug. 26, 1938.

in zadrugal land to women, with the growth of the new custom of providing dowry in land for brides, and with the decline in the size of the family, there has been an increasing tendency to treat the zadrugal property as if it were individual property. Until about 1890 it was rare for women to receive dowry or inheritance in land; even after that time such dowry or inheritance might be sold and the proceeds given to the bride in cash, to avoid bringing into the zadruga the disturbing element of individual property in land. Today, however, as in Neudorf, every biological, or small-family counts on receiving land from the bride's family as well as from the groom's. Even the practice of providing the older members of the divided household with a definite contractual support for life, here called the "uživanje," is almost as common in Rokovci as in Neudorf. Thus the evolution of the zadruga in a German and a Croatian village of the same region has been essentially identical, except that the Croatian village has been a little slower in changing its customs and has still preserved one or two fair-sized zadrugas, one of twenty-three members.[9]

An interesting illustration of a similar change in the rules of inheritance is found in the hamlet, or "mahala," of the Stoynevi, in the village of Kopanitsa, Radomir district, western Bulgaria. Here until recently the custom prevailed of paying a bride-price to the bride's father, whose duty it was to give the bride an outfit of clothes, bedding, towels, and so forth, together with a chest to keep them in. The daughters had no claim to inherit any share of the land so long as there were any male heirs. About 1930, however, married daughters began demanding and receiving their legal share of the patrimony; according to the Bulgarian code of 1889, a daughter is entitled to a share equal to one-half that of a son. Once a sister has demanded and taken her legal share of the patrimony, her brothers are naturally forced, in compensation, to demand the shares to which their own wives are entitled by law; and thus in a few years the entire custom of land inheritance in Kopanitsa has been turned inside out. When a wife brings her own land or the expectation of inheriting land to her husband's household, her position within that household is naturally quite different from what it was when she brought merely her hands and her marriage outfit. When several wives bring different quantities of land, strong

[9] Recorded Aug. 26, 1938.

pressure arises for the division of the zadruga into its component small-families. Each small-family, instead of looking to the joint cultivation of the zadrugal property for its livelihood, turns to the creation of a new unit, based on the combination of the wife's and the husband's shares of their respective patrimonies. Inequalities of property among the wives accentuate still further the disintegrating tendencies within the zadruga and make its continued existence problematical.

There is one common method of compromise which aims to preserve the zadruga without depriving its individual wives of their dowry or heritage in land. It is illustrated in the case of the zadruga of Petar Pavlev, with twenty-four members, in the same Bulgarian hamlet. When in 1937 one of the wives, Zora, inherited twenty dekars of her father's land in the somewhat distant commune of Pernik, the zadruga undertook to work the land for her on shares. The zadruga provided the seed, and turned over something more than one-half the net product to Zora, who in turn used that separate income to pay school expenses for two sons and to buy extra things for her small-family.[10]

An even more systematic elaboration of the same type of compromise between the communal zadruga and individual inheritance is illustrated in the case of the Varžić zadruga, in the village of Zelčin, Valpovo district, Slavonia. Here, although nearly every wife has property of her own in land or livestock, it is not exploited by the zadruga itself, but by outsiders working on shares. Manda, Jozo's wife, has no land, but when she married in 1917 she received a cow, which she sold, and with the proceeds she bought two breed sows. These are kept by a neighbor in his own pen; when litters of sucklings are sold, she receives one-half the money, and with this non-zadrugal, or individual income she buys additional sewing materials and dyestuffs toward preparing the marriage outfit, or "otpremnina," for her daughter, over and above the equal provision made by the zadruga for each of its marriageable girls. A more complicated case is presented by Kata, wife of Marko, in the same zadruga. After her wedding she received two sows, two cows, two calves, and three Joch, or "jutara," of land from her father. The land is worked on shares by a neighbor; Marko sold one cow and the calves and bought another Joch of land, which is also worked

[10] Recorded Sept. 4, 1938.

on shares by a fellow villager. From the income Marko's wife buys additional articles of clothing, and Marko provides himself with city-made shirts, cigarettes, and medical treatment. Usually when a girl marries out of the zadruga, dowry in land is provided by the girl's own mother out of her own dowry or heritage; in one case, however, the Varžić zadruga decided to buy a Joch of land with zadrugal money in order to provide a suitable dowry for one of its girls whose mother had married into the zadruga before the giving of land in dowry had become the rule.

It is interesting to note that this personal income, derived by individual couples within the Varžić zadruga from land and livestock received by the wives as dowry or heritage, merely supplements the identical allowances made by the zadruga itself to each of the six wives in it. Each wife receives 300 dinars in April, 300 in September, and 300 before Christmas to buy sewing materials for the needs of her small-family. In the autumn each wife shares in the sale of surplus chickens, which are disposed of to reduce the carry-over. In the spring each wife is assigned as many furrows of flax as she wishes to work; from the produce she makes linen for her family, and she may also sell the surplus flaxseed to add to her pocket money. As is plainly to be seen, this zadruga has worked out an elaborate compromise between the communal and the individual interests of its component small-families. The Varžić zadruga is, by the way, unusually prosperous and well organized. Its leaders are active in running the affairs of the village, the land community, the drainage coöperative, and the Croatian Peasants' party. They are quite aware that their zadruga of 26 members is an exception today and they strive deliberately to preserve it. For example, all its members but one, who provides his own tobacco out of his wife's separate property, have given up smoking and drinking. "If we should smoke and drink, we should have to lay out money for tobacco and wine, and then there would be quarrels about how much each consumed, and the zadruga would be in danger of breaking up," said Djuro, the co-elder of the household.[11] Their elaborate arrangement for harmonizing the continued existence of the zadruga with the development of female inheritance in land is thus only a part of the highly self-conscious and purposeful attitude of its members toward the zadruga as a whole.

[11] Recorded Aug. 27–28, 1938.

The problem of the change in the customs of land inheritance deserves special emphasis because it has been, in many regions of the Balkans, a central factor affecting the continuance or dissolution of the zadruga. It also shows how the zadruga and the small-family exist in the same social environment and according to the same customary rules and are not two distinct institutions, each with its own rules, as ethnographers and legislators have often assumed. It is also interesting to note in passing the tremendous influence which this change over in inheritance custom exerts on the very serious problem of checking the rapid subdivision of peasant holdings, and hence on the problem of maintaining the efficiency of peasant agriculture. The zadruga is likely to have its land in a few large fields, with all the advantages which that implies. The small-family, with its landholding formed by combining the heritages of both husband and wife, is likely to possess a rapidly increasing number of small, even tiny strips. To counteract the evil effects of excessive subdivision, consolidation, or "commassation," has been applied in some regions, notably in Slavonia and in a few villages of Bulgaria. But from the experience of the consolidations made in Slavonia during the twenty-five years before 1914 it is plain that, because of the decline of the zadruga and the consequent rapid partitioning of peasant holdings, consolidation loses its beneficial effect within two or three generations and has to be carried out all over again, with all the expense which it entails. The growth of the new custom of female inheritance in land, together with the decline of the zadruga, represents a broad, underlying cause of parcellation, which the purely technical procedure of consolidation is unable permanently to counteract.

The broader question of the break-up of the zadruga, aside from the development of female inheritance in land, would require extended treatment. In brief, it may be pointed out that any investigation of this problem should distinguish between two easily confused processes, the dissolution and disappearance of the zadruga and the normal process of subdivision. The very large zadruga is, and always was, the exception, although zadrugas of fifty, seventy, even eighty-three members have been studied in the course of this survey. The zadruga of ten to twenty members is much more usual, however. A zadruga may increase to such size that the forces of disintegration outweigh the integrating tendencies. It may become difficult to control and coördinate the work of a large zadruga, the degree of blood relationship may have become rather remote, or a considerable part of the zadrugal land newly brought under cultivation may lie at some distance from the communal homestead. In these circumstances the overgrown zadruga is likely to split into several smaller ones, or into a number of small-families, out of which new zadrugas may in turn grow. In widely separated parts of the Balkans the peasants liken this process to the swarming of bees.

The dissolution of the zadruga is quite a different process. As shown above, it may in some regions grow out of a change in the customs of inheritance and dowry; in this case it is strongly influenced by the refusal or the failure of the written law to accept and sanction the customary law of the peasant family, even where the legislators may have attempted to protect the zadruga, as in Croatia. It may be due to an increase in the practice of working outside the household. When outside wages are an exception, they are readily turned into the common fund, but when working for hire becomes an essential element in the household economy, the zadruga is almost certain to dissolve into its component small-families. In general, proletarianization is far more likely to be fatal to the zadruga than prosperity, although cases are recorded in which growing prosperity has led to the break-up of the zadruga. As a special subtype of this category of social change, it is interesting to note the destructive effect exerted on the zadruga by large-scale emigration to and return from America, as illustrated in southern Albania, Dalmatia, and parts of Croatia. So long as the emigrant is absent from the village, his family remains under the protection of the zadruga. On his return he is eager to set up for himself, he has acquired new habits, and finds it difficult to readapt himself to the routine of the communal household. Other factors, such as increasing education, experience in the army, growing contact with the cities, give rise to new demands and to individual ambitions. Not infrequently the result is that the zadruga, like the native costume, is discarded merely because it is "old-fashioned." Besides the general causes at work to preserve or disrupt the zadruga, local factors may play a decisive part. For example, in some villages of Bosnia in 1918 the destruction of the seignorial control exerted by the Mohammedan landlords was accompanied by a rapid division of the zadrugas. In the upsurge of release, the peasants were eager to cast off all bonds, including those of the zadruga. In Montenegro and northern Albania the system of clan rights of usage relating to the forests, pastures, and fisheries is not on the whole favorable to the large household, while the control and protection exercised by the clans reduce the importance of similar services rendered elsewhere by the zadruga.

In retrospect, the zadruga with its large and coördinated supply of labor, has played an important part in bringing Balkan land under cultivation and in the settlement of the area. Under conditions of a predominantly natural economy, the zadruga, with its elaborate division of labor and its high degree of coöperative self-sufficiency, represented an ideal way of life for the peasants, because of its economic and protective strength and because of its power to provide local leaders and to preserve strong nuclei of national life at the peasant level. The zadruga played an important part in the wars of liberation of the Balkan peoples, for the large household could keep one or two fighters in the field and equipped, without its livelihood being disrupted. The zadruga has also left its mark on the political concepts of the Balkan peoples. One can hardly understand the long rivalry between the Obrenović and Karageorgević families in nineteenth-century Serbia without remembering that for the Serbian peasant the king was a kind of zadruga elder on a national scale, and far removed from Hapsburg and Bourbon conceptions of monarchy. Today the zadruga contributes much to the vitality and beauty of village life in the Balkans. While there are strong tendencies running counter to its existence, the zadruga has shown, in some regions, a remarkable degree of adaptability to local conditions of life and work, and a notable capacity to absorb new agricultural techniques and to take the lead in the modern development of the village. Even when the zadruga disappears, it usually leaves a spirit of mutual help, which finds expression not only in the traditional coöperative labors of the peasantry but also in the modern coöperative organizations which are developing in the more progressive regions of the Balkans.

THE PEASANT FAMILY: THE CHINESE LARGE-FAMILY, ITS ROLE AND RECENT TRENDS

KNIGHT BIGGERSTAFF

FAMILISM, defined by Kulp as "a form of social organization in which all values are determined by reference to the maintenance, continuity, and functions of the family groups," [1] is perhaps the descriptive term which may most correctly be applied to traditional Chinese society.

While very little is known today of the earliest Chinese social organization, we have enough reliable information concerning ancestor worship and family inheritance among the rulers of the ancient city-state of Shang to be able to say that the importance of the family and of family relationships was recognized, at least by the ruling classes, as early as the fourteenth century before Christ.[2] Under the feudal system of the Chou period (twelfth century?–256 B. C.), a highly organized family system was an organic necessity to the feudal aristocracy, and it is quite possible, as Granet suggests, that such characteristics of the Chinese family system as the special emphasis on the father-eldest son relationship and the clear and detailed definition of large-family relationships originated in the political necessities of this period.[3] Confucius (551?–479 B. C.), striving to reinforce the crumbling feudalism of his time, proclaimed filial devotion and respect for elders to be the very foundation of his socio-ethical philosophy; and Mencius (372?–289? B. C.), second only to Confucius as a formulator of the Ju (the so-called Confucian) ideology, even more forcefully emphasized the fundamental importance of these familial virtues.[4]

During the Han dynasty (206 B. C.–220 A. D.) two books of great

[1] D. H. Kulp, II, *Country Life in South China* (New York, 1925), p. 188. The present paper is intended primarily for the use of persons unfamiliar with Chinese social institutions, so it has seemed unnecessary to cite material written in Chinese and Japanese.

[2] H. G. Creel, *The Birth of China* (London, 1936), pp. 127–28, 174 ff.

[3] Marcel Granet, *La Civilisation chinoise* (Paris, 1929), pp. 367, 378.

[4] W. E. Soothill, *The Analects of Confucius* (Yokohama, 1910), p. 121; James Legge, *The Life and Works of Mencius* (London, 1875), p. 251.

significance to familism came into general use which have continued to enjoy universal popularity down to the twentieth century. The first was the *Hsiao-ching* (*Classic of Filial Piety*), which appears to have been widely used as an elementary textbook during the Han dynasty and was finally elevated to the classical canon in 838 A. D. The second was the *Li-chi* (*Book of Rites*), an elaborate manual of social conduct which was used as a more advanced textbook and later also became a part of the orthodox Confucian canon. Between them they record many of the traditional ideas and obligations of the Chinese family system, and the importance of their influence on social and political thought and conduct during the centuries since Han times can hardly be overstated.[5]

The student of Chinese history encounters in the course of his research such compelling evidence of the importance of the role of the large-family in practically all aspects of Chinese life that, in order to understand the social setting in which historical events and movements have taken place, he is obliged to examine the nature and functions of the traditional family system. Such is the purpose of this paper, although the limitations of space demand great brevity. Besides analyzing the old family system and pointing out its most obvious strengths and weaknesses, an attempt will be made to summarize the more important factors which have in recent years been threatening the destruction of the large-family.

The small-family unit of father, mother, and minor children (sometimes called the marriage or biological family) plays only a subordinate role in the traditional family system, where its sole purpose is procreation—the production of sons for the benefit of the large-family. Marriage is a civil contract arranged and strictly controlled by parents or grandparents, a daughter-in-law being chosen primarily for her anticipated ability to bear many sons and to serve her parents-in-law well, although an effort is also made to obtain a bride who will be compatible with the other members of her husband's family.[6]

[5] H. G. Creel, ed., *Literary Chinese by the Inductive Method, I* (Chicago, 1938), 36. For English translations of the *Hsiao-ching* and the *Li-chi*, see those of James Legge in F. Max Müller, *The Sacred Books of the East*, III (Oxford, 1879), 465–88, and XXVII–XXVIII (Oxford, 1885), especially Book 10, entitled "The Pattern of the Family."

[6] Kulp, *Country Life in South China*, pp. 142–43, 169, 180; Hsiao-tung Fei, *Peasant Life in China* (London, 1939), pp. 30, 41–42; H. D. Lamson, *Social Pathology in China*

The really basic Chinese family group is the "chia," which term is generally translated by the sociologist as economic, or expanded-family. Ideally the chia consists of five generations living together, although the achievement of this ideal very rarely occurs, two or three generations being most common. The essential characteristic of the chia is that the property and other forms of wealth of the whole group are held in common, owned in the name of and administered by the chia-chang, or head, who usually is the father or the eldest uncle—at any rate the oldest effective male member of the group. Chia are of all sizes, ranging in number of members from one to over a hundred, who may live together under one roof, under a number of roofs about one or several courtyards, or even in entirely separate establishments. Each chia is administered as a single economic unit, with each member contributing his labor and even his outside earnings to the common cause, and each in turn having his requirements supplied by the chia-chang.[7]

The authority of the chia-chang extends beyond merely economic matters, for he is responsible for the conduct of all members of the group and so may not only direct them in everything they do but may even punish those who are guilty of misconduct. Theoretically, he has the power of life and death over the members of the chia, although there actually are both legal and social restrictions on his exercise of it. The chia-chang's wife in practice shares his power, in

(Shanghai, 1935), p. 497; G. Jamieson, *Chinese Family and Commercial Law* (Shanghai, 1921), pp. 34, 44 (material on p. 34 is translated from section 101 of the *Ta-Ch'ing lü-li* [*General Law Code of the Ch'ing Dynasty*]). Under the stress of current economic maladjustments, farm families sometimes obtain brides sixteen years of age or older for their pre-adolescent sons, in order to provide additional farm hands at low cost, and even well-to-do peasant families have been known to acquire concubines for the same purpose. See *Agrarian China: Selected Source Materials from Chinese Authors*, trans. into English (London, 1939), pp. 83–84.

[7] L. S. C. Smythe, "The Composition of the Chinese Family," *Nanking Journal,* V (1935), 371–93; Y. K. Leong and L. K. Tao, *Village and Town Life in China* (London, 1915), pp. 11, 13; Kia-Lok Yen, "The Bases of Democracy in China," *International Journal of Ethics,* XXVIII (1918), 199; Kiang Kang-Hu, "The Chinese Family System," *Annals of the American Academy of Political and Social Science,* CLII (Nov., 1930), 40. For figures on sizes of chia, see J. L. Buck, *Land Utilization in China* (Nanking, 1937), p. 368; A. B. Milam, *A Study of the Student Homes of China* (New York, 1930), p. 10; and Lamson, *Social Pathology,* pp. 553–54. For a case of a chia having members living in several different establishments, see Kulp, *Country Life in South China,* pp. 156–64. Once in a while, when there is no eligible male available, a woman acts as chia-chang. See *Ching Ho: A Sociological Analysis* (Peiping, 1930), p. 43; Kulp, *op. cit.,* p. 129.

fact she is often the real head, managing all the affairs of the home and directing much of the other business of the chia.[8]

A wealthy chia is less likely to split up than a poor one, although in a majority of cases after the death of the chia-chang the property is divided among the sons, who set up new chia of their own. Where there is much wealth, there is a tendency even after the death or retirement of the chia-chang for his sons and grandsons to continue as one economic unit under the headship of the eldest brother, working the fields in common and keeping the property of the chia intact. Poor chia sometimes are broken up even before the death of the chia-chang, although provision is always made for the care of the old people and for the dowries of unmarried daughters.[9]

Superior to the chia is the "chih," which term is probably best translated descendant or branch-family. It is made up of those chia which worship a common ancestor, and its primary function is a religious one. There is no formal chih organization, the direct male descendants of a not-too-remote ancestor merely meeting on certain designated days each year to perform the customary ceremonies before the tablet of their common ancestor. A chia may belong to a number of chih, one made up of the patrilineal descendants of the grandparents, another of the patrilineal descendants of the great-grandparents, and so on.[10]

[8] P. L. K. Tao, "The Family System in China," *The Sociological Review,* VI (1913), 48; P. B. Maybon, *Essai sur les associations en Chine* (Paris, 1925), p. 12; Ernest Alabaster, *Notes and Commentaries on Chinese Criminal Law* (London, 1899), pp. 153–68; Kulp, *Country Life in South China,* pp. 127, 322–23; Leong and Tao, *Village and Town Life in China,* pp. 7–8.

[9] Fei, *Peasant Life in China,* p. 66; Kiang, "The Chinese Family System," p. 40; A. H. Smith, *Village Life in China* (New York, 1899), p. 321; Jean Dickinson, *Observations on the Social Life of a North China Village* (Peking, 1927), p. 17. For an informing, even if not very scientifically conducted study of a peasant chia in Fukien during the nineteenth century, see G. E. Sîmon, *China: Its Social, Political, and Religious Life* (London, 1887), pp. 221–51. Legally, the property of the chia is divided equally among all sons, including those of concubines. See Jamieson, *Chinese Family and Commercial Law,* p. 16. Actually, customs differ in different parts of China. For example, in some places the shares vary in size according to the service previously rendered to the parents by the different sons (Fei, *op. cit.,* p. 67); elsewhere the sons of concubines do not fare as well as the sons of the wife (Kulp, *Country Life in South China,* p. 159); and in still other places the eldest son is given two shares because of his special responsibilities regarding ancestor worship (Sîmon, *op. cit.,* p. 230). Smith (*op. cit.,* p. 327) says that the father who divides his chia before death may make the division more or less as he pleases.

[10] Kulp, *Country Life in South China,* pp. 145–48; Lin Yüeh-hua, "Ts'ung jên-lei-hsüeh ti kuan-tien k'ao-ch'a: Chung-kuo tsung-tsu hsiang-ts'un" ("The Chinese Clan-Village Investigated from the Anthropological Point of View"), *Shê-hui-hsüeh Chieh* (*Sociological World*), IX (Oct., 1936), 133–34.

The largest family group is the "tsu," which term, while frequently translated clan, is probably better translated sib. The tsu is the inclusive patrilineal kinship group, its members sharing the same surname and tracing their relationship to an early common ancestor whose tablet holds the place of highest honor in the tsu ancestral temple.[11] In South China, where the family system has been more firmly intrenched than in the north, the so-called clan-village is common, a village in which practically all residents belong to one tsu which dominates the economic, social, political, and religious life of the entire community. The center of group activity in this type of village is the tsu ancestral temple, and, in fact, the entire life of the village is controlled by the council of elders which is chosen by the tsu to take charge of temple affairs. The temple frequently has an endowment, left by the founder or contributed by some other member or members, the income from which is used to maintain the temple, pay the expenses of the seasonal sacrifices, refurbish the ancestral cemetery, and sometimes to run a school for the promising children of the sib or to lend financial assistance to impoverished members.[12]

While each of these major family groups is represented in traditional Chinese society, it is by no means true that they always follow exactly the types herein described, that they all are to be found in every locality, or that a clear-cut distinction can invariably be drawn between them. Oftentimes the chia is identical with the marriage-family, and it is not impossible to find a group which is at the same time a marriage-family, an economic-family, and an independent religious-family.[13] In South China, especially in so-called clan-

[11] Lin, "The Chinese Clan-Village," p. 133; Kulp, *Country Life in South China,* pp. 143–45; Kiang, "The Chinese Family System," p. 42.

[12] Lin, "The Chinese Clan-Village," pp. 129, 134; C. M. Wilbur, "Village Government in China" (unpublished dissertation for the degree of Master of Arts, Columbia University, 1933), Chap. III: "Government by the Clan"; Sing Ging Su, *The Chinese Family System* (New York, 1922), pp. 88–89; Yu-yue Tsu, *The Spirit of Chinese Philanthropy* (New York, 1912), pp. 78–83. Kulp's book, *Country Life in South China,* often cited in this paper, is a study of the clan-village of Phenix [Fêng-huang?] in Kuangtung province. Lin Yüeh-hua's study of the clan-village of I-hsü in Fukien province, which was presented as a dissertation for the degree of Master of Arts at Yenching University in 1935, has not yet been published, although some of its conclusions are summarized in Mr. Lin's article, cited above.

[13] Kulp, *Country Life in South China,* pp. 143, 145. Fei reports (*Peasant Life in China,* pp. 28–30) that, as a result of the difficult economic conditions of recent decades, fewer than 10 percent of the chia in the village which he investigated include more than one married couple. However, as he points out, these small chia still differ

villages, all the different groups described are to be found. But in the northern and central sections of the country, where social and political disruptions caused by foreign invasion have been frequent, family cohesion has not been so strong, and some of the groups do not appear at all. Furthermore most of the villages in northern and central China are occupied by families representing more than one sib, and the term tsu appears sometimes to be applied to groups which in South China would undoubtedly be called chih.[14] The Chinese large-family is invariably patrilineal and also, at least theoretically, exogamous. Membership in it is established by birth or by adoption, the latter bringing into the group brides for sons and sons for sonless couples. Both wives and adopted sons are considered by society to have given up membership in the families into which they were born.[15]

Before taking up the role of the large-family, it may be well to discuss briefly the two institutions, religious and social, upon which the Chinese family system is based: namely, ancestor worship and filial piety.

Ancestor worship [16] is the ceremonial manifestation of the relationship between the living members of the family and their patrilineal ancestors, who, although dead, continue to be considered

---

from the American small-family in that the married sons generally do not leave their parents, and finding a bride for the son continues to be a parental obligation.

[14] E. T. Williams, "Chinese Social Institutions as a Foundation for Republican Government," *Annual Report of the American Historical Association for the Year 1916*, I (Washington, 1919), 428; Wilbur, "Village Government in China," pp. 35–36; Fei, *Peasant Life in China*, p. 84. Buck feels that at the present time the family system is stronger in the north than in central and southern China because modern disruptive forces have made less headway there (*Land Utilization*, pp. 365–66). See also C. M. Chiao, "Rural Population and Vital Statistics for Selected Areas of China, 1929–1931," *Chinese Economic Journal*, XIV (1934), 312–15; G. H. Danton (*The Chinese People*, Boston, 1938, p. 309) says that the 47 percent of Chinese villages designated by family names are clan-villages. As opposed to this, J. B. Tayler reports that in only 2 of 123 villages in northern and central China in which this matter was investigated were all the surnames the same. While he does not list the villages, undoubtedly many of them were family-name villages ("The Study of Chinese Rural Economy," *Chinese Social and Political Science Review*, VIII [1924], 208).

[15] Kulp, *Country Life in South China*, pp. 143–45.

[16] Cheng Wang prefers the term "ancestor reverence," and there is some justice in this view. See "A Preliminary Study of the Disintegration of the Chinese Family under the Impact of Western Ideologies" (unpublished dissertation for the degree of Master of Arts, Stanford University, 1930), p. 74. However, his argument that it is not a religious rite appears less valid. See Lin Yutang, *The Importance of Living* (New York, 1937), pp. 184–85. I am indebted to Professor R. T. La Piere, of Stanford, for calling my attention to Mr. Wang's dissertation.

members of the family and interested in its welfare. Each chia, rich or poor, has a shrine in which are preserved tablets bearing the names of immediate ancestors, female as well as male. The larger family groups also have shrines or temples in which the tablets of more remote ancestors are kept and to which the heads of the participating chia repair on ceremonial occasions to perform the sacrifices and rites prescribed by long-standing custom. While ancestor worship is in part commemorative, it is also believed to contribute directly to the well-being of the ancestral spirits, and no greater calamity can befall a family than to have the line die out, leaving no direct male descendant to perform these religious duties.[17]

Filial piety, as originally conceived, appears to have been limited to the attitude of obedience and devotion of children toward their parents, but it soon came to mean the complete subordination of the wills and interests of the younger members of the large-family to those of their elders. Finally it developed into the intricate system of family relationships by which the obligations, responsibilities, and rights of each member vis-à-vis every other member are fixed. The most important relationship continues to be that between father and son, and the most insistent demand that for the care of elderly or ailing parents by their children; but a very significant social by-product of the universal emphasis on filial piety has been the deference expected of youth toward age in all matters, a requirement by no means confined to the family circle. Filial piety, like ancestor worship, lays great stress upon the necessity for male offspring—to perpetuate the family and to provide security for old age.[18]

[17] T. T. Lew, "The Family," in *As It Looks to Young China* (New York, 1932), p. 20; Wang, "A Preliminary Study . . . of the Chinese Family," pp. 78–80; Fei, *Peasant Life in China,* pp. 30, 76–77; Kulp, *Country Life in South China,* p. 146; Lin, "The Chinese Clan-Village," p. 134; Tao, "The Family System in China," p. 49; M. K. Griffing, "Farm Households in Central China" (unpublished dissertation, Cornell University, 1931), p. 42; Sophia H. Chen Zen, in *Symposium on Chinese Culture* (Shanghai, 1932), p. 310; W. H. Mallory, *China: Land of Famine* (New York, 1926), p. 88. For a brief study of ancestor worship, see J. T. Addison, *Chinese Ancestor Worship* (1925); for a much more detailed study, see J. J. M. de Groot, *The Religious System of China* (Leyden, 1901), Vol. IV. For a description and illustrations of Fukienese ancestral tablets, see J. Doolittle, *Social Life of the Chinese* (London, 1868), pp. 167–69.

[18] D. K. Lieu, "The Social Transformation of China," in C. F. Remer, *Readings in Economics for China* (Shanghai, 1922), pp. 68–70; Kulp, *Country Life in South China,* pp. 108, 136–37; D. K. Lieu, "The Chinese Family System," *The China Critic,* I (1928), 329; Fei, *Peasant Life in China,* pp. 90–91. In China there is a distinctive name for virtually every family relationship, near or remote, by blood or by mar-

We turn now to an examination of some of the strong points of the Chinese family system. The traditional obligation of coöperation among family members has been a boon both to the individual and to the family as a whole. Not only are the aged, the infirm, and widows and orphans taken care of by the chia, but even the victims of such misfortunes as famine, banditry, and the loss of a job feel free to call upon relatives for assistance. The spirit of mutual helpfulness among kinsmen often provides the basis for coöperation in such enterprises as mutual loan groups, business ventures, schools, and the like. And the much greater economic efficiency of the large chia, resulting from a division of labor among the various members and the communal use of animals, tools, buildings, boats, and so forth, provides the economic justification for the continuation of this type of familial organization.[19]

In the Chinese Empire many of the tasks which in a modern Western state are performed by government were taken care of by the family. Wherever possible, civil law cases were settled by arbitration within the framework of the family system, litigations being taken to court only on the rare occasions when informal negotiations failed. Even in criminal cases it was customary to lodge a com-

---

riage. For studies of this relationship system and of relationship terms, see T. S. Chen and J. K. Shryock, "Chinese Relationship Terms," *American Anthropologist*, n.s. XXXIV (1932), 623–69; Han-Yi Fêng, "The Chinese Kinship System," *Harvard Journal of Asiatic Studies*, II (1937), 141–275; and two short articles by Hsiao-tung Fei: "The Problem of Chinese Relationship System," *Monumenta Serica*, II (1936–37), 125–48, and "Note on Chinese Relationship Terms," in the appendix of his book, *Peasant Life in China*, cited above (pp. 287–96). Mencius declared the failure to provide descendants to be most unfilial (Legge, *Mencius*, p. 250). However, in the absence of a natural son, both custom and law sanction the adoption of an heir. When any amount of property is involved, a chia-chang is expected to adopt one of his own kinsmen (Kulp, *op. cit.*, p. 144; Leong and Tao, *Village and Town Life in China*, pp. 14–16; Alabaster, *Notes and Commentaries*, pp. 168–70).

[19] Leong and Tao, *Village and Town Life in China*, p. 27; Lew, "The Family," p. 22; Su, *The Chinese Family System*, p. 89; Fei, *Peasant Life in China*, pp. 268–69; Cheng Ch'eng-k'un, "The Chinese Large Family System and Its Disorganization," *Social Forces*, XVII (1939), 539; Lien Chao Tzu, "Some New Factors That Affect the Old Values of the Chinese Family," *International Journal of Ethics*, XXXVIII (1928), 346; J. L. Buck, *An Economic and Social Survey of 102 Farms near Wuhu, Anhwei, China* (Nanking, 1923), p. 10; J. L. Buck, *An Economic and Social Survey of 150 Farms in Yenshan County, Chihli Province, China* (Nanking, 1926), pp. 28–30; Dickinson, *Observations*, pp. 5–6; Griffing, "Farm Households in Central China," p. 48. An examination of modern urban families (this type is something of an innovation in Chinese society, which has always been basically agricultural) shows that the large group tends to be less, rather than more, efficient than the small group (H. D. Lamson, "The Standard of Living of Factory Workers," *Chinese Economic Journal*, VII [1930], 1249).

plaint with the miscreant's family, if known, for the family could be depended upon to make every effort to make amends in order to save its reputation, not only punishing its guilty members but even reimbursing the injured party for losses or damages, rather than have the affair aired before the magistrate.[20]

Very little policing was necessary on the part of the central authorities, for the families—and in stable times practically everyone in a community belonged to a family—did most of the policing themselves, under the law making the chia-chang responsible for the conduct of all members of his group. Virtually all the other functions of local government were also performed by families, either singly in the various so-called clan-villages or jointly through their representation on the boards of elders of villages occupied by members of more than one tsu. Under the empire, local government was, except perhaps in the few cities, truly self-government, for it was customary for the central authorities not to interfere as long as taxes were paid and local disorders did not get out of hand. The comparative stability and continuity of Chinese institutions, even through dynastic upsets and other national catastrophes, were in large measure made possible by this tradition of local self-government based on the family system.[21]

Another major function of the Chinese family has been the cultivation of good social relations, children being given careful home training in those habits of duty, courtesy, and mutual adjustment which would be useful to them in the wider relationships of adult life. The well-ordered family has always been looked upon in China as the model of the well-ordered state, and there can be no denying that the social attitudes and disciplines fostered by the family have contributed greatly to both the social and the political stability of the country.[22]

Finally, the Chinese large-family, as a historical institution with roots deep in the past and with a definite stake in the future, has always identified its own continued existence with that of the tradi-

[20] Lin, "The Chinese Clan-Village," p. 134; Su, *The Chinese Family System*, pp. 89–90; Cheng, "The Chinese Large Family System," p. 538; Sîmon, *China*, pp. 55–56; Tao, "The Family System in China," p. 51; Kulp, *Country Life in South China*, p. 322.

[21] Alabaster, *Notes and Commentaries*, p. lxx; Tao, "The Family System in China," pp. 50–51; Leong and Tao, *Village and Town Life in China*, pp. 4–5; Wilbur, "Village Government in China," pp. 36–38, 54; Tsu, *Chinese Philanthropy*, p. 77.

[22] Lew, "The Family," p. 28; Lin Yutang, *My Country and My People* (New York, 1935), p. 176; Williams, "Chinese Social Institutions," p. 430.

tional culture of which it has been so integral a part. In view of the great emphasis placed on the familial virtues by orthodox Confucianism and of the legal as well as political support given the family in all its customary relationships and activities by the imperial government, it is only natural that the family should have become one of the chief bulwarks of Chinese culture. In fact, it probably is no exaggeration to say that the large-family has been the most effective single instrument in Chinese life for the preservation and perpetuation of traditional ideas and institutions.[23]

Let us now consider some of the less fortunate aspects of the Chinese large-family system. The subordination of individual to family interests, while in part productive of social stability, is exceedingly discouraging to the exercise of initiative by the more intelligent and energetic members of the group. Control by the older members of the family would have tended toward conservatism in any case, but this tendency was greatly aggravated by the custom, reinforced until recently by law, which made a family responsible for the acts of each of its members. In such a situation even the slightest deviation from accepted and customary behavior was not only frowned upon but was drastically suppressed by the family, which, moreover, had the economic power to make its will effective.[24]

Another serious charge which may be leveled against the old family system is that it encourages parasitism. Lazy persons, taking advantage of the recognized obligation of the family to care for its members, have been known to live off their relatives for long periods without themselves contributing anything more than gratuitous advice and complaints. Some of the worst abuses of this kind have arisen from the demands of poor or indolent relatives upon persons fortunate or energetic enough to attain public office or positions in commercial enterprises. Driven by social pressure either to find jobs for or himself support such importunate kinsmen, a Chinese official or business man frequently has had to create jobs

[23] H. T. Hodgkin, *Living Issues in China* (New York, 1932), p. 69; L. K. Tao, "Social Changes," in *Symposium on Chinese Culture* (Shanghai, 1932), p. 299. Education, essentially classical and considered primarily as preparation for the civil service examinations, was almost entirely a family responsibility. Cheng, "The Chinese Large Family System," pp. 539–40.

[24] Lew, "The Family," p. 22; Jameson Chen, "Reconstruction of the Chinese Family," *The China Critic*, I (1928), 134; D. K. Lieu, "The Chinese Family System," *ibid.*, p. 330.

for those he could not get rid of. Government and economic enterprises alike have as a consequence been cursed with a virulent nepotism which has wrecked efficiency and poisoned morality.[25]

The demand of filial piety and ancestor worship for the breeding of as many male children as possible to assure care of the aged and uninterrupted performance of the ancestral sacrifices has been a tremendously heavy economic burden to all but wealthy families. Under the Chinese law of inheritance, the family property was divided among all the sons, with the result that once adequate landholdings were within a few generations reduced to such small size as to be utterly incapable of providing a living for the families dependent upon them. Disease, civil strife, and natural calamities have helped to counteract the high birth rate to some extent, but even these have not succeeded in preventing grave overpopulation, which is the primary cause of Chinese poverty.[26]

The overemphasis on the importance of the male, which is a natural result of the demands of ancestor worship and of the economic liability of daughters who must be cared for in childhood only to be lost to another family by marriage upon reaching the age of possible economic usefulness, also has unfortunate consequences in the Chinese social system. Boys frequently are pampered and spoiled, with a resultant weakening of the moral fiber, and the position of woman is definitely that of a social inferior whose chief claim to respect is derived from her ability to produce male children. The institution of concubinage, which finds its moral justification in the demand for numerous sons, is responsible for a good deal of jealousy and dissension in many homes, although it is true that only comparatively well-to-do families can afford the luxury of concubines.[27]

25 Tao, "The Family System in China," pp. 52–53; Jameson Chen, "Reconstruction of the Chinese Family," p. 134; L. K. Tao in an article in the *Peking Leader* (1918) quoted in Milam, *A Study of the Student Homes of China*, p. 20; Lew, "The Family," pp. 22, 25; Kiang, "The Chinese Family System," pp. 44–45; H. D. Fong, *Industrial Organization in China* (Tientsin, 1937), pp. 6–7.

26 Mallory, *China*, p. 88; J. L. Buck, *Chinese Farm Economy* (Chicago, 1930), p. 335; Griffing, "Farm Households in Central China," p. 82.

27 Lew, "The Family," pp. 27–28, 34; Pearl S. Buck, "Women in China," speech before the Tientsin Women's Club, reported in the *Peking and Tientsin Times*, March 1, 1932, pp. 11–12; Richard Wilhelm, "The Chinese Conception of Marriage," in H. Keyserling, *The Book of Marriage* (New York, 1926), p. 127; Fei, *Peasant Life in China*, p. 47; Cheng, "The Chinese Family System," p. 539; Lin Yutang, *My Country and My People*, p. 163; Lamson, *Social Pathology in China*, pp. 513–18.

In the old Chinese family system, where the emphasis was primarily on intrafamily responsibility and where each family was absorbed in its own affairs, there was little place for social conscience or civic responsibility. As everyone was at least theoretically taken care of within the framework of some family group, family members themselves felt little concern for the welfare of those persons who actually were without family connections or whose kinsmen were unable or unwilling to render assistance to them in time of need. As regards civic responsibility, it is but natural that a family-centered social system like that of the Chinese should be characterized by extreme provincialism. Universal pride in Chinese culture appears seldom to have included a sense of national responsibility, even foreign invasion evoking little interest outside the area immediately affected.[28]

During the past half century or more, China, like many other countries in which traditional beliefs and institutions have long held sway, has been feeling the pressure of those modern ideas and practices which we generally call Western. Under the impact of a variety of economic, political, and social forces, the Chinese large family, like the society built upon it, has begun to crumble. While modifications are still scarcely discernible in the more remote sections of the country, revolutionary changes have occurred in those places where external influences have been most strongly felt.

Probably the most immediate causes of the breakdown of the large-family are economic, and some of these can be traced back to a time long before the appearance of so-called modern tendencies. During the prosperity and comparative peace of the eighteenth century, the population of China increased enormously, whereas there was only a slight increase in the acreage of cultivable land. The resulting decrease in the size of landholdings under the law of equal inheritance soon produced a situation in which it became impossible for a chia to obtain an adequate living from its land, and various measures had to be resorted to to make ends meet, measures which were in themselves weakening to the traditional family system. Abortion and female infanticide, for example, though contrary to accepted practice, were widely resorted to to limit the number of mouths which had to be fed from a family's limited resources. And

[28] Lin Yutang, *My Country and My People*, p. 180; Danton, *The Chinese People*, p. 110; A. H. Smith, *Chinese Characteristics* (New York, 1894), pp. 113–14.

there was large-scale migration of young men to foreign countries and to the comparatively uncrowded lands of some of the border areas—in spite of the Confucian admonition against leaving one's parents—not only to reduce the number of persons having to live off a tiny plot of land, but also to secure extra income for the family in the form of the surplus earnings of the emigrants.[29]

Equally injurious to the economic stability of the large-family have been the political and economic disorders which, in varying degrees of intensity, have persisted through the past century and a half of Chinese history. To mention a few: there have been political corruption and rapidly increasing governmental expenditures, with a consequent rising tax burden; unbalanced foreign trade, unrestrained price manipulation by big operators, and official currency debasement, resulting in an upset price balance; uncontrolled exploitation of the common people by monopolistic merchants, money lenders, and landlords (frequently with official connivance); and widespread banditry and civil warfare. All of these have contributed to the destruction of family wealth and have also interfered with that smooth tenor of life most conducive to social equilibrium. One very serious social consequence of family impoverishment has been the necessary curtailment for economic reasons of those ceremonial activities, such as weddings, funerals, birthdays, and even ancestor worship itself, which play such an important part in the maintenance of family cohesion and morale.[30]

Since the beginning of the twentieth century, industrialization has increasingly contributed to the undermining of the old family system. It is true, of course, that the concentration of wealth by means of industry and commerce has economically strengthened the comparatively few families participating in ownership and management, but the vast majority of Chinese families have been corre-

[29] K. S. Latourette, *The Chinese: Their History and Culture* (New York, 1934), II, -9; Lamson, *Social Pathology*, pp. 557–63; Fei, *Peasant Life in China*, pp. 33–34, 43–4; Smith, *Village Life in China*, p. 308; *Agrarian China*, pp. 47, 158, 255–58; Kulp, *Country Life in South China*, pp. 42–44, 47–49; Ta Chen, *Emigrant Communities in South China* (Shanghai, 1939), *passim*.

[30] *Agrarian China, passim;* G. E. Taylor, "The Taiping Rebellion: Its Economic Background and Social Theory," *Chinese Social and Political Science Review*, XVI (1933), 549–81; Fei, *Peasant Life in China*, pp. 131–32. For discussion of the growth of the "little bride" system, under which a girl joins the family of her fiancé while she is still a child, freeing her parents' family of the expense of keeping her while she grows to maturity and relieving her new family of the cost of an elaborate wedding, see Fei, *op. cit.*, pp. 53–55, and Doolittle, *Social Life of the Chinese*, p. 69.

spondingly weakened. In the first place, this rapid accumulation of wealth and the gradual impoverishment of rural families all over the country have combined to create a tremendous increase in absentee-landlordism, as industrial and commercial profits have been invested in farm mortgages. Large numbers of families have in this way had their already inadequate incomes further decreased by having to pay the high rents demanded of Chinese tenant-farmers. Secondly, there has been a gradual increase in the proportion of farm income which has had to be devoted to the purchase of necessities not produced on the farm. This has come about in large measure because of the increasing necessity to substitute manufactured goods for things previously made by handicraft methods or not used at all. Thirdly, the rise of industry has attracted men, women, and children from poverty-stricken rural families to work in factories, taking them for extended periods out of the environment in which family influences can be effectively exercised, and treating them as individuals rather than as members of family groups. Although family connections are retained and even a part of the individual's pay is contributed to the large family (when it can be spared), the idea as well as the actuality of a communal economy is severely undermined, and family ties are weakened.[31]

The political attacks on the old family system have been even more far-reaching than the economic ones, although their effects are perhaps not so immediately felt. The overthrow of the empire in 1911 and the establishment of a republic, based on the Western pattern, contributed to the decline of both the political and the social power of the family. In the new concept of democracy the individual is the basic unit; and family responsibility has been impaired by the appointment of officials and police to take over the control of local government. Furthermore, to meet the threat of foreign economic and political aggression, the leaders of "new China" have been driven to champion nationalism as a means of unifying the country for defensive purposes, with the result tha

[31] Tao, "Social Changes," pp. 296–98; H. D. Lamson, "The Effect of Industrialization upon Village Livelihood," *Chinese Economic Journal,* IX (1931), 1025, 106[illegible] 1074–76; H. D. Fong, "Rural Industries in China," *Problems of the Pacific, 1933* (Chicago, 1934), pp. 306–12; *Agrarian China,* pp. 8, 60, 158, 226–27, 242, 255; Chen Hanseng, *Landlord and Peasant in China* (New York, 1936), *passim;* Augusta Wagner *Labor Legislation in China* (Peking, 1938), pp. 14–15; Lamson, *Social Pathology in China,* p. 548; Danton, *The Chinese People,* p. 107; Fei, *Peasant Life in China,* pp. 6[illegible] 234; Lew, "The Family," p. 31.

family loyalties have come into conflict with the newly demanded loyalty to the state. And while some leaders have tried to reconcile the two, most have recognized their incompatibility and have frankly demanded that the old give way to the new.[82]

A further political blow to the traditional family system is to be found in the new law codes. The legal existence of the large-family continues to be recognized, but individual rights are so protected as to make the individual member more important than the family. Ancestor worship is ignored, marriage is freed of family control, concubinage is not recognized, and the traditional discrimination between male and female is removed, even to the extent of granting married daughters equal rights of inheritance. While it is true that the new laws still are widely ignored and that even judges of the higher courts sometimes modify their effect by the application of traditional doctrines, yet a new legal framework has been set up which may be expected to receive more general acceptance as time goes on.[83]

Finally, and probably most inimical to the old family system, have been the changes in social thinking which are the product of the present age. For nearly a century, Western ideas antagonistic to the accepted mores have been pouring into China, slowly at first, through the medium of a small body of Christian missionaries and a few translations of Western books, and then in increasing volume as schools for the teaching of Western subjects were opened, as Chinese began going abroad in large numbers to work and later to study, and as newspapers, books, and other disseminators of the new ideas appeared in increasing numbers. Political and educational reforms were introduced by the government soon after the turn of the century, but little was done regarding social reform un-

[82] Kulp, *Country Life in South China*, pp. 323–24; Fei, *Peasant Life in China*, pp. 09–16; Tao, "Social Changes," pp. 299–303; C. M. Chang, "A New Government for Rural China," *Nankai Social and Economic Quarterly*, IX (1936), 279, 282–88; Sun Yat-sen, *San Min Chu I* (trans. by F. W. Price), (Shanghai, 1928), *passim*. For an attempt to reconcile conflicting loyalties, see Sun, *ibid.*, pp. 114–15.

[83] M. H. van der Valk, *An Outline of Modern Chinese Family Law* (Peking, 1939), *passim;* Karl Bünger, "Die Familie in der Chinesischen Rechtsprechung," *Sinica*, X 1935), 22–31; M. H. van der Valk, "Freedom of Marriage in Modern Chinese Law," *Monumenta Serica*, III (1938), 1–34. Parts 4 and 5 of the new civil code, which are concerned with the family and succession, have been translated into English by C. L. Hsia: *The Civil Code of the Republic of China, Parts IV and V* (Shanghai, 931). Fei, *Peasant Life in China*, pp. 82, 95; Kulp, *Country Life in South China*, pp. 39–40; M. H. van der Valk, "The Revolution in Chinese Legal Thought," *Pacific Affairs*, XI (1938), 78–79.

til after the 1911 revolution. It was mainly in response to the mind-liberating activities of the Chinese renaissance movement, dating from 1917, and under the stimulus of various Western writers and social concepts, that a widespread conscious movement for social reform got under way in the 1920's.[34]

In this brief and somewhat sketchy description of the Chinese large-family system, the writer has leaned most heavily upon the few scientifically conducted studies of Chinese social institutions which have been published. Before generalizations concerning Chinese social phenomena can be made with real assurance, however, the sociological data scattered through the great mass of Chinese historical writings must be isolated and studied, and many careful sociological investigations must be made of present-day conditions in different parts of the country. Fortunately the past few years have seen substantial beginnings in both these directions, under the competent leadership of such eminent scholars as Chen Ta, Chen Han-seng, L. K. Tao, K. A. Wittfogel, and Wu Wen-tsao, and the work continues to be carried on, even in the face of the difficulties raised by the current Sino-Japanese War.

[34] C. H. Peake, *Nationalism and Education in Modern China* (New York, 1932), pp. 3–59; E. R. Hughes, *The Invasion of China by the Western World* (London, 1937), pp. 104–10; Wang Yü-ch'üan, "The Development of Modern Social Science in China," *Pacific Affairs,* XI (1938), 351–62; T. C. Wang, *The Youth Movement in China* (New York, 1927), pp. 1–18. For some examples of conflict within the family arising out of changing social conditions, see the last chapter of Chen I-fu, "The Old Chinese Family, A Study in Familial Control" (unpublished dissertation for the degree of Master of Arts, University of Chicago, 1934).

THE PEASANT HOUSEHOLD UNDER THE MIR AND THE KOLKHOZ IN MODERN RUSSIAN HISTORY

LAZAR VOLIN

NO OTHER institution of nineteenth-century Russian rural society was so much in the spotlight of public attention and controversy, scientific and political, as the Russian land commune—the "mir," or *obshchina.* No other institution was so much idealized or so much disparaged; none had so many friends and so many enemies in all political camps—conservative, liberal, and radical alike. Today the traditional Russian mir, which so recently pulsated with life, is dead, replaced by a more thoroughgoing collectivism.

As a result, while it was formerly an object of intense interest on the part of scholars in diverse fields, economists, sociologists, and students of law, as well as historians, the mir today is relegated entirely to the post mortems of historical research. Such research, however, not only can make a valuable contribution to general historical knowledge but can also contribute through comparative analysis to a better understanding of contemporary Soviet agrarian collectivism. I propose to attempt such a comparison in a tentative and necessarily sketchy fashion, from the standpoint of the peasant household as the social unit naturally closest to the individual. It should be borne in mind that I am not concerned here with an analysis of the theoretically possible or ideal forms of collectivism, but with institutions that actually existed or exist.

Now what were the essential characteristics of the Great Russian mir system as it existed in the nineteenth century? In the first place, the title to land was vested in the mir, which, as a type of rural organization, was carried over from serfdom by the emancipation legislation of the 1860's. The mir usually consisted of former serfs and their descendants settled in a single village, although sometimes a village included more than one mir and, conversely, several villages sometimes constituted a single mir.

In the second place, all members of the mir had a right to an allotment, on the same basis, of a separate family holding, which was separately cultivated. Moreover, the peasant household held, in addition, the home and kitchen garden in hereditary possession. Thus, except for common pasture and sometimes meadows and forests, there was no joint or coöperative farming of the mir land as a unit, but family peasant farming. In the third place, as a consequence of its collective tenure, the mir had the power to repartition the land from time to time among its constituent households on some uniform basis. Here we have the outstanding peculiarity of the Russian mir system.

The repartitional mir type of land tenure predominated among peasants of Great Russia and Siberia, while over a large part of the Ukraine and other western provinces the peasant family had its holding, as a rule, in hereditary possession and not in temporary possession at the discretion of the mir. Approximately three-fourths of all peasant households in the fifty provinces of European Russia (exclusive of Congress Poland and Finland) held more than four-fifths of the "allotted" [1] land in repartitional tenure and the rest was held in hereditary tenure, according to official data on land-holdings in 1905.

The basis on which land repartitions were made by the mir and their regularity or frequency varied from region to region. Not all mir communes repartitioned their land at regular intervals and some did not repartition at all, although the power to do so remained and was, in fact, increasingly wielded with the growing pressure of population on land. For instance, a study of data for 6,830 mir communes in 66 scattered districts of European Russia indicated that whereas during the 1880's, 65 percent had practically not repartitioned their land, during the period 1897–1902 only 12 percent failed to do so; 59 percent repartitioned largely on the basis of the number of males in a family, 8 percent on the basis

[1] Land held by peasants, whether in repartitional or in hereditary tenure, constituted a separate category of the so-called "allotted" (*nadel'naia*) land, i. e., land allotted to the peasants after the emancipation from serfdom in the middle of the nineteenth century and subject until 1907 to redemption payments. Such "allotted" land, even when held in hereditary tenure, was hedged by legal restrictions that distinguished it from land held as individual property in fee simple. The latter type was owned during the second half of the nineteenth century predominantly by the nobility and less so by business classes and corporations, but peasants were also purchasing such land. According to official data in 1905, there were in 50 provinces of European Russia about 275,000,000 acres of land owned in fee simple (of which peasants owned individually or coöperatively over 66,000,000 acres) and 375,000,000 acres of "allotted" peasant land.

of working adults, 19 percent on the basis of the total number in each family and its working power, and 2 percent resorted to partial repartitions.[2]

Blood relationship was not a basic factor in the modern Russian mir, as it is in the zadruga of the southern Slavs, although some students have traced its genesis to just such family association, while others have denied any historical affinity. However, the highly controversial problem of the origin of the mir, the question of how ancient it was, to what extent it was affected by the intervention of the state and landowners prior to the abolition of serfdom in the 1860's, are outside the scope of this paper.[3]

There were certain administrative and municipal functions of the mir that need not detain us, but one task assigned it was far too important to be left unnoted. This was tax assessment and collection, under the principle of joint unlimited liability of all members of the mir. The mir, therefore, was not only an institution of repartitional land tenure but equally an organ of fiscal administration.

The imprint left by the fiscal factor on Russian agrarian history, and especially on the emancipation reform that abolished serfdom

[2] P. Veniaminov, *Krestianskaia Obshchina* (*Peasant Commune*) (St. Petersburg, 1908), pp. 119–21. Based on material collected by K. P. Kocharovsky.

[3] The Russian literature on the subject of the mir is enormous. For valuable bibliographical material, consult E. I. Yakushkin, *Obychnoe Pravo* (*Customary Law*) (Iaroslav and Moscow), issues I, 1875; II, 1896; and III, 1908. See also a list of references given by the late Professor A. A. Kaufman in his article, "Sel'skaia Pozemel'naia Obshchina," in *Entsiklopedicheskii Slovar T-va, Br. A. i I. Granat i Ko.* 7th ed., Vol. XXXVIII. One work deserves special mention because of the part it played in the popularization of the mir among the Russian intelligentsia, August, Freiherr von Haxthausen, *Studien über die innern Zustände, das Volksleben und insbesondere die ländlichen Einrichtungen Russlands,* Vol. I–II, Hanover, 1847; Vol. III, Berlin, 1852. Translated as *The Russian Empire, Its People, Institutions and Resources,* 2 vols., London, 1856. Haxthausen performed a service for the Russian mir somewhat similar to that which Frederick Jackson Turner performed for the American frontier—he placed it definitely on the intellectual map. By a curious twist, not uncommon in the history of social thought, this treatise of a conservative Prussian scholar proved most helpful theoretically to the founders of Russian agrarian socialism (Narodnichestvo), Alexander Herzen and especially N. G. Chernyshevsky. Haxthausen and the Russian conservative proponents of the mir, such as the Slavophiles, for instance, valued this institution as a means of preventing the development of a propertyless proletariat in Russia and consequently as a bulwark against socialism. Herzen and Chernyshevsky, on the contrary, saw in the mir an embryo of socialism, which they believed could develop by skipping over the capitalistic stage of the Marxian evolutionary scheme. See Chernyshevsky's review of Haxthausen's *Studien* in *Sovremennik,* No. 7, 1857, republished in N. G. Chernyshevsky, *Polnoe Sobranie Sochinenii* (*Collected Works*), III (St. Petersburg, 1906), 270–310.

in the middle of the nineteenth century, is well known. How the peasants were burdened with heavy redemption payments for the land allotted to them and how these payments, together with taxes, sometimes exceeded the income from the land is a story that has often been told.[4] Now the primary task imposed on the mir by the government was to make the Russian peasantry bear this heavy fiscal burden; and from this fact stemmed much of the land-repartitioning and equalizing activity of the mir, as well as most of the fetters on the personal freedom of the peasant that remained after the emancipation and that legally set him apart from other more privileged classes of the community.

With land distribution and tax collection, the important functions of the mir came to an end. Not the mir but the peasant household was the actual farm unit. It owned or hired draft power and implements, performed all the farm operations on the land allotted to it, and disposed of its produce on a free market, without hindrance, if it had anything to dispose of. The peasant household was the actual unit of land allotment and had a voice through the head of the household in the governing body of the mir. The mir dealt with the household, not with the individual. We shall have to bear in mind this position of the peasant household vis-à-vis the mir when we discuss the *kolkhoz* (collective farm).

There were, of course, various limitations on the independence of the peasant farm unit under the mir. Thus the landholding could be changed both in size and in location by the mir, through either partial or general repartition. The allotted land could not be sold, mortgaged, or inherited by the peasant household. The latter, moreover, could not refuse to accept a holding allotted by the mir, as it was sometimes tempted to do when the income from the land was less than the various payments due. In other words, the right of the peasant household to be allotted a landholding entailed a correlative duty to accept an allotment.

There was also the very serious limitation on the independence of the peasant household arising from a compulsory cropping system, due to the unenclosed, scattered character of the holdings, consisting of a number of narrow strips, intermingled in each field with

[4] For an excellent account of the Russian emancipation reform by an American scholar, see G. T. Robinson, *Rural Russia under the Old Regime, A History of the Landlord-Peasant World and a Prologue to the Peasant Revolution of 1917*, New York, 1932.

strips of other holdings. Such a system, coupled with the use of the stubble for common pasture, made the planting in any particular field of crops with a different growing season and maturity practically impossible. The division of fields into strips under the mir had the definite purpose of equalizing the holdings with respect to quality of the soil, topography, distance from the village, and so forth. The strip system, however, was characteristic not only of the mir but also of hereditary peasant tenure prevailing in certain sections of Russia. As a matter of fact, it was convincingly argued that under hereditary tenure the evil of scattered strip holdings was even less easily corrected than under the mir system, where excessive scattering of the strips usually led to a general repartitioning of land.[5]

As would be expected, arrears in the payment of taxes was responsible for most of the intervention on the part of the mir in the affairs of individual households. To insure payment, the mir could hire out a member of the defaulting household or could remove the head of the family, appointing in his place a different member of the household.[6]

Removal of an individual as head of a peasant household in practice occurred also for other reasons. Thus the head of the household was but an administrator, removable by the mir, though an administrator with easily and frequently abused autocratic powers while at the helm. This position of the head of the household demonstrates not only the power of the mir but also the tremendously important fact of the joint family ownership of the property of a peasant household.

The institution of family property among Russian peasants owes its origin to custom, which was recognized and preserved by the courts, and also to some extent by the emancipation legislation itself. It had disadvantages, as well as advantages, for the individual. For instance, all his earnings from whatever source, if he was not legally separated from the household, were supposed to go into the common pool[7]—a serious matter, considering the prevalence of

[5] George Pavlovsky, *Agricultural Russia on the Eve of the Revolution* (London, 1930), p. 83.

[6] A. A. Leontiev, *Krestianskoe Pravo* (Peasant Law) (St. Petersburg, 1909), p. 201.

[7] The earnings of women were excepted, but they were supposed to provide their own clothes and dowry for their daughters. This explains the paradoxical fact that peasant women, with their notoriously inferior status, had personal property rights

migratory work in the overpopulated Russian village. Even peasants who had long lived and worked away from the village were often forced to continue their contributions to the household of which they legally remained members. The weapon here was the famous Russian passport, which hung like the sword of Damocles over the head of any peasant who wanted to leave his native village. For to receive or to renew the much-coveted passport, he had to obtain the permission both of the head of the household and of the mir.

But the traditional Great Russian large peasant family, zealously guarded by the master for economic reasons during the period of serfdom, began to feel the disintegrating impact of individualism following the emancipation. This was manifested in numerous family divisions, in spite of the undisputed economic advantages possessed by a large peasant family. In the 1880's the government became so alarmed over the adverse effects of family divisions that it tried to restrict them by law. Such restriction, however, was unavailing and served only to provide an additional source of vexation to the peasant.

It is hardly surprising that the mir system, as it existed in reality, seemed to its critics an extension or projection of the old servile order, rather than an embryo of the future socialist commonwealth as envisaged by the earlier Russian non-Marxian socialists, the *Narodniki*. This view of the mir as a germ of socialist development was staunchly opposed by the younger school of Russian socialists, the Marxists (among them Lenin, the father of Bolshevism), who came to the fore in the 1890's and who accepted and applied to Russian conditions the orthodox Marxian dogma imported from Western Europe. The mir, according to the Marxists, retarded but did not prevent the evolutionary development that, in their view, doomed small peasant farming as small-scale production generally and that resulted in the splitting of the village, as of the town, into two antagonistic social classes: the bourgeoisie at the top and the proletariat at the bottom. On the other hand, the mir fell out of favor with conservatives, who had, prior to the revolution of 1905, looked upon it as the bulwark of law and order in the village. They blamed the mir for keeping alive the idea of general repartitioning

denied to men. For evidence from different sources on this point, see A. F. Meiendorf, *Krestianskii Dvor* (*Peasant Household*) (St. Petersburg, 1909), pp. 6–9.

of all land, the so-called *chernyi peredel,* which inspired the rising of the peasantry against the landlords and the state. Moreover, the opinion, not new in itself, that the mir with its repartitions and scattered-strip system was a serious obstacle to agricultural progress gained increasing adherence in conservative and official circles.

The government wanted to create a new class of peasant proprietors who would form a barrier against agrarian revolution and who could also utilize the advantages of an improved agricultural technique, for which the strongly fostered consolidation and segregation of scattered holdings paved the way. And finally, with the abandonment of the joint liability of the mir for taxes and the discontinuance of redemption payments, the mir was no longer needed as an organ of fiscal administration. Hence the famous Stolypin laws, with their slogan of the "wager on the strong," attacked the mir, and in the same sweep the institution of peasant family property. Some of the legal disabilities of the peasants were also removed. There is no space to deal here in detail with this legislation and the tendency toward the individualization of the Russian peasant agriculture that it ushered in.[8] Anyway, the victory of the individualistic system of land tenure, which the Stolypin laws promoted, was short-lived.

The revolution of 1917 gave the mir a fresh lease of life. The mir, in fact, was an active instrument of the revolution in the agrarian sphere, since it helped to carry out the partition of estate land among peasant cultivators. The ties that bound the individual to the peasant household, and both to the mir, as this emerged from the turmoil of the revolution and war communism into the brief breathing spell of the regime of so-called New Economic Policy (NEP), were looser than in the old mir. The sweeping away of the landlord, the partial restoration of the free market—which had been legally abolished during war communism—and the retention of various limitations on the development of capitalistic farming (such as the prohibition of the sale or mortgage of land, which legally remained nationalized, steep taxation, and the like) turned the period of the New Economic Policy into the heyday of very small peasant family agriculture. The number of peasant households, in fact, showed an extremely rapid growth from some 16,000,000 be-

[8] The subject has been admirably treated in G. T. Robinson, *Rural Russia under the Old Regime,* Chap. XI.

fore the revolution to over 24,000,000 in 1928.[9] However, just as the Stolypin laws were but an episode between the two revolutions of 1905 and 1917, so was the New Economic Policy but an interlude between the early Soviet war communism and the intensified collectivism of the five-year plan.

The process of collectivization of Russian peasant agriculture was not carried out by the Kremlin via the mir, as it might have been. On the contrary, by a government decree of July 30, 1930, the mir was to be liquidated in R.S.F.S.R. (the largest of the constituent republics of the Soviet Union), if not less than 75 percent of peasant households were collectivized. The rights and functions of the liquidated mir were to be transferred to the village soviets. By a subsequent decree, requirements for liquidation were lowered to 68–70 percent of collectivized poor and middle-class peasant households (i. e., exclusive of the "kulaki"), including not less than 75–80 percent of the peasant sown area.[10] In view of the speed with which collectivization was generally carried out,[11] the liquidation of the mir may be accepted as an accomplished fact. Thus the very demise of the mir, which had been sought by Stolypin and his friends in the name of individualism, was brought about a quarter of a century later by the Bolsheviks in the name of socialism. And yet it is at least open to doubt whether collectivization, involving as it did a profound agrarian revolution, could have been effected so speedily, even with the very liberal use of force, if the mir system had not hindered the crystallization of a concept of stable individual property rights in land among the Russian peasantry. There is good reason to believe, therefore, that in spite of the Bolsheviks' hostility and contempt for the mir, their agrarian collective system is indebted to it.[12]

[9] I treated this period in greater detail in "Agrarian Individualism in the Soviet Union: Its Rise and Decline," *Agricultural History*, Jan. and April, 1938.

[10] *Collection of Laws and Decrees of R.S.F.S.R.*, Part I, no. 51, Dec. 6, 1930, item 621; and no. 65, Nov. 10, 1931, item 465 (in Russian).

[11] In 1928 only a little over 400,000 peasant households out of an estimated total of 24,500,000 were collectivized; in 1932 the figures were respectively 14,900,000 and 24,200,000. By 1937, 18,500,000 peasant households, out of a diminished total of 19,900,000, were in 243,700 collective farms. I discussed the problem of collectivization in detail in "Agrarian Collectivism in the Soviet Union," *Journal of Political Economy*, XLV (Oct. and Dec., 1937), 606–33, 759–88.

[12] For an interesting defense of the mir under Soviet conditions by a well-known economist and publicist, N. I. Sukhanov, see his article, "Obshchina v Sovetskom Agrarnom Zakonodatel'stve" ("The Mir in Soviet Agrarian Legislation"), *Na Agrarnom Fronte*, no. 11–12, 1926. Also the reply by M. Kubanin in the same publication.

We saw that under the distributive collectivism of the mir organization the peasant household was the keystone of the farm system. Now what is its position in the integrated collectivism of the modern *kolkhoz?* First of all, the kolkhoz and not the peasant household is the basic farm unit, carrying on, often with the help and supervision of the state machine-tractor station, the actual farming operations. The peasant household plays a decidedly subordinate role in the kolkhoz, although by no means a negligible role in the economic life of the collectivized village.

Consequently the kolkhoz, unlike the mir, deals primarily not with the peasant household but with the individual peasant worker, man or woman, who is entirely independent of the family in his work relations with the collective. The worker is assigned to a brigade, or more recently, to the smaller unit, *zveno,* into which the labor force of a kolkhoz is subdivided. For his work on the collective farm the peasant is credited with the so-called *trudodni,* or "labor days," which are arbitrary units representing performance of specific tasks and used for calculating his eventual income in kind and in cash. This system of payment is based on results and is differentiated according to the skill required for various jobs, so that skilled workers are better paid than the unskilled.

In general, then, the relation of the peasant to the kolkhoz differs fundamentally from the relation of the peasant farmer to the mir and resembles that of a worker to a factory using a system of payment by results. It differs, however, from the position of the Soviet factory or state farm worker in that the latter, even though a pieceworker, receives a money wage at regular intervals, while the collective farmer is merely a residual claimant to the income of the kolkhoz after all the obligations to the state have been met and expenses defrayed.

Thus the collective farmer has neither the advantage of a specified income that the Soviet industrial worker possesses, nor has he the degree of independence of the small peasant farmer. Having said this, I must enter some exceptions. A young peasant, who may have been merely a cog in the family farm system, may be somewhat more independent on the collective farm. This is likely to be the case if he or she joins the ranks of skilled workers, tractor or truck drivers, combine operators, and the like. Such opportunities for skilled, better-paid occupations, formerly rare in Russian agriculture, have greatly increased with the collectivization and mechanization of farming and have continued to grow, as can be seen, for instance, from the increase in the number of tractor drivers and combine operators from 235,000 and 11,000 respectively on January 1, 1934, to 870,000 and 125,000 on June 1, 1938.[13]

This situation, however, has provided a new basis for economic stratification in the collectivized village, because of the higher earnings of the skilled workers. Whereas, for example, a large majority of collective farmers in 1936 and 1937 earned in cash less than one ruble (20 cents at the overvalued legal par of exchange) per "labor day" and many of them much less, tractor drivers were guaranteed a minimum of 2.5 rubles per "labor day." The same differentiation prevailed with respect to payments in kind. The introduction of the so-called Stakhanovist speed-up, or more intensive methods of work, often bringing large returns to the "shock" workers, has tended on the whole to accentuate economic inequality in the kolkhoz. And so, while much was made by Marxist critics of the failure of the old mir to prevent economic or class stratification in the Russian village, in the kolkhoz economic inequality has the official blessing so long as it is inequality in the distribution of income that stimulates productivity. Conversely, egalitarianism, *uranilovka* as it is contemptuously termed in Soviet parlance, is deemed to have an adverse effect on productive efficiency and therefore to be a petit bourgeois vice that has no place in the socialist economy of the kolkhoz.

Another exception to what was said concerning the loss of independence by the peasants is furnished by the poorest households of the precollective era, especially households that lacked livestock and implements. Such semiproletarian peasants, who constituted in some regions a third or more of all peasant families, had little to lose but their poverty on entering the kolkhoz. It is probably true, however, that for the mass of collectivized peasantry there was some real loss of independence, even remembering the limitations of the mir system.

How does the peasants' security of status and privilege of self-government in the kolkhoz compare with that in the mir? The history of collective farming is replete with evidence as to the in-

[13] *Pravda*, Aug. 13, 1939. These figures do not include state farms, or *sovkhozy*, which had 68,800 tractor drivers and 22,000 combine operators in 1938.

security of the peasant family. Expulsion from the kolkhoz, which often, as the Kremlin itself has publicly admitted, entails starvation,[14] always stares the collective farmer in the face. On occasions, as during the Great Purge of 1937–38, expulsions have assumed epidemic proportions. From time to time, and notably in 1935 when a new collective charter was adopted, legal safeguards have been erected against arbitrary expulsions; but, for the most part, they appear to have failed in their objective. In practice, then, the ties that bind the peasant to the kolkhoz are less stable than those that bound him to the old mir, and this lessened stability has not worked to his advantage.

In theory, the governance of the kolkhoz is more democratic than that of the mir, since the governing body consists not merely of the heads of the households but of the whole membership. Moreover, the mir was often, and rightly, criticized for being the tool of the well-to-do peasants ("kulaki") and the *chinovnik,* the government functionary; but the self-government of the kolkhoz appears to be, if anything, even more of a fiction. A new collective charter in 1935 aimed to insure the elective character and a degree of security of tenure of the officers of the kolkhoz, who were, in fact, frequently appointed and removed by the Soviet officials at will.

Yet the new law, which was hailed as the Magna Charta of collective democracy, has also been continually violated according to numerous reports in the Soviet sources; and the officers of the collectives have, on the whole, remained the tools of the Soviet bureaucrat, just as the officers of the mir were the tools of the Tsarist chinovnik.

Government interference in the affairs of the kolkhoz is, if anything, much more active and minute than it was in the mir. So long as the mir paid the taxes, the government as a rule was little concerned with its internal economic life. It is true, toward the end of the nineteenth century administrative regimentation increased and began to be extended even to such economic matters as household divisions, repartition of land, and the like. But even this was a far cry from the detailed control exercised over the working life of the

[14] See a Decree of the Council of Peoples Commissars of the U.S.S.R. and of the Central Committee of the Communist Party of April 19, 1938, entitled "Concerning the Prohibition of Expulsion of Collective Farmers from *Kolkhozy,*" published in *Izvestiia* and *Pravda,* April 20, 1938. I discussed this matter in "Effects of the Drought and Purge on the Agriculture of the Soviet Union," *Foreign Agriculture,* May, 1939.

kolkhoz. There is hardly a question within the whole gamut of farm management and practice, whether of crop rotation or cultural methods, of remuneration of labor or its most effective employment, that does not come within the range of government control and attention.

No problem, however, has attracted so much official attention as the division of the product of collective farming in which the state shares. The satisfaction of the claims of the state takes precedence over everything else and is, according to Stalin, the "first commandment" of the collective farmer, to which obedience has been ruthlessly exacted. As a result, the Soviet government, through the combined power of taxation, price fixing, the monopoly of ownership of tractors, and the direct control over collective farming, has been able to procure mounting quantities of farm products at low prices. For instance, it increased its vitally important grain collections from less than 12,000,000 short tons in 1928 to 32,000,000 tons in 1937, obtaining the great bulk of this quantity from the collectives. Thus the kolkhoz, no less than the mir, is in its own way a fiscal handmaid of the state.

However we view a kolkhoz—whether as a state-organized and controlled producers' coöperative, or as a form of collective share-tenancy with the state acting as the landlord—the fact remains that it must function within the framework of a planned state economy, to which it must be fully attuned. Here is another contrast with the mir, which, although sanctioned and long protected by the state, was nevertheless a precapitalist survival in an increasingly capitalistic world. Hence, when the government in the early years of the present century became seriously concerned with the improvement of agricultural technique, an added motive arose for destroying the mir, which was considered from a capitalistic standpoint an obstacle to progress. Technical, as well as social, revolution in agriculture, on the other hand, was at the root of Soviet collectivization, with its consolidation of the numerous scattered strip holdings into large fields, and its emphasis on mechanized, scientific farming.

The spearhead of this technical revolution was the tractor, in spite of much inefficiency in its utilization and operation. Furthermore, the tractor also greatly helped to strengthen Soviet control over collective farming, for the government owns all the tractors, combines, and other complicated machinery, concentrated in over 6,400 machine-tractor stations. These tractor stations not only service more than three fourths [15] of all collectives, but constitute the backbone of the local agricultural planning and administration and are a valuable source of revenue to the state. It is an interesting paradox that the peasants, by slaughtering their horses during the early years of collectivization, made the tractor more vitally necessary, thus unwittingly helping the cause of agrarian regimentation to which they were opposed. Thus it has come about that Lenin's prophecy twenty years ago of the vital role of the tractor in collectivization has been fulfilled.

The old mir knew no such powerful centralizing weapon as the tractor to transform its distributive collectivism into a more integrated large-scale type, as many of the Russian non-Marxian socialists hoped might be done. Interestingly enough, one of the earliest and ablest defenders of the mir, the famous Russian publicist Chernyshevsky, believed that machinery would facilitate the development of coöperative farming in the mir and pinned great hope on the steam plow.[16] But as it turned out, it was the internal-combustion engine of the tractor and not the steam engine that did the trick; in the meantime the mir was gone with the wind in the process.

Essentially, the kolkhoz is an economy of socialized production and individualism in consumption. While the kolkhoz performs certain welfare and cultural functions (libraries, theaters, clubs, child nurseries, and so forth) that come under the heading of communal consumption, still its present *artel* form is an institution primarily of production and not of consumption, which is left to the peasant household. In this respect the artel type of collective farm organization differs from a completely communistic form, the so-called commune.

The artel, moreover, unlike the commune, does not provide for complete socialization of production. As Stalin pointed out in the commission that drafted the model or standard charter of the kolkhoz in 1935: "If you do not have as yet in the *artel* an abundance of goods and you cannot give to the individual collective farmers and

[15] In 1937, 78 percent of all collectives comprising 91 percent of the total collective sown area were serviced by machine-tractor stations.

[16] Article on land tenure in the magazine *Sovremennik,* no. 9, 1857. Reproduced in N. C. Chernyshevsky, *Polnoe Sobranie Sochinenii* (Collected Works), III, 477–80.

their families all that they need . . . then it is best to admit openly and honestly that a collectivized peasant household must have its own small personal farming." [17] Hence, in addition to the collective farm, each collectivized peasant family is supposed to have a little plot of land and a few animals of its own. Any surplus beyond their own needs the collective farmers have a right to sell on the limited local market (from which the middleman is legally tabooed) or to the government. Thus the peasant household in the kolkhoz is not merely a consumption but also a farm-production unit of a sort and is recognized as such in the Soviet law.

In theory, of course, the personal farming of the collectivized peasants is supposed to have a strictly supplementary character, subsidiary to the basic economy of the collective farm. In practice this economic dualism in the kolkhoz may and does result in competition and conflict between the collectivist and the individualist elements which the artel organization of collective farming is supposed to reconcile.

Obviously, the smaller the return a peasant family receives from its work in a kolkhoz, the more it will tend to concentrate on its own personal farming, compensating for its small size by its highly intensive character. This is reflected especially clearly in such an intensive branch of agriculture as animal husbandry. According to official estimates in 1938, most of the livestock in the collectives, except horses, was in the individual possession of the collective farmers, although they planted only 13,000,000 acres to crops as against 290,000,000 acres of collective sowings. Personal farming of collectivized peasants, however, accounted for over a fifth of the officially estimated gross farm output of the Soviet Union in 1937.

The Kremlin's attitude, which since the promulgation of the new collective charter in 1935 had been favorable to such personal farming, shifted after the XVIII Communist Party Congress in the spring of 1939, on the ground that personal farming "in some places began to outgrow the collectivized economy and became the basic part, whereas collective farming, on the contrary, became secondary." [18]

In May, 1939, the Kremlin issued a decree which aimed to curb

[17] A. N. Nikitin, A. P. Pavlov, and A. A. Ruskol, editors, *Kolkhoznoe Pravo* (*Kolkhoz Law*) (Moscow, 1939), p. 342.

[18] Speech by A. A. Andreev at the XVIII Party Congress, *Pravda,* March 14, 1939.

the alleged illegal expansion of the personal farming of collective farmers.[19] It reiterated the requirement that the plots allotted to the farmers for their personal use should in no case exceed the limits specified in the 1935 charter—0.6 to 1.25 and in some regions 2.5 acres per household.

Accordingly a new land survey in the collectives was ordered during the summer of 1939, and all land found to be in excess of the prescribed limit was to be confiscated. Likewise land allotted to those who had not worked continuously in the collectives was to be forfeited and used for allotment to collective farmers having insufficient personal holdings. In general a careful demarcation of the common land of the kolkhoz from the area available for legitimate personal use of the collective farmers was decreed.

The common land of the kolkhoz could be increased, but under no circumstances reduced without the official permission of the government, and thus it was to be protected against the encroachment of personal (i. e., individual) farming. Where, as a result of these restrictive measures, a shortage of land available for allotment for the personal use of collective farmers might develop, emigration to sparsely settled regions was "recommended." Collective farmers who had farmsteads outside of the village (the so-called *khutor*), as was often the case in the Ukraine, Belorussia, and other western regions, were to be speedily moved into the village, where presumably they would be easier to control. Finally, a minimum of "labor days" to be earned by each able-bodied member of the collective (not by each family) was set up, and those who fell below the minimum were to be expelled.

These measures and the jeremiads that preceded and accompanied them serve to underline the fact that the peasant household, although shunted to an inferior place, still remains a serious rival of the kolkhoz in its present artel form of organization.

[19] Decree of the Central Committee of the All-Union Communist Party of May 27, 1939. "On Measures for Safeguarding Common Collective Farm Land against Squandering," published in *Pravda* and *Izvestiia*, May 28, 1939.

THE EMERGENCE OF THE FIRST INDUSTRIAL CITY: MANCHESTER, 1780–1850

LEON S. MARSHALL

THE impact of the industrial revolution in the cotton industry produced in Manchester the first industrial city and the first center of diffusion of cultural materials developed in the industrial city milieu. Before its first factory was erected by Richard Arkwright in 1780, Manchester was a typical and thriving provincial market town; fifty years later, Manchester was a unique element in English society, a factory town, and its history was the pattern of development which was already beginning to recur, as the industrial revolution touched other communities. A contemporary observed in 1858:

> Manchester streets may be irregular, and its trading inscriptions pretentious; its smoke may be dense, and its mud ultra-muddy; but not any or all of these things can prevent the image of a great city rising before us as the very symbol of civilization, foremost in the march of improvement, a grand incarnation of progress.[1]

Productive power, massed population, and the progressive elaboration of industrial techniques underlay the influence of Manchester over England in the nineteenth century. In 1820 the value of cotton goods exported from the United Kingdom exceeded that of all other manufactured exports, and during the next thirty years the average annual value of manufactured cotton exports rose from £17,067,000 to £27,719,000. In population Manchester and its satellite, Salford, grew from 25,000 in 1772 to 367,232 in 1851. Only London exceeded this agglomeration of people, and the number residing within a radius of forty miles closely approached that within the same area around London. As capitalists in the woolen, silk, tool, brewing, and other manufactures adopted the new industrial methods, they created new factory towns whose development and, consequently, whose problems were in general similar to those of Manchester in transition. This repetition of social ex-

[1] *Chambers Edinburgh Journal,* 3d series, IX (1858), 251.

perience is the fundamental background of the "movements" in nineteenth-century British history, for such agitations as free trade, ten hours, political reform, public health, and national education were reactions to the problems of an emerging industrial society. Their meaning in social and cultural history must therefore be studied in the milieu from which they were diffused.

The creation and shaping of this new culture center was the work of entrepreneurs whose methods differentiated them from the traditional capitalistic classes. Their success made them an economic and social interest dominating both old and new interests in the city and in the kingdom. From the middle of the eighteenth century Manchester cotton merchants and manufacturers, individually and collectively, encouraged the invention of new productive tools and machinery. Their Committee for the Protection of Trade gave rewards for new inventions, and the Manchester Literary and Philosophical Society discussed the application of scientific discoveries to the arts of industry. It published the researches of Dalton, Henry, and Wilson on dyeing and bleaching. The entrepreneurs in the cotton industry were both eager and skillful in adapting technological improvements not only to the cotton manufacture but also to other industries and in organizing them and labor in integrated productive processes. The factories of Richard Arkwright, the first of the new industrial millionaires, were such integrations.

The success of Arkwright's Manchester factory and the defeat of his patent suits led several merchant-manufacturers to erect factories in the vicinity of Manchester after 1785. In 1790 a Mr. Grimshaw combined two heretofore separate technological advances by installing a Boulton and Watt steam engine in his cotton factory at Manchester. The use of steam power made possible the exploitation of the town's increasing labor force and established Manchester as a factory town. By 1820 the manufacturers had erected sixty-six cotton, six silk, and six woolen spinning mills in the community.[2] The elder Sir Robert Peel's use of rollers in printing, and the application of Berthollet's and Dalton's discoveries to the bleaching and dyeing processes, extended factory methods to those branches of the cotton industry. Almost ignoring Cartwright's invention of the power loom (1785), the manufacturers allowed weaving to remain a domestic and workshop industry until the 1820's. In that

2 Richard Burn, *Statistics of the Cotton Trade* (London, 1847), p. 25.

decade factory spinning became unprofitable unless combined with weaving, and the manufacturing capitalists began to install an improved power loom and to integrate the spinning, weaving, and finishing branches in single establishments employing from 300 to over 1,000 hands. There were over 100 such factories in Manchester and Salford in 1845.[3]

As the factory owners brought the cotton manufacture under their control, so the cotton industry drew old trades into dependence upon it and created new industries to supply its needs. In 1795 Dr. Aikin observed that six foundries in Manchester were occupied in casting wheels and pipes for steam engines and shafts and that tinplate workers, braziers, and harness makers were engaged in making parts for spinning frames.[4] From about 1817 a steady stream of engineers came to Manchester, and of them Richard Roberts, James Nasmyth, William Fairbairn, Joseph Whitworth, and T. C. Herries founded machine-making factories whose output supplied the materials for the spread of the new industrial techniques through the north of England. The trades which could be utilized by the factories themselves were most susceptible to the influence of the cotton manufacture, and from the service of the industry and its population Manchester developed important railway, brewing, chemical, building, coal, and wholesale businesses.

The competition of rural mills forced the Manchester factories to share their markets, but the Manchester capitalists soon extended their domination over the surrounding country through the facilities of the town as a center of communication and a source of capital. As the center of a network of canals by 1795, Manchester was ideally located for commanding the distribution of raw material and for the marketing of goods in various stages of manufacture. This position was strengthened in 1830 by the completion of the Liverpool and Manchester Railway, which was sponsored by the Manchester chamber of commerce and business men, who combined motives of profit and local patriotism. By 1845 five railway lines entered Manchester. The Bank of England established a branch in Manchester in the late twenties, and patriotism and profit combined to produce four joint-stock banks in the thirties. The Manchester Ex-

[3] People's Journal, II (1846), 270.

[4] John Aikin, *A Description of the Country from Thirty to Forty Miles around Manchester* (London, 1795), pp. 176–78.

change moved from a crowded open street known as "Penniless Hill" into a building of its own which had to be twice enlarged before 1850.

To be near this center of transportation, capital, and marketing, the Peels of Bolton, the Ashtons of Hyde, and other manufacturers of near-by towns set up factories and warehouses in Manchester and joined the chamber of commerce. The interlocking of Manchester capitalism with the enterprises of the surrounding country was further developed as Manchester manufacturers built factories in the neighboring towns and villages. Manchester at this time was more than a factory town; it was an industrial metropolis, the capital of a manufacturing empire with world markets.

The needs of expanding business and the pressure of population gave a new pattern to the town, making it conform to the requirements of the industrial entrepreneurs. Those requirements included sites for the factories, habitations for their "hands," and facilities for the concentration of business activities. During most of the eighteenth century the greater part of the inhabitants had lived within a quarter of a mile of the medieval center of the town, the Marketplace and the parish church, but in the second half of the century leading inhabitants began to complain of the congestion of the streets and courts leading into the Marketplace. The center of the town began to move in the last decade of the century, when the merchants, in order to secure more open locations, turned some of the residences of the wealthy on the periphery of the old town into warehouses. The new Exchange abandoned the Marketplace, while other new institutions such as the Literary and Philosophical Society, the police office, and the Portico, took up quarters on streets leading around the old center. By 1850 the administrative and cultural center of the town had enlarged and shifted nearly a quarter of a mile to the south of the Marketplace.

Warehousing concentrated on the higher ground to the east and southeast of the Marketplace. According to the *Manchester Guide* in 1816:

> The active genius of Sir R. Peel, Bart., effected the change. . . . He erected a warehouse in a situation where land was cheap, but which immediately experienced an unprecedented advance. Building after building arose, and dwellings after dwellings were metamorphosed into warehouses, which have spread till Cannon-street, High-street, Duke-

street, Marsden square, a great part of Church-street, and the upper end of Market-street, have banished the accustomed *Lares,* to make way for the God of Trade.[5]

As mills were erected along the rivers and canals, the new population burst through the limits of the old town and settled in slums around the factories. By 1821 Ancoats, formerly a village but now Police District Number One, was the most populous section of the town, with 21,000 inhabitants, nearly a fifth of the total. More than two-thirds of the residents lived in the outer parts, while the two central divisions, Collegiate Church and Exchange, had declined in population to about 5,000.[6]

In the 1830's Manchester absorbed the near-by villages and took on the concentric pattern of today's metropolitan urban area. Withington and Crumpsall, on the higher grounds and out of the line of the prevailing winds which blew the smoke alternately to the east or west, were dotted with the parks and homes of wealthy manufacturers. Closer in, Broughton and Cheetham became middle-class suburbs. Meanwhile the laboring classes, pushing outward in an expanding circle about the town, filled up Hulme and Ardwick in the twenties and thirties, and Miles Platting and Stretford in the thirties and forties. The physical aspect presented by this concentric arrangement, common today, was new and strange enough in 1850 to excite comment:

First, the railway traveller perceives a dull, leaden canopy encroaching upon the bright blue sky, and the number of station shows the increasing density of the population. . . . Then the tall chimneys begin to rise around you; the country loses its fresh rurality of look. . . . Further on, you shoot through town after town—the outlying satellites of the great cotton metropolis—all of them identical in features; all of them little Manchesters; all of them dotted with vast brown piles of building, distinguished by the dull uniformity of their endless rows of windows, their towering shafts, with pennons of smoke, and the white gushes of waste steam continually blowing off. . . . you are whirled along the roofs of a vast net-work of mean, unadorned streets; everywhere broken by the eternally recurring black masses of the mills; . . . until, in a few minutes, you find yourself discharged from the train, in the very centre of the city of Manchester.[7]

Although this growth appeared to be chaotic and planless, actu-

[5] Joseph Aston, *A Picture of Manchester* (Manchester, 1816), p. 221.
[6] *Manchester Courier,* July 16, 1831.
[7] *Littell's Living Age,* XXXVI (1853), 242.

ally it followed a clear principle of cultural development. The dominant social interest in the industrial city, acting in terms of its economic needs and its social outlook, merely shaped the physical arrangement of the community to serve these needs and to conform with this outlook. Thus, as the industrial capitalists rose to wealth, prestige, and power, they created a new form of community organization both in physical pattern and in flow of social interaction. The new industrial city, when seen against the historical background of rural villages, temple cities, fortress cities, and port cities, was a social milieu containing potentialities for great changes in every aspect of behavior and thought.

Before 1780 Manchester society had developed slowly under the impact of the commercial revolution upon medieval agrarian institutions. A small number of gentlemen and wealthy merchants, assisted by clergymen, lawyers, and physicians, dominated the town. The most numerous of the inhabitants were tailors, wool combers, worsted weavers, shoemakers, dyers, joiners, silk weavers, and hatters. At the bottom of the social scale were porters, unskilled laborers, and a growing number of cotton weavers and shopkeepers.

Industrialization not only drew together a vast new population, but also reconstituted the social structure of the community. In the 1840's factory owners, bankers, merchants, and wealthy shopkeepers occupied most of the seats in the corporation council, served as directors of the town's philanthropic and intellectual institutions, and in the chamber of commerce spoke authoritatively to Parliament of Manchester's interests. The old professional classes and the new ones—newspaper editors, teachers, commercial clerks, overseers, and engineers—propagated the views of the business men and administered their enterprises.

Because of the influx of workers from the farms and the dying crafts of post-Napoleonic England and Ireland, the factory working class was far larger than had been the artisan class in the old town. The sharp differentiation of this labor force in origin, economic situation, and social outlook from the working class of the old town made it the distinctively new element in the social structure of the industrial city. Its members, culturally uprooted from their traditional communities, were peculiarly open to the influences of the new social milieu.

Of the adult population of Manchester in 1851, only 28 percent had been born in the town.[8] Almost a fifth were natives of Ireland, of whom Richard Cobden expressed the prevailing opinion:

. . . The quarter in which they congregate is . . . a nursery of all the customs that belong to savage life. In the very center of our otherwise civilized and wealthy town, this place [sic.] which has acquired for its *locale* the title of Little Ireland, exhibits all the filth, depravity, and barbarism that disgrace its patronymic land. Nor is the evil confined within such limits. Its influences are felt in the adulteration of character, and the lowering in the standards of living of our artisans generally.[9]

Landless laborers, distressed artisans, enterprising persons converged upon Manchester because industrial wages were higher than agricultural wages and Manchester wages were higher than those of the surrounding industrial areas. The construction and supervision of the machinery in the factories drew in artisans and mechanics; every improvement of a machine which enabled a child, a woman, or an unskilled laborer to operate it created a demand for this type of worker; and, finally, the servicing of the new population required builders, tailors, tradesmen, messengers and porters, and commercial clerks. From two-thirds to three-fourths of the inhabitants were wage earners drawn to Manchester by its active labor market.

The basic characteristic of this labor market was freedom, of which James Ogden wrote in 1783 ". . . perhaps nothing has more contributed to the improvement in trade here, than the free admission of workmen in every branch, whereby trade has been kept open to strangers of every description, who contribute to its improvement by their ingenuity." [10] The industrial capitalists of the cotton manufacture consistently strove to maintain the freedom of contract between the employer and the individual laborer and to facilitate the mobility of labor. When the factory spinners became discontented in 1816 and formed a union, W. D. Evans, stipendiary magistrate of Manchester, in enforcing the Combinations Acts against them, emphasized the point of view that the men were interfering with the freedom of individuals to sell their labor.[11] Although some Man-

[8] *Census of Great Britain* (1851), I, clxxxiii.

[9] Richard Cobden, *England, Ireland, and America* (Manchester, 1835), pp. 11–12.

[10] James Ogden, *Description of Manchester* (Manchester, 1783), pp. 43–44.

[11] W. D. Evans, *A Charge to the Grand Jury at the Quarter Sessions . . . at Preston . . 16 . . . July, 1817* (Manchester, 1817), p. 4.

chester capitalists supported the repeal of the Combinations Acts in 1824, their aim was to weaken rather than strengthen the unions. In their struggles with the unions in the thirties and forties, the masters constantly appealed to the public and the government for support, on the ground that the unions by "dictating" to the masters were interfering with the freedom of trade.

The Manchester factory owners energetically supported the measures which ended the restraints imposed upon the mobility of labor by Elizabethan legislation. In 1813 they petitioned Parliament for the repeal of the Act of Apprentices. Edwin Chadwick, nephew of a Manchester manufacturer, was the guiding spirit of the Poor Law Commission, and the local factory owners coöperated enthusiastically with those Boards of Guardians which sought under the New Poor Law to find employment for their poor in Manchester. Manchester business men were always aware of the importance of poor laws to the supply of labor. The use of parish apprentices from Yorkshire and London furnished the first factory laborers, and removals of migrants from Manchester for lack of settlement were not customary. The manufacturer, as a purchaser of labor, aimed to control his market by encouraging competition among those who had labor to sell.

Both the newness and the complexity of the factory system required an extension of control over the laborer by his employer. In prefactory industry the needs of the family and its physical capabilities determined the conditions of labor in unregulated industries, but the efficient management of a factory demanded that the hours, place, and tempo of labor be fixed by the requirements of the machinery. Factory overseers set the tasks and in accordance with elaborate codes assessed fines for lateness, leaving before the machinery stopped, waste of light and water, and breakage of materials, machinery, and fixtures. That the installation of this system of control produced a considerable shock to the laboring classes is shown by the fact that most factory owners declared that they employed women and children not because they were cheaper but because they were more submissive to factory discipline than men. Finally, the rule of the machine and the power of its owner were extended beyond the confines of the factory through black-lists of those who refused to conform.

In replacing familial controls by the discipline of the factory, the industrial capitalists effected a social revolution. Labor units ceased to be households dominated by an adult male; the unit was now the "hand," and the "hands" were mostly women and children. Of every 100 employed in 63 Manchester cotton mills in 1836, 40 were under eighteen years of age, 34 were women, and only 26 were men.[12] Over a third of those employed in the sixteen leading occupations in 1851 were women.[13] The employment of women was not a new thing, but under the old system they had been employed at home under the supervision of the head of the family; the substitution of another control weakened the unity and power of the family. As early as 1800 it was said that the women employed in factories lacked domestic training, and in 1831 Dr. Gaskell declared that home was becoming merely a shelter for meals and sleeping. Other contemporary observers noted that the earning of wages caused children to be insubordinate and to leave home at an early age. Rowland Detroiser, a former factory operative, put the age of separation from the family at from fourteen to sixteen.[14] Conservative observers, fearful of the consequences which might follow the collapse of this ancient institution, were impelled to call the densely packed masses created by the free labor market "the social and moral Frankenstein of the nineteenth century" and to ask, "Will it become the master, or the minister, of the genius which evoked it?" [15]

No description of the conditions of life which prevailed among these masses is possible in this brief paper. At their heart, however, was the decisive fact that now great numbers of human beings were dependent upon the continuous sale of their labor, in order to obtain the means of subsistence. They were at the mercy of the labor market. If they did not obtain a price for their labor sufficient to permit them to buy subsistence or if they were, at times, unable to sell their labor at all, they suffered. Unemployment, variable in amount of course, was continuous and, as more than one observer noted, distress became endemic in Manchester's slums and dependent industrial villages.

Economic insecurity and social distress were important but not decisive factors in the lives of the workers of the industrial city, for combining with them were new occupational routines, new social

[12] G. R. Porter, *The Progress of the Nation* (London, 1836–43), p. 224.
[13] *Census of Great Britain* (1851), I, 648 ff.
[14] Royal Commission on Factories, *First Report* (1833), D2 115; E72.
[15] *People's Journal,* III (1847), 244.

controls, new opportunities for social organization, and a new access to new knowledge. If, on the one hand, the new industrial capitalists ruled the new community mainly by economic power, the new industrial masses began an evolution which meant, at some future date, a reorientation of behavior and thinking which are the web and woof of society and culture.

To control the social forces impacted in Manchester, the industrial capitalists and their allies had to wrest existing institutions from intrenched interests, to create and extend new institutions, and to fight off or compromise with the newer elements in the community. In local government this amounted to a municipal revolution.

As a market town, Manchester was recognized under the common law as a vague entity existing within the township of the same name. The township was one of thirty townships in the parish of Manchester, which, in turn, was a division of the Hundred of Salford. The local government was an interlocking directorate of vested interests in the town, parish, and county (the hundred being an illy defined part of the county of Lancaster). Since Manchester was part of a manor, the government of the town itself was the private property of a lord; this had been delegated in 1301 to a jury chosen by the lord's steward and known as the Court Leet. The justices of the peace, representing the county, seldom resided in Manchester, and the members of a small clique rotated in the manorial and parish offices, filling the subordinate positions with retainers and dependents. Although many of the manorial officers, magistrates, and parish authorities were public-spirited, coöperative, and intelligent, the growing mass of administrative detail and the limitations upon their authority forced them to neglect necessary services and to delegate others to untrained and unsupervised deputies. The latter, of whom deputy constables Richard Unite and Joseph Nadin are notorious examples,[16] frequently took advantage of the system to "job" and tyrannize over the defenseless portion of the inhabitants. Patronage, almost the only integrating force in this confusion, was so closely associated with the respectability of the ruling aristocracy that reform was hardly possible.

The congestion of population brought new problems of com-

[16] Sidney Webb and Beatrice Webb, *English Local Government: The Manor and the Borough. Part I* (London and New York, 1924), p. 104 n.

munity service and health protection to the leaders of Manchester early in the transition from the old town to the new city. The first attempts to make reforms along these lines occurred before the close of the eighteenth century. After some success in opening the Marketplace was won by statutory enactment, Manchester obtained, by act of Parliament in 1790, the creation of the police commission. This body, composed of the £30-ratepayers, was authorized to improve streets, to supervise the lighting, the watching (by night only), and the cleansing of the streets, and to regulate traffic. The success of the police commission—gradually dominated by the new business men as the character of property interests in the town changed—and its plans for further improvements caused it to replace the Court Leet as the principal governing body of the town. By 1825 a small group of radical manufacturers, principally Dissenters, allied with the shopkeepers of the town had "democratized" the parish vestry; by tumultuous invasions of the parish church during the quarterly meetings and a vigorous and constant criticism of parish finances, they badgered the churchwardens into opening their ring to manufacturers, accounting regularly and publicly for their expenditures, and conceding considerable powers to the police commission.

The police commission was the government of Manchester in the twenties and thirties. At the request of shopkeepers in 1817, the commissioners extended the commission's gas plant (erected in 1807 for lighting the streets) in order to sell gas to private consumers. The profits from this enterprise enabled the police commission to enlarge its improvement program, and at the same time precipitated a bitter struggle between the wealthier business interests and the shopkeepers for the control of the police commission. The former wished to use the profits from the sale of gas for street improvements, and the latter for reducing the price of gas. This conflict developed into the first recorded controversy over private or public ownership of a public utility and then into a struggle for the control of the town.

When the shopkeepers, because the property qualification for voting was high, failed to force the police commission to reduce the price of gas, they attempted to obtain from Parliament an act to permit the establishment of a private company to manufacture and sell gas. However, when they discovered that the projected company was a speculative "job" at the expense of the consumers who had bought shares in the company but who were not given any voice in its management, they abandoned the bill. And, nine years later, when they dominated the police commission, they successfully thwarted a proposal by some of their old opponents to sell the gas works to a private company.

The issue of this struggle was not the relative efficiency of public as compared to private administration, but whether the consumers or a vested interest should control one of the most important services of a modern city. During the conflict both parties so flooded the police commission with new qualifiers that its operations broke down under the weight of numbers. A compromise between the shopkeeping democracy and the wealthier manufacturers and merchants finally produced a new constitution, which provided for a representative system dominated by property, and extended the power of the municipal government to make improvements.

As Manchester expanded in the thirties, the weakness of the police commission became a serious matter. It could not govern the townships, now four in number, which had been engulfed in the city's growth; they had their own police commissioners, as well as the vestiges of their traditional governments. In 1833 the *Manchester Guardian* remarked on this division of power as it affected the maintenance of public order: "The most dangerous riots may exist in one township, possessing a very limited force of police officers; and the inhabitants may look in vain for the assistance from the other towns that they ought to expect." [17]

The conflicting views of the shopkeepers and the industrial capitalists also weakened the government. When the shopkeepers dominated the police commission, they reduced expenditures for improvements. When the wealthy manufacturers migrated to the suburbs, they became ineligible for the manorial offices, so that coöperation among the manorial, parish, and police authorities broke down. This situation persisted until 1838, when the Privy Council granted a charter of incorporation. This advance was largely the result of the efforts of Richard Cobden, who, in 1836, had revived an earlier project for incorporation. He sought support for the project by promising the vote to all ratepayers, a more efficient police, and many improvements. His opponents, the Tory

[17] *Manchester Guardian,* Dec. 28, 1833.

interests of the manorial and parish regimes, the trade unionists, and the shopkeepers carried the fight to the Privy Council; the favorable action of the Council was taken only after it had discovered that the weight of property was slightly on the side of incorporation. In 1844 the new corporation completed the transfer of local government to the industrial capitalists and their allies by purchasing the manorial rights.

It is significant of the integrating tendency of the industrial urban milieu that these capitalistic entrepreneurs, who founded the Manchester school of free trade and laissez faire, extended, when acting as members of the police commission and corporation, the authority of government over property and private enterprise in order to solve the problems which their economic activity had created. These problems were not new; they were traditional—want, disease, disorder, and distress, and, quite as important, individual aspiration for self-advancement. But these problems now existed in the presence of new economic and social facts. The production of wealth was more orderly than ever before, and the capacity to produce wealth was steadily increasing. Scientific advance was continuous and the diffusion of scientific knowledge was accelerated. Consumption commodities were constantly diversified. Riches and poverty had always existed in close proximity, but under these circumstances, there seemed less justification for the wide gap in living standards between the few and the masses than ever before. The magnitude of the social problems revealed in a new light by these circumstances implied a concentration of forces that would move for their solution, greater than any which had appeared in the past. And the integrating tendency of the new milieu drew these forces ever toward action. If the industrial city brought new problems it produced also motives for and modes of dealing with them.

An epidemic of fever in 1790 first attracted public attention to the factories and congested dwellings, as factors affecting the health of the inhabitants. Six years later physicians, magistrates, town officials, and several wealthy townsmen formed the board of health to check the inroads of fever. The board of health published a valuable series of reports on sanitary conditions, promoted the erection of a fever hospital (1801), and recommended preventive measures to be taken by families and owners of property when an epidemic broke out. Opposition to and neglect of its program, however, rendered the board inactive, and the growth of unhealthy conditions far outran the improvement of sanitary facilities until the crises of 1831–33.

At that time, criticism of the factory system, industrial unrest, and a cholera epidemic—amidst the tension created by the Reform agitation—caused the governing classes of Manchester to make the first attempts at scientific investigation of the problems of the city. These investigations, published in such works as those of Dr. Kay, Gaskell, and Adshead,[18] and in the reports of royal commissions and select committees on factories, poor laws, education, drunkenness, and health of towns, revealed in startling manner the critical nature of sanitary and health conditions in Manchester. Of 700 streets inspected in all parts of the town in 1831, 250 were unpaved and 350 contained "stagnant pools, ordure, and heaps of refuse." One-eighth of the houses examined had defective drains, one-third required whitewashing, and nearly a third had no privies. Dr. Kay estimated that the mortality rate had risen from 21 to 30 per thousand between 1821 and 1831.[19] Witnesses gave to select committees of Parliament sensational testimony from their own experience on the increase of crime, drunkenness, and sexual promiscuity. The gravity of the situation disclosed by these investigations led Dr. Kay, the Greg brothers, manufacturers, and Benjamin Heywood, banker, to organize the Manchester Statistical Society in 1834, for the promotion of improvements by the scientific analysis of conditions and the shaping of proper ameliorative measures. The investigations of the thirties also revealed serious weaknesses in the traditional philanthropic and social institutions of the city.

From the point of view of social administration, the municipal revolution was a socialization of the local government to perform tasks which private and associative enterprise could not accomplish. The superiority of the police commission over the Court Leet in performing the tasks of lighting, watching, cleaning, and improving the streets, and of managing the municipal market, reduced the manorial government to an anachronism. In turn, the corporation

18 James P. Kay, *Moral and Physical Condition of the Working Classes Employed in the Cotton Manufacture in Manchester* (London, 1832); P. Gaskell, *The Manufacturing Population of England* (London, 1833); Joseph Adshead, *Distress in Manchester* (London, 1842).

19 Sir James Phillips Kay-Shuttleworth, *Four Periods of Public Education* (London, 1862), pp. 4–7.

surpassed the police commission in reducing crime, paving and opening streets, and providing new markets. In 1844 the corporation extended the police commission's experiment in municipal ownership by purchasing the rights and property of the Manchester and Salford Water Company. By 1850 the municipal authorities had taken over the management of three great parks and a library and had obtained the power to regulate new construction.

Actuated by the principles motivating the Statistical Society, the inhabitants extended and reorientated their social institutions. Under the influence of the humanitarian movement of the eighteenth century, local philanthropy had founded the Royal Infirmary (1752), Sunday schools (1784), soup kitchens (1801), monitorial schools (1809), new churches and chapels, and numerous other charities. In the 1820's the medical charities were extended by the creation of free dispensaries, and education was provided for young children by means of infant schools. The popularity of thrift in contemporary thought, supported by the findings of the various investigations previously noted, tended to the displacement of almsgiving by institutions encouraging the poor to support themselves. Of this character were the Savings Bank (1817), the District Provident Society (1831), and the Ministry of the Poor (1833). On the other hand, an investigation of education in Manchester by the Statistical Society in 1833 revealed that the Sunday, dame, and monitorial schools were providing very inadequately for the education of only one-third of the children in the town.[20]

Even before the Statistical Society's "Report on Education," business and social leaders had attempted to remedy some of the obvious defects of the Sunday and monitorial schools. In 1825 Benjamin Heywood and several manufacturers established a Mechanics Institution to instruct mechanics and artisans "in those branches of science which are of practical application in the exercise of their several trades, . . . enabling them more thoroughly to understand their business, giving them a greater degree in the practice of it, and leading them to improvement with a greater security of success." [21] Manchester business men expected schools to supply their industries with much-needed engineers, designers, and technicians

[20] Great Britain, Parliament, House of Commons, *Report of Select Committee on Education* (1835), App. 2.

[21] Mabel Phythian, *The Manchester Mechanics Institution* (Typescript of thesis, Christie Library, Manchester University), I, 110, quoting the first annual report.

and at the same time to contribute to the well-being of the laboring classes by providing opportunity for self-advancement. The effectiveness of the industrialists' control over education therefore depended upon their ability to popularize their educational theory. When the Mechanics Institution, although democratized and popularized in the thirties, failed to attract many of the working classes, the manufacturers and merchants gave support to new institutions such as the Athenaeum (founded in 1834 by Richard Cobden) for the education and recreation of clerks and white-collar workers. Except as the increase in number of small private and endowed schools improved the situation, the effectual extension of educational facilities awaited the establishment of a national school system for which the Lancashire Public School Association, founded in Manchester in 1848, agitated. Meanwhile, the rulers of Manchester gave more and more attention to those institutions, by which the spiritual, emotional, and intellectual aspirations of the inhabitants might be controlled.

Conforming to the pattern of English life in the eighteenth century, Manchester institutions before the Evangelical movement made but little appeal to the religious. Although a large variety of sects provided amply for current differences in religious belief, not more than a fraction of the inhabitants could have been accommodated in the churches and chapels of the town. Under the stimulus of Evangelicalism, church-building progressed rapidly during the period of the Napoleonic wars, when also branches of the Society for the Promotion of Christian Knowledge were active in circulating the pamphlets of Bishop Paley, Hannah More, and their local imitators. At the same time the attitude of the governing classes was hostile to mass amusements: the borough reeves, constables, and magistrates discouraged cockfighting, bear baiting, and the horse races on Kersal Moor, probably because they feared the combination of large crowds, drinking, and industrial discontent. When peace came in 1815, out-of-door recreations revived; the Manchester Golf Club was established in 1815, cricket matches and the races were resumed, and the Botanical Gardens were planted in the twenties. To preserve something of the open spaces for the recreation of the poor, the editor of the *Manchester Guardian* and several of his correspondents in 1822 prevented Ardwick Green from becoming the site of a block of tenements, and three years later another group of business men formed the Society for the Preservation of Ancient Footpaths.

Because opinion, informed by the reports of the Select Committees on Drunkenness and Public Walks, held that the growth of intemperance, brutality, and crime was due to the disappearance of the traditional amusements of the village green and tavern, the philanthropists of early industrial Manchester undertook to provide "rational amusements" for the poor. The character of these amusements was determined by the new urban milieu. The Music Festival, first held in 1828, was opened to the poor, and workingmen's concerts were started by the Philharmonic Institution in 1846. About this time, also, the Liverpool and Manchester Railway offered excursion rates to the Liverpool Music Festival and to beaches on the coast. Subscribers to the Botanical Society forced its directors to open the gardens to the public on Sundays; these men and their associates in other philanthropic enterprises also obtained the town's first park in 1840. But business enterprise was even more active than philanthropic enterprise in providing amusements—not always "rational"—for the new working classes. As the city grew, music halls, dancing rooms, and cheap theaters—operated for profit—appeared in increasing numbers. The "palaces," where both male and female workers gathered in thousands to drink, sing, and dance, and to see and hear Ethiopian serenaders and low comedians, were the show places of Cottonopolis. Gas light and mechanical musical instruments gave them the glitter and the clatter that were to become enduring characteristics of the amusement places catering to the new urban masses wherever they formed.

The diffusion of literacy among the working classes was a notable aspect of intellectual development in the industrial urban milieu. In 1790 the intellectual interests of Manchester's upper classes were served by the Literary and Philosophical Society, a subscription library, concert and assembly rooms, a theater, and two newspapers; but the intellectual interests of the poor were limited to the fare provided by the churches and Sunday schools. The traditional fear of the upper classes that the spread of literacy among the lower orders would lead to political disorder was abated somewhat when the education of the masses was undertaken by the well-disciplined monitorial schools and the Sunday schools. The Society for the Promotion of Christian Knowledge and the Society for the Diffusion of

Useful Knowledge first made cheap books available to the people. Circulating libraries for the workers appeared in the twenties. A cheap press found an outlet among the masses, for both newspapers and books, in the thirties. A modern public library was established, when in 1852 an Act of Parliament authorized the corporation to take over the management of the library of the Mechanics Institution.

The effects of this intellectual development were clearly evident in the formation of a newspaper-reading public. During the Napoleonic wars both the number and the circulation of Manchester newspapers increased, and during the political agitations after 1815 the newspapers changed from advertising sheets to organs for the dissemination of news and the discussion of public issues. Cobbett's *Political Register,* which found some local imitators, the chief of which was the *Manchester Observer* (1818–22), stimulated this change. In 1821 five manufacturers established the *Manchester Guardian,* with John Edward Taylor, one of the founders, as editor. Advertising revenues were invested in developing an improved news coverage, and soon it outstripped the older sheets in both circulation and prestige. Taylor made the *Guardian* the organ of the town's business and industrial interests. Its success led to the establishment of other papers to speak for other local interests. The first working-class newspaper in Manchester, the *Poor Man's Advocate,* was founded in 1828 by John Doherty, the leader in an early attempt to organize trade unions among the cotton "hands." By the forties the Manchester newspaper press reflected the opinions of every articulate interest in the community—the traditional aristocracy, the industrial and financial capitalists, the shopkeepers and tradesmen, the trade unionists, the Owenites, and the Chartists.

The inhabitants of Manchester had built up, by 1850, a diversified set of institutions that organized their lives in new patterns. To the middle and wealthy classes the development of the factory, the revolution in the local and national governments, and the expansion of intellectual and recreational facilities had given wealth, political power, and a sense of social and personal responsibility and fulfillment. The new fields of activity opened to the working classes were no less significant. In general, the standard of living of the working classes was both raised and broadened, not only through the widening of the margin between wages and prices but also through the supplying of greater facilities for recreation and education. At the same time the interstimulation among dense masses of people in factories, crowded streets and saloons, and congested dwellings produced new forms of social activity.

> One distinguishing feature of the manufacturing system is its tendency to make men co-operate for mutual protection and benefit. It may interfere with domestic enjoyment; it may break in upon fireside happiness; but it leads men to form associations.[22]

Lodges, coöperative and socialist societies, and mass meetings were popular forms of expressing mass interests in varied forms.

Broader possibilities of enjoyment and new group interests transformed individual and group behavior. The appearance around him of desirable things to have and familiarity with the careers of persons who had acquired fortunes made the Manchester workingman less content with his lot in life than the pre-industrial poor man. Accepting the dominant Benthamite philosophy, he often tried to increase his power in the labor market by thrift and education. Following another philosophy current in many places, he demanded, as his right as a producer of value, a greater share in the earnings of industry. Even while the operative accepted and tried to conform to the laws of the free labor market, he became more aggressive in his demands, as his confidence in his associations increased. Socialist societies and trade unions shaped these demands in the form of propaganda, strikes, and demonstrations, and these modes of expressing discontent displaced the spontaneous and leaderless riotings that had accompanied the famines of the pre-industrial era. The control which these associations exercised over their members is clearly evident in the fact that the riots of the forties—for example, the Plug-drawers riots of 1842—were directed by skillful agitators with very definite objectives.

In contrast to the discipline of custom, tradition, and force of pre-industrial society, the basic social control in early Manchester was regimentation; not regimentation by order supported by force, but regimentation developing under the integrating power of the urban milieu. The factory enforced a system of management through a routine of work and a minute division of labor. The codes and fines were incidental aids to support this regime and, in time, they became unnecessary. The cheap press and new forms of

[22] *People's Journal,* II (1846), 271.

recreation organized pervasive standardizations of belief and emotion. Since the accommodation of the most families in the least space was the governing principle of the jerry-builder's unalterable architecture—rows of apartment houses, back to back, with two rooms upstairs and two rooms down—the working class residential areas were models of physical uniformity. It was, however, no greater than the uniformity that pervaded working-class life as a whole. The source of this regimentation was the industrial process itself and the interest of the entrepreneurial class, to which, in fact, the economy of uniformity was essential. Working-class leaders, such as John Doherty, Rowland Detroiser, and David MacWilliams, having learned the techniques of regimentation from the industrialists, adapted them in the organization of unions. The social ideals embodied in the now-current term "masses," namely, solidarity and uniformity, have their roots in these social controls which were shaped in the early industrial city and have spread through society as an ever-larger proportion of the population has come to live under the industrial urban milieu.

The tendency of the industrial city to emphasize individual and group aspirations moved hitherto politically inactive elements of society to challenge the authority of the vested interests in government. The entrance of the industrial capitalists into national and local politics was facilitated by the ability of British society to adjust its conceptions of property so that new interests could be integrated into its government. On the other hand, the growth of the urban working class, with its own problems and demands, occurred too rapidly for such adjustment, and so the political activity of the working class developed a revolutionary aspect. In the 1790's the Manchester workers, acting as a mob, could be roused to attack political reformers and to support Tory interests. During the depression years 1812–20, the working classes took up radicalism and became allies of the manufacturers. Detroiser instituted lectures on political economy and philosophy in his New Mechanics Institution in 1829, and a year later the original Institution discontinued its policy of avoiding political subjects. After 1832 the working class was becoming politically independent, and its support was bid for by both sides. In the election of a member to the Reformed Parliament, the popular party won the show of hands for their candidate, William Cobbett, and frightened the Whig-Liberals by threatening to split their votes with the Tory candidate in the poll. Recognition of the political activity of the workingmen came in 1834 from the conservative interests of Manchester, when they attempted to consolidate their temporary alliances with the radicals by forming a Conservative Association of workingmen. The preparedness for and the experience in political action of the Manchester masses made the town a focal point of the Chartist agitation, but the ten-pound franchise, the corporation, and—in the great crisis of 1839—Sir Charles Napier's artillery, restrained working-class political action to sporadic agitation, while the industrial capitalists, organized in the Anti-Corn Law League, drove forward to national leadership.

Between 1820 and 1850 the industrial capitalist became the dynamic force in British politics. In the former year Manchester business men joined the merchants of Liverpool and London in free-trade petitions to the House of Commons and in the next year formed the Manchester chamber of commerce to observe national policies from the point of view of the local industry. Four manufacturers or former manufacturers were elected to the Reformed Parliament, and several others to succeeding parliaments. The Anti-Corn Law League (its headquarters were in Manchester) made the problems of Manchester business enterprise the political issues of the nation. Six years after the repeal of the Corn Laws—when the last vestiges of the Navigation Acts had been swept away, when national finance had been grounded on the income tax, and when agitation for factory legislation had been relaxed—an enthusiastic admirer of the manufacturer in politics wrote: "The whole kingdom has seen that district which it contemned as a region of grinding capitalists, without a thought save of cotton and stunted serfs, . . . suddenly dart into magnificent political energy and power; found a new economic and social system; and by the peculiar clear-headedness of the views, and the still more peculiar working energy of its people, triumphantly direct the policy of the land." [23]

The victory of the Anti-Corn Law League signalized the extension of the interests of industrial capitalists and of the conditions of life under their rule over England. Parliament debated the "Condition of England" question in terms of the industrial population —unemployment, class conflict, new moral standards, and public

[23] *Littell's Living Age,* XXXVI (1853), 241.

health. It enacted legislation dealing with public health, education, and municipal improvements, thereby recognizing that problems which had come to public attention as municipal conditions had become national problems. Foreign policy discovered investment overseas as an interest to be considered along with the sale of manufactured goods. Literature, although still paying homage to chivalry, accepted labor as a subject; furthermore, it recognized that the laboring man, no longer bound to his position in a class structure, could advance in life—at least, he could and should aspire to be a capitalist. In fact, not only was the dominant interest of the industrial city identified with the national interest, but the outlook upon life organized in the industrial urban milieu harmonized old elements of the national culture with innovations in a new unity.

THE CORPORATION: AN INSTITUTIONAL FACTOR IN MODERN HISTORY

STEPHEN RAUSHENBUSH

WITHIN the past eighty years the corporation has become one of the most important institutions in the United States. It represents a concentration of economic power which few of its early sponsors foresaw. Because of that unification of power, it has played a major part in the transformation of this country from a semiagrarian to an industrialized metropolitan community. It has been powerful enough to prevent or frustrate many of the attempts to bring it under the control of the political state. The very fact of its concentrated power has in recent years apparently increased the tempo of our depressions. When a large corporation shuts up shop, more people go down with it, more economic effort is halted, than would be the case in a realm of many small enterprises.

The rise of an institution to new importance can be measured in terms of the displacement and replacement effects on the older institutions in existence at the beginning of that rise. We have seen the progress of many institutions: monarchy, commercial colonizing companies, the church, the family, the army, town meetings, slavery, the modern political state itself. Each of them has focused or created loyalties, influenced attitudes, habits, customs, developed and expressed power in political and other cultural forms. Their vitality at any time can be measured, in a dynamic society, by the extent to which they become receiving stations for attitudes and emotions previously centered around other, older institutions. An institution does not grow in a desert. It grows by shoving other institutions aside to make way for itself, or by absorbing them.

The rise of the one-party, all-absorbing totalitarian state in modern Europe is the one vivid example of the process before us; it became vivid to us because of the speed of the process quite as much as by its completeness. Church, corporation, labor unions, democratic institutions, were all rendered impotent, or absorbed, in an attempt to prevent the very competition, among institutions, for loyalty and power which all other rising institutions in our experience have had to undergo, and which has delayed their growth. Like any competent study of any other institution, a study of the growth of Fascism, Naziism, or Communism must be partly in terms of the inadequacy of the older institutions to hold their own against the newcomer.

In the United States the corporation, the economic organization of much of our modern society, has come to maturity more slowly. It has ridden the tide of popular belief in progress, of American belief in efficiency, of that long period when all wanted the natural resources of the nation to be used rapidly, and the rapid use could most easily be secured by those who had unified the financial resources of others in corporation form.

Now, we are told, some few hundred corporations and some few score individuals control over half of our industrial power. Yet little scholarly attention has hitherto been directed toward a development which the historians of the future may consider to be as important to our era as the swing of political power from the South to the West and North was to the era of a hundred years ago.

The growth of the corporation has brought a change in business mores and in economic relationships. The multitude of economic activities carried on within the corporation are organized by administrative direction rather than by market forces. Sheer size, and the reduction in the number of independent enterprises in fields where corporate production predominates, have placed the corporation in a position to make decisions which have significant impact on the economy.

Corporate growth, too, has brought major social changes. The great migration into the cities has meant a change in the way of life of many people and the growth of many new problems. The character of the liberty that people formerly possessed to become and remain independent in the process of earning a living has been changed. In terms of democratic theory, the growth of the corporation has meant, for many people, a termination of participation in important decisions affecting their lives. By diminishing the independent opportunities for small men in trade and manufacture and forcing them into the more dependent service occupations, it has changed the character and status of the middle class. By the tempo of its technological improvements, it has contributed to the problem of unemployment. Industrial discipline has imposed a regimentation and dependence on authority in the lives of the working people which has no parallel elsewhere in our society outside of the military services. In each instance the problems created by the growth of the corporation are left for solution largely to the political state.

The corporation is an institution which still has a great future before it. Like every other vital institution, it is still reaching out for power, for without continually increasing power it cannot assure its future against the vicissitudes and uncertainties of competition from other corporations or other institutions, such as the political state.

Already there are a whole series of points of frictional contact with the state, which shift with the changing impingements of the corporation and the state alike on the life of the people. Already there is an attempt on the part of some of the spokesmen for the younger institution to capture the patriotic sanction from the government, which represents the state in the minds of the people. When the authoritarian parties in Italy and Germany were able to do that, their importance in the social complex increased enormously. Those who know the one-company steel or coal town recognize the battle-cry, "What is best for the corporation is best for the community." On the national scale it reads, "What is good for business is good for America." What is happening here is that the institution is measuring the nation in terms of its own welfare. It is one, or perhaps two, steps from combating everything which conflicts with the institutional interest as "unpatriotic," to fighting it out with the state for the right to exclusive possession of that sanction.

The relations between the modern corporation and the state should lend themselves to profitable study. The first institution has in its later days been able to throw most of its depression burdens upon the latter, with the result of weakening the political state and of making its continued life and health difficult. In its earlier days, it throve on the gifts of the state's resources. There seems, however, at the moment to be no Hamiltonian bargain that the former wants to keep the latter strong for purposes of support.

On the contrary, the spokesmen of the modern corporation want the state kept weak. In that weakness, they believe with the eighteenth-century liberals, lies the only guarantee of liberty and action for themselves.

In his paper, "The Corporation and the Rise of National Socialism," which Dr. Gerhard Colm presented at the 1939 meeting of the American Historical Association, he dealt with the German experience of the corporation and the weak state:

> Business leaders tried to extract from the republic whatever advantage they could but decried all attempts at an active economic policy as "cold socialization." Business made concessions, it is true. It agreed to agricultural tariffs, but only to get the political support of the landed aristocracy. It agreed to social security legislation, since something had to be given to labor. It made concessions to all kinds of pressure groups, but no concessions to the government as such. When a prominent representative of business took charge of the government (Stresemann), the majority of business turned violently against him. They fought with all the means at their disposal whenever the government tried embarking on a constructive program which would have taken care as well of those classes of the population which were less organized as, for instance, the small farmers, shop-keepers, small-sized businesses, and the unemployed. In a world of restricted competition, of international tension and powerful domestic pressure groups, business still preached a laissez-faire attitude. Laissez-faire under such conditions means mainly laissez-faire for the various pressure groups.
>
> In this period of modern industrial organization no government can avoid some sort of business regulation. The question is only how much regulation is necessary, who should direct the regulation and in whose interest it should be invoked. Business apparently wanted to agree to regulation if its own representatives would direct regulation for their own benefit. The short and unsuccessful episode of the Papen government proved the impracticability of such an attempt.
>
> If we wish to find out what the real relationship is between corporate business in Germany, on the one hand, and the victory of National Socialism, on the other, then the answer is that corporate business too short-sightedly believed that it could exert greater influence on a weak government, and did not recognize that the legal order, on which all business activities are based, depends on a strong government determined to pursue a far-sighted policy of adjusting the economy to present technological and organizational conditions. The German case proves that in our age of industrial organization a weak government with a laissez-faire attitude cannot survive; but a democratic government need not be a weak government.

The significance of this disastrous experiment with a weak state by those who expressed corporation power in Germany has been little appreciated in the United States. Here, as there, before Hitler, the spokesmen for the younger institution have an abounding confidence in their ability to survive in a weak state. They have not accepted the evidence that a weak state tends to be superseded, rather rapidly in modern industrial society, by a strong state. They see only the evidence that a strong state, in our time, does not tolerate economic decisions which are beyond its control and yet vitally affect its destinies.

The growth of the corporation as an institution has to be evaluated, at any one moment of time, by the relative contemporary importance of its decisions with the decisions of the institutions upon which it impinges. In the 1940's the corporation decides when to operate its plants and when to close them. The importance of these decisions is not restricted to its own employees, but extends to the other industries whose products these employees purchase. It decides how much money to invest in new plant and new technological processes. These decisions again extend beyond the immediate environment. It decides price policy, sometimes in coöperation with competitors, with effects upon the whole economy. It decides to move the field of its operations from one town to another, with huge local after-effects. It decides, with or without effective consultation with the employees, what wages to pay. It decides, with or without effective consultation with the stockholders, what part of earnings to distribute in the form of profits, and what form of political activity its officials should engage in. In times of national crisis, when the nation needs the corporation's resources, the latter is in a position largely to determine the terms upon which its resources will be made available. All these enormously important decisions are taken outside the democratic system, and are powers exercised separately (except, in some instances, for price and wage policy) by each corporation. They have never consciously united in their decisions, with the result of creating a constantly increasing growth of employment and purchasing power. Until they do that, the political state will presumably be called upon to bear the burdens in relief expenditures of various kinds for the failure of the corporation decisions to produce a functioning economy, and will be drained and weakened by the expense, derided for its failure to do something it had not been created to do—guarantee the functioning of the economy—and fought for its attempts to do so.

In the United States the institution upon which the corporation is impinging most at present is no longer the small independent enterprise, but the political state. The latter has for over a hundred years yielded powers to the corporation, without imposing any responsibility upon its creature. In recent years the state has attempted to influence a few of the minor activities of the corporation (safety, minimum wages, maximum hours, compensation for idleness), but has, on the whole, kept out of the major decisions. Yet the state has a series of powers, which it has slowly and only recently been allowed by the courts to exercise, which are probably adequate today for control of the major economic decisions of the corporation in times of peace almost as thoroughly as they are in times of war, when the safety of the modern state automatically involves control of all the major corporation decisions. In other words, while the recent rise of the corporation in the United States has been accompanied by an actual weakening in the ability of the state to carry continued or new burdens of depression there has, at the same time, been a theoretical strengthening of the power of the state to control the decisions which result in these burdens.

The student of modern history may expect to find himself observing more and more clearly the simultaneous development of the two institutions in terms of conflict over control of the major decisions of the corporation, which, at one remove, create the major decisions of the modern political state.

THE SOCIAL HISTORY OF THE CORPORATION IN THE UNITED STATES[1]

THOMAS C. COCHRAN

RECENT institutional history frequently has suffered from overabundant materials. Like surface veins of coal, obvious and easily available sources have been exploited while those requiring greater effort in selection and synthesis have been neglected. Corporation history is a conspicuous example. Corporate influences that plumb the depths of social organization have been ignored. Only the business and legal aspects of the subject have been studied in detail. Such specialization, to be sure, has been necessary for more comprehensive work. Nor should business and legal matters be excluded from social history. It is time, however, to incite analysis of the undeveloped areas. It is time scholars began to explore the impact of corporations upon cultural traditions, political procedures, and the larger aspects of social change.

Fortunately, many of these neglected fields may be cultivated without awaiting new research techniques. Historical study has been directed often before into new and fruitful channels simply by the reëxamination of well-thumbed records in the light of fresh objectives.

Some may think the time not yet ripe for the study of the comprehensive social history of the corporation. In 1932 Kenneth Porter, for instance, wrote in the *Journal of Economic and Business History:*

> Perhaps when a sufficient number of business biographies and case histories of business firms have been prepared, business history may come to be considered in more general terms, but at the present time it is still in the early stage in which biography is all important.[2]

Mr. Porter's conclusion seems unnecessarily pessimistic, even for 1932. It would apply still less today, to some degree because of the

[1] In the revision of this manuscript for publication, the author was aided by William Miller.

[2] Kenneth W. Porter, "Trends in American Business Biography," *Journal of Economic and Business History,* IV (1932), 584.

work Mr. Porter himself has participated in at the Harvard Graduate School of Business Administration.[3]

Though some of the required history has been written, it still needs to be reinterpreted, for most of the useful secondary material is not explicitly on the social history of the corporation.[4] Nor has recent scholarship tended to correct this. In the six latest volumes of Grace Griffin's *Writings on American History,* only five items appear in the indices under the heading "corporation." Four are legal essays, and one, a brief business history of an early period.[5] Yet the corporation has come to dominate almost every phase of modern life. As the Middle West Utilities Company proclaimed: "From birth to death, the modern man is served every waking and sleeping hour by corporations of one kind or another." [6] It is high time we found out how the corporation achieved its present power and what the exercise of this power has meant in modern life.

Besides the secondary material, there are innumerable sources available that have never been explored with broad social considerations in mind. A specific description of these is obviously impossible in a short paper. A perusal of Henry P. Beers's *Bibliographies in American History* [7] will yield thirty or forty lists, all readily accessible. Among them are a score or more of short type-

[3] "Harvard Studies in Business History," edited by N. S. B. Gras, include: Kenneth W. Porter, *John Jacob Astor, Business Man,* Cambridge, 1931; Henrietta M. Larson, *Jay Cooke, Private Banker,* Cambridge, 1936; Kenneth W. Porter, ed., *The Jacksons and the Lees, Two Generations of Massachusetts Merchants, 1765–1844,* Cambridge, 1937; N. S. B. Gras, *The Massachusetts First National Bank of Boston, 1784–1934,* Cambridge, 1939; Ralph M. Hower, *The History of an Advertising Agency, N. W. Ayer and Son at Work, 1869–1939,* Cambridge, 1939.

[4] There is a wealth of corporate social history in such writings as: Arthur H. Cole, *The American Wool Manufacture,* 2 vols., Cambridge, Mass., 1926; Melvin T. Copeland, *The Cotton Manufacturing Industry of the United States,* Cambridge, 1912; or Caroline F. Ware, *The Early New England Cotton Manufacture,* New York, 1931. Also in good biographies of business men, such as the series edited by N. S. B. Gras, cited in n. 2 above, or the studies of special firms cited in later notes.

[5] Harold W. Stoke, "Economic Influence upon the Corporation Laws of New Jersey," *Journal of Political Economy,* XXXVIII (Oct., 1930), 551–79; Edwin Merrick Dodd, Jr., "The First Half Century of Statutory Regulation of Business Corporations in Massachusetts," in *Harvard Legal Essays,* written in honor of Joseph Henry Beale and Samuel Williston (Cambridge, 1934), pp. 65–132; Joseph G. Blandi, *Maryland Business Corporations, 1783–1852,* "Johns Hopkins University Studies," LII, no. 3 (Baltimore, 1934); Shaw Livermore, "Advent of Corporations in New York," *New York History,* XVI (1935), 286–98; Shaw Livermore, "Unlimited Liability in Early American Corporations," *Journal of Political Economy,* XLIII (1935), 674–87.

[6] Middle West Utilities Company, *America's New Frontier* (Chicago, 1929), p. 72.

[7] Henry Putney Beers, *Bibliographies in American History,* New York, 1938.

written or mimeographed lists by the Division of Bibliography of the Library of Congress. Government publications, including court records, reports of investigating committees, legal briefs, and statistical studies by various departments, offer mines of unused material.[8] Private business papers, even those already worked over, undoubtedly contain much that has not been used because the historian has not had a social objective in mind.[9]

One obstacle in the way of writing comprehensive corporate history is the traditional disinclination of executives to permit publication of detailed business records. Sometimes this has been due to justifiable fear of competitors. More often, it seems simply to result from traditional secrecy. In either case, it presents the historian with a dilemma: he must write from outside sources only, or submit to censorship that vitiates his work and robs it of social usefulness.[10]

In one way, however, this lack of inside records need not bother the social as much as the strictly business historian. For the social effects of corporate action must necessarily be felt and judged largely from the outside.[11] Often the only real deprivation is not to know exactly why certain policies were pursued. The social consequences of those policies will be apparent without the records of the corporation.

Merely to call attention to available literature, of course, will

[8] As for example: the Report of the Senate Committee on Education and Labor, 76th Congress, 1st session, Report no. 6, *Violation of Free Speech and Rights of Labor,* or the Federal Trade Commission *Report on Utility Corporations,* Senate Document 92, 70th Congress, 1st session. Among United States Library of Congress bibliographies are such as: "List of References on Fraudulent Practices in Promotion of Corporations and the Sale of Securities," 1915; "List of References on the Pension Systems of Corporations and Firms," 1931; "Short List of References on Business and Professional Ethics," 1924; and so forth.

[9] Almost all of the large manuscript collections contain business papers, letters, and so forth, that have never been worked over. The Baker Library, at Harvard, probably has the most important collection of this kind.

[10] In such works as Ralph Hower, *The History of an Advertising Agency,* the author has had fairly satisfactory access to the records, but has been censored in the use of them, see review by Thomas C. Cochran in *Pennsylvania Magazine of History and Biography,* XXXVIII (1914), 122–25. It is a hopeful sign that the economic historians at the University of Minnesota have recently undertaken to "stir up interest in the collection of business history materials and in making business men themselves aware of its importance," *Mississippi Valley Historical Review,* XXVI (1940), 655.

[11] Statistical research like that of William Miller on early Pennsylvania corporations may be of considerable value to the social historian. See, for example, William Miller, "An Introduction to the History of Business Corporations in Pennsylvania, 1800–1860," *Quarterly Journal of Economics,* LV (Nov., 1940).

not convince anyone of the need for a new type of study. What problems will this new approach clarify? That is the basic question. In the case of the social history of the corporation, it is obvious that the list can be almost infinite, and must vary according to the interests and imagination of the student. N. R. Danielian, for example, in his critical study of the American Telephone and Telegraph Company,[12] lists the following aspects of that company's activities as social: (1) the extent of accountability to the public; (2) the scale of wages paid; (3) employee's opportunity and security; (4) policy toward old age; (5) respect for worker's right to associate in unions; (6) effect on scientific progress; and (7) policy toward preservation of such benefits as civil liberties, free speech, freedom of the press, peaceable assembly, and the like. This list includes many factors bearing on business or government as a whole, rather than the particular element of corporateness. Other problems, however, seem to result directly from the apparently indissociable attributes of corporateness and bigness. Some of these we will pursue further. They may appear obvious and elementary, but deeper understanding can come only from further study. One of the more important points to emphasize is that if scholars will concern themselves with the social history of the corporation, we shall accumulate data now so limited [13] and get many fresh ideas and inspiring, fruitful conclusions. The whole area of group behavior and personal escape from responsibility, for instance, is one in which the psychologist must now rely heavily on the historian. If the latter approaches his work with the needs of the psychologist in mind, there will be great mutual benefit.[14]

[12] N. R. Danielian, *A. T. & T.; The Story of Industrial Conquest,* New York, 1939.

[13] From the end of the period covered by Joseph S. Davis, in *Essays in the Earlier History of American Corporations,* 2 vols., Cambridge, 1917, until near the end of the nineteenth century, there is a great dearth of monographic material. Scattered exceptions to this statement can be found in J. G. Blandi, *Maryland Business Corporations, 1783–1852,* Baltimore, 1935; Guy S. Callender, "Early Transportation and Banking Enterprises of the States in Relation to the Growth of Corporations," *Quarterly Journal of Economics,* XVII (1903), 111–62; G. H. Evans, Jr., "The Early History of Preferred Stock in the United States," *American Economic Review,* XIX (March, 1929), 43–58; Shaw Livermore, *Early American Land Companies,* New York, 1939; S. E. Howard, "Stockholder's Liability under the New York Act of 1811," *Journal of Political Economy,* XLVI (1938), 499–514; and William Miller, *An Introduction to the History of Business Corporations in Pennsylvania, 1800–1860,* cited above.

[14] The social psychologists are in the position of needing larger-scale experimentation than can be performed in a laboratory. Historical accounts can, perhaps, fill this need to a limited degree. For discussions of the present level of social psychological

came the great merger period around the turn of the century, the consequent flood of criticism of corporations, and a return to the arguments of early times.[20] These infected theorizing politicians and statesmen, and from that time to this the dualism in corporate personality has been stressed, with emphasis on the governmental, not enterprising features.[21]

Despite this trend, corporations continue to be personified simply as enterprising individuals. This attitude persists, especially among writers friendly to complete autonomy for modern business corporations and anxious to justify their unrestrained action in society. Thomas Lamont, for example, writes of his fellow Morgan partner: [22]

> . . . Henry Davison had for the Bankers Trust Company a feeling that was almost a passion. This trust company was his creation—his child. . . . What he wanted to realize for the Bankers Trust Company was an institution which, if it could have been personified, would be such a man as Davison proved himself to be throughout his life: active, fine, imaginative, cautious, yet full of courage—always looking the worst in the eye and daring any course that seemed constructive and helpful.

The playfulness of such language is clear enough to those who write it, but it produces misleading overtones of continuity of character, moral qualities, and intelligence which simply do not exist.[23] Could one look the Bankers Trust Company in the eye, even in those early days? Did it, as a company chartered under the banking act of New York, have a fine imagination? Did it have a

[20] W. Z. Ripley, *Trusts, Pools, and Corporations,* New York, 1905, bibliographical article by C. J. Bullock. Also, John P. Davis, *Corporations, A Study of the Origin and Development of Great Business Combinations and of Their Relation to the Authority of the State,* 2 vols., New York, 1905; and John Moody, *The Truth about Trusts,* New York, 1904.

[21] Woodrow Wilson, for example, in addressing the American Bar Association at its annual meeting in 1910, pointed out the duality of corporate personality and stressed the governmental aspect. This same approach is continuously emphasized in such writings as W. Z. Ripley, *Main Street and Wall Street,* Boston, 1927; A. A. Berle, Jr. and G. C. Means, *The Modern Corporation and Private Property,* New York, 1932; Maurice Wormser, *Frankenstein, Incorporated,* New York, 1931; Thurman Arnold, *The Folklore of Capitalism,* New York, 1938; and N. R. Danielian, *A. T. & T.,* New York, 1939.

[22] Thomas W. Lamont, *Henry P. Davison* (New York, 1933), pp. 51, 56. See also Edward Hungerford, *The Story of the Baltimore and Ohio Railroad,* 2 vols. (New York, 1928), II, 166; and H. J. Thornton, *The History of the Quaker Oats Company* (Chicago, 1933), p. 180, for the use of similar language.

[23] See Thurman Arnold, *The Folklore of Capitalism,* pp. 185–206.

conscience, a moral code, a willingness to suffer for ideals? To raise these questions is to see the difficulty of Mr. Lamont's flight of fancy. The Bankers Trust Company was an organization committed to making a profit from a sound banking business. No chairman or director had a right to ask the stockholders to suffer for a moral principle. No fine imagination could envisage changing its function, altering it, let us say, from a banking house to an art museum. Personification directs attention to the clothes and bearing of the corporation. It obstructs searching analysis of its inner nature and its true role in society.

Specific topics for investigation may be divided into four groups: (1) Problems concerning administrative structure and operation that are common to both political and business government: (2) the specific interactions, overt and *sub rosa,* of private corporations and the state; (3) the effects of the development of corporations on the morals and ethics of business and business men, and hence on the social community in general; (4) specific miscellaneous problems, such as the relation of corporations to population movements and labor policies.

Why did the democratic features of many early corporation charters fail to survive, at a period when democracy was growing stronger in politics? Why could it be reported by the Pujo Committee in 1914 that "None of the witnesses was able to name an instance in the history of the country in which stockholders had succeeded in overthrowing the existing management in any large corporation"? [24] Accounts have been written of the final degradation of the democratic corporate dogma, to a point where it is scarcely upheld even in theory.[25] How account for this shift from the conditions in the early nineteenth century? At that time the desirability of democracy within the corporation was recognized in many charters. In one case, the larger stockholders of a corporation had smaller voting power per share, and no individual could cast more than 100 votes.[26] Some early charters even gave an equal vote to all stockholders, regardless of the size of their hold-

[24] Quoted from Louis D. Brandeis, *Other People's Money* (New York, 1932), pp. 59–60.

[25] N. R. Danielian, *A. T. & T.*, pp. 33–34; W. Z. Ripley, *Main Street and Wall Street* (Boston, 1927), pp. 84–90.

[26] William O. Scroggs, in *Facts and Factors in Economic History,* by former students of Edwin F. Gay (Cambridge, 1932), p. 404.

ing.[27] How account for the progressive departure from this condition, particularly in the twentieth century, when many devices were adopted to divorce management from stockholder control at a time roughly contemporaneous with the introduction into political government of initiative, referendum, and recall? [28]

While there have been thorough investigations by political and constitutional historians of the development of the administrative machinery of government, little if any historical study has been made of the parallel development in big business. Yet, as Professor Bullock indicated in 1905,[29] noncompetitive business was bound to develop all the administrative ills of government, including bureaucracy and lack of enterprise.[30] Men having practical experience with the situation have emphasized the tendency toward the bureaucratic shift of responsibility in large corporations. J. B. Sheridan, for many years director of the Missouri Committee on Public Utility Information, writes: [31]

> We are raising a lot of thoroughly drilled "yes Ma'am" in the big corporations, who have no minds of their own, no opinions. As soon as the old individualists die, and there are not so many of them left, I think corporations will have a lot of trouble in getting good executives. After a man has served 20 to 30 years in one of these monstrous corporations he is not liable to have a mind of his own.

There has been, however, no attempt to synthesize the available material in a way that would shed light on the historical evolution of bureaucracy in large-scale noncompetitive or semicompetitive business.

A much larger field for further study is that of the social as-

[27] Shaw Livermore, *Early American Land Companies* (New York, 1939), p. 328; Joseph S. Davis, *Essays*, II, 323–24.

[28] W. Z. Ripley, *Main Street and Wall Street* (Boston, 1927), pp. 78–118.

[29] In *Trusts, Pools, and Corporations* by W. Z. Ripley (New York, 1905), pp. 458–61.

[30] A great deal of helpful material on this difficult subject has been assembled in receivership proceedings and government investigations. Some of this has been well presented for the general historian in such books as Max Lowenthal, *The Investor Pays*, New York, 1933; Ernest Gruening, *The Public Pays*, New York, 1931; J. B. McFerrin, *Caldwell and Company*, Chapel Hill, 1939. Fragmentary treatments of the question of bureaucracy and other administrative failings can be found in many of the histories of railroad companies. For example, F. C. B. Bradley, *The Eastern Railroad* (Essex Institute, 1922), pp. 82–89. A further suggestive approach to this subject is O. H. von der Gablentz, "Industrielbureaukratie," in Schmoller's *Jahrbuch*, L (München, 1926), 539.

[31] Quoted from Carl D. Thompson, *Confessions of the Power Trust* (New York, 1932), pp. 14–15.

pects of the relations between corporations and the state. Despite numerous treatises of a legal nature, Professor Beard is justified in saying: "The history of the tug of war between states and their corporate creatures has never been written."[32]

What have been the social effects of certain state charter policies, of various Supreme Court interpretations, of state ownership of corporate stock?[33] While Federal participation in business during the World War and the recent depression is in every student's mind,[34] the widespread early nineteenth-century state participation in corporate stock holding has generally been slighted.[35] Nor has any work been done to trace and interpret the question of why government has alternately gone in and out of business, and the social meaning of such changes in policy.

There is an abundant and highly respectable literature by historians and social scientists describing and criticizing government interference in business. Whole sets of studies, which it would serve no purpose to mention here, seem to have been executed with this consideration in mind. But there is very little scholarly literature about the other side of this reciprocal relationship—the interference of private corporations in government. Yet any objective scholar of American history must be in doubt as to which of these activities has been of greater importance over the years. Certainly from the Civil War until very recent times corporate influence in politics would seem to have been more important than political influence in business. Danielian points out that the American Telephone and Telegraph Company, for instance, subtly guided by public relations experts, is really in politics everywhere. Education pamphlets, press releases, specially written articles, and editorials are its defenses against the only competitors

[32] Charles A. Beard, "Corporations and Natural Rights," *Virginia Quarterly,* XII (July, 1936), 345.

[33] There are discussions of recent phases of this history in "A Comparative Study of the Corporation Laws of the States of New Jersey, Delaware, and Maryland," by V. W. Westrup, *New York University Law Quarterly Review,* XI (1933–34), 349 ff.; and *Brandeis,* by A. T. Mason, Princeton, 1933.

[34] See H. A. Van Dorn, *Government Owned Corporations,* New York, 1926; Arthur E. Cook, ed., *A History of the United States Shipping Board, and Merchant Fleet Corporation,* Baltimore, 1927; and John Thurston, *Government Proprietary Corporations in the English Speaking Countries,* Cambridge, 1937.

[35] Except for discussions such as John Ray Cable, *The Bank of the State of Missouri,* New York, 1923; James H. Johnston, *The Western and Atlantic Railroad of the State of Georgia,* Atlanta, 1932; and an excellent article by Guy S. Callender, referred to in n. 13.

that it really need fear, the governments of the states and the United States.[36] As for the earlier period, how arresting is the offhand statement of F. C. Oviatt, that the Protection Insurance Company's Ohio Office was, after 1825, "a sort of headquarters for prominent Whig politicians." [37]

It is important to emphasize the fact that the corporate form of organization is not limited to business companies. All scholars in the academic world, in colleges and universities as well as institutions for endowed research, are familiar with its use in education.[38] Perhaps as important from the standpoint of incorporated education are certain pressure groups specifically devoted to affecting public policy. These range from organizations such as the National Association of Manufacturers,[39] which seeks to impress upon the whole of society the philosophies and aims of business, to such a comparatively simple group as the Society for the Prevention of Cruelty to Animals.

Studies have been made listing the principal activities of some of these nonbusiness corporations,[40] but no effort has been made to assemble the whole picture of their general influence on social development. A problem of interest to psychologists and historians

[36] N. R. Danielian, *A. T. & T.*, pp. 271–333. See also Carl D. Thompson, *Confessions of the Power Trust,* New York, 1932; Henry H. Klein, *Politics, Government and the Public Utilities in New York,* New York, 1933; Bruce Raup, *Education and Organized Interests in America,* New York, 1936; George W. Norris, "The Power Trust in the Public Schools," *Journal of the National Education Association,* XVIII (1929), 277; and Edward L. Bernays, *Crystallizing Public Opinion,* New York, 1923, and *Propaganda,* New York, 1928.

[37] F. C. Oviatt, "Historical Study of Fire Insurance," *Annals of the American Academy of Political and Social Science,* XXVI (1905), 168.

[38] See Ernest V. Hollis, *Philanthropic Foundations and Higher Education,* New York, 1938; Jesse B. Sears, *Philanthropy in the History of American Higher Education,* United States Bureau of Education Bulletin, no. 26, 1922; Eduard C. Lindeman, *Wealth and Culture,* New York, 1936; and Thorstein Veblen, *The Higher Learning in America,* New York, 1918.

[39] An interesting study of the National Association of Manufacturers might be made from its own publications. See also Clarence E. Bonnett, *Employers' Associations in the United States,* New York, 1922; and Report of the Senate Committee on Education and Labor, 76th Congress, 1st Session, Report no. 6, Washington, 1939.

[40] As, for example, Kenneth M. Sturges, *American Chambers of Commerce,* New York, 1915; J. A. Swisher: *The American Legion in Iowa, 1919–1929,* Iowa City, 1929; Belle Zeller, *Pressure Politics in New York,* New York, 1937; National Consumers' League, *The National Consumers' League; First Quarter Century, 1899–1924,* New York, 1925; Harold C. Coffman, *American Foundations,* New York, 1936; F. P. Keppel, *The Foundation: Its Place in American Life,* New York, 1930; Kenneth D. Crawford, *The Pressure Boys,* New York, 1939; and "Pressure Groups and Propaganda," ed. by H. L. Childs, *Annals of the American Academy of Political and Social Science,* CLXXIX (1935).

alike is the extent to which the actions of such groups have been dictated by their corporateness, particularly the attendant freedom from personal responsibility.

Another aspect of the relations of corporations to the state and to the functions of the state is the development of the company-dominated city or town. This field offers abundant material and opportunities for further work. Some excellent studies have been made recently,[41] but these tend to document only the implications of absentee ownership, brilliantly set forth by Veblen. Other aspects of this development have as yet hardly been explored. Such a problem as the influence of the personnel policies of locally dominant corporations on the educational and social ideals encouraged in the community indicates one type of study still to be made. It should be said that this influence need not be malevolent,[42] but certainly in towns such as Pullman, Hershey, or Kohler there can be little doubt that an element has entered into local political and civic affairs not as yet included in the popular conception of the spirit of American Government. It is the task of the historian at least to record this change. As yet he has not done so.

No student can long avoid the fundamental question as to what participation in corporate activity has done to undermine old individualist standards in ethics and morals.[43] Men like Daniel Drew and Jay Gould were pioneers in illustrating the decline of the old standards, based on individual responsibility, but it was not until a generation later that Thorstein Veblen supplied the philosophical background for the new relations.[44] E. A. Ross soon added

[41] As, for example, Vera Shlakman, *Economic History of a Factory Town,* "Smith College Studies in History," Vol. XX, 1935; Constance M. Green, *Holyoke, Massachusetts,* New Haven, 1939; Almont Lindsey, "Paternalism and the Pullman Strike," *American Historical Review,* XLIV (Jan., 1939), 272–89; Robert S. Lynd and Helen M. Lynd, *Middletown,* New York, 1929. And, on a more popular plane, Robert Leighton, *Five Cities,* New York, 1939; Omar P. Goslin and Ryllis A. Goslin, *Our Town's Business,* New York, 1939.

[42] Horace M. Bond, in his *Negro Education in Alabama,* New York, 1939, points out that the United States Steel Corporation greatly assisted the education of Alabama Negroes. The fact that the steel corporation did this for its own economic advantage does not detract from the social benefit.

[43] From Mark Twain and C. D. Warner's novel, *The Gilded Age,* 2 vols. (New York, 1873), to Max Radin's *The Manners and Morals of Business* (Indianapolis, 1939), this has been a theme for fiction and essay writing.

[44] That is, relations that made the directors of large enterprises feel no personal responsibility for the actions of remote underlings. The theory was that the stockholders, as the ultimate owners, bore the responsibility. See Thorstein Veblen, *The Theory of*

a sweeping and clever denunciation of corporate amorality, together with a plea for the recognition of new social "sins." [45]

One problem suggested by such writings is the tracing of the effects of corporate environment in the lives of important executives, or their agents, the men who, "acting for the company," had to do the things that led to the "new sins." Everybody illustrates at least slight differences in personality when acting in different capacities, but submersion of the individual in the corporate personality during business hours allows a much more complete split, the more perfect dramatization of a role. As Floyd Allport has noted, corporations permit a kind of fractional behavior.[46] The man, as idealist, humanitarian, and paternalist, may become simply the man, as business manager, when he sits with a board of directors or carries out their decisions. For this shedding of the "better" qualities of his character, he feels no responsibility; he is hired to protect the interests of the stockholders, and they (unknown to themselves) symbolically bear the burden of guilt.[47]

There is, as already cited, an abundance of literature bearing upon this specific social dilemma,[48] but there has been very little historical study of the problem itself. I know of no biographer who has employed detailed records, combined with recent psychological knowledge, to contrast the character of the business man in his various business and nonbusiness roles, with a view to determining what considerations limited his activities in each sphere.[49] How much light might be thrown on economic history

---

Business Enterprise, New York, 1904; W. Z. Ripley, *Main Street and Wall Street,* Boston, 1927.

45 Edward A. Ross, *Sin and Society: An Analysis of Latter-Day Iniquity,* New York, 1907.

46 Floyd Allport, *Institutional Behavior* (Chapel Hill, 1933), pp. 29–48.

47 It is interesting to note that in an unidentified opinion of Mr. Justice Brandeis, Professor Ripley quotes him as saying: "There is no such thing to my mind as an innocent stockholder. . . . He accepts the benefits of the system. It is his business and his obligation to see that those who represent him carry out a policy which is consistent with the public welfare" (*Main Street and Wall Street,* p. 79).

48 See previous references to E. A. Ross, W. Z. Ripley, Thorstein Veblen, Berle and Means, and Max Radin.

49 The following may be consulted for modern psychological theories regarding group activity: Gardner Murphy, L. B. Murphy, and T. M. Newcomb, *Experimental Social Psychology,* New York, 1937; Carl A. Murchison, *Handbook of Social Psychology,* Worcester, 1935; Edward A. Strecker, *Beyond the Clinical Frontiers,* New York, 1940; Ruth Benedict, *Patterns of Culture,* New York, 1933; Gordon W. Allport, *Personality, a Psychological Interpretation,* New York, 1937; Kenneth Burke, *Attitudes toward History,* 2 vols., New York, 1937.

and the development of American patterns of social action, if the activities of corporate manipulators could receive the painstaking study that Douglas Freeman has lavished on General Lee or Albert Beveridge on Marshall and Lincoln! [50]

Since the late eighteenth century, some type of corporation has almost invariably been the *deus ex machina* directing the movements of American population. The role of the railroads and land companies in growth and settlement has, of course, received considerable attention, but there are many other types of companies whose influence has been largely neglected. The Middle West Utilities Company predicted, with an optimism born of 1929, a rapid decentralization of industry, due to long-distance power transmission by public utility holding companies.[51] Certain it is that the opening and closing, or moving of a plant employing 30,000 or 40,000 workers produces a population shift equal to any of the old-style real estate booms. But besides these direct influences there are more subtle ones. Very little has been written, for example, on the influence of insurance-company investments in the westward movement. Yet, as Charles Abrams remarks:

> . . . Twenty-five billion dollars of institutionally-held mortgages take on a profound importance to the national economy by reason of sheer magnitude alone. The growth of these institutions and their freedom from federal control present a major political challenge.[52]

Terence O'Donnell and Burton J. Hendrick, in their histories of life insurance, touch upon the origins of this investment, but their accounts can hardly be rated as satisfactory histories of the situation.[53]

The relations of corporations with labor, and with labor unions, which are, in effect, corporations themselves, have so extensive a literature that only the specialized scholar can estimate what remains undone. This has been the one great field for the study of corporate social history, although it has not been called by that

[50] Detailed study will be made difficult by a relative shortage of personal letters, in the case of many business men, but Kenneth Porter's *John Jacob Astor* and Henrietta Larson's *Jay Cooke; Private Banker* show what may be done in this field.

[51] Middle West Utilities Company, *America's New Frontier,* Chicago, 1929.

[52] Charles Abrams, *Revolution in Land* (New York, 1939), p. 113.

[53] Terence O'Donnell, compiler, *History of Life Insurance, in Its Formative Years,* Chicago, 1936; Burton J. Hendrick, *The Story of Life Insurance,* New York, 1908.

name, and most of the scholars have concerned themselves only incidentally with the larger aspects of the corporate picture.[54]

All the foregoing suggestions hinge to a large degree upon the need for more case histories of all kinds of associations, emphasizing as far as possible every ascertainable relationship, and upon more critical and complete biographies of corporate leaders. Such studies need not, in fact should not, be confined to profit-making business corporations. Women's clubs, lodges, chambers of commerce, veterans' organizations, trade associations, reform associations, philanthropic foundations, and educational institutions all represent important aspects of corporate social behavior.[55]

If institutional studies are to be really thorough, if they are to consider the corporation in its environment, they can probably cover only a brief span of years, but this is perhaps an advantage. A comparative study of two periods, such as the Lynds' *Middletown,* can be truly historical without filling in all the intervening incidents.[56]

Such studies must necessarily be approached by the historian in the role of social scientist as well as that of chronicler. He must lean heavily on the aid that can be given by psychology, sociology, and economics, and not hedge his writing in by self-imposed artificial barriers. The purely business and legal aspects shackle corporate study today, just as the political and military themes restricted the old history texts. Corporate study in the future should be not only business history, psychological history, or political history. It should disclose how all of these related facets affected corporation history, or, in turn, were affected by the growth of the corporation.

[54] Two exceptions to the above statement are to be found in the United States Department of Labor, Bureau of Labor Statistics, Bulletin no. 634, *Characteristics of Company Unions,* Washington, 1938, and John Randall, *The Problem of Group Responsibility to Society; an Interpretation of the History of American Labor,* New York, 1922.

[55] See Frank D. Watson, *The Charity Organization Movement in the United States,* New York, 1916; A. G. Warner, *American Charities,* New York, 1908; E. T. Devine, *Organized Charity and Industry,* New York, 1915; and also the material referred to in notes 38–40 above.

[56] Comparative graphic studies such as Otto Neurath's *Modern Man in the Making,* New York, 1939, offer suggestive possibilities to the social historian dealing with the complex relationships of corporations.

THE GERMAN ARMY OF THE SECOND REICH AS A CULTURAL INSTITUTION

ALFRED VAGTS

HARDLY an army, whether of past or present times, has been set up for the purposes of warfare alone and, contrary to most readily expressed convictions, the Prusso-German army before 1914 was perhaps least of all designed for purely martial ends. A tabulation of modern wars would bring that out very clearly. For whereas, in the hundred years from 1815 to 1914, unmilitary England undertook the greatest number of wars, Prussia-Germany, the most military of all the great powers, was involved in the smallest number of wars.[1] What was true of Germany was true, in a varying degree, of other countries as well: armies are planned with other than the strictly military goal in mind. They may exist for themselves merely—"the army for the army's sake"—or for what may be largely the same, the peace-time purposes of the ruling society. Of such a state of things, the ruling groups, or, for that matter, the potential foreign enemies of such societies are seldom so consciously aware as the typically critical or oppositional groups in a given country. This inner contradiction, nevertheless, has had far-reaching effects: where it has not actually annihilated armies from within, as has sometimes been the case, it has often enough decreased their usefulness for war, since army government is peculiarly apt to deteriorate into over-government, if the commanding groups are not open to criticism and advice from below or around them.

Armies, viewed in this twofold aspect as war instruments and as governing instruments, involve a double managerial problem. The plan and control of an army to fulfill both peace-time and war-time requirements—requirements which usually overlap and must be faced at one and the same moment—constitute a highly complex problem of employment and occupation, often indeed, the largest single managerial problem of the country in question.

[1] Charles Hodges, "The Changing Background of World Politics," *Our World*, VI (Dec., 1924), 14–20.

One may, therefore, legitimately compare some issues in the military sphere with others in the industrial, and employ the unusual but still befitting term, "military management," to cover the principal problems to be dealt with in this article. The following series of questions, translated from military into industrial terms, will be raised and then discussed, if not finally answered, with special reference to the pre-war German army.

What is the supply of workers (or recruits) available for the purpose of the army? Which are the best among them? And where do they originate? One historical military personnel problem is whether the rural recruit provides a better soldier than the urban one. Better, that is, for the true goal of the soldier, war, and not as far as the preferences of the individual officer or officer body are concerned, or, for that matter, the inclination of the laborer for military service.[2]

What officers or officer material is available? Are the most obviously available ones, the traditionally available ones, the best from the technological point of view, since the modern officer is a "destruction engineer"? Must some officers be chosen and accepted, even though they may not be the best fitted, while others are excluded, for extraneous reasons, perhaps because they are not "well-born" or of sufficient social rank and "presence"?

What is the most desirable morale in armed bodies, whence is it to be derived, by what means is it to be instilled and preserved? Which elements in the nation provide best and most efficiently the discipline and authority which is required in each and every large body of men, and most so in an armed body?

Which is the best and most productive working time—in military terms, the service period which prepares a soldier best for the most likely sort of war? Is there perhaps one requirement for the peace-time soldier and a different one for the war-time soldier?

Which age groups provide the best workers—alias soldiers—for a specific job: young, very young, middle-aged, old employees? And are requirements different for officers and men? This involves the perpetual problem of rejuvenation and also the question of whether generals should be young, to keep pace with war technology, or old, to preserve authority.

[2] I would conclude tentatively that in countries where men have the choice of enlistment, the rural recruit is more apt to volunteer in peace time, the urban one in time of war.

What is to be done with employees after working hours? Is the *dopo lavoro* perhaps older in the military field than in the civilian?

What should be the pay and other emoluments of the officer and the common soldier? What shape should be assumed by the extra-pecuniary rewards which both forms of enterprise have to offer, except perhaps under the most outspokenly laissez-faire entrepreneurs?

What are the effects of military employ or service on the individuals who undergo this service, freely or involuntarily, or on the nation as a whole? How does such employment affect their health, thought, fitness for nonmilitary pursuits?

What is the effect, good, bad, or indifferent, of armies, on the economy of a nation?

In times like the present, when *Wehrwirtschaft,* the organization of national economy in preparation for war, is spreading everywhere, the dividing line between military or war economy and private economy has become so blurred that these questions may not appear as clear-cut as they have at certain times in the past. For the purposes of exemplification as well as clarification, it would seem advisable to go back to the period of relative simplicity, beginning about 1600, in which the large-scale employment problems arose. This was the age of what is called *Manufaktur* in industrial history, the early attempts to gather several processes and considerable groups of workers under one roof, often through capital and initiative provided by the state, as in the case of France. Manufacturing was the intermediate step between the small craftsmen's booths and the modern factory, with a real, though primitive division of labor, centralizing the production and marketing processes under the direction of a capitalistic entrepreneur. Large-scale employment was, however, earlier in armies; as Marx and Engels insisted, not without justification, such principles as the division of labor and the application of machinery were evolved first among military masses [3] in the sixteenth century, the age of hired *condottieri* and imported troops of Swiss and *Landsknechte.*

Manufacturing was characterized in its first stages by the coöperation of skilled artisans within the large shop. The laborer

[3] *Zur Kritik der politischen Oekonomie* (ed. Stuttgart, 1919), p. xlvi; Alfred Vagts, *A History of Militarism* (New York, 1937), p. 34.

in this in-between period of industrial development was indeed forced into the shop through want of sufficient capital of his own, but he was still in a good bargaining position because the "manufacture" needed his special knowledge and abilities and was often willing to bring him a long distance, giving him many privileges. He frequently was costly, but worked well, efficiently, reliably, and made delivery of goods certain.

The conditions under which soldiers were employed in armies at a comparable period were similar. One of the main differences between industrial manufacture and the armies of that period would appear to lie in leadership: there was a greater gulf between the sovereigns who, so to speak, placed the order for an army with someone, and those who actually commanded the troops as experts, than there was between the capitalists and the heads of shops, if indeed the two were not identical. On the other hand, the state tendency to control industries and, if necessary, to create royal factories, may be compared with the efforts made at the same time to bring armies from feudal to royal hands.

In the more industrialized countries like France and Holland, there was not enough available man power—at least, that was the notion of the times—to serve both industries and armies. The constant need of foreigners, whose pay depleted the royal treasury of France, gave governors like Sully the idea that the further development of industries should be stopped and the mass of the people brought back to the land, in order to restore and nurture the warlike strength of the French. For "France is not fitted for such baubles," he said. "This sedentary life of the manufactures does not make good soldiers." It was actually decreed in 1635 that all building should cease for a time, in order to force the masons to became soldiers.[4] But such orders of so-called statesmen did not halt industrial progress; they did, however, bequeath to later times a heritage of resentment against industry as the destroyer of military man power, a feudal grudge that was not to die out before the World War, and a belief that the peasant always makes a better soldier than the industrial worker.

That military men do not generally progress *pari passu* with industrial development becomes obvious at this early stage; when the industries presented new means of warfare, it took the military

[4] Max Jähns, *Heeresverfassungen und Völkerleben*, 2d ed. (Berlin, 1885), p. 260.

leaders long years to create corresponding forms of warfare, to subdue and coördinate the instruments of destruction. This problem of coördinating industrial organization and products with military leadership was solved for the first time in the Dutch Revolution.

In this revolt of a mercantile people against Spain, various features of industrial organization were reflected in military fields. Foreign soldiers were hired and persuaded by regular payment to perform the tasks set by the military leaders of Holland. On land, the perfection of this organization was finally achieved by Maurice of Orange through his system of drilling and tactics, which brought about effective coöperation.[5] The specifically Dutch elements, water and earth, were applied to build the cheapest, quickest, and strongest fortifications of the time, consisting principally of earthen walls and broad ditches, behind which Ostend, for example, could defend itself for forty-two months. The employment of the soldiers was planned more systematically than before; sometimes movements were designed with the help of tin soldiers and other models, and thought out with something of the rigor of modern shop efficiency.

In certain respects there was even more standardization in the Dutch army than in contemporary manufacture. Thus Dutch guns were reduced to three or four calibers, which largely settled the types of gunnery until the introduction of rifling and breech loading.[6] There were far more foremen, or officer supervisors of efficiency, in the army than in the workshops of the day. They taught the soldiers to perform to perfection the "exercitia Mauriciana" (thirty-two movements for the pike and forty-three for the musket), demanding a dexterity of motion in which the army again preceded industry. Under these regulations, the soldiers became much more industrious than those wild fellows who had formed the dense crowds of the early sixteenth century when, as the story is told of the battle of Ravenna (1512), the agile Spaniards jumped on top of the heads of the densely massed *Landsknechte* and fought them from above.[7]

[5] G. Roloff, "Moritz von Oranien und die Begründung des modernen Heeres," *Preuss. Jahrb.*, CXI (Berlin, 1903), pp. 255–76.

[6] Max Jähns, *Geschichte der Kriegswissenschaften* (München, 1889), pp. 1138, 995 f., 1004.

[7] Hans Delbrück, *Geschichte der Kriegskunst im Rahmen der politischen Geschichte*, Part IV (Berlin, 1920), p. 198.

The standing armies before and after 1700 were far from carrying to further perfection this Dutch model of war efficiency. For the former were not conceived for efficiency above everything else, but rather for providing more constant employment and payment than a crisis-shaken economy could provide for the landholding nobility and their sons, elder and younger—a group that was on the verge of annihilation. What took place may be called a refeudalization of the armies—one of the several refeudalizations which bourgeois society has undergone in modern times. The Dutch themselves, after they won their independence from Spain, the great land power, allowed their army to decay like a factory for which there was little use; of the two fighting forces, the navy was thenceforth considered the only profitable and—incidentally or not—the truly national arm.

It is not possible to discuss here the influence of the Dutch example upon Brandenburg-Prussia—with Calvinists as electors and kings at the head of the state. There has always been a good deal of international "tutoring" in the military field; this imitaion, however, has, on the whole, taken place primarily in the echnological field and far less in the sphere of "commanding," of discipline, organization, and the like, which to a large degree have been evolved from within. Whereas the ruling class in the Netherlands was a commercial oligarchy, in Prussia it was a landowning oligarchy, commonly called the Junkers; if on occasion it was thought that the bureaucracy ran the country, it was at any ate run in the interest of the Junkers. It was this group which, on the whole, applied its experience and convictions about the management of an army as a large-scale enterprise. In great part hese convictions were carried over from their own economic background, large-scale agriculture, the only form of considerable nterprise existing originally and for a long time in Prussia, unless, s the eighteenth-century saying insisted, war was the only industry of that country. The "Old Dessauer," Leopold I of Anhalt-Dessau died, 1747), the foremost drillmaster of the Prussian army, was at the same time one of the largest landowners and grainproducers in Prussia, having abolished noble landholding in his own principality. That the Prussian armies then and later bore the marks of this origin, in their personnel and direction, will be vident if we consider these armies in terms of the questions posed at the beginning of this chapter.

First, who did supply the common soldiery? In 1653 the Elector of Brandenburg came to an accord with the Estates, whereby they agreed to grant taxes for the upkeep of the *miles perpetuus,* receiving in return the grant of the perpetual serf.[8] In this deal the towns later joined—they were to pay taxes and win exemption from military service. The unfree peasant, after he had been trained in obedience by the nobility, became in turn the Prussian conscript soldier, often serving in the company of a captain whose family he had served on the estate. Military service was thus sandwiched in between early and later serf duty. The other part of the common soldiery, in Prussia as elsewhere, was imported from other lands and very largely consisted of what in modern language would be called urban proletariat. For all of them, the old right of free contract no longer existed; unlike the "willful" Swiss and the independent *Landsknechte* before them, they could not insist upon terms—"pas de monnaie, pas de Suisse." The new discipline meant, among other things, that the higher partner to the service contract did not necessarily have to keep his part of the bargain. After 1807 this arrangement, penurious as it was, proved too expensive for improverished Prussia; the foreigners were dismissed and the whole Prussian nation—though nation it hardly was as yet—was conscripted. Some privileges were, however, allowed the citizenry, whose sons, if they acquired a certain grade of higher education, were obliged to serve only one year in the army instead of the three years required of the common soldier. Such burgher sons supplied officers for the *Landwehr* and Reserve formations. Even after 1807 the officers preferred the rural recruit to the industrial worker, hiding their aversion for the latter behind the claim that the health of the rural recruit was better than that of the city man, a statement for which the statistical proof has always remained of dubious character.[9]

The preferred officer in the Prusso-German armies has at all times been the nobly born officer; the noble cadet was the one most readily accepted, even if his education was faulty, and he was taken very young—down to 1807 the Junker (young master) could enter the army at the tender age of twelve, thus enabling him to

[8] Vagts, *A History of Militarism,* p. 47.

[9] L. Brentano and R. Kuczynski, *Die heutige Grundlage der deutschen Wehrkraf[t],* Stuttgart, 1900; Kuczynski, *Ist die Landwirtschaft die wichtigste Grundlage der deu[t]schen Wehrkraft* (*Volkswirtschaftliche Zeitfragen,* Heft 213), Berlin, 1905.

procure a captaincy fairly early in life. Nor could he easily be too old: Field Marshal von Schwerin died in action before Prague at the age of seventy-three; Blücher was seventy-one in 1813, Hindenburg sixty-seven in 1914. Privates were likewise sought in their youth, as soon as their physical health allowed them to stand the rigors of military service. For the rest, the requirement of youthfulness, desirable for military reasons, was inextricably joined with the disinclination to use the *Landwehr,* in which men in the thirties were serving. The latter had often started to think for themselves politically; consciousness of this on the part of the Prussian officer body led to the rejuvenation of the *cadres* of the Prussian army in the army reform of 1862.[10]

Foreign noble officers, like the Marquis de Galliffet, envied Prussia an army "où la hierarchie militaire se confond avec la hierarchie sociale."[11] This principle largely—in time of peace absolutely—excluded promotion from the ranks. After a period of permissible moderate Liberalism in the nineteenth century, represented in the army by men like General von Stosch, onetime organizer of the young Reich navy, party conservatism became a *conditio sine qua non* for the officer, with a growing tendency to include the Reserve and *Landwehr* officer in this expectation. And then even in the navy of the Reich, the nobility, ever hungry for the higher positions of officialdom, was gaining ground, despite Pascal's warning that on board ship one does not choose the man from the oldest house to direct the vessel.

At no time in its history has the exclusiveness of this army gone so far as to shut out all personalities who could bring and transfer the ideas necessary for military progress. Little of this thought has come from Prussia proper; practically all the great leadership has risen elsewhere, a fact that might be phrased in the semblance of a law: Prussia has been carried on and saved by non-Prussians or by Prussians who had at least a non-Prussian, non-noble streak

10 With the memory of 1848–49 still vividly before his eyes, the later King and Emperor William I asked the Prussian ministry in 1859: "Why have all the Landwehr battalions of the Guard stood to their oath? Because the three years' service term has been enforced in the Guard corps without interruption. Infantry regiments of the line, however, have wavered. . . . However of all the cavalry regiments of the line not one has wavered in its loyalty even for a moment. Why? Because they as well have preserved the three years' service." Johannes Ziekursch, *Politische Geschichte des neuen deutschen Kaiserreiches* (Frankfurt am Main, 1925–30), I, 36.

11 Felix Priebatsch, *Geschichte des preussischen Offizierkorps* (Breslau, 1919), p. 56.

in them. Unadulterated Old Prussianism wrecked the Kingdom in 1806 and played havoc with the Reich before 1914. Prussian exclusivism insisted in the 1900's that the army must not be enlarged in accordance with the available manhood; the Prussian ministry of war explained that there was not enough "reliable" officer material to command such an increase and that, if the army were expanded, "unreliable," democratic elements must be drawn upon for the officer corps. This rigidity caused a serious, probably fatal, shortage of men at the outbreak of war in 1914, which was further increased by the cry of the big landholders of Eastern Prussia for protection when their province was invaded. The three army corps thus drawn away to the East were sadly missed in the first Marne battle, and also arrived too late to help in the battle of Tannenberg at the end of August, 1914. By contrast with this Prussian mismanagement, one may ask who, on the contrary, have been the saviors of Prussia, before Adolf Hitler, the Austrian? Not Old Prussians of the 100-percent variety. Bismarck had a mother from the bourgeoisie, a simple Mencken. To restrict ourselves to military leadership: Blücher, Scharnhorst, Gneisenau were non-Prussians; Bülow von Dennewitz was an illegitimate child; the nobility of Clausewitz is fully as dubious as that of Steuben, and may in fact be called fictitious; Roon's patent of nobility was so shaky that he did not care to have it investigated; that of Yorck von Wartenburg was hardly better; Moltke was born in Mecklenburg and entered Danish service before he was admitted to the Prussian army as "a poor acquisition." Such men carried the technological and managerial progress achieved elsewhere to an army in which the typical officer mind was closed to such advance. It might be recalled on this occasion that the intellectual contributions of the nobility generally and of the German nobility in particular were appallingly small, by comparison with the large opportunity which the nobility enjoyed.

If personal observation is worth anything to the military historian—and Hans Delbrück used to say that one year of military service was the equivalent of several years of abstract research—the author would say that, in his case, it confirmed the conclusions drawn from literature: that on the whole the noble Prussian officer was, as if by birth, typically gifted for the leadership of the small unit, from the company to the division; that beyond such units, as well as in the more technological tasks, the non-noble officer was superior. Names of commanders of German armies in the World War are misleading in such a case—the true directors were the chiefs of staff and so-called "I A-officers." To this might be added another observation: that the higher nobility in Germany, from the rank of count upward, have presented practically nothing to military leadership, except figureheads, since the eighteenth century.

One of the reasons that the rural recruit was considered the most desirable by the prewar German army was the fact that he had been "broken in" by the conditions of rural life and authority, before he came to the barracks; he had not felt the influence of the nonauthoritarian life, not to speak of the positive counter-indoctrination which the Social Democratic Party tried to give its youth before they joined the colors.[12] Part of the antagonism between the officer and the urban recruit was due to the largely rural forms of authority and discipline which he tended to impose and which were his own, historically speaking, reinforced by those of the village parson and the village schoolmaster. The latter was, however, largely unthanked. After the victories of 1864, 1866, and 1870–71, the bourgeoisie, proud of its education, wished to ascribe these victories to the schoolmaster (who, by the way, was the least respected of all officers serving in the army); but Moltke asserted from the rostrum of the Reichstag in 1874:

> Not the schoolmaster, but the educator, the state, has won our battles, the state which now for nearly sixty years has educated for the purposes of physical strength and mental vigor, for order and punctuality, for loyalty and obedience, for patriotism and agility. You cannot do without the army, and that in its whole present strength, even within the nation for the educative purposes of the latter.[13]

In rural life the instruments and symbols of authority were almost constantly visible, and little retreat or concealment from them was possible. In urban life the individual could at that time retreat from supervision into the anonymity of the city. As against this partial withdrawal from authority, noble officers insisted that "the officer must be of that master race whose decisive

[12] For the story of the army life of a young Social Democrat, see August Winnig, *Preussischer Kommiss. Soldatengeschichten,* Berlin, 1910.

[13] Gustav Tuch, *Der erweiterte deutsche Militärstaat in seiner sozialen Bedeutung* (Leipzig, 1886), pp. 172–73.

influence is felt even if its personality is not immediately seen or heard." [14]

Inextricably bound up with the problem of authority and discipline was the question of the length of army service. The Liberal parties contended that a three years' service was a waste of time on the part of the soldier and of money on the part of the nation, entailing a loss of productiveness to industry; that the general progress in education and intelligence easily warranted a shortening of the period. But for some twenty years the governors of the Reich would not hear of it. Nothing illustrates this determination better than a letter from Moltke to Bismarck in 1879, referring to the unusual strengthening and reorganization of the army in Russia, despite the recent close of a victorious war, when the establishment of armies is customarily reduced. "Whether this measure is intended against something abroad or at home, must be left undecided." Bismarck's marginal note, "not against [something] at home, for it is combined with a shortening of the service period" shows *in nuce* the identity of the three years' term and its antirevolutionary function at home. Moltke went on to say that perhaps in Russia the calling to the colors of the largest possible part of the population was considered as the most adequate school for their education (Bismarck: "No") but at any rate this remains a danger for the neighbors (Bismarck: "Yes"). "The shortening of the service period in the Reich is opposed by this principle that we must not in any case pay for a numerical strengthening of our army by a reduction of its intrinsic efficiency." [15]

The two years' service term was introduced against the strong opposition of Bismarck by his successor, Caprivi, general and chancellor. As a parliament deal, it was the price paid for a considerable army increase, the largest after the victorious wars. Military and political conservatives had soon to admit that their pessimism was unjustified. For one thing, "the outcry about the damaging effect of the two years' service calmed down when the fact became known that the number of punishments had decreased steadily and considerably ever since its introduction," as the later General Keim, the military "press agent" of this

[14] Reisner von Lichtenstein, quoted by Freytag-Loringhoven, *Folgerungen aus dem Weltkriege* (Berlin, 1917), pp. 84 f.

[15] Reichsarchiv, *Der Weltkrieg. Kriegsrüstung und Kriegswirtschaft.* Anlagen zum 1. Band (Berlin, 1930), pp. 22 f.

measure and one of the later Pan-German ex-officer agitators, writes in his *Memoirs*.[16] From the 1890's on, the question of army strength was continually discussed between the Prussian war ministry, contemplating party fights at home and consequently emphasizing the need of a *better* and thoroughly reliable army, and the general staff, which considered competition abroad and therefore called for the *largest* possible army, regardless of what the war minister thought about the shrinking supply of officer personnel. During the World War, then, it had to be admitted that rather short periods of drill had to suffice, and in fact did so; that in retrospect it appeared that even the so-called *Ersatzreserve*—men who were supernumeraries or who had showed slight bodily defects at the muster—might have been useful if that body had received a drilling of even some months, instead of having being completely unutilized as "military proletariat."

Liberals considered a part of military service sheer waste—the more liberal the conviction, the larger the proportion regarded as waste—and the industries saw in it not only a reduction of the labor market, including the effect that military service had on the inclination of families to emigrate before their sons reached military age, but also the occasion for the loss of skill and dexterity acquired earlier. It was the heavy industrialists who were the first to evidence an inclination to view the positive good in military service, which military writers were eager to proclaim and recommend after the Revolution of 1848 with its "mad Radicalism and Communistic liberty mania." [17] Men like the Krupps and Stumm perceived the uses of such service; the latter, called the "King of Saarabia," declared that:

It has often been maintained, that there is no analogy between factories and the army. I insist on the contrary. . . . In both cases, discipline is a wholly unavoidable first condition if successes are to be achieved. . . . If a manufacturing enterprise is to flourish, it must be organized in a military, not a parliamentary way. . . . As the soldier estate includes all the members of the army from field marshal down to the youngest recruit, and all together march against the enemy, when their king calls them, thus the members of this plant stand together like one man when the time has arrived to fight competition

---

[16] Generalleutnant Keim, *Erlebtes und Erstrebtes* (Hannover, 1925), p. 74.

[17] Reinhard Höhn, *Verfassungskampf und Heereseid. Der Kampf des Bürgertums um das Heer* (Leipzig, 1938), p. 335.

as well as the sinister powers of the Revolution. If we are victorious, that is to the advantage of all; if we lose out, we all suffer, and you far more than I myself. Victory, however, calls among ourselves, as well as in the army, for the severe upkeep of discipline, which here as well as there is not only compatible with loyal comradeship but forms the real basis thereof.[18]

Like the army, which forbade the reading of certain newspapers and the use of certain inns and public houses said to be frequented by labor unions and other organizations, Stumm tried to control the after-working hours of his militarily ruled workers, who were not allowed to join Socialist or Catholic parties. In this interest of the industrialist and the army in the supervision of their employees' after-service time, the historical roots of the Fascist *dopo lavoro*, after-work organization, must be sought.

In a free economy, competition determines, on the whole, the wage and pay of the employee. The pay of the bureaucrat is largely removed from the sphere of economic competition, and its level is subject to considerations which must be called political, by and large. A history of military pay would offer one of the most fascinating fields for study, even though it would constantly run into such difficulties as the comparative value of military and other forms of income, the former including any number of not strictly monetary items of revenue, like the free servant. In comparing military pay with that in other occupations, it would be necessary to take account, for example, of the relatively early beginning of pay and relatively cheap education, as compared with the academic profession. These and similar advantages would have to be balanced against the disadvantages of slow promotion, of early pensioning off—in which, on the whole, the noble officer came out better than the non-noble—and, of course, the greater risk to life and limb in the military career. Extra-monetary rewards, like the honored position in society, would be considered as making up for low income, even where such position did not enhance the officer's standing in what the Germans called the "Heiratsmarkt" (marriage market). The wage of the private before 1914, low and merely nominal as it might have seemed, was traditionally, and remained in essence, an agricultural wage. In the early 1880's, for instance, the average yearly cash income of

[18] Fritz Hellwig, *Carl Freiherr von Stumm-Halberg* (Heidelberg, 1936), pp. 295 f.

male workers on large estates in the Reich amounted to 198.18 M., on smaller farms 178.92 M., as against a soldier's yearly pay of 126 M., which breaks about even, if we consider that the worker had to procure his own clothing and the soldier did not.[19] Part of the payment of the long-serving noncommissioned officer was the expectancy of a position in the state or other bureaucracy, a use of personnel that largely contributed to the harsh and uncivilian character of German bureaucracy.

It is not possible to determine with anything like statistical certainty the effects of military service upon the fitness of persons for nonmilitary pursuits and upon the economy as a whole. For one reason, in the past, no one was really interested in providing the basis for certain statistics about military service. The answers up to now have depended upon the political standpoint of the observer and judge. Enemies of the army have pointed to the harmful effect of the service on working habits or, worse still, on the morality of the individual, who not infrequently might become familiar through garrison life with urban prostitution. Officers have indulged not a little in self-praise when discussing the favorable effects of army life on the citizen and his country.[20] But no one has sung the praises of the army more eloquently than its civilian and political friends, like Adolf Hitler, who, before he came to power, wrote in *Mein Kampf:*

> What the German people owes to the army may be simply summed up in one single word, namely: everything . . . in the swamp of a generally spreading softening and effeminacy, out of the ranks of the army there shot up every year 350,000 vigorous young men who in two years' training had lost the softness of youth and had gained bodies hard as steel.[21]

It is possible to judge with somewhat greater certainty the effect of the German army on private economy. Even before the World War a certain anticapitalistic sentiment had entered the German services and had taken hold on some officers, particularly those with a background of bureaucracy or family poverty. An officer poet, Detlev von Liliencron, wrote in 1888: "This infamous

[19] Tuch, *Der erweiterte deutsche Militärstaat in seiner sozialen Bedeutung,* p. 357.

[20] A convenient ex-parte statement may be found in General von Hartmann, *Die allgemeine Wehrpflicht,* Heilbronn, 1879.

[21] Adolf Hitler, *Mein Kampf,* unabridged ed. (Reynal and Hitchcock, New York, 1939), pp. 384, 386.

bourgeois, I hate him, as only a Social-Democrat can hate him." [22] Such officers fully shared the convictions that led German bureaucracy to the establishment of the several institutions of state socialism and favored measures which were even more anticapitalistic, such as the "field-gray socialism" of war economy. This state socialism, or state control of industry and the rest of the national economy, so fully and fatefully developed in the *Wehrwirtschaft* of 1933 and succeeding years, grew in the last analysis out of the safety of the officer's tenure, the certainty of receiving salary and pension, which could not be taken away even for high treason committed against the Weimar Republic. It grew out of the officer's own "social security," a position which made him independent of, if not superior to private economy and its considerations.

[22] *Die Neue Rundschau,* XXI (Berlin, 1910), 663.

PART FOUR: THE CULTURAL ROLE OF IDEAS

INTRODUCTORY NOTE

THE WRITING of history, because of the sources from which material is derived, has always largely reflected the history of ideas. Techniques for getting at the opinions and attitudes of leaders have been vastly superior to those for observing behavior that was not translated into articulate thought and expression.

Economic determinists, reacting against the tendency to tell the history of a people in terms of the thought of its successful members, have laid stress upon processes largely independent of individuals and their ideas. Instead of regarding literate leaders as the source of events, they have regarded them as the product of forces over which individuals have little or no control, viewing ideas as rationalizations of a situation rather than as dynamic elements in the situation. At the same time, there have been strong adherents of the opposite tendency who have sought to invest ideas with mystic power. The present generation has seen the political reflection of those two opposing interpretations of history in Soviet Russia on the one hand and Nazi Germany on the other.

In recent years, two factors in particular have given a new basis for understanding the role of ideas. Psychology has revealed something of the process of idea-formation in the mind of the individual; new techniques of mass communication have provided a laboratory experiment in the possibilities of manipulating conduct by means of ideas. Advertising and propaganda have shown that ideas are, indeed, potential "weapons" and that they play a very definite cultural role.

But more important than either psychology or propaganda as a factor in shaping a view of the role of ideas in cultural development is the concept of culture itself. This concept assumes that mentality is a social product and performs a social function. The philosophical, religious, and scientific traditions of Western culture, on the other hand, emphasize the individualistic quality of intellectual activity. The application of the concept of culture to a study of mentality as a social phenomenon, therefore, calls for a significant departure from traditional forms of analysis.

One of the main functions of ideas in cultural development is to establish the direction which intellectual activity will follow. In a given cultural situation, individual mentalities, both speculative and investigative, are conditioned by the content of their intellectual heritage. This heritage, in turn, exists in a social milieu which includes (1) the organization of social relationships and means of communication, (2) the array of special interests which attempt to establish their positions through institutions and intellectual conceptions, (3) the accumulation of new data of experience from widened contacts or new investigations, and (4) a well-established routine of specific acts and accompanying emotional accents which repeats itself in the daily lives of the great body of the population. In any cultural situation each of these four aspects of the social milieu may be changing; altogether, however, they establish a pervasive social orientation for the individuals who live within the milieu.

In the interaction between the intellectual transmission from the past and the play of factors in the social milieu, ideas become the organizing factors which (1) bind new experience into old, preserving intellectual continuity, or (2) reorient old ideas in terms of new experience, or (3) summarize new experience in new generalizations which may look toward a possible reorganization of social relationships.

From this point of view, ideas may be seen as organizing an intellectual structure which, although it changes or develops, endures through time; such structures, when considered in relation to the institutions which they justify and the technology which they make possible, constitute the cultural traditions which are permanent organizing forces in human life.

Basic modifications in these structures occur mainly as new social groups arise and adapt ideas to the service of their interests. Ideas thus have a special role to play in social conflict. They may serve to justify the position of an established interest or to promote action to establish a new interest. The competition among conflicting social groups for the sanction of the cultural tradition which is common to these groups is a primary aspect of both political and intellectual activity. It is this conflict which commonly brings about the reorientation of old ideas in terms of new interests.

In terms of the concept of culture, social and intellectual history may be seen in a single focus, social change affecting intellectual development and intellectual change organizing social development into a cultural tradition. Thus interests and ideas are discovered to be more significant in interaction than as separate factors in any cultural situation.

The two chapters in this section explore the role of ideas in two ways. The first takes a period, the Middle Ages, and, by posing the question of how far medieval ideology was ecclesiastical and how far secular, examines the way in which the ideas current in that period entered into the formation and modification of cultural traditions. The second takes a single idea, liberalism, and examines its present historical position by analyzing its basic postulates, its changing content, and the cultural situation essential to its existence and survival. In addition, the three chapters of the following section deal in part with the role of ideas in the processes of cultural change.

MEDIEVAL INTELLECTUAL HISTORY: ECCLESIASTICAL OR SECULAR?

GRAY C. BOYCE

THE chief concern of intellectual history is, I take it, the discovery, analysis, and comprehension of the ideas which affect the thought and action of thinking men. One must give also full consideration to what ensues when ideas—inherited or developed—and the more concrete manifestations of a civilization act and react upon each other. Though in essence abstractions—concepts, attitudes, ideals—the facts of intellectual history are none the less real than are those more immediately perceptible realities of the political, institutional, and economic historians. Indeed, without the facts of intellectual history, the other historical disciplines would be at a loss, and, without them as an actual frame of reference, intellectual history could have little, if any, meaning—unless, by some inconceivable aberration, historians acquiesced in accepting that philosophical anomaly Kant so abhorred: facts without concepts and ideas devoid of content.

The question to which this paper is addressed is: to what degree were the High Middle Ages secular or ecclesiastical? Or, to be more explicit, to what degree were the ideas of thinking men secular or ecclesiastical? Though valid and challenging, the question is not an innocent one. It is a query loaded with the latent prejudices of our own and earlier ages. We must, I would insist, be ever aware that it is a secular age that poses the question and also one that most commonly holds that the terms "secular" and "ecclesiastical" are mutually exclusive. That they are not necessarily so the Middle Ages proved, unless, perchance, we are prepared to deny the assertion that "the shape that ideas take is relative to the culture and era in which they develop and are used." [1]

Professor Thompson [2] has shown that during the Middle Ages

[1] Max Lerner, *Ideas Are Weapons: The History and Use of Ideas* (New York, 1939), p. 8.

[2] James Westfall Thompson, *The Literacy of the Laity in the Middle Ages*, "University of California Publications in Education," Vol. IX, Berkeley, 1939.

greater literacy prevailed among the laity than historians were formerly inclined to admit; yet can it be said that, prior to the thirteenth century, these men credited with some degree of intellectual accomplishment influenced contemporary thought and turned into new channels the currents of prevailing ideas? How often they reflect merely the source from which their ideas were derived, the fount of their inspiration, the pattern of an ecclesiastical mold! Although Sir Charles Oman [3] has recently insisted that "new ideas percolate downwards, not upwards" and implies that they descend to a less rarefied air than that in which they were born and first nourished, is it not also true that often the germ of their being is to be discovered in the active world of man? It would be hard indeed with all we know of keen business men, conniving lawyers, hard-headed barons and scheming bankers, to say naught of those fascinating *Goliardi,* to discover that nothing of their worldly attitude left its imprint on those contemporaries whose thought squared more exactly with ecclesiastical ideal. Since men of this type are primarily men of action, they are rarely conscious of, or at once interested in, the ideas implicit in what they do. Yet their secular world refused to be ignored, and eventually it forced men of intellect to face in a thoughtful way the problems of a newer social order in their eternal debates on the nature of things. It may be for such a reason, therefore, that the implications of the active secular life of the twelfth century became the meat on which the intellectually minded of the thirteenth and fourteenth centuries had to chew.[4]

The late Hermann Kantorowicz remarked not long ago that "men possess thoughts but ideas possess men." [5] With this aphorism in mind, let us ask the question: What ideas possessed the thinking men of the High Middle Ages, of this age, as many would have it, of a European renaissance? Perhaps the first, but not the sole idea was that they belonged to an ordered universe, controlled by and subservient to power by nature divine and supernatural—an idea so prevalent that for many it has tended to exclude any significance that may be attributed to ideas intruding

[3] *On the Writing of History* (New York, 1939), p. 254.

[4] Cf. Richard McKeon, "Renaissance and Method," in *Studies in the History of Ideas,* ed. by the Department of Philosophy, Columbia University, Vol. III (New York, 1935), *passim.*

[5] Lerner, *Ideas Are Weapons,* p. 3.

from the secular world. But this is not all, for the secular character of European civilization and the secular elements in its thought and ideas were clearly apparent even as late as the seventh century. Even when, after that time, these were obscured by what seemed to be an omniscient, all-pervading ecclesiastical sentiment, the possibility of a secular tradition survived in the memory of Rome and an antique heritage.[6] This tradition emerged with renewed vigor from the vicissitudes of intervening centuries to challenge thoughtful minds of the twelfth and thirteenth centuries. It is identified by a historical succession, connecting in unbroken line men of the medieval world and their forefathers of ancient times; by an ancient literary, legal, and philosophical heritage, enriched by the recovery of Aristotle and augmented by Greek and Roman science preserved and developed in the Moslem world.

Many years ago Rashdall[7] declared that the key to the history of medieval Europe at large was the continued existence of the Roman Empire. Faced with this fact we must not overlook nor forget how secular were many of the ideas abiding in the term *imperium*.[8] This is not the place, nor am I competent to discuss moot points of political theory, but is it not true that in the concept of empire lay the chance and opportunity for the play of secular minds? The long struggle over investitures and the political history of the age not only forced to the front secular reaction, but solidified or at least precipitated the expression of secular ideas in clear and often convincing terms, frequently upsetting the balance more favorable to an ecclesiastical point of view.[9]

I have heard it said that neither the law nor lawyers can with propriety be called intellectual. Be that as it may, for the student of intellectual history the law and the lawyers, at least when they are concerned with principle, furnish not only food for thought but positive clues to the mutable relations between secular and ecclesiastical ideas. Even the arts schools of Italy had early absorbed

[6] Cf. Henri Pirenne, *Mohammed and Charlemagne* (New York, 1939), pp. 118–44.

[7] Hastings Rashdall, *The Universities of Europe in the Middle Ages*, new ed. (Oxford, 1936), I, 94.

[8] *Cf.* Fritz Kern, *Kingship and Law in the Middle Ages*, trans. by S. B. Chrimes, "Studies in Mediaeval History," ed. by Geoffrey Barraclough (Oxford, 1939), IV, 48–49. Cf. also *ibid.*, p. xxiv, where Chrimes writes, "It was, then, the struggle between the *sacerdotium* and the *regnum*, and the interaction of secular and ecclesiastical ideas that made possible the intellectual conditions necessary for the emergence of the modern sovereign State, and therefore, in the long run, of modern constitutionalism."

[9] Cf. *ibid.*, pp. 95–96, 113 ff.

something of the Roman law into their curriculum, and those who followed the courses there lived in an atmosphere pregnant with secular ideas of an order older, yet forever real. In the age of the universities, the highly trained ecclesiastic was not to be unfamiliar with or untouched by this secularizing influence. Honorius III might ban civil law at Paris, but many a cleric destined for high position would meet the challenge of its precepts elsewhere. And in the discipline of canon law is there not evident much indicating the penetration of secular fact that remolded or reshaped canonical principle in a more worldly pattern? [10]

Recently Landry has attempted an analysis and evaluation of the literary heritage of antiquity, as it was used by twelfth-century authors, and his contentions are of interest in any consideration of secular influences and their relation to ecclesiastical ideas.[11] Rightly impressed by the wide knowledge of and enthusiasm for Latin writers that he discovers in the works of men like Abelard, Hildebert, Marbode of Rennes, Peter of Blois, the satirists, and writers of romance, he finds these writings on the whole to be little more than class-room exercises and fundamentally divorced from the realities of contemporary life. The author of the *Moralis philosophia,*[12] for example, does write with the pen of an ancient. To those easily deceived, his dialogue between Timor and Securitas (a rather pert lady, by the way) may reflect the dignity of stoic self-discipline. "Thou shalt die," chants Timor in sepulchral tones. But Securitas remains unmoved, answering each booming "*morieris*" with quick retort. Timor, one senses, becomes progressively more fearful of self, as Securitas throws her quips with easy, confident aim. The list of Roman authors from whom high ideal has been cribbed may be impressive; yet nowhere is there any indication of a twelfth-century outlook or of a morality touching the life of the author's age. Here, for Landry, is a very rational juxtaposition of stoic thought and attitude, which in no way

10 Rashdall, *The Universities of Europe,* I, 100–2; cf. Roscoe Pound, "The Church in Legal History," Part I, *Jubilee Law Lectures, 1889–1939,* School of Law, The Catholic University of America, Washington, 1939.

11 B. Landry, "Les Idées morales du XIIe siècle: Les Écrivains en latin," *Revue des cours et conférénces,* 40e Année (1939), 1re série, pp. 385–98, 491–504, 614–24; 2e série, pp. 82–96, 127–36, 263–70, 343–61, 432–48, 526–47, 641–66, 709–22.

12 Landry ("Les Idées morales," 1re série, p. 621) attributes this to Hildebert of Le Mans or William of Conches. The text is found in Migne, *Patrologia Latina,* Vol. CLXXI, cols. 1003–56, where it is listed as by Hildebert.

seems to challenge the writer. He has his faith and at the same time admires Seneca. Affirming the dignity of man and extolling wisdom as the greatest good, these writers of the twelfth century followed the course of Dr. Jekyll and Mr. Hyde. Their enthusiasm for antique letters and their sympathy with antique ideas seem locked in some secret chest, opened only for their own delight and edification, in a sense held as a means of escape from the realities of ecclesiastical idea and ideal which they are all ready to admit. These writers, insists Landry, were nothing more than dilettantes playing at something that exalts their ego, while at the same time extolling the ecclesiastical virtues of virginity, celibacy, and withdrawal from common society and the active life of the world. They were, he says, all clerics—clerics writing for clerics, playing with things that had no basic meaning for their own class and that were kept away from the nonclerical world, where they could have taken root in fertile ground.

Landry's pages are filled with penetrating comment and brilliant suggestion and deserve careful attention. But has he not missed a point? Though the men encountered in his pages did accentuate those elements in antique authors that made these fit more readily into the ecclesiastical concepts of a contemporary world, in doing so they preserved the antique and made of it a vital, although incomplete force in the development of medieval attitudes. The twelfth century could make a god of Cicero—a Cicero, to be sure, who extolled withdrawal from active life and who ennobled *otium* in the face of *negotium*. Had this been naught but of the books, had the Cicero as a guide to morals and "as the ideal monastic scholar" not attained such fame and aroused deep feelings of affection, would the historical Cicero (rediscovered in the thirteenth century) have given rise to such furor in the mind of Petrarch or brought such consolation to the more civic-minded society of later days? [13]

In our attempt to evaluate the secularizing force of the antique heritage on the twelfth and thirteenth centuries, we may be confused by the conflicting and somewhat contradictory views we encounter and by the variable values used to interpret the same

[13] Cf. Hans Baron, "Cicero and the Roman Civic Spirit in the Middle Ages and the Early Renaissance," *Bulletin of the John Rylands Library*, XXII (April, 1938), 3–28; cf. also Nigel Abercrombie, reviewing Etienne Gilson's *Héloïse et Abélard* in *Journal of Theological Studies,* XL (July, 1939), 296, 297.

facts. There are, for instance, those who admit the presence, the authority, and the force of this heritage, but who are of the opinion that when all is said and done, the antique is completely absorbed by and into the ecclesiastical frame of reference—enriching it, perhaps, certainly adorning it, but leaving the whole still a pattern essentially ecclesiastical. Here, unless I have been deceived, I would place Landry. Then there are those, like Nordström [14] and Schramm,[15] who proclaim the new age a renaissance, humane and effectual in restoring the dignity and worth of older concepts amidst the realities of a medieval world. It is men such as these who bring down upon their heads the wrath of a Siciliano [16] and the more reasoned censure of a Panofsky.[17] If the values used by men of this group in forming their judgments are the true ones, the powerful secular elements taken over from a Roman order into twelfth- and thirteenth-century intellectual life cannot be given a minor place.

There is, however, another attitude toward this problem held by scholars like Erwin Panofsky [18] and W. S. Heckscher,[19] who prefer to speak of the age as a proto-renaissance, an age "by no means blind to the visual values of classical art, and deeply interested in the intellectual and poetical values of classical literature." [20] Yet these scholars could hardly accept the theory that the juxtaposition of the antique and the medieval, if the latter implies an ecclesiastical frame of reference, would result in a secularization of the medieval. If I do not misunderstand their arguments, they are impressed by the way in which medieval man, completely incapable of seeing antiquity as a historical period and obsessed with the *principium unitatis*, absorbs the past, the antique, the secular into his own medieval consciousness, with which it be-

[14] J. Nordström, *Moyen âge et renaissance: Essai historique*, Paris, 1933; also G. Paré, A. Brunet, P. Tremblay, *La renaissance du XIIe siècle: Les Écoles et l'enseignement*, "Publications de l'Institut d'études médiévales d'Ottawa," III, Paris and Ottawa, 1933.

[15] Percy Ernst Schramm, *Kaiser, Rom und Renovatia: Studien und Texte zur Geschichte des römischen Erneuerungsgedankens vom Ende des karolingischen Reiches bis zum Investiturstreit*, 2 vols., "Studien der Bibliothek Warburg," hrsg. von Fritz Saxl, Vol. XVII, Leipzig and Berlin, 1929.

[16] Cf. Italo Siciliano, *Medio evo e rinascimento* (Milan, 1936), esp. pp. 35–53.

[17] Cf. Erwin Panofsky, *Studies in Iconology: Humanistic Themes in the Art of the Renaissance*, (New York, 1939), Chaps. I and IV.

[18] *Ibid.*

[19] W. S. Heckscher, "Relics of Pagan Antiquity in Medieval Settings," *Journal of the Warburg Institute*, I (Jan., 1938), 204–20.

[20] Panofsky, *Studies in Iconology*, p. 18.

comes as one. "So far from destroying the pagan charm," writes Heckscher,[21] "the church absorbed its powers into her own and sometimes even superimposed upon an ancient image a new type of magical function." [21] Furthermore he seems to deny secularizing potentialities in such a process, in stating that "to the medieval mind, the cult of the antique meant not so much a revival of a thing which had died as the removal of obstructions which impaired the maintenance of things extant." [22] In contrast to a writer like Schramm, Panofsky and Heckscher find no true spirit of "renovatio" in medieval man and dwell at length on the dichotomy evident when the Middle Ages not only permitted, but freely sanctioned, largely because of its nonhistorical attitude, a disparity between a theme and the motif in which it finds expression, a disparity removed only by the Renaissance, imbued with the spirit of "imitatio." [23] This is in direct contrast to opinions of more sociologically minded writers. "So closely is the literary form tied to the culture out of which it has grown," says one, "that when another culture attempts to take it over there is a tendency toward a transfer of the ideological patterns of the older culture." [24]

The thirteenth century was consciously aware of the fundamental distinction between the lay and clerical orders in its society, and the history of its politics and social life furnishes much evidence that the distinction was well understood. Then the laity did not complacently step aside in face of ecclesiastical challenge. It held its own ground, in the hope of regaining or even retaining spheres which the church claimed for its very own. Is this not noticeable in connection with the heresy rampant almost everywhere as the century opened? Heresy was, indeed, deeply rooted in and expressive of secular idea. Though in general not characteristically intellectual, it could be so described when it emerged from the clamor of the schoolroom and the debates of university professors.

Probably the greatest secular force in the intellectual life of the thirteenth century was Aristotle, returned in new garb. What if he was a thirteenth-century Aristotle—he returned to be censured, admired, adored, remaining always a positive challenge

21 "Relics of Pagan Antiquity," p. 215.

22 *Ibid.*, p. 206.

23 Panofsky, *Studies in Iconology*, p. 26.

24 Lerner, *Ideas Are Weapons*, p. 419.

to the pretensions of ecclesiastical minds. The twelfth century had its renaissance of classical authors; the thirteenth one in philosophical studies, in which secular points of view demanded to be heard. Its most profound result was, perhaps, a complete change in the manner of thought. This was, too, the age of the development and rapid expansion of universities. The cloistered atmosphere of the monastic schools and the somewhat restricted activities of cathedral centers gave way to the more secular climate in which university life was to flourish. As Professor Baron so pertinently remarks:

> A cleric, writing in civic surroundings, would contemplate his studies in quite a different light from a writer in a monastic cell. He would not feel them to be a secular parallel to religious contemplation; he would consider his own literary work as a service to the community—as a parallel in the intellectual sphere to the politico-social work of a citizen.[25]

Though thought and universities are two concepts that have not always had much in common, this could hardly be said for the Middle Ages, since much of the intellectual history of the period following 1200 cannot be divorced from university activity and influence.[26] The students—if not those who ultimately became the dominant scholars—tended to represent wider elements of contemporary society than had been the case in earlier centers of learning. Their secular background, secular aims, and secular desires are evident. This is especially apparent if we follow the history of that most important, as well as most numerous Faculty of Arts. Here the newer philosophical studies gradually, but firmly found their place. Ecclesiastical authority might stand in the way, but in the end it acceded to the force of current opinion. The penetration of the new Aristotle into the university curricula was to have its effect not only on young boys, first bewildered, then amazed at its implications, but especially upon those headed for that ecclesiastical goal, training in theology. These theologians, themselves often actually teachers of the arts, had to face this new

[25] Hans Baron, "Cicero and the Roman Civic Spirit," p. 13.

[26] Cf. Rashdall, *The Universities of Europe;* "Le Moyen âge et le naturalisme antique" and "Philosophie médiévale et humanisme" by Etienne Gilson, appended to his *Héloïse et Abélard* (Paris, 1938); and his *Christianity and Philosophy* (New York, 1939), *passim;* Sydney Herbert Mellone, *Western Christian Thought in the Middle Ages* (Edinburgh and London, 1935), Chaps. III and IV; and Georges de Lagarde, *La Naissance de l'esprit laïque au déclin du moyen âge,* 2 vols., Vienna, c. 1934.

force, and their theology could not and did not remain impregnable to its attacks. It did, in fact, profit from the experience.

Yet how far did all this sense of authority, found in the *auctores* and in Aristotle, lead man to a more secular way of thought? Few could deny that it all might help rationalize an ecclesiastical position, but did it secularize theology? Theology, in its scholastic form, became, as a result, more rational in its answer to secular query and plainly showed that secular philosophy and lay thought might even be handmaids in the fulfillment of its own desires. But is it a contradiction in terms to stress the problem of theology in any consideration of secular tendencies and influences in cultural development? I think not. Though essentially concerned with matters pertaining to God, theology is not unmindful of man; it is, after all, of his invention; its methods are of his design, and its history reflects his secular as well as his ecclesiastical mind.

Scholasticism can be explained historically, and would not closer scrutiny of its aims show the historian how the challenge of the secular world forced medieval men to give answers that were reasonably intelligent and intelligible to queries concerning the order of the universe? Is there, perhaps, in St. Thomas's restoration of the world of nature to a rightful place a reflection of the force of secular idea on ecclesiastical concept? Nature is restored, man is in his proper place, and God is in his heaven. The result, as a leading Dante scholar puts it, is a "humanism that can accept the Cosmos as a whole, and yet see in Man the horizon between God and Nature, a being utterly one and yet linked by his sense to the world of matter, by his mind to the world of thought, and by his spirit to the world of Mystery." [27]

Nor must one forget those men of science, minds redolent with secular potentialities. Here too the authority of an ancient tradition and the impact of newer Moslem learning hold the secular world of nature before the vision of medieval men. These produced in due time Franciscan experimentalists and explain in part the development of tolerance in faith and matters of religion, so evident in "the easy agnosticism of Frederick II and his

[27] Gerald G. Walsh, "Dante as a Mediaeval Humanist," *Thought* (Sept., 1939), pp. 384–400. Cf. Lagarde, *La Naissance de l'esprit laïque*, I, 186: "Le synthèse thomiste, notamment, en accentuant l'unité de la nature et de la surnature, avait fait percevoir plus clairement que jamais, combien il était nécessaire de les distinguer."

entourage." [28] Yet where medieval science is most alluring is where its fundamental implications were least explored, where it foreshadows the positive elements of later inductive methods. For the most part it fits into the picture of the medieval intellectual world, with its aspiration to bring order out of chaos and to give meaning to what it had, rather than always to explore new worlds. It was, however, in many cases exploring new worlds, even if not always appreciating just what those worlds were.

Surveying the whole, one sees in the intellectual realm of the High Middle Ages what Professor Lerner [29] would call its rational phase, "where men are in possession of ideas, using them to clarify their world and subject it to order." There is also its irrational phase, "where certain ideas are in possession of men." May it then be said, by way of conclusion, that the secular elements in this realm of the intellect were rather unmedieval in their tendency to upset the balance of a perfect order? Or, on the other hand, by remaining medieval were they seeking to balance ecclesiastical forces to preserve the unity of the whole? The latter, I believe, describes more accurately their culminating effect, if not their conscious aim. Perhaps, too, there is here evidence of that "lag between intellectual change and the awareness of it." These men, however, did not, could not, see that, in an endeavor to keep the balance even, the ecclesiastical tended to remain fixed, while secular forces increased with the passing of time.

[28] Lynn T. White, Jr., *Latin Monasticism in Norman Sicily*, "Mediaeval Academy of America," Monograph no. 13 (Cambridge, Mass., 1938), p. 73.

[29] Lerner, *Ideas Are Weapons*, pp. 3–4.

THE HISTORICAL POSITION OF LIBERALISM [1]

GEORGE H. SABINE

THE greatness of the liberal tradition no one will deny; that is a matter of history. But for at least forty years, and therefore long before the day of the present dictators, the opinion has existed that liberalism had served its turn and was being superseded by radicalism from one side and by nationalist imperialism from the other. Today its position is more problematical than ever and its future more threatening. Yet because of the many values associated with the name, it is not easily relinquished. An analysis of the historical position of liberalism, therefore, calls for an answer to the question of whether liberalism really is a finished chapter of history, or whether it can still be regarded as a vital force in politics for today and for tomorrow. If the latter, under what circumstances, partly within the control of liberals, might it go forward to a future influence comparable with that which it has had in the past?

To give an acceptable definition of liberalism is practically impossible. The name has been attached to many reforms and policies, and even to more than one political philosophy. Its history is strewn with the wreckage of constitutional devices and political apparatus, all of which proved disappointing in the light of the ardent hopes that they once inspired. The separation of powers, the priority of the legislative power, the independence of the judiciary, the extension of the suffrage, economic individualism have all been important parts of historical liberalism, but they certainly cannot now be regarded as of its essence. This subject cannot be discussed at all if liberalism must be tied down to a set of supposedly unchangeable institutions. Liberalism has been an attitude toward political institutions and public questions and a philosophy of the social relationships on which these institutions depend. Even that philosophy cannot be fully outlined in a short paper. It has seemed to me best, therefore, to select a single phase of liberal philosophy, that which most completely typified the liberal's attitude toward the many reforms with which, from time to time, he concerned himself. In short, I have tried to find a focus for liberalism, a center around

[1] Reprinted from *The American Scholar,* Vol. X, No. 1, December, 1940.

which its subsidiary doctrines arrange themselves. Even in respect to this central principle, however, I wish to suggest that liberalism was by no means static. It moved under the impact of its experience in applying its own principle. Doubtless it must do so still if it is to persist.

Throughout its history liberalism has been, first and foremost, a belief in the supreme social value of intelligence. This belief itself included several related, but distinguishable, ideas. First, it included a belief in the great utility of intelligence or reason as a force in social and political progress. Institutions require constantly to be renewed, for custom is inert and the undirected drift of institutions is blind. From Locke to John Dewey liberals have regarded intelligence as the only reliable means of solving problems, social problems above all others. Liberalism as a political and social doctrine was only one side of a much larger idea, very characteristic of modern philosophy, which Francis Bacon summed up in his aphorism, "Knowledge is power." The fact-finding investigation used as a guide to legislation might almost be called a liberal invention, as, for example, such work as Edwin Chadwick began for the English Poor Law Commission a century ago.

In the second place, however, liberals never believed that social intelligence could be made either safe or effective if it were monopolized by experts. Behind the expert, they felt, there is needed an informed and critical public opinion. The reason for this is that some vital questions in politics cannot be left wholly to experts. An intelligent man who has to live with and under political institutions ought to know some things about them that an expert cannot tell him. In Aristotle's homely comparison, a man does not have to be a shoemaker to know whether his shoes hurt him. Moreover, there has to be some guarantee that expert knowledge will be put to useful purposes, and liberals have always insisted that the only effective guarantee lay in the general intelligence of the community. Certainly public opinion is not infallible, and it becomes utterly fallible if it is set to do what only expert knowledge can do. But even Machiavelli, who was perhaps no great liberal, insisted that on the right kind of question public opinion was on the whole a safer guide to sound policy than the opinion of princes.

In the third place, liberals have argued that there is only one way to have an intelligent public opinion, and that is by allowing free and open discussion. The reason is that knowledge about public questions is like all knowledge: it is never finished and it advances by pooling and criticizing many opinions. In order to have such discussion, it is necessary that every interest should have the right to air its grievances and state its own case. For no man, and no class of men, is either good enough or wise enough to be made the irresponsible guardian of other men's interests. Obviously the liberal must assume that the common fund of intelligence and good will is great enough to insure that free discussion will, in general, issue in a wise decision. He has argued, of course, that, after all allowances have been made for the failures, there is no better criterion of wisdom than what Justice Holmes called the market value of an idea. The civil liberties necessary to free discussion, therefore, are the foundations of liberalism; the political liberties and liberal political institutions follow them. For public opinion is useless unless it has some leverage to influence government and to hold rulers responsible for their acts.

I have purposely left until last, however, the moral aspect of the liberal belief in intelligence, both because this is in reality the crux of the matter and also the point that is most difficult to establish. However liberals may have developed their argument, they did not in fact depend altogether, perhaps not even chiefly, upon the proved utility of either intelligence or public opinion. They were actuated by a profound moral conviction that intelligence is the core of personality, the distinctively human faculty in man, and the part of him that could not be limited without crippling all his higher powers. Liberalism was built upon the moral postulate that men have a right to be convinced, to understand and evaluate the demands that are laid on them, and if possible to consent to them. This is at bottom a moral judgment transcending utility, a preference for a kind of character in which action flows from conviction and conviction is reached by intelligent consideration of means and ends. The whole liberal doctrine of freedom rests upon the belief that normal men can in some degree achieve this kind of character, that they become morally self-directing in the degree in which they do so, and that their power to enjoy and contribute to a civilized life depends chiefly on their having such a character. They become sociable beings in proportion as they have it. Consequently, the declared object of liberal reform has always been the removal of hindrances to this kind of living. So true is this that it is hard to see how liberalism could survive if this sort of moral preference were radically to diminish.

Now it must in frankness be admitted that this high valuation set on intelligence and the belief in its social worth are not inevitable in the sense that everyone invariably shares them. The proposition can be denied and in fact is denied today. It is denied outright by the counterbelief that societies are made good and great by a daemonic will that is not controlled or directed by intelligence but serves the inner drive of national or racial instinct. It can be denied in effect by the assertion that, however desirable reasonableness may be, most men are incapable of attaining it in a degree sufficient to make it an appreciable force in social and political matters. It is denied in practice by acting on the supposition that the consent and conviction required for social cohesiveness are more surely produced by suggestion and propaganda than by appealing to intelligence. In order to be effective, liberalism must face these facts and come to some sort of terms with them, and any political philosophy has to be effective if it is to survive. There can be no justification for a liberalism that holds up the ideal of social intelligence but fails to consider realistically how intelligence can be evoked and put to work. For even intelligence is no God-given faculty. Like everything else it has its conditions, and there are other conditions that make it impossible or nugatory. Liberalism itself has taken two distinct attitudes toward this question, and fundamentally the difference lay between two ideas about what were the great hindrances to free and rational living.

The first period of liberalism, perhaps its classic period, was that in which the object was to protect individual freedom against oppressive governments. The story is too well known to need repeating. In this period liberals sought to embody the fundamental liberties in bills of rights that should put them beyond the reach of distrusted governments, to secure the completest possible freedom of business enterprise, to extend the suffrage, to increase the power of popularly elected representatives, and to make constitutions having an elaborate system of checks and balances. It became a liberal axiom that governments are best when they govern least, and that in a good society every man will have the greatest amount of freedom compatible with keeping peace and order. Around every

individual there is a circle of rights within which he must be pro
tected not only from the incursions of other individuals but more
particularly from the incursions of the government that exists to
protect him. The ideal relationship in a free society is contract, for
here the individual freely binds himself and assumes voluntarily
the obligations to which he may rightly be held. Now in promul
gating this program liberalism was undoubtedly effective. Govern
ments were oppressive and the need for political and civil liberty
corresponded so obviously to the requirements of the time that i
was one of the great driving forces of political and social reform.

What I wish to point out, however, is that the liberal theory o
political and economic freedom depended upon a certain idea
about the way in which intelligence could be made socially effec
tive. Moreover, though that idea was perhaps true enough to work
the circumstances being what they were, it eventually reached the
limit of its working and had to be revised. The liberal picture o
society was extraordinarily intellectualized. Every individual wa
believed to act only in the light of his greatest advantage; each
understood what his interest was, or could be made to do so by
education; each was able to attain his interests if only the govern
ment would leave him to himself. But though human beings were
represented almost as calculating machines, the role of intelligence
in society was singularly and arbitrarily restricted. Every single
item of human behavior was computed down to the least incre
ment of pleasure, but its integration into an effective social whole
was imagined to be the almost miraculous result of natural har
mony, which apparently worked best when no one thought abou
it at all. Reason was looked upon as an individual faculty with
which men were simply endowed; it was treated as having no socia
antecedents except the lack of restraint, and its social consequence
accrued indirectly and deviously through the beneficence of en
lightened self-interest.

Everyone knows how this older type of liberalism suffered ship
wreck. Long before it was abandoned in theory, it was eaten awa
by social legislation which, advocated partly by liberals who were
more interested in results than in theory, was mainly carried b
the rising political influence of organized labor. In every case legis
lation of this kind was a restriction upon freedom of contract
though its intent was clearly liberal in the sense that it sought t

extend the opportunities for a humane standard of living. To keep oneself and one's family in health, to have education and to educate one's children, to work in safety and to enjoy a reasonable security and leisure—surely these opportunities were liberties if anything were. The day was long past when it was possible tacitly to assume that the most serious hindrances to freedom were governments, or that it was feasible to exclude government from whole areas of modern social and economic life. Consequently, when a new upswing of liberalism occurred both in England and America shortly before the war in 1914, it took a definitely new line. It argued that liberty is not merely a negation, the right not to be interfered with, but an opportunity to enjoy and achieve something intrinsically satisfying and worth doing. In 1913 Walter Lippmann wrote that it is the business of statesmanship to create "opportunities for the expression of human impulses" and of government "to carry out programs of service, to add and build and increase the facilities of life." Thus the state took its place in the category of social services and had for its special function such regulation of the other essential services on which society depends as would open to more persons the chance for satisfying activity, without which a sense of frustration arises and social disorder results.

What I wish more particularly to point out, however, is that this change of purpose represented another step in the experience of liberalism with its fundamental postulate, the belief in the social value of intelligence. In the first place, it implied that an intelligently ordered society must be envisaged as a whole—must, if you like, be planned. For it is evidently not reasonable to suppose that even the most intelligent self-interest will work out automatically to intelligent coöperation, unless intelligence be applied also to the relationships that produce coöperation. And in the second place, it assumed that neither intelligent self-interest nor intelligent public opinion can arise or operate in a society that does not provide the conditions for them. The older liberal notion that self-help and individual initiative will of themselves lift whole classes out of a state of misery had been proved a myth. It appeared evident that the more miserable a class becomes, the more surely it can be coerced under the guise of free contract. Neither native capacity nor the development of native capacity can be regarded as the properties merely of an individual person. They depend upon external conditions—material, moral, and intellectual—within which they must be applied and developed and over which, except to a limited extent, voluntary choice and effort have no control. The possibility of either having intelligence or using it is inherent in the state of the society in which an individual lives. In consequence, though intelligence may be socially beneficent, it is no panacea, because without an adequate moral and social underpinning it will infallibly fail to assert itself.

This conclusion, it is important to notice, was inherent in the internal development of liberal thought itself, evolving within the changing cultural scene, not something foisted on it from the outside. At the same time it introduces a basic question, namely, the prospects of liberalism for the present and future. This is the question whether, in a time of great social and political stress, it remains possible to make a vigorous attack on contemporary problems without discarding most of the political achievements and methods that have been called liberal in the past. Otherwise stated, it is the question whether liberalism is not, as is often asserted, a philosophy for political fair weather which is bound to be superseded in a revolutionary situation. I do not see how a liberal can be quite certain in advance that this will not prove to be true in a given case. There unquestionably is a point, in any society that approaches political or economic paralysis, where the processes of liberal government become impossible. Where this point will lie depends partly on the severity of the crisis and partly on the degree in which compromise and coöperation have become well-settled political habits. The latter, in turn, depends largely upon the amount of experience that a people has had in making liberal institutions work. Where this is considerable, a liberal can claim at least a reasonable probability for the assumption that the fund of intelligence and good will is great enough to permit a peaceful settlement of pretty fundamental issues. No one will deny that this is the best working hypothesis, so long as it is plausible at all. But it is surely a matter of elementary precaution, where liberal governments still exist, not to palter with conditions that reduce the factor of safety. This is not a doctrine of repression but of prevention.

This amounts to saying that the persistence of liberalism depends in no small degree on the will of liberals. The low esteem in which liberalism is now so often held depends, unless I am mistaken, on the suspicion that, though liberals talk about removing the hindrances to opportunity and the good life, they cannot be depended on to do anything about it. There is also the suspicion that they have never really counted the cost of even approximating to their ideal and that they are inhibited by a kind of nostalgia for the older forms of economic individualism, even though they know that these are impossible. In a period of political difficulty this is the most injurious of reputations. Where liberalism has been destroyed, there has always been a conviction that liberal government is feeble. In the days when liberalism was strong it certainly had no such reputation; it was strong precisely because it combined the two qualities of intelligence and will. And this is one of the conditions for the effective persistence of any political philosophy. It must be at once an analysis of remediable grievances, a program of intelligent adjustment, and an incitement to go forward on the line that the program marks out.

Though liberalism is rather an attitude toward political questions than a specific set of institutions, it cannot coexist with any and all kinds of institutions. In the liberal conception politics is essentially a medium in which grievances may be aired and their redress sought. Consequently, the essential institution of liberal politics is the opposition, the critic and the competitor of the government and its potential successor. As a means to this end there is no known device except political parties and the various forms of free association by which political parties can be influenced. Liberalism cannot be imagined as existing or as coming into being in any of the governments that permit only a single party. It is quite true, however, that the existence of political parties is no infallible assurance of continuing liberal government, for there have been only too many cases in recent history of parties that were designed expressly to destroy other parties and the liberal system through which political parties have to work. A civil society in which large numbers of persons can be attracted into parties that are dedicated to the tactics of rule-or-ruin has passed beyond the possibility of liberal government. Such parties create an insoluble dilemma. Either they capture the government or they force other parties to adopt repression and terrorism on pain of being extinguished. In either case liberal government becomes impossible.

This fact brings the analysis of liberalism back to the point already stressed. The liberal belief that government ought to depend on intelligent decisions formed in the light of free discussion depends upon a moral presumption from which it cannot escape. Discussion and the formation of an intelligent public opinion are possible only on the basis of fair dealing and mutual respect. The sense of unity that holds parties and factions together in a civil society must be strong enough to overlap and include the divergent and separatist interests of the parties. Without this element of moral restraint political tactics become simple terrorism. This amounts to saying that the ultimate basis of civil society is an intangible but effective moral community holding its members together and that liberalism is possible only so long as this is so generally acknowledged that no considerable number of persons refuses to act on it. Obviously this moral basis of government can fail, and does fail when the stresses and strains upon a political society become too great. When it fails there is no substitute for it, least of all a substitute that will support liberalism. It may perhaps be restored, but there is no known technique for recreating it. The most that liberal statesmanship can hope to do, where liberal statesmanship exists, is to prevent, if it can, a breaking down of the political and economic structure that brings this moral degeneration with it.

The crux of the question about the present position of liberalism lies, I believe, in the region of economic liberalism, for the test of any present political movement is its capacity to deal constructively with the economic paralysis that from time to time threatens modern society. The burden of insecurity arising from this condition forms the head and front of the grievances that now require relief. No government has dared or will dare to refuse the responsibility for finding this relief. Can there be a social situation more dangerous to the foundations of a liberal society than one in which a considerable proportion of young men and women, upon the completion of their education, find no work to be done, no satisfying career in which they can expand the energies natural to their age, and no means of gaining a competence that will permit them to set up families? Or again, can there be a situation more morally corroding than one in which considerable numbers of men and women, with no deficiency of training or skill or willingness to work, can find no employment that offers security for themselves and their families? For this situation quasi-charitable relief is no solution, even though it be the best stopgap available. For though it provides the minimum necessary for life, it does not remove the sense of frustration which inclines men to desperate remedies. Nor is it to be expected that this burden will be borne with that resignation which human beings can always muster to face an evil that they accept as inevitable. The point is that they do not accept it as inevitable. On the contrary, they become more and more convinced that the material means and the technical knowledge already exist to provide a decent opportunity for everyone. They suspect that there are faults in the institutional structure of modern economy that act as a clog on the social power of production and as a bar to a more equitable distribution; there is a growing belief that political action, if sufficiently wise and vigorous, can modify and improve that institutional structure.

This belief is by no means confined to peoples that live under those governments which it is now the fashion to call democracies. It is an even more powerful motive where, for one reason or another, the political and economic systems have come close to shipwreck and where great portions of the middle class have found themselves dispossessed of the security they formerly had. Unless I am quite mistaken, some sort of social revolution is in progress over large parts of Europe in which the drive of social idealism is furnished by just this aspiration for greater security, with all that security might mean for human happiness and humane living. There is unfortunately no guarantee that this inchoate idealism will find a wise or an effective outlet. It can be exploited by ignorant and unscrupulous leadership. It can be fobbed off with security in a miserable subsistence, because production is turned to ends that destroy the possibility of a humane life. It can pursue security with a reckless disregard for civil and political rights without which its own success cannot be permanently insured. But is it necessary that these disasters shall befall the honorable hope that an increasing number of men shall enter securely into the heritage of modern civilization? Whatever the answer to this question may be, the future, I believe, belongs in

PART FIVE: THE DYNAMICS OF CULTURAL CHANGE

INTRODUCTORY NOTE

A MAJOR preoccupation of historians of all periods has been with change. While some historical writing has laid little emphasis on change and has served primarily to enlarge the experience of individuals in one society by allowing them to view contrasting societies of other times and places, historians have for the most part been concerned with the sequence of events, and with sequential relationships.

The terms in which the past is studied necessarily determine the terms in which the processes of change are viewed. Political history follows the sequence of political events; national histories focus on changes in the position of nations and in the balance of power.

By the same token, cultural historians are necessarily concerned with the processes of cultural change. They must inquire into the slow, evolutionary processes, and the cataclysmic events, which modify or destroy old institutions, old value structures, old group and class relationships.

In virtually all cultures, even the most closely integrated and stable, seeds of cultural change are present both in the divergence or conflict between the interests of different groups in the society and in disparities in the relationship among the several aspects of the culture. Cultural changes, more or less basic in character, grow out of the effort of a group to make the institutions of a culture serve better the interests of that group, and out of the tendency of one aspect of the culture, say the political aspect, to make adjustments so as to conform to another aspect, such as the economic or religious.

It is through these two channels that innovations, entering a society either through importation from without or invention within, permeate the society and bring adaptations in its culture. Individuals or groups who are in a position to take advantage of the innovations rise to riches, power, and prestige. Their drive is so to modify old institutions, attitudes, and habits as to give themselves the greatest opportunity to exploit the new situation and to entrench their new position. In this process the circumstances under which many other people have been accustomed to live may be drastically changed. New types of work, new divisions of labor, new types of communities are required. People are drawn out of their old occupations and old communities and into new situations which create new conditions of life. To all of these things all who are affected by the changes react. New interest groups challenge the dominance of old groups, and at the same time find among them those whom they can enlist as allies. Innovations occur in some one aspect of the society, but are soon transmitted to other aspects. Politics changes its pattern; agitation finds new causes; idealism reaches for new goals; philosophy develops new principles; literature discovers new personal and social situations; religion attempts to realize old values in new ways. Altogether these reactions, which, in turn, give rise to innovations, organize new patterns of thought, emotion, and action. At first these tend to be integrated so that they serve the dominant new interest, but other new groups and interests arise as the result of change and, in time, press for a new integration in terms which better serve their interests.

Even fairly widespread changes of this sort may occur, however, without effecting a cultural change of major significance. Changes may affect a large number of activities, and may even shift the balance of power among groups in the society, without altering the terms in which the culture as a whole is integrated. Major cultural changes are those in which a reorientation of a culture has occurred. The multiplication of industrial, urban activities in a predominantly agricultural society, for instance, assumes the character of a major cultural change at the point where the integration of the culture takes place in terms of urban rather than of agrarian institutions, attitudes, and values.

The three chapters included here pose the problem of cultural change in three forms. The first looks at the industrial city as the spearhead of cultural change in the modern world—the milieu which has most radically altered the basic cultural relationships of pre-industrial society, where innovation comes and whence it spreads through the whole society. The second compares the impact of western culture on two oriental societies, those of China and Japan, observing contrasts in the manner and levels at which the impact of the West brought cultural change in these two societies. The third takes a specific cultural phenomenon, the so-called "Flowering of New England," and inquires into the various factors which may have played a part in producing that phenomenon.

THE INDUSTRIAL CITY: CENTER OF CULTURAL CHANGE

RALPH E. TURNER

IN 1832 the *Manchester Guardian,* commenting on an exposure of bad living conditions among the factory population, offered as an apology for their existence the following observation: "The manufacturing system as it exists in Great Britain, and the inconceivably immense towns under it, are without previous parallel in the history of the world." This recognition of the industrial city as an unprecedented phenomenon was developed, not as an apology for bad living conditions, but as an explanation of the general changes under way in society, by two English observers of early industrialism, namely, William Cooke Taylor and Robert Vaughan, both of whom, it is worth noting, were historians. Taylor wrote a general history of civilization under the title *The Natural History of Society* (1841), besides many textbooks; and Vaughan, before he became president of the Lancashire Independent College at Manchester, was professor of history at the University of London. In a sense, therefore, it may be said that the view of the industrial city as a center of cultural change belongs peculiarly to historians.

Taylor held that the industrial town was a "new element" in society, which could not develop without deranging old institutions and relationships. It exhibited, he said, "a system of social life constructed on a wholly new principle, a principle yet vague and indefinite but developing itself by its own spontaneous force, and daily producing effects which no human foresight had anticipated." Above all, he was impressed by the formation of the urban masses who, developing new habits of thought without external aid or guidance, would ultimately, like the slow rising and gradual swelling of the ocean, "bear all elements of society aloft upon its bosom." But, although these masses lacked guidance, they were, in his opinion, no worse off than their superiors who, however educated, found little in past human experience of use in understanding the unforeseen innovations of the factory towns. The Greek verse, said Taylor, meant nothing in Manchester, and philosophy knew no circumstances like those which prevailed there.

Vaughan, who pointed out the fact, none too well recognized even today, that rural and urban populations have played different roles in the growth of civilization, argued that in the "unavoidable intercourse" of the new towns there was occurring an education of the people that would stimulate science, advance self-government, improve the arts and literature, and raise the general level of popular life. "Such, indeed, is often the astuteness acquired in the exercise of this greatest of free schools," he said, "that the smith of Sheffield, or the weaver of Manchester, would frequently prove, on any common ground, more than a match for a college graduate." Vaughan saw the new industrial towns as centers of "vast experiments" like those which had occurred in the cities of other lands and ages.

For us who live today in the midst of what is a chaos understood badly if at all, the views of Taylor and Vaughan may provide a point of departure for a consideration of the prevailing confusion. At least, it is clear that, if the English industrial city of the 1840's was a scene of "vast experiments," today, with similar cities having become the dominant type of community in all industrial nations, "vast experiments" have probably been carried further than they had gone in the early nineteenth century. Similarly, if, as Taylor said, the urban masses will ultimately bear all society aloft, it is probable that the tendency of this bearing is more clear today than when he noted it.

An examination of the industrial city as a center of cultural change may indicate something of these "vast experiments," may possibly show the general direction the urban masses are tending. It is the purpose of this paper to sketch the outlines of such an examination.

The postulates of the examination are to be found in the concept of culture, as developed in recent social thought, especially by anthropologists and sociologists. According to their views, "a culture" is a socially organized and transmitted structure of behavior and thought. The structure is integrated functionally, that is, its elements provide more of a unity than of a conflict of services to life and have coherence psychologically in terms of a relatively clearly focused outlook on life. The basis of this integration is a process of social interaction, through which individual interests and needs are organized into collective forms or patterns. In the growth of culture, the social process impels individuals to new modes of action and thought—innovations, they are called—and these new modes, in turn, become organized as enduring patterns, through selection in the social process. The evolution of any structure of human behavior and thought, when viewed in historical perspective, is recognizable as the evolution of a cultural tradition which, from time to time as new social conditions arise, assimilates new elements in what may be called a reorientation of the tradition. The newly assimilated elements, it may be believed, seldom outweigh those persisting from the past.

This conception of the evolution of behavior and thought also predicates that, although cultural development goes forward constantly both by the loss of old elements and by the assimilation of innovations, there may be far-reaching disturbances in a cultural tradition which, disorganizing a long-persisting integration, produces finally a new integration. At the base of such new integration, setting its pattern and tendency of growth, is the social process through which individual behavior and thought are originally organized and finally assimilated into transmitted materials. In the words of A. A. Goldenweiser,

> In its constituent elements culture is psychological and, in the last analysis, comes from the individual. But as an integral entity culture is cumulative, historical, extra-individual. It comes to the individual as part of his objective experience, just as do his experiences with nature, and, like these, it is absorbed by him, thus becoming part of his psychic content.[1]

It is from the point of view of these predications that the industrial city can be seen as having special significance for cultural development. Relative to the life that prevailed in the traditional countryside and the old market and port towns, it is not difficult to understand that the industrial city tends to organize a new structure of behavior and thought. The original patterns of this structure, as they emerged in Manchester, England, have been sketched in another essay in this volume; [2] here it is important to emphasize that the industrial city, as a focus of technological, eco-

[1] A. A. Goldenweiser, *History, Psychology, and Culture* (New York, 1933), p. 59.
[2] See Chap. X.

nomic, political, intellectual, and esthetic changes, organized cultural influences from many sources in a social process in which the constantly increasing populations participated. Whatever the influences of industrial cities, these influences move in the social interaction that arises in city populations, as individuals carry on their occupations, pursue their interests, and obtain their satisfactions. In terms of the concept of culture, the industrial city is, then, a milieu which everywhere has the same general elements and everywhere supports the development of a structure of behavior and thought from these elements. Because it is a predication of the concept of culture that both behavior and thought, although individually expressed, are socially organized, this milieu may be conceived as bringing about, through time, the transformation of the various organizations of behavior and thought carried in the traditional culture. Thus, for example, the organizations of behavior and thought characterizing the historic sociocultural types—the peasant, the noble, and the priest—are transformed into new structures of behavior and thought, which, however different for workers, technicians, and entrepreneurs, are nevertheless the common base of their lives.

Some of the aspects of this developing structure of behavior and thought may be briefly noted. Its primary elements are evident in the intricate division of labor, which, instead of standardizing and routinizing work as commonly supposed, gives it a manifold variety of forms which make the new urban workers not a "uniform mass" but a composite of diversified types. In contrast to the historic peasants, the members of the new industrial working class possess individuality in a great variety of forms. This developing structure of thought and behavior is also evident in new social services, in new amusements, in new intellectual and artistic pursuits, as well as in new technological and economic procedures. Also the new structure of behavior and thought is embodied in new standards of consumption, in new relationships of the sexes and the members of families, in new positions of the several age groups, in new circumstances affecting health, and in new causes of death. For individuals, these aspects are elements of a changing behavior and mentality; for the industrial city milieu, they are attributes fixed upon individuals coming under its influences.

From the point of view of cultural development, it is necessary to conceive of the beginnings of this structure of behavior and thought as appearing in the early industrial cities, of its elements spreading and maturing as industrial cities have grown, and, finally, of these elements becoming integrated through an intellectual outlook upon or a feeling for life shaped in terms of the frame of reference organized in experience as it goes on among the masses who now live in industrial cities. This matter may be stated in another way. If the industrial city, considered as the social milieu of a new structure of behavior and thought, is influencing ever larger parts of national populations, this influence is evident, on the one hand, in the dislocation of old forms of behavior and thought in the several national traditions and, on the other hand, in the appearance and spread of new forms. However, at the moment, because the dislocation of the old forms intensifies the emotional attachments to them, the new ones are not recognized. If at the moment such is the case, the prevailing confusion is understandable in the feeling that, although the old modes of behavior and thought no longer serve life, there is nothing to replace them. In truth, however, the modes of behavior and thought of a *new* culture may be implicit in the industrial city, requiring only recognition and acceptance to become the basis of conscious action. In the words of Robert H. Lowie, the anthropologist, "Culture, it seems, is a matter of exceedingly slow growth until a certain 'threshold' is passed, when it darts forward, gathering momentum at an unexpected rate." [8] The present disturbed situation in western culture, where the industrial city originated and has had its fullest development, may be only the approach to such a "threshold."

Before turning to a consideration of some of the aspects of industrial-city life which may be factors at the "threshold" of a cultural change, it is well to note that no one meant to create the industrial city or, as currently designated in the United States, the "metropolitan urban area." It arose as entrepreneurs pursued their interest—profits—and engineers served that interest by technological ingenuity. But once created, it became something other than a center of business and machine industry, that is, it became a milieu having the power to organize socially a structure of behavior and thought for those coming under its influence. For this reason the industrial city may ultimately react on business and in-

[8] Robert H. Lowie, *Culture and Ethnology* (New York, 1917), p. 78.

dustry, giving them new forms, in spite of the interests of entrepreneurs. It seems that commonly men do two things when they perform an act, first, what they intend to do and, second, what they do not intend to do. And often the second thing is more important than the first. Certainly this seems to be the case with those persons who, while their intentional activities were chiefly concerned with making money, unknowingly created the industrial city, which, as a social milieu, is now the matrix of cultural change.

An examination of the development of industrial cities shows three classes of factors which may be considered as having significance for further cultural development. Although these factors may not have originated completely in the industrial city, their influence in contemporary life is focused in its milieu, so that they must be considered as elements of a complex of urban psychological influences. These three classes of factors may be designated: (1) the paradox of economic liberalism, (2) conditions having origin in machine technology, and (3) conditions of urban association. Each of these classes of psychological factors ramifies through contemporary society, having many manifestations and exciting many comments. However, only in the industrial city or the metropolitan urban milieu can they be viewed objectively.

By the paradox of economic liberalism, the central predications of which are too widely accepted to require statement here, is meant that entrepreneurial activity has created conditions which not only restrict the freedom of individuals but also reveal that the presumptions that universal competition promotes the automatic realization of a constantly advancing well-being are false. The restrictions on individual freedom of action have objective form in the hierarchies of employment which have appeared as technological developments have brought together ever larger units of capital. For individuals employed in these hierarchies, economic advancement is more a matter of rising from grade to grade than a shift from the status "employee" to the status "entrepreneur." Moreover, in these hierarchies economic power is exercised from the top downward. Through the "right to fire," the qualities of behavior that bring advancement become less and less those summed up in the phrase "individual initiative" and more and more those implied in the word "loyalty." Actually "conformity" rather than "initiative" is the quality desired in an ever-increasing body of individuals who occupy the status of employee. It is also important to note that economic power exerted from the top of these hierarchies upon individuals in the lower levels of employment does interfere upon occasions with the exercise of personal liberties in areas of life quite beyond that of the economic functioning of the hierarchies. The effect of this interference is to impose upon more and more individuals a regimentation in terms of private interests. Indeed, in many ways the current assertion of the doctrines of economic liberalism is merely a defense for economic power that functions as private regimentation.

Probably no more concise statement of the contradiction between the theory of economic liberalism and the fact of the private regimentation which prevails among the populations of industrial cities can be cited than the following words from Walter Lippmann's column, "How Liberty Is Lost":

> To have economic independence a man must be in a position to leave one job and go to another; he must have enough savings of some kind to exist for a considerable time without accepting the first job offered. . . . the industrial worker who has a choice between working in one factory and not working at all, the white collar intellectuals who compete savagely for the relatively few private positions and for posts in the bureaucracy—these are the people who live too precariously to exercise their liberties or to defend them. They have no savings. They have only their labor to sell, and there are very few buyers of their labor. Therefore, they have only the choice of truckling to the powerful or of perishing heroically but miserably.[4]

Who are the great to whom these workers shall truckle? The private employers or the politicians who promise jobs? The economic and political crises which have already swept away some liberal regimes, and which now threaten the remainder, root in this social soil.

In this connection, it is worth observing that, from the cultural point of view, the mere criticism of a social order cannot be the basis of social reconstruction. Indeed, if a program of social reform or amelioration can be successfully based on a critique of a social order, progress away from the conditions giving rise to the paradox of economic liberalism should have been rapid, since the rise of the early industrial cities, for the eloquence of the writers of

[4] *New York Herald Tribune,* July 16, 1938.

those times on these conditions has not been surpassed by writers of the present century. But to be able to point out social evils—even, in fact, to understand their origin—is not to become adequate to deal with them. For they cannot be dealt with in terms of themselves or even in terms of the institutions which give rise to them. In other words, the evils cannot be dealt with merely as problems of distress, unemployment, and the like, or as aspects of a social order retaining the essential characteristics described in the doctrines of economic liberalism; they must be dealt with in terms of the potentialities of cultural change, implicit in the industrial city milieu. To know these potentialities involves not the emotional excitement raised by pointing to the evils, but a technique of analysis of the factors in cultural development. And to the development of this technique few social critics have made contributions.

In turning to a consideration of the two other classes of factors which are elements of the industrial city milieu, namely, conditions having their origin in machine technology and conditions of urban association, it is necessary to point out that the items listed under these headings have been arrived at in a certain way. This way has been an isolation of the repetitive, or recurring elements in industrial urban life, or, in other words, the finding of its continuously pervasive elements. This mode of analysis has been adopted on the ground that a culture, as an integrated and persisting structure of behavior and thought, is constructed psychologically upon a relatively stable order of stimuli, in terms of which patterns of reaction are developed. To such repetitive stimuli the great part of an industrial population react, and the recurring reactions become the determining tendencies of the development of the urban structure of life. Culture, it must be remembered, is both a psychological and a social phenomenon.

This way of analysis is not unfamiliar in American historiography. In fact, the classic essay, *The Significance of the Frontier in American History,* by Frederick Jackson Turner, which has received the lip, if not the mind service of a generation of students of American history, embodies it. The fundamental postulate of this essay is that a persisting underlying influence gave distinctive patterns to national life and furthermore created an intellectual outlook which unified the national culture. Certainly the following excerpts can be so understood.

> The existence of an area of free land, its continuous recession, and the advance of American settlement westward explain American development.
>
> Behind institutions, behind constitutional forms and modifications, lie the vital forces that call these organs into life and shape them to meet changing conditions. . . .
>
> The frontier individualism has from the beginning promoted democracy. . . .
>
> The result is that to the frontier the American intellect owes its striking characteristics. That coarseness and strength combined with acuteness and inquisitiveness, that practical inventive turn of mind, quick to find expedients, that masterful grasp of material things, lacking in the artistic but powerful to effect great ends, that restless, nervous energy, that dominant individualism, working for good and for evil, and withal that buoyancy and exuberance which comes with freedom, these are traits of the frontier, or traits called out elsewhere because of the existence of the frontier.[5]

In terms of the concept of culture, the fact of "free land" may be understood as having established patterns which, as the frontier was pushed westward, were worked into the various phases of national life and, as individual experience and behavior were organized in these patterns, came to embody a pervasive psychological reaction which was the source of the subjective tradition of the national culture. In a sense, therefore, an analysis of current American developments in cultural terms is not greatly different from the mode of thinking which led Turner to his view of national development.

In every culture the integration of man with physical nature, in terms of technology, is significant in the life of the people who carry the culture. From this integration flows the wealth which supports the social order and certain basic judgments on life that have entered always into social attitudes, religious beliefs, and moral practices. There is no need here to discuss these phenomena, as they have long existed in cultures having an agrarian base. From contemporary technology come, it seems, at least three recognizable

[5] "The Significance of the Frontier in American History," *The Early Writings of Frederick Jackson Turner*, compiled by E. E. Edwards (Madison, 1938), pp. 185–229, at pp. 186, 220, 227–28.

conditions that may contribute to the shaping of new cultural forms:

First: The sense of human control. Machine technology is operated by energy produced and controlled by man; in fact, it represents the fullest expression of his rationality. He creates power, orders its flow, governs its movement, and determines its resultant. In this circumstance exists ground for the assumption that what man achieves in one field of action, he may also do in another field. As a result of man's triumph in technology, it may be that he feels more able to command his fate socially. The emergence of the concept "planned economy" roots at least partly in this circumstance.

Second: The utility of objective knowledge. That knowledge is power is appreciated by the simplest mechanic; in terms of a special body of knowledge, every machine operator or machine fixer performs his task. This circumstance boldly insists that it is knowledge which functions to give success in every situation, that myth, tradition, and special interest must give way to knowledge—and the knowledge meant is worldly, factual, and utilitarian. By implication, therefore, machine technology supports the view that social distress exists either because of lack of knowledge or because of the unwillingness to apply what is at hand.

Third: The increasing capacity to produce wealth. With the advent of machinery and applied science in agriculture and industry, man's capacity to produce wealth expanded enormously. For example, between 1920 and 1930 the agricultural population of the United States decreased by 4,000,000 persons, while agricultural production increased by 25 percent; now agricultural economists estimate that the agricultural population, not counting the back log of persons who would have migrated to cities if jobs had been available, could be decreased by at least 3,000,000 persons without seriously affecting the agricultural production necessary to maintain national consumption at present standards. It has been estimated that since about 1870 the capacity to produce in manufacturing industries has increased 3 percent per year. Especially important is the fact that the increase of productivity has gone on steadily during the present depression decade. This fact is relevant to the present situation, which finds industrial production near the 1929 level without the employment of an equal number of workers.

These three conditions having their origin in contemporary technology—the sense of human control, the utility of objective knowledge, and the increasing capacity to produce wealth—point more and more directly to an economy in which human control, exercised with knowledge rather than with self-interest, may utilize the new capacity, to produce wealth for the support of a more secure life.

In closing this comment on the new conditions of life that have come with contemporary technology, it should be noted that one does not need to be a philosopher in order to know them, for they run constantly in the experience of all who actually work at the production of real goods. In other words, these conditions are part and parcel of the life of the masses of industrial cities.

The conditions of urban association are certainly no less significant for setting the direction of cultural change than those arising in contemporary technology. In fact, because they have existence in social interaction, they are primary to these influences which, after all, are reactions of men to physical nature and not of men to men. Culture, it may be noted, stands between man and nature, whereas man comes to culture through the social process.

From this point of view four conditions of industrial urban association are significant:

First: The disintegration of localism and tradition. Innumerable social stimuli flow through the contemporary urban population. Newspapers, movies, and radio pour the world into their eyes and ears; from these visual and aural images there is no escape. By the number and impact of these social stimuli, local prejudices and old traditions are disintegrated. By this wearing away, the urban masses are freed to take on views which harmonize with their social environment—the industrial city as a whole, not merely as a place where labor is sold and a profit is made. Indeed, the rise of propaganda, i. e., the organized control of mass opinion, has its origin in this circumstance, for as the masses are released from local and traditional opinions, they become free to move in new directions. Propaganda is organized by special interests in order to determine this direction. In the end, however, the movement of mass mentality will necessarily be in the direction set by the milieu which exists in the going experience of thousands of individuals.

Second: The cult of uniformity. As social stimuli flow continuously through the urban masses by way of machine-made commodities and routinized social services, manners, customs, and tastes are shaped into a wide conformity. This conformity is the necessary base of the organization of a complex social order among a large population; it makes for frictionless movement among large aggregates of individuals, who can, as a result, move together in actions not possible for them when they were embedded in local communities. Conformity serves the need for orderly coöperation in the intricate processes of urban society.

Third: The diversification of individual behavior. In communities antedating industrial cities, refinement, elegance, and taste were, in the main, attributes of small classes; to belong to these classes meant the possession of an explicit moral code, special forms of dress and manner, and particular intellectual affectations. In some respects these class attributes survive now, but among urban masses individual tastes find release from such controls. Thus there appear among urban populations innumerable groups pursuing self-selected interests, and individuals are permitted wide variations from all norms of conduct. The modern urban milieu is fostering a diversification of intellectual, artistic, and amusemental pursuits, unheard of in earlier types of communities. Individual energies are free to find expression in more ways than ever before. The industrial city well exemplifies the sociological principle that as social organization becomes more complex, individuals necessarily have more opportunity for development.

Fourth: The reorientation of the right of property. From the point of view of the concept of culture, the social rather than the economic factor is decisive in historical development. Thus it need cause no surprise that the social milieu of the industrial city is affecting the right of property—indeed, the whole relationship of men and wealth. The prevailing concept of property was derived from societies mainly agrarian in their economic and social organization. It is a concept developed mainly in terms of tangible goods, for it emphasizes possession on the ground that from possession flow the benefits of ownership. Now it appears that property in this sense has been becoming less and less important in the lives of all urban dwellers. Urban dwellers, even those having great wealth, can own very little of the property upon which their lives continually depend. The rich and the poor alike are dependent upon a continuity of services—water, food, light, heat, protection—which are maintained only through social coöperation. And they demand not ownership of these services, but their continuous functioning, regardless of ownership. Similarly, the owner of tangible property, whatever it may be, can produce little with the property that contributes to real satisfaction. His property probably functions to create any wealth that gives real satisfactions only through a minute division of labor, and such wealth is produced only through the maintenance of this division of labor. Finally, since the individual in the modern urban economy, no matter who he may be, can command few real goods through the possession of real property, he must possess some claim upon wealth which can be executed in diverse ways; for only by such execution can he acquire the diversity of real goods which supports urban modes of living. Thus it appears that in the modern industrial city the ownership of property is far less important to the support of individual life than the maintenance of certain fundamental economic services and the establishment of some kind of claim on currently produced real goods. In fact, the elaboration of the modes of ownership through various kinds of legal claims—securities, trusts, insurance annuities, and social security claims—is an adjustment to this growing social orientation of the right of property.

However confused and clouded this exposition of the factors in the industrial urban milieu has been, it has made these factors far more clear than they are. Actually they exist today as part of the chaos previously noted. They are vaguely felt impulses, uncertain judgments, and befogged visions; they are neither defined nor oriented. However, they run in the experience of urban masses, as life goes on in terms of the labor market, machine technology, and urban association; and, as combined in a day-by-day routine, they form a frame of reference which for these masses, without conscious effort on their part, becomes the point of departure of feeling and thinking. Thus from this frame of reference issues, in the life of the masses, new attitudes toward their problems, new definitions of their interests, and new concepts of what life ought to be like. More important still in the day-by-day routine of behavior, as organized under the influence of this complex of urban forces, are the elements which may be combined in new patterns of behavior that will constitute the culture which is correlative with the modes of thinking and feeling set in this frame of reference. In other words, the frame of reference, as the subjective content of life shaped by the complex of urban forces, and the day-by-day routines of behavior, as the objective content of life shaped by this complex, together form the psychological basis for the integration of thought and behavior in a new culture.

In the concept of culture, it is postulated that at any time there are a limited number of possible modes of thinking and acting; therefore, as far as the contemporary world is concerned, if the old forms of thought and behavior are to be displaced (as, indeed, they are being displaced), the complex of urban forces which shapes this frame of reference and day-by-day routine of behavior of the urban masses fixes the possibilities for the future. It is pertinent to state here that because this frame of reference and this day-by-day routine of behavior are organized through social interaction, they affect, to some degree, the smaller specialized urban groups as well as the urban masses; for this reason contemporary cultural change is not merely an adjustment to the rise of a new social class. It is, in fact, far more fundamental, for it is touching all classes, compelling those which have been dominant to alter the forms of their control if they are to remain dominant. The twentieth century cannot have just any kind of social order; it must have one oriented in terms of the contemporary industrial urban milieu.

If one seeks a general heading under which to sum up the most significant aspect of the cultural change under way in nations whose chief communities are industrial cities or metropolitan urban areas, it would seem to be the phrase "a reëducation of the masses." Before the rise of industrial cities, the overwhelming proportion of population in all lands consisted of peasants—socially isolated, superstitious, tenacious of the land, and illiterate. As industrial cities grew, the peasant element declined and the urban masses formed. It should be recognized that, as the masses shifted to the cities, they brought with them the mentality of peasants; this has been a primary condition in their reëducation which, even today, the contrivers of propaganda know how to use. But, once

THE MODERNIZATION OF CHINA AND JAPAN: A COMPARATIVE STUDY IN CULTURAL CONFLICT

HU SHIH

IN RECENT years I have published some of my reflections on the modernization of Japan and China.[1] The following paper is a summary and a restatement of what I have been thinking on this fascinating subject during these years.

First of all, we must state the problem of our inquiry. What special aspect of the modernization of China and Japan arouses our curiosity and requires our study and explanation?

Generally speaking, there are two aspects of the question that have puzzled the outside world and demanded some explanation.

For many decades, down to very recent years, the question often asked was: Why was Japan so successful in her task of modernization, and why was China so unsuccessful? That is the first aspect of the question which has called forth many explanations.

But in recent years the problem has radically changed. After almost a century of hesitation and resistance, China has emerged as a modern nation, not sufficiently westernized, it is true, in her material aspects, but fully modern in her outlook on life and feeling completely at home in the modern world. On the other hand, Japan, after seventy years of apparently rapid modernization, is suddenly discovered by the outside world as having never been transformed in all the fundamental aspects of her national life. Professor G. C. Allen, one of the most sympathetic interpreters of Japan, said:

> If the changes in some of the aspects of her [Japan's] life have been far-reaching, the persistence of the traditional in other aspects is equally remarkable. . . . The contrasts between these innovations and the solid core of ancient habit are as striking as ever they were.[2]

Professor Emil Lederer and Emy Lederer-Seidler, in their joint work on *Japan in Transition,* another most sympathetic interpre-

[1] Hu Shih, *The Chinese Renaissance* (Chicago, 1934), pp. 1–26; Hu Shih, "Can China Survive?" *Forum,* XCVII (1937), 39–44; Hu Shih, "The Westernization of China and Japan," *Amerasia* II (1938), pp. 243–47.

[2] G. C. Allen, *Japan, the Hungry Guest* (London, 1938), p. 39.

tation of Japanese life, have dwelt on the most strange phenomenon in Japan, namely, her "immunity to the dialectic play of deep-lying evolutionary forces," [3] her being "devoid of dialectic and dynamic," [4] and her ancient civilization "offering strong resistance to the facile assimilation of foreign elements." [5]

In short, the new problem is just the opposite of the older puzzle. It is: Why has China at last succeeded in overthrowing her old civilization and in achieving a Chinese renaissance? And why has Japan, after seven decades of extraordinarily successful modernization, yet failed to break up her "solid core of ancient habit"? That is the second aspect of the problem.

Any theory that attempts to explain the first set of questions must also explain satisfactorily the second set of questions. And vice versa.

In 1933 I was trying to solve the first set of puzzles: Why and how has Japan succeeded, and China failed, to achieve a speedy and orderly cultural readjustment and bring about the modernization necessary for national survival in the new world? The explanation I offered then [6] was that China and Japan had been going through two distinct types of cultural response. The modernization in Japan I described as the type of cultural transformation under centralized control, made possible by the existence of a powerful ruling class—the feudal militaristic caste—from which came the leaders of the reformation, who not only decided for the nation what to change and what not to change, but who also had the political power to carry out their decisions. On the other hand, I pointed out, China, because of the nonexistence of a ruling class and because of the thoroughly democratized social structure, could only go through the slow and often wasteful process of cultural transformation through the gradual and diffused penetration and assimilation of ideas and practices, usually initiating from a few individuals, slowly winning a following, and finally achieving significant changes when a sufficient number of people were convinced that the new ideas and practices were superior in reasonableness, convenience, or efficacy.

The advantages of the Japanese type of modernization under

[3] Emil Lederer and Emy Lederer-Seidler, *Japan in Transition* (New Haven, 1938), p. 47.

[4] *Ibid.*, p. viii.

[5] *Ibid.*, p. 190.

[6] Hu Shih, *The Chinese Renaissance*, pp. 1–26, especially pp. 23–26.

the centralized control of a ruling class are easy to see. It is orderly, economical, continuous, stable, and effective. But, I point out,

it is not without very important disadvantages. The Japanese leaders undertook this rapid transformation at so early a time that even the most farsighted of them could only see and understand certain superficial phases of the western civilization. Many other phases have escaped their attention. And, in their anxiety to preserve their national heritage and to strengthen the hold of the state and the dynasty over the people, they have carefully protected a great many elements of the traditional Japan from the contact and contagion of the new civilization. Much of the traditional medieval culture is artificially protected by a strong shell of militant modernity. Much that is preserved is of great beauty and permanent value; but not a little of it is primitive and pregnant of grave dangers of volcanic eruption.

The disadvantages of the Chinese type of cultural change through gradual diffusion and penetration are numerous: they are slow, sporadic, and often wasteful because much undermining and erosion are necessary before anything can be changed.

But they have also undeniable advantages. They are voluntary. From the lipstick to the literary revolution, from footwear to the overthrow of the monarchy, all has been voluntary and in a broad sense "reasoned." Nothing in China is so sacred as to be protected from the contact and contagion of the invading civilization of the West. And no man, nor any class, is powerful enough to protect any institution from this contact and change. In short, this process of long exposure and slow permeation often results in cultural changes which are both fundamental and permanent.

This, in general, was my theory regarding the modernization of China and Japan. Japan was modernized under the powerful leadership and control of a ruling class, and China, because of the nonexistence of such control from above, was modernized through the long process of free contact, gradual diffusion, and voluntary following.

We may ask, Can this theory satisfactorily explain all the four phases of our main inquiry? Can it explain the marvelously rapid westernization of Japan and at the same time the unchanging solid core of medieval Japan? Can it explain both the long failures and the recent successes in China's modernization? I think not only that it can, but that it is the only hypothesis which can satisfactorily resolve all the apparent contradictions of the problem.

According to my theory, the early and rapid successes of the Meiji reformation were brought about by the effective leadership and powerful control of the ruling class, which happened to coincide with the militaristic class of feudal Japan, and which naturally was most anxious and at the same time best fitted to undertake the adoption of the Western armaments and methods of warfare. As Professor Lederer has pointed out, "it could hardly be foreseen at this early stage that in this case one step leads inexorably to a second."

> Since a modern military state is possible only on condition that it is an industrialized state, Japan had to develop in that direction. But industrialization, by reason of the economic interrelationship between various types of production, means also the development of branches of industry which are not essential to the conduct of war. Just as militarism reaches beyond itself into industry, so the technological system of industrialism has far-reaching implications for the social system.[7]

The leaders of Japanese westernization started out with the desire of adopting Western militarism, and have thereby brought about what Professor Lederer calls a "militaristic industrial system."

Of all the non-European countries with which the European civilization has come into contact, Japan is the only nation that has successfully learned and mastered that one phase of the occidental civilization which is most coveted by all races, namely, its militaristic phase. Japan has succeeded where all these other non-European countries have invariably failed. This historical mystery can be explained only by the fact that no other non-European country was so favored by the existence of a militaristic caste, which has been the governing class of the country for over twelve centuries.

But this militaristic caste was not an enlightened or intellectual class. Its leaders were courageous, pragmatic, patriotic, and in some cases statesmanlike. But they were limited in their vision and in their understanding of the new civilization that had knocked at their doors. They thought, just as Lafcadio Hearn thought, that they could build up a Western war machine which should be made to serve as a protective wall behind which all the traditional values of Tokugawa Japan should be preserved unaltered.

[7] Lederer and Lederer-Seidler, *Japan in Transition,* pp. 179–81.

Unfortunately for Japan and for the world, the military successes of Japan against Russia and China tended to vindicate these narrow-visioned leaders. The result has been an effective artificial protection and solidification of the traditional culture of medieval Japan against the "dangerous" contact and influence of the new ideas and practices of the ever-changing world. By the use of the modern means of rigidly controlled education, propaganda, and censorship, and by the use of the peculiarly Japanese methods of inculcating the cult of emperor-worship, Japan has succeeded in reinforcing and consolidating the "solid core" of unchanging medieval culture left over from the 250 years of Tokugawa isolation. It was the same centralized leadership and control which made possible the rapid and successful changes in militarization and industrialization and which has also deliberately protected and solidified the traditional values and made them "immune to the dialectic play of deep-lying evolutionary forces."

The same theory also explains the history of modernization in China. The early failures in the Chinese attempts at westernization were almost entirely due to the absence of the factors which have made the Japanese Meiji reformation a success. The Chinese leaders, too, wanted to adopt Western armaments and methods of warfare and to build up the new industries. Their slogan was "Fu Ts'iang" (Wealth and Strength). But there was in China neither the militaristic tradition nor an effective and powerful governing class to undertake the leadership and direction in such gigantic enterprises. China had come out of feudalism at least twenty-one centuries ago; the social structure had been thoroughly democratized; and governmental policy, religion, philosophy, literature, and social usage had combined to condemn militarism and to despise the soldier. Whereas the Samurai was the most highly esteemed class in Japan, the soldier ranked lowest in the Chinese social scale. Therefore the new Chinese army and the new Chinese navy of the eighties and nineties of the last century were doomed to failure. With the destruction of the Chinese navy in 1894–95, all the new industries—the shipyard, the merchant marine, the government-operated iron and steel industry—which were to feed and support the new war machine, gradually came to naught. The government and the dynasty were thus discredited in their early efforts in modernization. After the failure of the reforms of 1898 and the tragedy of the Boxer Uprising of 1900, the discrediting of the dynasty and the government was complete. From that time on, China's main endeavor was to destroy that center of ignorance and reactionism—the monarchy and its paraphernalia—and then to build up a new center of political authority and leadership.

Thus, while Japan's first successes in westernization were achieved under the leadership and control of her feudal-militaristic class, China has had to spend three or four decades in the effort of first removing the monarchy and later destroying the newly arisen militarists. It has been found necessary for China to bring about a political revolution as the pre-condition for her modernization.

In 1911–12 the revolution succeeded in overthrowing the alien rule and the monarchy, together with its historical accompaniments. The political revolution was in every sense a social and cultural emancipation. In a country where there is no ruling class, the overthrow of the monarchy destroys the last possibility of a centralized control in social change and cultural transformation. It makes possible an atmosphere of free contact, free judgment and criticism, free appreciation, free advocacy, and voluntary acceptance.

What has been called the Chinese renaissance is the natural product of this atmosphere of freedom. All the important phases of cultural change in China have been the result of this free contact and free diffusion of new ideas and practices, which are impossible in Japan under rigid dynastic and militaristic taboos. The net outcome is that modern China has undoubtedly achieved more far-reaching and more profound transformations in the social, political, intellectual, and religious life than the so-called "modern Japan" has ever done in similar fields.

Time permits me to cite only one important and fundamental fact, in illustration of the character of the cultural change in China. I refer to the spirit of free and fearless criticism which the leaders of China have applied to the study and examination of their own social, political, historical, and religious institutions. It is no accident that all the men who have exerted the greatest influence over the Chinese nation for the last forty years—Liang Ch'i-ch'ao, Ts'ai Yuan-p'ei, Wu Ching-heng, Chen Tu-shiu, and others—have been men who know our historical heritage criti cally and who have had the moral courage ruthlessly to criticize its evil and weak aspects and to advocate wholehearted changes. Not Confucius, nor Lao-tze, nor the Buddha, nor Chu Hsi; not the monarchy, nor the family, nor religion, is too sacred to be exempt from their doubt and criticism. A nation that has encouraged honest doubt and free criticism, even in matters touching the sacred and most time-honored institutions, is achieving a modernity undreamed of by its neighbors, whose intellectual leaders are persecuted and punished for having taught thirty years ago a certain theory of constitutional law or for having suggested that certain sacred treasures at a certain shrine might be of doubtful authenticity.

To sum up, the modernization in China illustrates the view that, in the absence of centralized control from above, cultural changes of basic importance may take place through the process of free contact and slow diffusion. It is the reverse side of what has happened in Japan: the breakdown of the monarchy and its paraphernalia has removed the possibility of artificial protection and solidification of the old culture, which is thus thrown open to the natural processes of cultural transformation through free contact and voluntary acceptance.

If I have any moral to present, it is this: freedom of contact and choice is the most essential condition for cultural diffusion and change. Wherever two civilizations come into contact, there are the natural tendencies (or laws) of each people learning and borrowing from the other what it lacks or recognizes as of superior utility or beauty.[8] These natural tendencies of cultural diffusion will have free play only if the peoples are allowed free contact with the new ideas and practices.

Where such freedom is denied to a people, where artificial isolation and solidification are consciously and effectively carried out with regard either to a whole culture or to certain specially prized aspects of it, there arises the strange phenomenon of the "solid core of ancient habit" "devoid of dialectic and dynamic," such as has been found in present-day Japan.

There is really no mystery in this unchanging Japan after sev-

[8] Hu Shih, "Indianization of China: A Case Study in Cultural Borrowing," in *Independence, Convergence and Borrowing in Institutions, Thought and Art* ("Harvard Tercentenary Publications," Cambridge, 1937), pp. 219–24. There I tried to formulate these natural tendencies and natural limitations in cultural borrowing.

enty years of marvelously rapid change in the militaristic industrial system. There is no truth in the theory, for example, that the Japanese civilization has been able to resist change because it has its peculiar vitality and has attained "the completed perfection of its forms." [9] The fashion of men's clothing in the Western world does not change so rapidly as that of the women—but can we say that men's clothing has achieved special vitality and "the completed perfection of form"? In the same way, sitting on the floor, for example, was discarded in China so long ago that historians have difficulty in dating the first use of chairs and tables: but the Japanese to this day continue to sit on the floor. That does not mean the custom of sitting on the floor has any special "vitality" or has attained "completed perfection in form."

Nor is there much truth in the view that the Japanese are naturally clumsy in understanding and conservative in their outlook. Lack of understanding never prevents a people from accepting new fads. Japan probably never understood the various schools of Buddhism when she accepted them. (Certainly China did not understand some of them when she adopted them.) Besides, a people can always learn. European observers in the seventeenth century recorded that the Japanese knew "nothing of mathematics, more especially of its deeper and speculative parts." [10] But we now know the Japanese can become accomplished mathematicians.

As to their native conservatism, the history of early Japanese contacts with Korea, China, and Europe only proves the contrary. They learned from these foreign peoples everything they could learn, not excluding things affecting their social, political, and religious institutions. In recording the success of the Jesuits in sixteenth-century Japan, Sansom said:

> though a number of their converts were beyond all doubt genuine to the point of fanaticism and adhered to their new faith in the face of great danger, one cannot but suspect that it had, by one of those crazes which have often swept over Japan, become the fashion to ape the customs of foreigners, including their religion. We know that rosaries and crucifixes were eagerly bought and worn by many who

[9] Lederer and Lederer-Seidler, *Japan in Transition,* p. 190.

[10] G. B. Sansom, *Japan: A Short Cultural History* (New York and London, 1938), p. 411, quoting Kaempfer.

were not Christians, even, it is said, by Hideyoshi himself; and it was modish to wear foreign clothes and to be able to recite a Latin prayer.[11]

I cannot therefore escape the conclusion that it will be the element of freedom that may yet someday break down the "solid core of ancient habit" in Japan, just as it has already broken it down in China.[12]

[11] Sansom, *Japan,* p. 413.

[12] Cf. Allen, *Japan, the Hungry Guest,* p. 245: "A policy of preserving without exact definition, the old ideological foundations of the State, and at the same time of allowing spiritual and intellectual freedom to individuals, would permit the gradual and insensible modification of these foundations as the temper and outlook of the people slowly changed. This policy was, on the whole, being followed down to 1930. But to attempt to base the State unequivocally on what must eventually become outworn symbols and to insist on the conformity of everyone to an ideology which, though for the moment fashionable, cannot forever survive the spread of a scientific attitude of mind, is to invite disaster. Men will, of course, conform for a time, but in conforming they will make mental reservations, and so the whole of public life will become riddled with insincerities. What can be the future of such a State?" Where I differ with Allen is that I seriously doubt the possibility of "spiritual and intellectual freedom" under a policy of "preserving the old ideological foundations of the State."

THE FLOWERING OF NEW ENGLAND

EDITED BY RALPH H. GABRIEL

FOR the purposes of the discussion which follows, the "flowering" was defined as the appearance in New England, in the middle period, of important religious developments eventuating in Unitarianism and transcendentalism, of a variety of humanitarian movements, and, in particular, of the creation of a body of literary writing which gave to America a position in the world of letters. The question posed was how should the historian explain this afflorescence? Were the causes social, economic, or intellectual, or a combination of all three? Was New England's "golden day" due to the chance appearance as neighbors and contemporaries of a few men of genius?

The several statements which follow do not constitute attempts to answer this question with finality. They were made as contributions to a lively discussion, and provide challenging hypotheses, rather than definitive conclusions.

Economic Ferment

EDWARD C. KIRKLAND

In tune with the current vogue in historical thinking, perhaps I should commence by giving the frame of reference within which my thoughts are operating. I shall have to confess, in the first instance, that I am a New Englander who thought during the formative years of his life that culture extended only as far as the Hudson River, or perchance Buffalo. In the second place, although I am an economic historian, I am not an economic determinist. If I must advance any connection between economic data and the flowering of New England, I think I should conceal that connection under the theory expressed by an associate of mine, "History is the mud from which the flower of literature grows."

It is quite clear that this discussion is proceeding under a fundamental assumption. We are discussing the "flowering of New England," not as an accident, not as the spontaneous appearance of genius, but as having apprehensible causes. One reason for this assumption, no doubt, is the group character of this New England activity. It could hardly have been the result of a mass coincidence of births. It might, to be sure, have arisen through discipleship, the leadership provided by a few accidentally great individuals. But here the individualistic character of the renaissance comes into play. Emerson contributed to it, for instance, but he did not cause it. I think we are safe in believing that the explanation is to be found outside the realm of individuals and accident.

Economic factors might have operated in either an indirect or a direct fashion to shape the flowering of New England. Quite obviously they played an occasioning part through factors which are not in themselves economic in character.

The role of Unitarianism in the flowering has often been stressed. This is clearly an intellectual movement, but that its appearance had some connection with economic status is clear from Mrs. Stowe's observation that all the elect of wealth and fashion thronged the Unitarian churches. This is simply a passing illustration. More important was the economic basis for the factor of nationalism. Everyone at all acquainted with the growth of American culture is at once aware of the importance of the nationalistic impulse. It underlay the scientific work of Audubon, the formation of arithmetic books, and the foundation of colleges. This nationalistic impulse was nation-wide. It came later to New England than to other sections. Its landmark in literature is commonly esteemed to be Emerson's essay on *The American Scholar*. But his note had been anticipated by others, among them Longfellow, and others had put his idea into practice.

In my opinion, the most important factor in explaining this arrival of the nationalistic impulse in New England, a retarded arrival, was the construction of the railroad. Before its time, New England was a geographic province, as much connected with the rest of the world as it was with the rest of its own country. It was the equivalent of the Hanseatic city-states of an earlier era. The railroad brought it in touch with America. The Western Railroad, opened in the forties, was not only a great engineering feat, in its day the equal of the Union Pacific; it was eventually a means for the breakdown of New England's American provincialism. When Emerson wrote that "from 1790 to 1820 there was not a book, a speech, a conversation, or a thought in the State" of Massachusetts, he might well have added that there was not a railroad.

Of the economic influences which operated directly upon New England culture, the omnipresent—and somewhat tedious—industrial revolution was the most novel. Lowell, a planned industrial community, was, after all, well within the sacred circle swung around Concord. It would be foolish to assert that the factory and the machine made an immediate dent upon New England thought. For, although Theodore Parker might belabor the results of industrialism with intense specificity, others seem to have ignored the changing economic scene, except for generalities. But there is plenty of evidence that they knew that it was there. The Fitchburg Railroad ran along the shore opposite Thoreau's Walden cabin; and as an artisan, he was interested in its work and its workers. Hawthorne saw fit to include the factory along with the dunghill as a place where a man could lose his soul. Emerson, who had invested in the New England railroads, saw them both as American art and American menace. But the industrial revolution is not important to the flowering because it gave subject matter. Rather it was one of the great transforming factors in New England, just as surely as Unitarianism and Jefferson republicanism were transforming factors. Like them it gave to New England life that sense of change and flux, of the old things and world giving place to new. It gave an *élan,* a dynamic character to the age which we know as the flowering of New England.

Basic Cultural Unity

ARTHUR E. BESTOR

Two years after Appomattox, Emerson turned his eye back over the epoch in New England's intellectual history that had already drawn visibly to a close. In a piece of sustained writing unusual for him, he set down his recollections of life and letters in the decades following 1820. "The ancient manners were giving way," he began. The era was one of conflict, between "the party of the Past and the party of the Future." The latter were "fanatics in freedom; they hate[d] tolls, taxes, turnpikes, banks, hierarchies, governors, yea, almost laws." And their criticism was directed not only to institutions, but also inward to the very secrets of personality. "The young men were born with knives in their brain, a tendency to introversion, self-dissection, anatomizing of motives." [1] Out of such intellectual ferment, Emerson implied, came the worthiest thought and the best writing of his contemporaries and himself.

It is easy to document such a conclusion. There were striking physical changes in New England life as the Yankees of the middle period explored new paths of commerce, applied their wealth and their ingenuity to manufacture, and sent their young men to found new commonwealths in the west. Spiritual stirrings became evident not only in religion, but also in the founding of utopias—collectivist like Brook Farm or individualist like Walden—and in numerous reform movements: for temperance, for peace, for the abolition of slavery, even for vegetarianism and hydropathy. We do not need the retrospective evidence of Emerson's "Historic Notes" in order to demonstrate that his writings were influenced by these fresh winds of change blowing across New England. The titles of the lectures into which he distilled his thought in the early 1840's tell the story: "The Present Age," "Politics," "Reforms," "Tendencies," "Man the Reformer," "The Times," "To the Temperance Society," "The Young American," "On Emancipation in the British West Indies." [2] The so-called flowering of New England affords no proof more substantial than Emerson's work of a connection between great literature and critical, dynamic tendencies in thought.

But before the historian explains this flowering too exclusively in terms of social and intellectual unrest, he should pay close attention to the spirit and the mood in which Emerson and his fellows wrote. For a literature based on dissent or criticism or

[1] Ralph Waldo Emerson, "Life and Letters in New England," in his *Works*, ed. by Edward Waldo Emerson (Centenary ed., Cambridge, 1904), X, 325, 327, 329. According to the editor (p. 572), "this paper was not a mosaic of many notes . . . , but . . . was continuously written, . . . probably about the year 1867."

[2] See James Elliot Cabot, *A Memoir of Ralph Waldo Emerson* (Boston, 1887), II, 741–51.

conflict, their utterances are strangely lacking in the tone of protest and controversy. When Emerson, for example, broke finally with established religious tradition by resigning his pulpit, he summarized his position on the Lord's Supper in these words: "I have no hostility to this institution; I am only stating my want of sympathy with it. . . . That is the end of my opposition, that I am not interested in it." [3] Can one imagine Luther stating so mildly his objection to any practice of the Roman church?

Once free of the pulpit, Emerson's antipathy to argument and controversy grew even more marked. "If they set out to contend," he wrote, "Saint Paul will lie and Saint John will hate." [4] Emerson was willing to accept whatever misconstruction might be put upon his views, rather than debate them. Defiantly he "would write on the lintels of the door-post, *Whim.* I hope it is somewhat better than whim at last, but we cannot spend the day in explanation." [5] The burden of proof, he felt, did not rest upon him. In similar vein, Thoreau "preferred that society should run 'amok' against me, it being the desperate party." [6] Instead of argument there was confident affirmation. Though these writers carried on controversy, they refused to be controversialists.

In the last analysis, Emerson refused because he could not believe that controversies were fundamentally real. At the heart of things, beneath all differences of opinion, there was oneness.

> Though your views are in straight antagonism to theirs [Emerson advised his fellow transcendentalists], "assume an identity of sentiment. . . . You will never do yourself justice in dispute. . . . But assume a consent and it shall presently be granted, since really and underneath their external diversities, all men are of one heart and mind.[7]

To Emerson this was truth, not paradox. Conflict he might stress, as in the statements with which this section began, but an underlying unity was always to be understood. These opposites, conflict and unity, lay always in the two pans of the balance with which the philosopher of "compensation" was accustomed to weigh the universe.

For the cultural approach to history this duality of emphasis

[3] "The Lord's Supper," *Works,* XI, 24.
[4] "Prudence," *Works,* II, 238–39.
[5] "Self-Reliance," *Works,* II, 51–52.
[6] Henry David Thoreau, *Walden,* in his *Writings* (Boston, New York, 1906), II, 190.
[7] Emerson, "Prudence," *Works,* II, 239.

has a significance that I feel is generally missed. Historians have been ready enough to connect the mood of dissent or rebellion in New England letters with the forces of change at work in society. But for these writers' correlative emphasis upon unity, scholars have been content to seek a philosophical rather than a social origin. What is sauce for the goose is sauce for the gander. If we examine society for the sources of a critical tendency in literature, can we refuse to look there also for explanation of a monism equally characteristic?

The fundamental unities of New England life, in other words, are as important as the disunities for any complete explanation of its cultural flowering. Emerson's own intellectual history demonstrates this. As the great creative period of New England waned, he became increasingly aware that it had been influenced by deep-lying concords as well as by those critical, questioning tendencies he emphasized in his "Historic Notes." Alongside the satisfaction he expressed in 1844 at the "heterogeneous population crowding on all ships from all corners of the world to the great gates of North America,"[8] one must place his bitter words to Carlyle twenty years later concerning "the wild Irish element, imported in the last twenty-five years into this country, and led by Romish Priests, who sympathize, of course, with despotism."[9] The Calvinism that he described in 1834 as a "sucked eggshell"[10] appeared to him a quarter of a century later as a necessary foundation of that cultural unity without which the literature of his generation could never have achieved greatness. "I sometimes think," he wrote James Elliot Cabot in 1859, "that you & your coevals missed much that I & mine found: for Calvinism was still robust & effective on life & character in all the people who surrounded my childhood."[11] And the man who had resigned his pulpit rather than administer a rite which he could not do with his whole heart, voted as a Harvard Overseer for the retention of

[8] "The Young American," *Works,* I, 370–71.

[9] *Correspondence of Thomas Carlyle and Ralph Waldo Emerson,* ed. by Charles Eliot Norton (revised ed., Boston and New York, 1884), II, 322.

[10] Emerson, *Journals,* ed. by E. W. Emerson and W. E. Forbes (Boston and New York, 1909–14), III, 324.

[11] Emerson, *Letters,* ed. by R. L. Rusk (New York, 1939), V, 145. This letter was called to my attention by Professor Perry Miller, who quoted it in the original discussion on which this chapter is based.

compulsory chapel.[12] Emerson, it seems clear, acted primarily to preserve those elements of unity which in earlier days he had been inclined to underrate, but whose passing, he felt, had had something to do with the decline of New England's greatness.

Such experiences as these—and they are important, of course, only if they prove upon fuller study to be in a measure typical —suggest both a hypothesis and a method of investigation for the student of cultural history. The hypothesis is simple. A society does not flower if it is torpid; that is, its highest expression does not arise from the mere unchallenged accumulating of tradition On the other hand, it does not flower if conflict strikes so deep as to rend apart the fabric of ideas and institutions, and interrup communication and common understanding between conflicting groups—as has happened in many unhappy eras of human history and as was to happen in America in the decades that followed Bleeding Kansas. Cultural flowering, in other words, occurs only at a moment when the traditions of a society, still alive for mos of its members, are challenged by forces, material or intellectual that are powerful enough to threaten, but not powerful enough immediately to destroy, the social unity of which the tradition are part.

If this hypothesis is valid, then from it follows logically a pos sible technique for the cultural approach to history. Instead o concentrating either upon the evolution of tradition or upon th evidences of change and conflict, the historian might well direc his attention primarily to the equilibrium between them. Wha types of balance have existed in periods of cultural flowering Within what minimum and maximum limits of intensity mus each component force be confined, if an equilibrium of this typ is to be maintained? Without setting as a goal any formulatio of quantitative laws, something might be learned by comparin New England in its period of flowering with colonial New Eng land on the one hand, and New England after the Civil War o the other, in terms of such factors as homogeneity of populatio extremes of wealth and poverty, degree of urbanization, and tot size in proportion to existing facilities of transportation and con munication. The situation in New England during its flowerin would undoubtedly prove to have been a mean between extreme

[12] Cabot, *Memoir*, II, 629–30.

The nature and the limits of that mean position could profitably be investigated.

Proceeding more subtly and less mechanically, the historian might well reëxamine, in the light of the hypothesis, those very cultural and social conflicts that seemed so shattering to contemporaries. Unitarianism and transcendentalism, which denied the Trinity and questioned even the Christian miracles, nevertheless preserved much more of the Protestant tradition than contemporary controversialists admitted. Utopianism, especially of the Fourierist variety, though denouncing the existing organization of commerce and the private control of productive wealth, would expropriate no one, would deny to no factor in production its reward, and would spread its system only through voluntary limitation. Abolitionism and the homestead agitation—two bogeys of Northern conservatives—proved in the end not incompatible with the basic concepts of the economic order in which these conservatives believed, but became, rather, allies in its spread.

To explain a changing world, the historian has often looked most closely at things that themselves were changing. The cultural historian, however, must guard against treating the forces of social change as absolutes. He must see them in their context, must weigh them against the things that at the moment were not changing. In the balance, perhaps, he may find the truest explanation of such a phenomenon as the flowering of New England. And is it too much to hope that out of such studies may also come some guidance for society amidst the conflicts of today?

The Social and Economic Characteristics of the Leaders

MERLE CURTI

Why did New England "flower" just when it did? This is the sort of question to which historians can never give a definitive answer, because the factors involved are so complex that no reasonable hypothesis could be proved right or wrong. Nevertheless proximate answers are worth seeking, because it is not by proved facts alone that historians make progress—interpretations are also important.

He who asks the question, why did New England flower when it did, will not find the answer in the brilliantly descriptive pages of Van Wyck Brooks. True, a few of his pages do throw light on the problem, and in his conclusion he ventures to offer a kind of explanation which apparently did not satisfy him, for he did not push it very far. One gathers that, so far as Brooks thought about the problem at all, he had in mind some Spengler-like notion of "the soul of the culture-city." He even speaks, vaguely, of rhythms and cycles. More penetrating, certainly more concrete, is his suggestion that New England enjoyed a homogeneous culture, and that her sons felt that this belonged to them, and they to it. Suggestive, also, is the idea Brooks touches on, when he intimates that the New Englanders had never entirely abandoned the old Puritan dream of a City of God, a land in which spiritual values became real. He calls attention, quite properly, to the fact that the Puritans and their descendants were given to writing, to reading, to study. They knew their Bible, their classics, their sermons; they kept their journals and diaries. They prized education. A people with such a bookish and other-worldly tradition would naturally produce intellectual leaders, and some unmanageable, quixotic souls. Van Wyck Brooks also makes something of the idea that the long-cultivated New England soil was in the early 1800's newly fertilized by contacts with the outside world, especially with the romanticism of Germany and France. Many studies have already explored these relationships, and we are in need of additional investigations.

But even if one grants that these were powerful influences, and I think they were, we must still explain why the flowering did not come several decades before it did. The reason in part may be found in the fact, which Parrington makes much of, that New England, under the guidance of her orthodox clergy, throttled the Enlightenment in an almost hysterical furor against all its values. Had the Morses and the Dwights and their kind not closed their gardens to the fertile seeds which the French-driven winds were scattering, the older Puritan habits of intellectual discipline, emotional intensity, and speculation might well have been transformed in the last decade of the eighteenth and in the early years of the nineteenth centuries. But this is, after all, an "if," and our problem is to explain not why something else did not happen, but why what happened, happened when and as it did.

One could make a good deal of the argument that New England flowered when it did because many New Englanders had found by the 1820's and 1830's that they had something to live on in the way of accumulating capital. The young men most ambitious economically were going West or establishing mills and factories. Those most ambitious for fame through literary and reform activities were enabled, by family support, to indulge their whims. The trouble with this thesis is that it is too simple. There were fortunes in New England long before the 1820's, and conceivably young men from some of the well-to-do merchant families might have turned in larger numbers than they did to literature and scholarship. Moreover, capital and leisure were also available in the middle states; and yet nothing that appeared there in the second quarter of the nineteenth century was comparable to that which emerged in New England. Nor should one, by the same token, make too much of the fact that by the twenties and thirties New England had cities and libraries, lectures, and the stimulus of intimate social contact, for this was also true of the middle states.

Yet it may well be that the social-economic approach does provide a key, if it is not oversimplified and if it is not pushed too far. Assuming that it might, I have examined the social and cultural backgrounds of the sixty persons to whom Van Wyck Brooks devoted more than passing mention. Of the fifty-one for whom I could without extensive search find data regarding their own economic status, seven were poor, or came from poor families, seven were well-to-do, and thirty-seven intermediate. Of the fifty-four for whom parental occupations could be readily found, eleven came from agricultural families, eleven from commercial families, two from industrial families, and thirty from the professions, with the clergy claiming eleven out of the thirty, the law eight, medicine five, and education four. Of fifty-nine, forty-one had been graduated from an academy or high school, and three had attended such a school for a time. Only three had had less than a full grammar school education. These data suggest that the men chiefly responsible for the flowering of New England were of the middle class, that they came largely from professional and mercantile families, and that they profited from the superior educational advantages associated with their segment of the middle class. The overwhelming majority were neither poor nor rich, but in between.

These data do not in themselves prove that the flowering was a middle-class phenomenon, for, as we have suggested, a similar middle class could be found in the east Atlantic states between New England and the Mason and Dixon line. But when the affiliations of the men whose achievement brought such distinction to New England are considered along with their religious affiliations, it is clear that the Puritan tradition is an important leavening influence. Out of forty-three, twenty-one were Congregationalist, twelve were Unitarian, three Presbyterian, two were Friends, two Episcopalians, and one Baptist. Of all the New England denominations, Congregationalism and Unitarianism thus provided the largest number of contributors to the flowering. The weight of the Congregationalists and Unitarians is out of proportion to their ratio to New England's population, if one relies on the unsatisfactory data of the census of 1850. It appears, then, that the men responsible for the flowering of New England were largely middle class and largely the immediate descendants of Puritans rather than Anglican or of such evangelical sects as the Methodist.

In this fact we have, perhaps, a clue of some importance. The religious and professional backgrounds of parents provided a strongly intellectual and idealistic environment for the children who grew up in such homes. The fact that so few were neither poor nor rich meant that it was not necessary to struggle with the bitterness of poverty nor to find playboy pastimes. The roots of the awakening, clearly, are in the intellectualistic tradition of Puritanism and in the middle class.

But the rising middle class was not homogeneous. The intermediate groups with idealistic, religious backgrounds were not likely to look with entire complacency on the materialism of the merchant, the banker, and the entrepreneur. Nor was the economic middle-of-the-road and religiously trained man apt to regard with equanimity all the social ailments which the emerging industrialism brought in its wake. The practice of the middle class failed to correspond with its ideal. Its ideal implied that merit always succeeds, that the good man is always provided for, that sobriety, industry, and frugality are always rewarded. It implied the doctrine of inevitable progress.

Such ideals and the facts at hand did not square. The ministrations of the Rev. Joseph Tuckerman and others of the time demonstrated that many slum dwellers were victims of environments beyond their control. And while the accumulated wealth of the upper strata in the middle class did enable New England cities to enjoy libraries, lectures, and the like, the plain fact was that the great and successful in the middle class only too often took on airs, or else abandoned themselves to crass materialism. Such conditions made for conflict in the minds of seriously educated people, and out of the conflict arose protest.

To these Puritans, protest might mean embarking on reform crusades. Or, if their temperaments were not those of reformers, they could seek in the pursuit of culture compensation for the materialistic emphases of the society which was, on the whole, indulgent toward them. In romanticism, in European culture, in transcendentalism, they could reconcile a conflict between their devotion to the old Puritan idea of righteousness and their loyalty to the middle class, which gave them much while it also irked their sensitiveness by its materialism and by the fact that its ideals did not square with its practices. The literary members of the middle class, in other words, could enjoy the opportunities provided by that class for travel, for study, for the publication of books, for the giving and hearing of lectures. They had enough of worldly goods, but not enough to glut sensibilities, to surfeit with materialism. They could enjoy their own pleasant leisure and inward glow; but while others lacked the necessities, they could not be complacent unless they found complete escape in culture. Those in a similar position, to whom mere culture was an inadequate compensation, could take the path of reform.

To put it another way, the rediscovery of the beauty of righteousness and of cultural values corresponded in point of time with the advanced state of education, at least in relation to other sections, with the patronage of a well-to-do class, with sufficient support to follow the intellectual life, and with values in the middle class that enlisted their support. But the rediscovery of the beauty of righteousness also stimulated the literary and reforming men responsible for the flowering to solve a conflict between their class loyalties and their ideals, a conflict born of the gulf between class ideals and practices on the one hand, and the Puritan afterglow on the other. This was a dynamic situation. It set a stage congenial to great acting and to great drama.

Boston's Puritan Heritage and Its "Flowering" in Literature and Theology

RICHARD H. SHRYOCK

It is to be assumed that there is something unusual about the "flowering" of New England as compared with the cultural attainments of other parts of the United States. If not, there is no reason why such a title should be employed; one might just as well discuss the efflorescence of the whole seaboard. Granting this, the explanation of the unusual achievement of New England for the given period (*c.* 1830–60) must be found in certain factors—or in combinations of factors—which were more or less peculiar to the region.

Economic influences were certainly at work. One can hardly imagine that the cultural level attained in the Boston area could have been built on anything less substantial than the rapid growth of wealth and population there, which was in turn based upon the whole expansion of trade, industry, and economic factors in general. These developments, however, were not in any way peculiar to Boston. Both New York and Philadelphia excelled it in these respects in this period. In like manner, political influences may have played their part in the story—the advantages of national unity, and so on—but there was nothing very unusual here in the Boston experience. Again, international contacts doubtless proved stimulating to the Bostonians—scholars seeking German libraries and doctors walking the wards in Paris—but such contacts were not unknown to other Americans.

What was peculiar to Boston, apparently, was not its economic, political, or international experience, but rather its religious background. Calvinistic Puritanism, with its moral and social implications, "carried on" in one form or another into the nineteenth century, and even those leaders who consciously revolted against the tradition can hardly be explained without some reference to it. Calvinism, to be sure, was shared with the Scots-Irish Presbyterians who were so influential in portions of the South, but in that section there were no urban centers comparable to Boston and hence less of an economic basis upon which to rise to higher things. Nor was there the same cultural unity in the South as obtained in New England. Perhaps one should say, therefore, that the Boston achievement was to be explained by the survival of a particular religious tradition in a homogeneous society and during a period of increasing economic advantage—a combination not found to the same degree in any other center in the land.

Calvinism, to begin with, stressed a tradition of learning. A learned clergy was essential, even in a wilderness Zion: hence Harvard College. Compare this with the Philadelphia story, where Quaker influence—with its stressing of the "inner light"—was long dominant. No one seems to have believed that the inner light needed a college education. A learned clergy preaches and writes, and preaching and writing soon became an essential part of the Puritan way. So, too, did that "New England conscience" which was at least in part an expression of Calvinistic zeal. The Boston leaders were still preaching, writing, and searching their souls on social reform in 1850, albeit in a more liberal and refined manner than did their forbears of 1700.

If this religious explanation of New England flowering is valid, one would expect to find negative as well as positive evidence in support of it. There were phases of culture in which the Puritans of Massachusetts did not excel, and in which they therefore did not hand down an especially strong tradition. Most obvious were the fine arts and the sciences. There was music in eighteenth-century Boston and science as well, but it is doubtful if one could claim any preëminence therein for this city. What is more to the point, the same thing may be said for the Boston of the best days—not its music, nor its painting, nor its architecture, nor its science was clearly superior to what could be found in these respects in either New York or Philadelphia. Indeed, preëminence might well be claimed for the latter two centers in certain given fields and periods.

The peculiar Boston flowering, then, was an important but

somewhat limited achievement in three major phases of culture: that is, in liberal theology, in literature, and in certain phases of social reform. Why, then, was this city so frequently viewed as the chief center of American culture in general—as "the Athens of America"? The answer is not far to seek. Those particular phases of culture in which Boston was more or less outstanding happened to be those which made the widest appeal to the educated public throughout the nation. The Americans of 1850 were still relatively a theologically minded people. In the North, at least, they were all likely to be caught in the current of humanitarian reform. And of all the arts and sciences, literature was by far the best known. There was some popular interest in music, and in science for that matter, but nothing comparable to that in *belles lettres.* The poet Longfellow was the friend of every school child, but the biologist Joseph Leidy was pretty much unhonored and unsung outside his own profession. Oliver Wendell Holmes, *both* a poet and a biologist, was known only in the former role, despite the superiority of his brilliant medical essays over most of his effusions in verse. In noting the popular appeal of literature, moreover, it should be recalled that this included the historical writings of the period; for history was then viewed as a branch of literature, rather than as one of the social sciences. New Englanders wrote the history of the land as well as its novels and verse, with the result that a New England version of our national story became widely current and survives to some extent to this day. All this added greatly to the popular reputation of the section.

What we are dealing with in this flowering of New England, therefore, is not simply the objective course of human events between 1830 and 1880, but also a subjective question as to the meaning of "culture." Defining this in sufficiently narrow terms, it may well be claimed that New England—or, more exactly, the Boston area, for Maine, New Hampshire, Vermont, and Rhode Island contributed virtually nothing—developed a culture superior to any other center in that day, and that it did so largely by virtue of the Puritan heritage. Literary historians can cite chapter and verse for this claim. But all this will have to be reconsidered on a broader scale if we extend the denotation of the word culture to include the other arts and sciences which now, at least, seem so significant. One may sum up the whole matter by observing that New England once excelled in cultural achievement, by the simple device of defining culture in terms of those things in which New England excelled.

Connecticut's "Flowering" in Science and Reform

C. R. KELLER

Insofar as intellectual achievements, Unitarianism, and transcendentalism constituted the "flowering of New England," this phenomenon was confined to a very limited area. It was not the flowering of New England, but only of a narrow section of eastern Massachusetts.

My special field of interest is Connecticut, where, in the first half of the nineteenth century, there was no transcendentalism, practically no Unitarianism, and no literary figures such as those who flourished in Concord and Boston. It occurs to me, therefore, that it will be worth while to consider some aspects of life in Connecticut which distinguished it from eastern Massachusetts and which might help to explain the flowering of the latter area. Parenthetically, let me say that the various humanitarian reform movements, also included as part of the flowering by the definition upon which this discussion is based, were widespread in Connecticut and will be considered later.

Connecticut differed from eastern Massachusetts in that Unitarianism was practically nonexistent within its borders. Only one Congregational church, Samuel J. May's church in Brooklyn, became Unitarian. This was no accident. Connecticut Congregationalism under the Saybrook Platform had a much more cohesive organization than the Massachusetts brand of New England Calvinism. There were the General Association and the county associations to which only the ministers belonged, and the important consociations in which the laymen figured. At the end of the eighteenth century religious leaders in Connecticut—and in other parts of the country, including eastern Massachusetts—were roused by the spread of infidelity let loose by the eighteenth century in general and by the French Revolution in particular. There developed in Connecticut and elsewhere what I call the Second Great Awakening. A remarkable series of revivals occurred, out of which came missionary, Bible, tract, and education societies, as well as Sunday schools. In Connecticut the embattled Congregationalists, with their effective organization, repulsed the invasion of unorthodox religious ideas, of which one form was Unitarianism. In eastern Massachusetts the Congregationalists also rallied and fought Unitarianism. But they were not so successful as their Connecticut neighbors. Literary achievements and transcendentalism thus appeared in an area where Unitarianism more than held its own in the religious struggle.

Another difference between Connecticut and eastern Massachusetts was that the former had Yale and the latter Harvard. Yale, under Timothy Dwight (1795–1817) and Jeremiah Day (1817–46), was closely allied with the Congregationalists and fought on the religious front against all forms of infidelity. Harvard, under John T. Kirkland (1810–28) and Josiah Quincy (1829–45), was more liberal theologically, and this helped to create the atmosphere in which Boston and Concord—Cambridge too—peopled with Harvard graduates, flowered. Yale, moreover, had no one comparable with Professor Edward Tyrrel Channing, who taught rhetoric at Harvard from 1819 until 1851 and who included among his students Emerson, Holmes, Lowell, Thoreau, Edward Everett Hale, James Freeman Clarke, Henry W. Bellows, Thomas Wentworth Higginson, and Richard Henry Dana, Jr. Professor Channing taught his students in a way quite uncommon in those days. Edward Everett Hale wrote of Channing,

> But Edward Tyrrel Channing, brother of the great divine, met his pupils face to face and hand to hand. . . . You sat, physically, at his side. He read your theme aloud with you,—so loud, if he pleased, that all of the class who were present could hear his remarks of praise or ridicule.[13]

Professor Kirkland has described the economic conditions which environed the flowering. Attention should be called to the fact that the economic developments to which he alluded were characteristic of the eastern end of Massachusetts and not of Connecticut. The railroad which bound the seaboard to the state of New

[13] Edward Everett Hale, *James Russell Lowell and His Friends* (Boston, 1899), pp. 18–19.

York ran through southern Massachusetts. Connecticut remained predominantly agricultural. In 1850 nearly 100 of the state's 148 towns were almost entirely agricultural. The value of the hay crop in 1845, as J. M. Morse has pointed out, "surpassed the appraisal of cotton and woolen goods, the two most extensive manufactures, by a million dollars." [14]

It should be noted, too, that Connecticut was much less in the world than eastern Massachusetts. The extent to which the flowering in the latter section was due to literary and transcendentalist developments in Europe has been passed over too lightly in the previous statements. Many of the intellectual leaders of Boston and Concord went to Europe and brought European culture back with them. Some of them corresponded with European literary figures. Connecticut young men, on the other hand, remained at home, with the exception of those who, like Benjamin Silliman, went abroad to study scientific developments. Connecticut had contact with Europe—especially England—through the religious publications from which the people learned about religious activities across the Atlantic. Connecticut's Second Great Awakening of the nineteenth century was much like England's Evangelical Revival of the eighteenth century, and Bible societies and missionary societies were modeled on similar institutions previously established in England.

Enough has been said to indicate why there was a flowering in eastern Massachusetts and not in Connecticut, insofar as the flowering comprised literary accomplishments, Unitarianism, and transcendentalism. But another aspect of the flowering was included in the definition here used, namely, the various humanitarian reform movements. In these Connecticut, as well as eastern Massachusetts, participated. Connecticut people supported the American Colonization Society and later the more radical aspects of the antislavery movement. Heman Humphrey, of Fairfield, Lyman Beecher, of Litchfield, and Calvin Chapin, of Rocky Hill, all Connecticut clergymen, were pioneers in the prohibition movement, while Beecher's daughter Catherine made significant contributions in the field of female education. The first deaf and dumb asylum in the United States was established in Hartford

[14] Jarvis M. Morse, *The Rise of Liberalism in Connecticut, 1828–1850* (New Haven, 1933), p. 3.

in 1817. There was also interest in prison reform and the peace movement, and in caring for the poor, widows and orphans, and the blind. Very important among the causes of these humanitarian reform movements was the renewed religious spirit which constituted the Second Great Awakening. Thus humanitarianism and reforms rose from the same source which helped to exclude Unitarianism from Connecticut.

There were in Connecticut during the first half of the nineteenth century people who were speaking loudly and clearly the language of John Calvin. As has been pointed out, under Presidents Dwight and Day Yale was the most important center of science in New England. Benjamin Silliman, founder of the *American Journal of Science,* and James Dwight Dana, who established the science of mineralogy, were as much a part of the flowering as Thoreau or Longfellow.

PART SIX: SOURCES AND MATERIALS FOR THE STUDY OF CULTURAL HISTORY

INTRODUCTORY NOTE

NO HISTORIAN, whatever his aim, can free himself from the limitations placed upon him by his materials. Any suggestion for methods of historical analysis and attention to aspects of society other than those to which the usual sources give access must meet the challenge, "Where are the materials which will throw light on these new problems and how may these materials be exploited?"

Many of the previous chapters of this book give a partial answer by the materials upon which these chapters are based. Other chapters pose problems and state hypotheses but do not indicate the sources in which evidence to solve those problems or to test those hypotheses may be found.

The types of material required for use by the cultural historian must have certain characteristics. These materials must throw light on mass behavior as well as on the behavior of individuals; they must reveal activities not ordinarily a matter of formal record; they must deal with the inarticulate as well as the articulate groups in society; they must make it possible to reach down into the home and community where the details of life are lived. Such materials, moreover, require techniques other than those commonly used to exploit the materials to which the historian is most accustomed. Techniques necessary for the critical examination of documents are of limited usefulness in dealing with mass data; methods of exploiting media other than the customary literate sources are essential to an understanding of non-literate groups; many of the concepts indicated in the preceding chapters constitute new tools with which to order and find meaning in both familiar and unfamiliar data.

The first two chapters of this section consider the process of writing history "from the bottom up," through the use of local materials and a local focus and through exploiting population data to reveal mass behavior. Local materials are among the easiest and the most difficult of access; local histories have often been merely antiquarian compilations, but occasionally have demonstrated the rich possibilities for interpretation available in local analysis. The treatment of local history in the first chapter of this section indicates the kinds of materials and the techniques for their use calculated to make the writing of local history yield rich results.

The treatment of population data in the following chapter indicates the ways in which these data may be drawn upon for an understanding of mass movements and mass behavior. Individual accounts of the settler, the migrant, or the farm boy making his way in the city may be set against the record of mass migration; individual genealogies acquire cultural meaning in terms of the birth and death rates and family types which characterize the society; the history of particular communities and areas may only be understood in the light of knowledge as to whether the population was increasing or decreasing, what its age composition was, and its rate of turnover.

The last five chapters consider sources by which to tap the culture of non-literate groups. Each of the media here discussed—folklore, folk music, documentary photography, speech, and Latin verse—has been customarily studied by specialists other than historians who have used these materials primarily for other than historical purposes. These chapters, therefore, contain not only a discussion of these materials, but some indication of ways in which they may be exploited through coöperation between specialists in those media and cultural historians.

THE VALUE OF LOCAL HISTORY

CONSTANCE McLAUGHLIN GREEN

FOR any true understanding of American cultural development, the writing and study of American local history is of primary importance. There lie the grass roots of American civilization. Because of our varied population stocks and their sharply differentiated cultural inheritances, the widely differing environments which the United States includes, and the rapidity of changes in our economic life, the problems confronting the social historian assume mighty proportions. American history in the past has been written from the top down, an approach feasible enough as long as scholars were content to write only political and diplomatic history. But the necessity of studying American life from the bottom up becomes obvious for the cultural historian. The story of how American people have lived as individuals and as communities must be told by details.

It is evident that detailed material may be assembled in various categories by various schemes. Data extracted from a specific locality are clearly local materials, but they may be used for a topical study which includes a number of separate communities. For example, a compilation of school laws and their educational effects in many widely scattered towns and cities may be multiplied until the historian has at hand the basic materials for generalization upon American education of a given era. Again, a study of one aspect of life in a particular community must employ local sources, as in the examination of the race relationships of a southern town, past and present. Still there remains the use of local materials for the study of a specific community in its entirety.

Such a study, local history simon pure, becomes the life history of a community. The student, using the local materials, sets himself the task of following out all the significant factors in the community's history and evaluating their relative importance. Confined within a frame imposed by geographic or jurisdictional limits, his study may be a complete social and economic history in miniature. In the focusing upon one locality, local historical research may make a peculiar contribution to American cultural history.

Obviously "locality" may be interpreted with considerable elasticity. Any community having clear geographic or cultural unity, however extensive in area, may come within the terms of any reasonable definition. Demarcation by political jurisdiction can be regarded as an accident growing out of a fundamental geographic and economic unity, although it is true that political administrative unity, once established, tends to exert an enduring cohesive influence which affects cultural evolution. The unit may be a scattered agrarian community—a county in Georgia, even the Great Plains of Webb's illuminating book—or a concentrated urban group, a region or a colony within a city. Not only a history of Chicago but a history of Greenwich Village within New York City comprises local history.

More thorough examination of local materials, whether directed at separate community life histories or at wider topical studies, is needed for adequate American cultural history. Our social history, as written to date, has been inaccurate in detail and lacking in pattern because generalizations have been based upon insufficient evidence and criteria. For example, it has been assumed that the West has been peopled by the push from the East. Immigrants, even peasants eager to take up farms in the Middle West and the Great Plains, have been supposed to have landed at Ellis Island and to have moved thence westward. Local studies indicate that numbers entered the port of New Orleans and headed north and west from there. Similarly, much of western New England was invaded direct from the Connecticut River and Connecticut ports, sometimes via Boston, sometimes not. Again, careful local studies in Kansas demolish the whole frontier population-movement thesis. A study of Cincinnati, in course of preparation by Daniel Aarons, suggests that the universal religious piety of America of one hundred years ago, as described by historians, is a myth.

In the field of American economic history there are many topics upon which specific information is badly needed to supply data for generalization. Since ours has become largely an industrial civilization, problems of the relations of capital and labor are manifestly important in their bearing upon American culture. We need local studies of conditions of labor and changes in the social status and attitudes of work people; exact histories of capital accumulation in various communities; the emergence of varying types of business leadership; careful analyses of the growth of that vague entity we call the American middle class; detailed examination of population movements from one community to another, whereby might be found surer clues to the whys and hows of labor migration. Without a number of thoroughgoing studies of individual localities, generalization upon these subjects must remain mostly guesswork. The inadequacy of business history has been recognized by scholars of late. Recently this situation has been partly corrected by detailed attention to individual business firms, but local histories of business communities must prove invaluable in meeting this want more fully.

Still more striking is the gap in our knowledge of the cultural role of the "statistically numerous, nondominant groups." The cultural historian early becomes aware of the difficulty of gauging the attitudes and influence, even the behavior, of the great mass of the inarticulate in America. Even the best local studies to date have contributed little there. Students of American life have sensed the weight of these groups, but an evaluation of their importance and effect upon cultural development has scarcely been attempted. Anthropological studies such as Hortense Powdermaker's *After Freedom* [1] may indicate the way and offer useful material for interpreting the present. But the problem of reconstructing and understanding the vanished past, of which few specific written records exist, is even harder. Class antagonisms, religious rivalries, emergence of a sense of social responsibility are admittedly essential elements in cultural evolution. Yet about these questions the most rigorously selected Gallup poll of the nation could elicit little valid information, since responses inevitably would derive from the articulate groups only. Hence the wisdom of localizing studies, seeking to cope with such tenuous and fragmentary data as must suffice for the interpretation of the way of life and modes of thought of persons who rarely wrote

[1] Hortense Powdermaker, *After Freedom, A Cultural Study in the Deep South*, New York, 1939.

letters and whose opinions have found scant expression in the press. Cultural history may not ignore these people. Careful collecting of scraps of evidence about them by the local historian would appear to be the surest means of viewing the character and significance of their part in the American scene.

Many of the topics listed in early paragraphs can be dealt with by the use of local materials without any special community focus. But for the effective interpretation of data dealing with the fugitive, evanescent stuff of the nondominant, inarticulate groups, the historian must consider the local setting with attention. Certainly by marking out a particular community for study, the probability of his achieving accuracy in depicting behavior and in gauging influence is greatly increased. Furthermore, I suspect that it is upon the mass of the inarticulate in American society that effects of environment are likely to be most marked. And to trace the influence of environment, natural and cultural, it is virtually essential to have a definite locality under the historian's microscope.

What are the peculiarities of environment which appear to impose a behavior pattern upon the people of one community differing from that of another? Why or wherein does a lumbering town in Maine differ from a lumbering town in the state of Washington? What makes a farming district in Iowa a contrast to one in Mississippi, a Waterbury, Connecticut, distinct from a Detroit and a Flint? Is the principal differentiating factor the difference in nationality stock, or the diversity or homogeneity of the population, the age or youth of the settlement, the accessibility to or remoteness from other communities? What are the effects of disparities of soil and weather conditions? The social historian must seek more than true pictures of American life as it has been; he must endeavor to explain the process, why it took those forms, what the directing forces were. Analysis of the natural and cultural environments of many communities, examined locality by locality, can best answer these questions with any certainty.

But emphasis upon local differences can induce confusion rather than clarity of any view of the whole of American cultural history. Multiply the number of studies in which differences are stressed, and the result might well be merely greater difficulty in finding any broad pattern for the whole. We must also seek similarities. We need to establish categories of communities, classified probably by general region and then by type within each. Perhaps the Turner sectional thesis may be usefully applied. May we not assume some fundamental geographical unity for each section of the United States? A tentative plotting of regions should be helpful, with a number of studies projected in each. As such studies progress, it might happen that some of the regions would be shown to have been falsely plotted. A shift would then have to be made. For example, one might project a local study in Maine as part of the industrial New England section, only to find that it belonged more nearly in the category of agrarian Michigan. The analysis of why that situation obtained might be illuminating.

In each region the various types of community should be studied, the agrarian areas, the agricultural market towns, the transshipping depots and commercial communities, the manufacturing cities, the lesser financial centers and the true metropolis of each section, mining towns, college towns as centers of intellectual life, perhaps artists' colonies, suburban communities, summer resorts. Possibly even trailer camps, as manifestations of the nonlocalized elements of American society, should be included. The fact that one locality could be characterized as belonging in several of these categories at one and the same time might prove provocative of valuable investigation. Certainly the rise of semi-industrial, semiagricultural communities, whether of the type of Henry Ford's vision or other, suggests a trend demanding study. Series of such local studies, compiled region by region, should furnish means of estimating the validity of the sectional thesis. And meanwhile such tentative classification should be a useful guide to the student of any individual locality.

For some vision of the relation of the local fragment to the whole, regional, national, or world-wide, is essential, if the local historian is to make his chronicle significant. American local history as written in the past has been so exclusively localized as to appear to have no meaning for any community but one. American town and county histories are legion. Scarcely a village founded over seventy years ago but has its own local chronicle. But self-glorification or antiquarianism, or both, have dominated their pages. The lack of perspective, the inability to see his own town as part of a larger community, has often made the local biographer's labors nearly sterile. Determination to paint his home town as a Garden of Eden, to enlarge upon the virtues of its leading citizens, and to portray its achievements as unparalleled, has rendered his work unsound and generally dull. The antiquarian's history, on the other hand, may be exhaustingly accurate in its detail, but the conclusions he derives from his lengthy factual compilation, if indeed he attempt any, seem lacking in any importance. Still, to the antiquarian's industry and enthusiasm the scholar with wider vision may be deeply indebted. While the genealogical tables and minutiae of property transfers as listed by the antiquarian, or his accounts of minor local episodes may in themselves be meaningless, from that detailed factual array the historian, gifted with perspective, may evolve a significant story. For example, genealogical tables, linked to data relating to occupation, activity, wealth, and participation of persons listed, should prove invaluable in following out the concentration or dispersion of capital in a community and in tracing the development of prestige groups. Detailed accounts of real-estate transfers might give clues to the emergence of special vested interests and serve to show that the venturesome, risk-taking pioneer business man, dear to American tradition, was rather a cautious soul whose shrewdness consisted only of gambling on a sure thing, a rise in land values. The antiquarian's findings supply the raw material which, digested and presented in connection with other data as part of a pattern, can tell a story of deep social import.

The historian who aspires to write local history from the broader point of view must supplement the antiquarian source with a great variety of other materials. He may well employ field study techniques, as worked out by the sociologists. Inasmuch as the historian, in contrast to the cultural anthropologist, must be concerned less with the immediate present than with the developments of the past out of which the present grew, one particularly useful borrowed device may be the questionnaire, or interview directed at some three different age levels. The social historian then has spread before him the reflection of the changes of attitudes of nearly one hundred years. Derived from one locality where natural environment can be assumed to be identical for all, such information may reveal the effects of the time factor. Unlike political history, cultural history is less a chronicle of deeds and misdeeds than a survey of human feelings and attitudes of mind and interrelationships. Personalities are of its very essence. The interpretation of these demands personal contacts. And, let me repeat, a definite setting for persons as part of the community in which they live makes that interpretation easier and surer.

For locating documentary evidence, the quantities of records being listed and described by Works Projects Administration workers on the Historical Records Survey will be of enormous assistance to the local historian. Specific methods of finding and evaluating additional local materials must be evolved by the ingenuity and common sense of the research worker. Careful mapmaking of the locality may reveal graphically startling truths. Assisted by the town directory—particularly if occupational data are included—and aided by lists of assessors' valuations and lists of directorates of local enterprises, the student can readily plot out a map of his community which will be thought-provoking. The juxtaposition of facts not before observed in any close connection, geographic or otherwise, should indicate further lines of inquiry. This method of finding and using material, possible to employ in a study of only one specific community at a time, emphasizes again the value for social history of a local focus. Other kinds of information are sometimes turned up in unexpected places. Travel books may offer interesting comparisons between one city and another and point the way to significant relationships. Not only news items and comment in the local press but changing types of advertisement over a span of years may bring to light facts and tendencies not easily observable elsewhere. Even the kinds of patent-medicine advertisement and the matrimonial-bureau notices might give clues to the habits of thought of a bygone generation. Collections of sermons, showing changes of theme over a period of years, the lists of acquisitions for the public library year by year for several decades, if such lists have been preserved, lists of membership of social clubs and fraternal organizations—these are merely a few of the sources which the alert local historian may tap.

The obstacles in the path of the student of local history in his search for material are, however, frequently disheartening. They may be those of the historian in any field: lack of evidence upon particular subjects, inaccessibility of material, opportunity to secure only data obviously unreliable, not representative, or irrelevant. But the special difficulties which the local historian encounters are born of the local character of his inquiry.

The first of these peculiar problems grows out of public indifference to his undertaking. Much of his material is likely to be in private hands. But who cares about the sources of the familiar local scene? Everyone knows about that. We threw out Grandfather's papers twenty years ago; they were a nuisance. Homely things are too close to be of interest. It seems unnecessary to give the research worker either full or especially accurate information. A little free advertising certainly, only let it be calculated to portray the family and the community in the most favorable light! There is likely to be a certain unconscious condescension on the part of local residents in dealing with the seeker for local historical light. He is marked as a person of little importance in the scholarly world. Else why should he concern himself with such trivia as this local story? Scholars write about the fall of the Roman Empire or the history of slavery or the theater in Shakespeare's time. Ergo, let's turn off this inquirer with the suggestion that he look in the public library.

Paradoxically, the local historian next confronts the antipodal difficulty of being at the mercy of the town wiseacres, who are convinced that Podunk is vitally important and that all that is significant in its history is at their tongues' tips or to be found among their family papers. And the result may be distortion for the historian, in spite of his best efforts not to be deceived. By way of illustration: when the Federal writers were collecting data for one of the state guide books, in one town the research man was frostily received by local leaders; only one small industrialist was at pains to be informing to the WPA writer. When the guide book appeared, the rest of the town's business men discovered with a shock of annoyance that their town was described as having only one important industrial enterprise, the establishment of the genial host who had talked so graciously to the writer.

Along with obstacles arising from public indifference and misconceptions are perhaps even greater ones growing out of fear.

Dead men tell no tales, and locked records reveal no unsavory secrets, no facts open to misinterpretation. Particularly does this point of view prevail among prestige groups, notably among business leaders. The business man has felt himself the special quarry of the academic and of reformers. In an endeavor to trace the growth of capital in a community, the student perhaps seeks access to corporation books which show the capital setups over a period of years. Not infrequently his request will be refused. The heads of the companies may explain: "Doubtless you as a scholar would be fair. If you found that for years we had paid stockholders 10 percent in dividends and that yearly we put back 25 percent of earnings into upkeep and expansion, you might not accuse us of greed. But how do we know that someone else wouldn't pounce on such facts in your book and cry, 'Bloodsuckers! Those profits should have been paid out in wages'? It is too risky." Evidence which might be used in derogation of business men as a class, even of the business pioneer of three or four generations ago, must be suppressed, lest it prove subversive of the social order. To combat that attitude is as necessary as it is difficult. Again, fear may close the mouths of the individuals best qualified to give information. Their jobs or their standing in the community they may feel to be jeopardized by revelations. No promise of anonymity will induce them to speak. The smaller the community the more likely are such personal apprehensions to exist.

Yet in spite of the probable closing of some avenues of inquiry, the local historian is only too likely to be overwhelmed by the mass of material available to him. We have the advantage over the European local historian in that rarely, if ever, are the origins of an American community so remote that patience will not suffice to produce fairly clear evidence of its beginnings. Gaps in the sources for the earlier periods there often are, and in later periods data may be so hidden as to prove difficult of access. More often, however, the problem of sources becomes one of choosing the significant. For the American local historian the chief problems consist of weaving together into meaningful pattern the numberless strands that go to make up an American community. How is the student to sift out the essential? Familiarity with the characteristics of the category into which his locality may be expected to fit gives him at once some basis of selection. A series of questions of why and how, as well as whence, must be perpetually before him. In using the answers he may work out, he must constantly ask himself: "So what?" It is wise to stress this point to the novice in local historical research—and here most of us are still novices—since more than in most fields the multiplicity of petty detail may easily obscure any larger vision. Why did Mechanicsville specialize in tool manufacture when a village ten miles downstream remained a dairy center—geographic factors, personality forces, accident?

In examining materials and presenting findings, recourse to the sampling method should be useful. The futility of trying to study in detail all the institutions, movements, and trends in a community seems self-evident. Which appear to conform to the pattern of the general classification the investigator experimentally assumes, which run counter to the type? Judicious selection from the mass may be determined by the existence of comparable material in another community, although unhappily the paucity of competent local histories makes the employment of the comparative method today enormously difficult. Only by comparison are the uniquenesses born of environment or of heredity to be seen. What are the features that are peculiar to any one community? What are shared by its neighbors? How significant is the unique, and what special circumstances created that uniqueness? If so, why? What is the unifying core? Sampling, however, may well be used without comparisons with another locality. The student will find it reasonable to restrict his analysis to the three or four churches that have obviously determined the religious atmosphere of his town, as he may then infer why other groups withered away. He may confine his investigation to the most vigorous of the local industries instead of attempting to study all, and within the principal industries he may trace the course not of all the companies but of the strongest, the weakest, those nearest the middle. Let him also, however, heed the failures, the ventures which proved ill-adapted to his town. For him as a historian, study of the non-successes may be as important as examination of the successful dominant. In part, his intuition must guide him in his selection of materials and in his relative emphasis in presentation. He must be sufficiently part of the community he is scrutinizing to be able to understand what has importance and meaning for its citizens and why. Perception of the values that obtain in his community should serve as a guide.

Indeed some feeling of oneness with the community of which he writes, some sympathetic comprehension of its attitudes, is probably an essential factor in writing sound local history. Many an unjustly hostile twist can be given to facts viewed by an alien observer. Local historians should write not only for the initiate and for the compiler of general history, they should also write for the local public. For "a knowledge of its own past is essential for any community to achieve cultural adulthood." History for the historian alone would be like law for the lawyers or the church for churchmen. If historians are to continue to pose as teachers, they must consider who is worthy of teaching. As citizens of a democracy, can they afford to disregard their neighbors in order to speak only to Lowells and Cabots?

Grant that the historian should give local citizens opportunity to gauge the part their community has played in the national drama; grant that justified local pride, coupled with critical judgment of a community by its own citizens, is a socially constructive force; nevertheless, since the local public will not read drearily written, dry history even of its own past, must the scholar lower himself to the level of the public mind? In answering this query, we may well quote the late Ulrich B. Phillips, "There is no law against having history interesting." The popular and the scholarly are not necessarily incompatible, although for wide popularity the writer must doubtless stress the colorful. And it is only when the community is aware of the interest and value of its local history that it will coöperate intelligently in making accessible the sources of that history. Such coöperation is frequently all-important. The public may find much of the truth about its past unpalatable, but it must also find such rough fare more nourishing than the sweet adulteration often dished up by the untrained enthusiast, to whom American local historical writing has been largely relegated.

The professional historian's disdain of the nonprofessional has not been conducive to the writing of better local history. Today the outstanding achievements of Works Projects Administration writers and workers on the Historical Records Survey should show the feasibility of enlisting the aid of the professionally untrained. But wider professional recognition of the importance of the field of local history is also needed. In writing cultural history, local historical research must take rank as a basic discipline.

THE USE OF POPULATION DATA

The Historical Context of Population Study

FRANK LORIMER

THE social sciences have developed as technical contributions (1) to general social theory and (2) to specific problems presented by the changing course of events in the modern world. The latter orientation has in general proved the more fruitful, being more conducive to critical inductive studies. Criticism of methods and implications has led to more technical research on fundamental issues. In any case, the development of the social sciences has been strongly influenced by their historical context. These tendencies are clearly apparent in the development of population studies.

Population study, as conceived by the founders of the Royal Society in 1662, was humanistic, diversified, and technical, developing in close association with the natural sciences. Halley's application of the calculus to the problem of survival gave us the life table, a corner stone of modern demography. The *Political Arithmetick* of Sir William Petty, recently invoked by Lancelot Hogben in presenting a collection of valuable population studies,[1] and Graunt's *Bills of Mortality* were kindred in spirit.

Population studies after the time of Malthus suffered eclipse through association with classical economic theory. The treatment of population remained theoretical, and interest was focused on a single phenomenon—the growth of population in relation to natural resources, especially land, as the basis of food supply. This concentration of attention naturally reflected the dominant trend of population change during the eighteenth and nineteenth centuries. This was the period of the most rapid population increase in world history. The people of Europe and their descendants increased from about 100,000,000 in 1650 to 700,000,000 at the present time—the era of European colonial expansion and the "great white peril" to the rest of the world. The population of

[1] Lancelot T. Hogben, ed., *Political Arithmetic; A Symposium of Population Studies*, London, 1938.

Asia also increased more rapidly than in previous centuries, but lacked the technical facility to protect itself against European expansion. To most Europeans these developments seemed only normal and presented no special problems for research; but some scholars, following Malthus, saw in this rapid increase of people the seeds of present and future misery. The last and perhaps most dramatic expression of these fears was set forth by Professor E. A. Ross.[2] It was customary to refer to "the population problem," meaning the pressure of population on resources. Little attention was given to scientific studies of the impact of technology and urban life on mortality and fertility.

Decline of fertility began at about the same time in France and in New England, at the beginning of the nineteenth century. It was followed by similar trends in the other nations of Western Europe about seventy years later, and more recently in industrialized areas in the East. This led to a new type of speculation, especially in France, and to practical efforts both for extending and for combating the trend toward smaller families. Interest in population, however, remained theoretical or humanitarian, with little technical advance. The Malthusian thesis was replaced by an equally attractive and sterile concept, the theory of "optimum population."

The systematic investigation of differential population trends in their dynamic interrelation with economic and social phenomena, the crux of contemporary population study, is a development of the last two decades. Serious attention to variations in the density of population, in relation to economic resources in various regions within as well as across national boundaries, and the significance of internal migration is also a new development. These interests are stimulated by and associated with movements for the social control of economic life, national and regional planning, and the development of more comprehensive social-political philosophies. The analysis of differential population trends becomes a matter of more than academic interest. In a world in which the most technically advanced nations are tending toward cessation of population growth and rapid population decrease while areas with low economic levels are characterized by rapid natural increase, and in which some social groups are having less than one-half the

[2] Edward A. Ross, *Standing Room Only?* New York, 1927.

number of children needed for replacement of the parent stock while other groups are still characterized by primitive reproductivity. Concern about national population trends is becoming a motive force of major political importance in many countries. Present population changes must also be investigated in their relation to maladjustments and strains in the present economic order. Population study offers one critical and objective avenue of approach to the understanding of current social changes. There has, therefore, been a remarkable growth of scientific population study in recent years.

The first responsibility of the modern demographer has been to develop satisfactory methods of measuring population change. Crude birth rates and death rates are very unsatisfactory for this purpose, because in large part they reflect variations in age distribution. For example, in the United States in 1937 there were only 11.2 deaths per 1,000 total population, but such a death rate would correspond in a stationary population, with normal age distribution, to a mean expectation at birth of 89.3 years, which is obviously absurd. A moment's reflection shows that the particular age structure of a population is a function of past birth rates and death rates, modified by migration. A stationary population with a high rate of births and deaths will have a large proportion of children and a relatively small proportion of aged persons, as compared with a stationary population with a low rate of births and deaths. An increasing population will tend to have a large proportion of children and a small proportion of aged persons, since the latter are the survivors of birth to a much smaller parent population. It is possible mathematically to determine the *normal* age distribution of the population corresponding to any particular set of age-specific fertility and mortality rates. This makes possible the calculation of *intrinsic* rates of birth, death, and reproduction, apart from the temporary influence of the particular age structure of the population. This technique was first fully described by Louis I. Dublin and Alfred J. Lotka in 1925.[3] It is also possible to show the future development of population on various hypotheses regarding the trend of birth rates and death rates, by applying age-specific survival ratios and fertility ratios

[3] "On the True Rate of Natural Increase as Exemplified by the Population of the United States, 1920," *Journal of the American Statistical Association*, XX, no. 150, n.s. (1925), 305–39.

to the constituent parts of any actual population. Population forecasts, as developed in this way by Warren S. Thompson and P. K. Whelpton and others, have far greater range and accuracy than the extrapolations of total population growth previously in use. Much progress has also been made in the accurate measurement of internal migration. These technical developments are dependent for their application on accurate basic data, which are available with increasing adequacy through the progress of census procedures in the United States and other civilized nations, and through supplementary field studies.

Population study still has slight academic status, outside of a few advanced institutions. It has been carried forward chiefly through the interest of independent scholars, foundations, social science institutes, and governmental agencies. The professional associations for the advancement of population research are all very young. The International Union for the Scientific Study of Population Problems was founded in 1931, and the Population Association of America in 1932.

Historical demography has, as yet, received little attention, but a survey of recent titles in *Population Index,* the current bibliography of population studies, shows a considerable and growing interest. This is not surprising. There has been much demand for population forecasts, but little public clamor for historical demography. Then, too, the inadequacy of the statistical data usually available for earlier periods is often discouraging, and at best makes large demands on the patience, ingenuity, and restraint of the scholars engaged in such studies. Nevertheless, as population policies become a subject of broad popular interest and as population studies advance, it becomes increasingly important to analyze population trends in their full economic, social, and cultural context. In this task, population research must be fortified by broad historical perspective. It is therefore evident that population studies are likely to profit more and more through historical research and, it is hoped, will more and more merit and receive the attention of competent historians.

Medieval Demography

JOSIAH C. RUSSELL

To the student of demography, the Middle Ages offer both peculiar advantages and disadvantages.[4] They contain the one long and fairly continuous period of depopulation available for careful study, which, since we seem to be approaching another decline, should be of exceptional interest to us now. In the terrible Black Death of 1348–49, there occurred probably the worst single epidemic suffered in historic times. During the period an increase of population took place from about 1000 A. D. for several centuries and was resumed after the adjustment to the Black Death was finished. In these variant developments can be studied the effects of such population changes upon the general course of history.[5] The paucity of sources for the early half of the period is a serious disadvantage, but this is remedied to some extent in the latter half. The actual course of population movement may be followed with fair certainty on account of the sharpness of movement. The long period of population decline from about 200 A. D. to about 700 or later was also a period of economic depression and of the development of the Catholic church to a position of predominance in European society. This coincidence raises a question in regard to their mutual effect.[6] Is it not possible that man's failure on earth may have turned his attention to the supernatural and caused him to entrust his life to those who claimed special power from the divine? May not celibacy be a rationalization of depopulation, and monasticism a rationalization of both depopulation and depression? Is not the saint as the highest type of man, according to the opinion of the Middle Ages, indicative of an age of material failure consoling itself in religion? Thus large questions about the effects of declining population are raised,

[4] For a discussion of the subject, see my "Medieval Population," *Social Forces,* XV (1937), 503–11. I have not seen A. Schück's *Befolkning under Medeltiden,* Oslo, 1938.

[5] General opinion has inclined to regard population as a result of economic and other forces, rather than a cause. For some exceptions, see A. Losch, "Population Cycles as a Cause of Business Cycles," *Quarterly Journal of Economics,* LI (1937), 649–62; H. P. Fairchild, "When the Population Levels Off," *Harper's Magazine,* CLXXVI (1938), 596–602.

[6] I have discussed this more at length in "Decline of Population, 200–700 A. D. and Its Intellectual and Social Consequences," *Communications Présentées, VIIIe Congrès des Sciences Historiques* (1938), II, 508–10.

which are well worth the attention of historians and demographers.

Following this period of decline came a period of increase, which should have reversed the tendencies induced by the period of decline. We have the cultural lag to consider here. Ideals change slowly, even though material conditions alter. So we find that the new wealth often, even usually, went into monastic and other ecclesiastical developments, so that a mighty age of church building ran from about 1100 to 1400. Only gradually did the secular spirit arise in what we usually call the Renaissance, probably because the Black Death set back population increase just when its influence upon European culture was beginning to make itself felt. Fortunately this period saw more forms of taxation, which yield information about trends in population: the poll taxes in England, hearth taxes in France, Spain, and elsewhere,[7] and descriptions of land known as extents.

England has better demographic sources than other countries, mostly at the Public Record Office. Much depends upon whether it is possible to use with any degree of precision the extents, describing numbers and classes of landholders, with occasionally the actual names of such tenants. Fortunately some of the poll-tax returns list persons by houses, so that it is possible to secure light upon the number to a house. By comparing these with numbers of tenants in extents of the same villages, it is possible to say that usually there was a house to a tenant, which makes the extents much more valuable. These include Domesday, the Hundred Rolls, and thousands of documents of lesser importance.[8]

The English are fortunate also in having another good source of demographic information in the inquisitions post mortem, which give the ages of heirs as well as the time of death. From these can be secured information about expectation of life and about times of birth and death. By combining the use of these inquisitions with the evidence of gross population from poll tax and extents, the adjustment of England to the Black Death can be followed. This disease recurred at intervals in epidemic form

[7] Beloch was much interested in population, especially in Italy. A part of his study has appeared posthumously as *Bevölkerungsgeschichte Italiens,* Berlin, 1937.

[8] During 1938–39, upon grants from the Social Science Research Council and the Penrose Fund of the American Philosophical Society, I studied these problems in England and have in preparation a study "British Population, 1066–1550."

and gradually became endemic before it died out for a time in the fifteenth century. Because of its terrible incidence and epidemic form, this allows us to examine the experience which mankind must undergo to make adjustment to any new disease. For this alone (rather than for its more morbid characteristics) this evidence deserves the closest study.

In the matter of migration, medieval developments often paralleled the early American. Professor Thompson has pointed out the similarity of the German expansion eastward to the American frontier experience.[9] The British advance into the Celtic regions of Wales, Scotland, and Ireland is also parallel in many ways, with their trading-post forts, constant border warfare, and mutual diffusion of ideas of conqueror and conquered. Only in the British Isles can one see the release from pressure upon the Celts, due to the ending of rapid population increase with the Black Death. European culture also saw migration from the countryside to the rising city, creating a greater trade and industrial development. Migration thus often affected the course of European states.

In the study of the demography of the Middle Ages, the student must bring information derived from unconventional (and therefore suspected) sources; from sociology, biology, and statistics, among others. Medievalists, confronted often by the poverty of information available, will not hesitate to accept the offer of data from unusual approaches to their history. Demography should assist in the exploration of many areas of medieval knowledge which are little known today. On the other hand, the demographer has a real need for information about the course of population in times of whose sources he is no master. The outlining of the human adjustment to the Black Death would be of great value to him. Knowledge of the effects of declining population would be stimulating in planning for future demographic policies, policies which occupy increasing attention from modern nations as time goes on. The coöperation of demography and history in the medieval field thus promises a great advance in human knowledge.

[9] James W. Thompson, *Feudal Germany*, Chicago, 1928.

The New South, 1880–1936: A Study in Population Movements [10]

RUPERT B. VANCE

Population movements constitute the mass aspects of a process that history has to deal with on a more selective basis. The decisions of leaders in peculiar political, military, or economic situations rest on the broad basis of mass movements, concerning which historians are always conscious but rarely specific. Nevertheless, history and population study have their temporal and spatial dimensions in common. History as narrative is concerned with the flow of events; demography, in studying the reproduction of generations, is concerned with the flow of population through time. The historian must delimit his area of operations on the map, usually in terms of a political area; and the demographer must study regional migration, the flow of population across the map. Both groups have their methods, and both, accordingly, have their ideas as to the perfect sources of data. The historian longs for the perfect set of primary documents, for he has methods of piecing documents together to create history. Mass phenomena are well fitted for abstraction and visualization by mathematical methods, and the demographer longs for the perfect series of statistics, delimited in space and time. From vital statistics, from statistics of migration, from the records of that decennial shutter, the Census, which periodically snaps population on location, the demographer visualizes the mass flow of the people as they move across the map and down the stream of time. Whether viewed from the collective or the selective aspect, it is just possible that their materials give historian and demographer more in common than they have yet realized.

The following discussion briefly summarizes the type of population information that is available and basic to an understanding of the historical development of a region in recent times, the "New South."

Into each region population flows by the entrances of birth and

[10] To a large extent, the treatment of this section is based on the work of the Study of Population Redistribution and the writer's *Research Memorandum on Population Redistribution within the United States,* Social Science Research Council, New York, 1938.

immigration. Out of each region, population flows by the exits of death and emigration. The level attained by these flows gives us an ever-changing regional balance of population. Such a view sees the region as a reservoir and views population movement, the migration into or out of the region, as an index of important economic and social changes.

The Southern population has taken part in three great migrations: one agricultural and two industrial. These are (1) the expansion westward of the Cotton Kingdom; (2) the great interstate migration to the northeast and middle states; and (3) the population movement to the region's own cities. The first is a familiar theme of historians of the Old South. It was characterized by the continued position of the East as a reservoir of population. In 1850 Virginia, the Carolinas, Kentucky, Georgia, and Tennessee were losing population by migration. By 1870 Alabama had become a state of net outward migration, to be joined by Mississippi in 1880, Louisiana in 1890, and Arkansas in 1920.[11]

The migration history of the agricultural areas appears to follow a uniform pattern.[12] About three decades after the first settlement, the immigration surplus reaches a maximum, and, after about three more decades of decreasing surplus, emigration sets in. This pattern is made clear by mapping states of surplus and deficit migration, from the state-of-birth data offered in the Census.[13]

A second movement from the Southeast has been the great interstate migrations to the northeast and middle states. It is difficult to realize the extent to which industry and cities have drained the population increases of the nation's countrysides. Before the depression, approximately 40 percent of farm youth, aged ten to twenty in 1920, had moved to towns and cities by 1930. Nearly 55 percent of the nation's rural migrants landed in four great metropolitan districts, those of New York, Chicago, Detroit, and Los Angeles.[14]

Migration to the rising industrial towns and cities of the New South has offered a third outlet for an increasing agricultural popu-

[11] Carter Goodrich, and others, *Migration and Economic Opportunity* (Philadelphia, 1936), Plate I-A, p. 676

[12] C. Warren Thornthwaite, *Internal Migration in the United States*, Philadelphia, 1934.

[13] W. S. Thompson, *Research Memorandum on Internal Migration in the Depression* (New York, 1937), p. 15.

[14] Thornthwaite, *Internal Migration*, pp. 32, 28–30.

lation. To gauge the force of this movement, we need figures on rural-urban migration that no bureau yet gathers. The rise of new cities and the growth of old ones in the South offers one familiar measure of this movement.

Differential rates of reproduction by social-occupational classes furnish the unequal flows into regional population reservoirs. The inflow of differential reproduction is largely from agricultural and lower skilled labor groups and reaches its highest point in the Southeast. Reproduction in inverse relation to economic condition can be shown for the whole country by regions, economic areas, social occupational groups, and by size of community, from the open country to the large metropolis. In 1930 the Southeast, Southwest, and Northwest held one-third of the population. This third, located in regions of lower incomes, accounted for 55 percent of the total natural increase in population from 1930 to 1935. The Southeast, with slightly over 20 percent of the 1930 population, accounted for almost 36 percent of the increase. The great industrial areas of the Northeast and the Middle States plus the Far West, possessed of 66 percent of the population, accounted for only 45 percent of the total increase.[15]

Although the Southeast has consistently been an area of emigration for many decades, the outward migration has not been sufficient in volume to offset the rapid natural increase of the region. In fact, the proportional emigration from most of the Southeast has been lower than that from the areas of slower natural increase in New England and the Middle Atlantic States from 1880 to 1930. As a result, although the Southeast has attracted relatively few migrants from other regions, there has been a rapid accumulation of population through retained, nonmigrant natural increase.

Population flow in its East-West, South-North, and rural-urban movements has followed lines of economic attraction. J. J. Spengler has used migration data in correlation studies of the rank of states in per-capita income, net replacement of native white population, and other factors of demography, migration, and cultural and economic status.[16] He finds, in general, that native-white migration has moved: (1) from states of lower to states of higher per-

[15] National Resources Committee, *The Problems of a Changing Population* (Washington, 1938), p. 120.

[16] J. J. Spengler, "Migration within the United States," *Journal of Heredity*, XXVII (Jan., 1936), 3–19; Tables I–III, pp. 8–10.

capita income; (2) from states that have a predominantly extractive economy (agriculture, forestry, and fishing) to states with a predominantly industrialized economy; (3) from states in which the true rate of natural increase is high to states in which it is relatively low.

Not the least among the many forces that have decreased the employment capacity of agriculture are the loss of many of agriculture's traditional tasks to the newly emerging industrial sector; the substitution of industrial for agricultural products, as coal-tar dyes for indigo and madder root, rayon for cotton, gasoline for oats (the substitution of gasoline for oats, hay, and corn fed to animals in the nation has resulted in releasing some 18,000,000 crop acres once devoted to growing feed [17]); increased output per agricultural worker, accompanying the shift of agricultural production from unfavorable to more favorable areas,[18] improvements in plant and animal breeding, and the increased mechanization of farms.

If this movement accounts for the push out of agriculture, changing employment capacity in other economic sectors accounts for the pull of the urban-industrial environment before 1930. Until 1920 the increasing proportion of gainful workers in manufacturing showed that the employment capacity of industry was increasing each decade, as an increasing output per worker met an increasing per-capita demand for industrial products. Moreover, until 1930 the trend of employment in the clerical, service, and professional group had been upward in many fields, for increasing demand had met improvement in quality of services but not a sustained increase of output per worker.

Migration in response to the pull of industry has not, however, been frictionless. "Sentiment, poverty, lack of knowledge, indecision, race barriers, and other restraints counteract the incentives which would lead people to seek new jobs, new homes, new occupations." [19]

Rural-urban migration has reflected both the push of agriculture and the pull of industry. Agriculture has undergone a long-

[17] Z. V. Pettit, *The Farm Horse,* Bureau of the Census, Washington, 1933.

[18] Karl Brandt, "The Employment Capacity of Agriculture," *Social Research,* II (1935), 1–20.

[19] H. Bowen, "Population Mobility and Economic Recovery," *Sociology and Social Research,* XXI (1937), 404.

time trend of diminishing employment capacity, because increasing output per worker has met no increased per-capita consumption of agricultural products and has met a declining export demand. For a long time forces have been operating to expel labor from agriculture. In 1887 it took nineteen people on the land to furnish the food and fiber supplies for one person in town. Now nineteen persons on the farm supply fifty-six persons in the urban United States, and five to ten persons abroad.[20] The percentage of the total employed population to be found in agriculture, fishery, and forestry, has declined from 72.3 percent in 1820 to 52.8 percent in 1870 to 21.3 percent in 1930.

Like populations, industries themselves have a way of moving across the map. Extractive industry must be located close to the sources of its physical resources, but manufacturing which assembles materials from many sources may well afford to move in search of markets and labor supply. The historian will, no doubt, seek some way of relating the migration of industries to the problem of his regional area. The movement of industry by communities, as measured by the proportionate increase in wage jobs, has been largely a diffusion from the center to the suburban periphery of established manufacturing areas and into counties of moderate industrial concentration. Interregional movements have taken place by the formation of new areas of concentration, rather than by dispersion into nonindustrial areas.

A survey of the proportionate gain in wage jobs from 1899 to 1933 indicates that the greatest gains were in the suburbs of the main industrial cities, followed by the 200 industrial counties of less concentration. The great bulk of the other 2,900 counties, containing 90 percent of the farming population of the country, had in 1933 only 27.0 percent of the industrial wage jobs. In 1899 they had 26.8 percent. The increased industrialization of the country, up to the present time, apparently has not meant the dispersion of industry through the nonindustrial areas.[21] It will be noted, however, that the 200 "industrialized" counties were chosen on the basis of 1929 conditions. In 1899 some of these counties were not industrialized; a few were not in existence. If the calculations had been based on a list selected as of 1899, the formation of new

[20] *Technological Trends and National Policy,* National Resources Committee (Washington, June, 1937), pp. 97–145.

[21] D. B. Creamer, *Is Industry Decentralizing?* (Philadelphia, 1935), p. 10.

areas of industrial concentration could have been presented as "dispersion." Gary, Indiana, it will be remembered, had not been formed in 1899, while Greenville and Gaston, textile counties of the Carolinas, existed only as areas of scattered industry.

History must also take account of the alternating cycles of depression and recovery, as they influence population mobility. In the main, one concludes that the effect of economic cycles on internal migration in the South or any other region has centered largely on rural-urban movements, which prosperity operates to accelerate and depression to slacken or reverse. With present birth rates and employment trends as before the depression, the push of agriculture—the normal flow of internal migration—is urbanward; but when the pull of industry becomes a push, migration flows to rural areas, even though agriculture be also depressed.

Depression has temporarily reduced Southern emigration, but the permanent slackening of this historical population movement is likely to occur only if the effects of continued industrialization on the area are combined with a sharply falling rate of population increase. Among all these changing conditions, it will be realized that birth rates themselves have not remained a fixed quantity. The rate of reproduction is now falling most rapidly among those groups in which it has been highest. Although the crude death rate in the Southeast from 1917 to 1936 has fallen from 14 to 10 per 1,000, the gap between birth rate and death rate has been decreased by a fall in births from 30 to 20 per 1,000 in the twenty-year period.

The contemporary materials which population students are now exploiting are slowly changing into background materials for the future historians of the New South. It is to be hoped that history as an art will secure the documents to infuse life into some of these movements, which in their treatment at the hands of demographers and statisticians have seemed somewhat desiccated.

Local Historical Studies and Population Problems [22]

JAMES C. MALIN

As a historian participating in the discussion of population studies, the first aspect I wish to emphasize is one of materials and procedure. For the most part, demographers have drawn upon the mass figures of the printed Census when dealing with the United States. Necessarily these are net figures, which do not reveal the contradictions or differences existing among the component elements of the population or among the local units other than the arbitrary political subdivisions into states and counties. The behavior of one element in the population or local unit may be canceled by that of another, or the net result of the mass data may be determined by the decisive behavior of a relatively small element of the whole. As in outline surveys or general histories, it is writing from the top down and partakes too much of the fitting of generalizations to particular cases rather than arriving at the generalization from the study of the underlying detail. Not only does American history as a whole need to be written from the bottom up, but population studies, as an aspect of history, need such treatment. The mass statistics tell only part of the story, and it is necessary to balance one type of procedure against the other, recognizing that both are essential to a complete and balanced treatment of population problems.

The local-community approach makes possible the analysis of units small enough so that they can be dealt with in the entirety of their behavior. As people do not live their lives in separate compartments—economic, social, cultural, or religious—the study of history and of population behavior must be envisioned as a whole. As single communities are small enough to make comprehensive studies practicable, but too small to afford the basis for generalization, a number of sample communities may be selected, each of which may be studied separately, and then the samples grouped together in sufficient numbers to afford a reasonable basis for statistical validity. The materials for such local studies are varied, including records of local government, of probate of wills

[22] The author wishes to acknowledge assistance from the Graduate Research Fund of the University of Kansas and from the Social Science Research Council, in financing the agricultural investigations upon which this section is based.

and settlement of estates, of churches, of schools and other organizations, of private diaries, newspapers, and so forth; but for population problems, in particular, land records and, most important of all, the original Census schedules, the manuscript record as it was taken down name by name, family by family, in the periodical enumerations by house-to-house canvass under either state or Federal authority, are appropriate. Kansas has taken a decennial state census from 1865 to 1925 inclusive. These are deposited in the Archives Department of the Kansas State Historical Society, Topeka, and the society has also the Federal Censuses of 1860 and 1870. All are open without restriction for the use of students of population problems. By statute, the Federal Government has closed the later Federal Census records to use by any but government employees. As decennial enumerations such as those of Kansas have not been made by the states generally, and as Kansas has abandoned its census,[23] it is highly desirable that the Federal Census records be opened for the use of accredited private investigators.

The present writer is engaged upon local studies, employing the materials and procedure described above, and some of the possibilities may be illustrated from results already published or in progress.[24] The studies of migration of population based upon mass statistics emphasize increasing interstate migration and mobility, while the local Kansas farm population studies demonstrate a high degree of stability of farm operators. The Kansas communities studied seem to pass through three stages: the frontier period of extremely rapid turnover, a second period of relative stabilization at low levels, and a third stage, entered upon by the older eastern communities about 1915, of a high degree of stability, which increased after the World War. The younger western com-

[23] Partly because of the overshadowing of the state by the extension of Federal activity and partly as an economy measure, Kansas abandoned its census in 1935, thereby breaking the continuous record of population data.

[24] James C. Malin, "The Turnover of Farm Population in Kansas," *Kansas Historical Quarterly,* IV (Nov., 1935), 339–72; "The Adaptation of the Agricultural System to Sub-humid Environment," *Agricultural History,* X (July, 1936), 118–41; "The Kinsley Boom of the Late Eighties," *Kansas Historical Quarterly,* IV (Feb. and May, 1935), 23–49, 164–87. Cf. A. D. Edwards, *Influence of Drought and Depression on a Rural Community: A Case Study of Haskell County, Kansas,* Farm Security Administration, Social Research Report No. VII, 1939, Washington, D. C. This study by Edwards applied the procedure of the present author, together with some improvements which were suggested by experience with the pioneer project.

munities of the semiarid west followed essentially the same pattern as the eastern communities sampled, but had not reached the same community age or quite the degree of stability of the older samples. The important point is that, for any given community age, the rate of turnover was essentially the same for any rainfall belt, whether in the humid east or the semiarid west. Seemingly the mass statistics and the local studies lead to opposite conclusions but in fact they are both valid. This is a striking instance of the importance of rounding out population studies by utilizing both approaches, and placing the whole in its historical perspective.

The Federal Census data on interstate migration is particularly defective because it records only the state of birth and the state of residence at the time of the particular enumeration. Attempts to measure, from mass statistics drawn from such sources, the volume and direction of migration cannot trace removals from state to state between these dates. These difficulties have been recognized, but not to their full extent, because there have been no means of filling the gaps, even in part. The Kansas state census enumerations, 1875–1925 inclusive, however, give both the state of birth and the state from which migration was made to Kansas. It is thus possible to scan the lists, name by name, and determine the numbers respectively who migrated direct or migrated by way of another state or states. In the case of large families, it is possible to go a step further in analyzing the indirect migration and, by examining the birth states of successive children, to trace with surprising completeness the record of the migration of such families through several states.[25] For present purposes, however, the discussion is limited to the simplest classification into direct and indirect migration from state of birth.

As Kansas is 400 miles long, reaching from the humid Missouri River to the semiarid high plains, sample townships were selected in seven successive stages of the westward push of population. In this way, if there are any substantial differences in the relation of these successive frontiers to the sources of migration, they should be revealed. The percentage curves follow the same general pattern, however, the proportion of direct migration rising after 1875 to a peak and then declining, the decline being quite sharp

[25] The manuscript Federal Census records, if they were open to investigators, would afford opportunity to make studies by means of this child-birth data.

after 1915. The principal difference in the curves is found in the exact date at which the high point of direct migration was reached. In the three successive groups of sample townships in the eastern third of the state, the high point is registered in the census of 1895, which means that this migration had reached its climax during the eighties and early nineties. In the central third the census of 1905 is the high point, and in the high-plains third, west of the one hundredth meridian, the crest was recorded in 1915.

Two types of conclusions may be drawn from these facts: first, regarding the nature of the migration; second, regarding the birth-residence index. On the first point, between the Civil War period and the high point in the direct migration curve, the migration to Kansas was increasingly of a type of people who had not been on the move before—obviously they were relatively stable people, in the sense that they had not wandered permanently from the state of birth. On the other hand, since those high-point dates, in increasing proportions the migrants to Kansas were of a type who had been on the move, to the extent of at least one removal prior to the census in which they were found in Kansas.[26]

Further analysis of direct native migration, on the basis of whether it came from substantially contiguous states (Nebraska, Iowa, Missouri, and Arkansas) or from noncontiguous states, reveals that the movement from contiguous states was a relatively small proportion of either the total native migration or of the direct migration until the census of 1905 and after, varying somewhat with the groups of samples. The movement from noncontiguous states was much the greater and for the most part increased in proportion to the whole native migration, following much the same curve as the total direct migration except that the peak and reversal of trend were reached in some groups about ten years earlier. By 1915 in some samples and by 1925 in others, the contiguous migration had increased to such an extent as to exceed the noncontiguous movement in the extreme eastern and extreme western samples. From its nature, the birth-residence index, based on the Federal Census, cannot give any indication of this fluctuation and composition character of interstate migration. It is evident that since the decline set in for direct migration to Kansas

[26] Neither of the above statements deals with intrastate movement, either in the state of birth prior to removal to Kansas or within Kansas after arrival.

from the state of birth, the birth-residence index has become more and more defective for Kansas and for any other state that may possess similar characteristics. For satisfactory migration analysis, it is essential to determine whether comparable changes took place or whether behavior was substantially different in other sections of the United States.

This analysis possesses significance for evaluation of the Turner frontier interpretation of American history, by which individuals are represented as following successive frontiers, each new frontier being peopled by the last adjacent frontier. None of the results for Kansas studies conform to this simple formula. At the peak, direct migration constituted 46 percent to 60 percent of the native migration in the several samples, and over 50 percent in four of the seven groups; and direct migration from noncontiguous states accounted for approximately half of the native migration at the highest point of its flow. If the increased direct migration is explained, as some of the Turner school have suggested, by the consolidation of railroads which promoted long-distance movement, then the still greater efficiency of transportation in later periods does not explain the reversal of the trend.

Still another aspect of population movement may be studied by tracing the succession of people who occupy any given community. Either the manuscript census records or local land records afford the material for such studies.[27] From the standpoint of sectional sources, emigrants from New England or from the lower South found difficulty in establishing themselves in Kansas and were rather easily displaced by Mid-Western native or foreign farmers. Farm occupants of urban origin likewise found difficulty in competition. Probably the most significant consideration from the standpoint of American agriculture is the outcome of racial competition. Negroes and Jews usually failed to maintain themselves as farm operators, while Germans, Scandinavians, and Czechs, those European rural immigrants among whom love of the soil was conspicuous, usually drove out Anglo-Americans, who to an increasing degree have lost their soil-hunger under the influence of urbanization of the United States and inefficiency in economic competition.

[27] A. B. Hollingshead, "Changes in Land Ownership as an Index of Succession in Rural Communities," *American Journal of Sociology*, XLIII (March, 1938), 764–77. Hollingshead used land records for this purpose, in a study of Nebraska communities.

There is no general appreciation of the extent to which these foreign racial strains influence or even dominate the agriculture of the trans-Mississippi West,[28] and only in part have the first and second generations of the native-born been sufficiently Americanized to lose the soil tradition. To what extent have the migrant American farmers, emphasized by mass statistics, been these native Americans who have failed in competition? To what extent have drought and depression been excuses, rather than reasons, for this migrancy, along with monopoly, trusts, railroads, money, and other traditional agrarian issues? There is peculiar irony in the fact that the operation of governmental policies over the last half century or more, in subsidizing the American tradition of the family-size farm, have aided these immigrant strains in the process of displacing the native Anglo-American farmers.

The manuscript census materials open new possibilities for the analysis of the internal structure of society, as well as of its population movements. In interpreting American history in terms of the frontier hypothesis, generalizations have been formulated which are in themselves contradictory, but so superficial have been the critical examinations of the composition of frontier populations that the inconsistencies have passed almost unchallenged. If the movement to new lands had been that of individuals migrating through several successive frontiers, then necessarily the newest frontier must have been composed of mature people. Yet it has been asserted more insistently that the frontier was young, composed in large measure of young married couples just starting out in life to grow up with the country, their children in turn to begin life on a newer frontier. Studies of farm operators in Kansas demonstrate a relatively normal age distribution. The median ages for men in 1860 (within six years of first settlement) was about thirty-five, and later Kansas frontiers to the westward (the fourth and fifth rainfall belts) were thirty-six and forty respectively. As the communities matured the median ages advanced, in some cases as much as ten years, then declined for a time, and between 1915 and 1925 most of the samples turned slightly upward again, but not above the earlier highs. In general terms, it might be said that the median age of farm operators stabilized between forty-three

28 The role of Asiatics on the Pacific Coast and of Southern Europeans in New England agriculture has received more attention.

and forty-five and that fluctuations were within a comparatively narrow range. In age distribution, the number of men under twenty-five was very small, and even the bracket twenty-five to twenty-nine was altogether too small to conform to the youth formula of the frontier hypothesis. On the other hand, the fact should be emphasized that, in samples of similar community age, the farm operator of 1925 was not older than the farmer of 1885 or 1895.

In the United States general interest in population problems is not only of recent origin, but it has spread under the influence of the abnormal conditions of the depression of the 1930's and has been too closely associated with social and economic planning. Some of the work has been scientifically and objectively done, but much of it, being inspired by a cause, has been controlled largely by zeal in promotion and defense of a particular type of social policy. Historians have neglected this type of investigation, and much of the work is in the hands of those belonging to the presentist school, who scorn history and tradition. Yet, without historical perspective, even the most careful investigators may misinterpret their results. The question of migration, discussed above, is a case in point. Many sensational things have been written about migrating farmers during the present depression, and grandiose schemes of resettlement have been proposed and some inaugurated. In the light of historical studies of farm communities, however, the Kansas farmers have achieved for the first time in history a high degree of stability. The sensational exploitations of migrant farmers deal with an extremely small minority, most of whom are of the type which in earlier times always have been on the move in larger relative numbers. The remarkable thing about this present depression, from the standpoint of population movement, is the relative minuteness of the volume in comparison with previous historical periods, either before or after the passing of the frontier. The fact that the Turner hypothesis has been used extensively as a justification for social planning, as a substitute for the frontier, gives particular pertinence to the fact that much that has been claimed for the significance of the frontier in American history does not bear investigation.

The rapid turnover of frontier population and the increasing stability in mature communities present many problems. During the early periods of extreme instability, little permanence or continuity in community organization and culture could be expected. With the coming of population stability, however, other disruptive forces appeared upon the scene. Automotive transportation was a leading factor in all but closing the country school and church and destroying the village as a rural community center. With school, church, trading, and entertainment focused upon large towns, the farmer's social and cultural life became urbanized. At the opening of the century, the country-life movement, under the pioneer leadership of Bailey and Butterfield, emphasized this characteristic and the resulting discontent with farm life among rural people. The factors dominating the fourth decade of the century only accentuate the tendencies then so conspicuous, and under the new circumstances the possibilities of preserving or readjusting a distinctly rural culture in the United States are even more remote.

FOLKLORE AS A NEGLECTED SOURCE OF SOCIAL HISTORY

B. A. Botkin

If We admitted no impediments to a marriage of true minds between folklore and history, the product of their union would be folk history. This is history produced by the collaboration of the folklorist and the historian with each other and with the folk; a history of the whole people, in which the folk are seen as people and as human beings, and people are seen in their folk relationships, among others; a history, also, in which the people are the historians as well as the history, telling their own story in their own words—Everyman's history, for Everyman to read. This is "collective" history, gathered from thousands of contributors, in all classes and ranks; it is collected and recollected history, recorded from the memory and the lips of informants. Drawn, as it is, from living sources, obviously this history can be written only in our own day, of the immediate past or present, but even so the whole field of American history since the Civil War is open to us. Something like it has been attempted successfully by Sandburg in his life of Lincoln, which draws largely on "the talk of men and women who had eaten with Lincoln . . . heard his jokes and lingo. . . . The folklore of Lincoln, the maker of stories." [1] A contribution to contemporary social history is the same author's *The People, Yes*—107 variations on the theme that

> The people is Everyman, everybody.
> Everybody is you and me and all others.
> What everybody says is what we all say.[2]

The book is mined out of the rock of American sayings and story-telling—wisecracks, allusions, metaphors, proverbs, quotations, anecdotes, jokes, boners, bromides. In *The American Songbag*, which is his third folklore contribution to social history, Sandburg defines the purpose of such collections as to give the "feel

[1] Carl Sandburg, *Abraham Lincoln, The Prairie Years* (New York, 1926), p. vii.
[2] Carl Sandburg, *The People, Yes* (New York, 1936), p. 26.

and atmosphere, the layout and lingo, of regions, of breeds of men, of customs and slogans, in a manner and air not given in regular history." [3]

The regular historian, however, goes to folklore principally as a last resort, when all other sources have been exhausted, or when dealing with times before recorded history, with myths of history which he may help preserve for their protective symbolic and patriotic value, or which he may turn around and debunk. This is the use of folklore as a prehistorical or extrahistorical source in the building up of national traditions and heroes, and points to a time when folklore or oral tradition was the first history, which, before the mixture of cultures, was still pretty reliable and authentic. After the mixture of cultures, however, legend and history became confused. At various times, however, as in the Elizabethan chronicles, history has returned to its anecdotage, and been all the livelier as a result. The folklorist, on the other hand, has often had the mildly historical pretensions of attempting to find in folklore traces of buried or distorted history, along with the other wreckage of culture (especially in so-called "historical legends" and "historical traditions"), and also—without much success—to use folklore to establish historical facts (as in George Laurence Gomme's *Folklore as an Historical Science*).[4] Modern folklorists, however, are content to rest their claims for folklore as a historical science on the use of the historical method in general and on the geographical-historical method of the Finnish school in particular.

For the separation of history and folklore, the folklorist, the literary historian, and the anthropologist, as well as the historian proper, must all come in for their share of blame. For one thing, the folklorist has taken from history considerably more than he has given to it. And for the rest, he has taken his cue from the literary historian and the social anthropologist who still largely dominate the folklore field, with the result that it has been studied chiefly for its motifs, patterns, survivals, and attitudes, rather than for its historical reference. Because folklorists are trained either in literature or in anthropology but seldom in both, their emphasis is still exclusively on either the esthetic or the cultural side of folklore—but seldom on both. In anthropology there is a natural

[3] Carl Sandburg, *The American Songbag* (New York, 1927), p. vii.
[4] London, 1908.

preoccupation with primitive mythology, while in literature comparative mythology and the English and Scottish ballad still divide the honors, with the proverb as a not-too-close third. Over both the anthropological and the literary scene, the shadow of linguistics hovers. In the folk arts and crafts, which in England and America are outside the field of folklore proper (though they are included in the German *Volkskunde*), the dead hand of the antiquarian reaches out. For this last reason an important source of social history has been neglected in household objects, implements, and tools.

As a result, we have the folklorist and the historian looking at each other wistfully or skeptically across a stone wall, mumbling something about "good fences make good neighbors." On the one side stands the folklorist himself, regarding folklore as auxiliary to, rather than an integral part of history and the other social sciences. On the other side there is the historian, regarding folklore as something to be kept at its proper distance, which is that of physical facts, archeology, and nonhistorical literature in general as an indirect source.

To lump all folklore together as an indirect source is to fail to distinguish between several divergent types and phases of folklore. Unfortunately, this is the fault of the word itself, which for most of us is associated with the past and is generally synonymous with archaism, anachronism, and antiquity. Even with regard to the past we tend to use the term "folk" indiscriminately in two quite different senses: first, to denote a survival from an earlier to a later stage of culture, with resultant loss of function and meaning; and second, to denote a variety of idiom or taste within our present culture, corresponding to a certain sphere or level of usage, acceptance, or currency—confined to a certain geographical area, nationality, or occupational group. In the second sense, folklore furnishes a more or less exact parallel to dialect, which is a modification of the standard language, peculiar to a locality, class, or minority. In the case of folklore, however, we must not exaggerate the coefficient of isolation or homogeneity, but rather stress the differentiations of cultural diversity. And just as we may distinguish between a true dialect and a literary dialect, which is in turn a modification of the former, so we may distinguish between "folklore" and "folk literature" proper (which is a primary source for the historian) and the "literature of folklore" (which is a secondary source). The latter includes, first, "literature about the folk"; second, "pseudo-folk works," imitating or adapting folk motifs, forms, and moods, as in pseudo Indian and Negro songs; and third, "quasi-folk works," mined out of folk tradition and fused with fine art tradition by individual artists, as in the songs of Shakespeare and Burns. All three of these are legitimate sources of social history, but require different criteria of evaluation and different techniques of utilization.

The picture is further complicated by the complex process of diffusion and acculturation, in which there is a two-way flow between the literate and the illiterate, the sophisticated and the naïve, the urban and the rural. Here we must distinguish a third quantity, the popular, midway between the folk and the academic traditions. The popular is distinguished from the folk by its wider acceptance and by its transmission through other than oral means; for example, the stage, the film, the radio, the pulpit, the newspaper, and the magazine. But the so-called lively arts—jazz, the comic strip, burlesque,[5] pulp-paper fiction, and the like—often have a folk basis, as notably in the case of the blues; or give rise to new folk creations, as in Mickey Mouse, Donald Duck, Krazy Kat, and the like. The shifts and vagaries of popular taste and usage, in relation to folk and academic traditions, provide some of the most fascinating phenomena for the social historian. In fact, because we have to deal here with quasi lore and quasi literature (such as local and homespun verse, of the village-bard or sweet-singer type), which tend to be neglected by the orthodox folklorist and literary historian, they are all the more the concern of the historian, to whom nothing human is alien as historical fact or historical data.

We may distinguish further between folklore of the past and folklore of the present. The former comes down to us in the present, to be sure, but as a survival, which survives not without value or meaning, but with an emotional or esthetic one, chiefly symbolic. Such is the case with Negro spirituals and animal tales, which still live among folk Negroes in the rural South but as an American cultural heritage. (Originally based on white models,

[5] See Geoffrey Gorer, *Hot Strip Tease and Other Notes on American Culture,* London, 1937.

the spirituals, in fact, have reverted to white tradition—having passed into conventional usage as concert and anthology pieces.) Folklore in the making, on the other hand, has a more direct relation to contemporary or recent social structure and is the expression of social change and culture conflict. This may be illustrated by the social songs (blues and reels) and the work songs and "hollers" of the Black South. The folklore of the past has acquired prestige value because it has the immunity of the old and the safe. Living lore, on the other hand, tends to be submerged below the usual submerged level of folklore by social taboos and scholarly inhibitions.

In the folklore of both the past and the present we may distinguish between the more symbolic elaborations of folk fantasy and the more realistic and materialistic expressions of folk knowledge. It is impossible, of course, to conceive of a folk fantasy that does not contain some folk knowledge, and vice versa. But we are concerned here with the function as well as the content of the lore. In the class of folk fantasy, we have fabulous tales, fairy tales, tall tales and whoppers, lying tales generally, which are told for entertainment and not to be believed in. These have an inverted relation to social history, but have to be turned inside out, as it were, for the historical truth to be extracted. Tall tales, for example, tales of artistic exaggeration told by "authentic liars," as in the case of the Paul Bunyan tales, have been described as having "just enough truth in them to make good story material and to incite the imagination to try to improve on actual happenings."[6] They have also been related to caricature—for example, Mody C. Boatright's *Tall Tales from Texas*[7] cartoon familiar Southwest phenomena such as rattlesnakes, sandstorms, jack rabbits, northers, twisters, and killings. They are also related to practical jokes and the pranking of tenderfeet, or, when told for consumption back home, to the habit of boasting. As Houston Peterson has said, you can boast because you have too little as well as because you have too much.

These lying tales are more realistic than another species of fantasy—the sacred tales of mythology, which in the time and

[6] *Folk-say, A Regional Miscellany,* ed. by B. A. Botkin (Norman, Oklahoma, 1930), p. 429.

[7] Dallas, 1934.

place out of which they sprang were accepted as true, but which may since have become part of poetic literature. "The veracity of the account," says Martha Warren Beckwith, "lies in its truth to the social experience and development of the group, not in its literal truth to life as we regard narrative." [8]

Coming now to folk knowledge, we find narratives in prose and verse which are told as true to happenings in the outer world, rather than in the inner invisible world. On the naïve level, these are represented by personal histories, reminiscences, and anecdotes, especially those of old-timers, dealing with the experience of the folk group—the own stories of eyewitnesses and participants who did or saw and heard these things themselves—the ultimate source of all history. The historian has been quick to take advantage of this rich and colorful body of source material in the writing of pioneer history. An example is Carl Coke Rister's *Southern Plainsmen*.[9] My only quarrel with these historical treatments of folkways is that they are still largely confined to paper history—to contemporary material in print (chiefly newsprint) and to manuscript material (letters and journals), and that they are still pretty static. The folkways are fixed in a certain moment in time and space, like flies in amber, and fail to give a sense of development. This fault is perhaps an inheritance from the folklorist, for whom time too often marches backward or stands still. The historian of folkways, in other words, has still to tap the oral sources of local anecdote and personal reminiscence and the lore of the folk in all its activities (not simply folk cures, weather and crop wisdom, pastimes, and place names, and other minutiae which are the favorite subjects for collectors). A folklorist like George Korson comes nearer to the functional approach, in *Minstrels of the Mine Patch: Songs and Stories of the Anthracite Industry*.[10]

On the sophisticated level there is the folk stuff contained in local collections of folklore and folk ways and in folkloristic and regional literature. In passing, it may be noted that folk novels often have greater historical value than historical novels, which are too often merely warmed-over history, served up with adventure and romance. I refer to folk novels in which the author draws

[8] M. W. Beckwith, *Folklore in America* (Poughkeepsie, 1931), p. 30.
[9] Norman, Oklahoma, 1938. [10] Philadelphia, 1938.

on his own folk experience and does not simply document his stories with folklore at secondhand.

Through the use of questionnaires, personal interviews, and sound recordings, the folklorist and the social scientist have worked out adequate techniques for the collection and recording of this folk-say and folk stuff, including the life histories that illuminate them. It now remains for the historian to work out adequate techniques for utilization and interpretation of the material.

What the historian must bear in mind above all in determining what is and what is not folklore is the fact that it is the history and not the origin of a given piece of lore—its history through diffusion and acculturation—that makes it folklore. Thus "Oh, Susanna," originally written by Stephen Foster as a pseudo-Negro song, became a typically American folk song only when it became the theme song of the forty-niner. Just why and how this particular song appealed to the miner in his particular socio-economic situation concerns the social historian as well as the folklorist. In this sort of thing folklore and social history are inextricably bound up with each other, and are not simply common ground but one and the same ground.

In fact, the historian has a real service to render the folklorist by rescuing folklore from the museum and the archive and from the folklorist himself and giving it back to the people and to history. At the same time, the folklorist can render the historian the service of taking history out of the realm of print and enlarging the concept of culture history to include, in the truly "finer things of life," not simply the expressions of individual fantasy but the expression of "buried culture" outside of books and the fine-art forms. This culture is buried not because it is dead, but only because it has been submerged by the flood of print, to which the historian is incidentally contributing. From its own point of view, in fact, folk culture is very much alive and kicking and can also give life and color and warmth to the dry bones of research.

Finally, the historian may derive from folk sources not only materials but a point of view—the point of view which regards history, like literature, in Constance Rourke's words, as based upon the "slow accretions of folk elements, the humble influence of place and kinship and common emotion that accumulates through generations to shape and condition a distinctive native consciousness." [11] In this way social history becomes not merely the history of a given society, but history that goes to the roots of society—society with roots and history with roots—roots as well as sources.

[11] Constance Rourke, "The Significance of Sections," *The New Republic* (Sept. 20, 1933), p. 149.

FOLK MUSIC AS A SOURCE OF SOCIAL HISTORY

CHARLES SEEGER

BY THE term "folk music" we customarily designate one of the three or four types of socially and historically determined music idiom found in most large culture groups, the others being primitive, fine-art, and popular.

It is quite impractical to discuss the external relations of one of these types of idiom without first showing something of the inner, technical relations of the whole collection of idioms within the various musics, which they crosscut, and at least plotting the external relations of these musics and the cultures of which they are elements. Since this has not as yet been done, I can only propose some hypothetical values to historical study which might conceivably (after the preliminary spade work has been done) render inquiry into folk music as a source of social history particularly worth while.

It may be to the point, however, first to inquire briefly here: (1) why has the study of music-culture relationships been neglected? And (2) how shall we go about remedying the situation in which we are at present?

As to the first question, it would appear at first sight that we must look primarily to the historian for an answer. Clearly, the general operations of any art in a culture fall within the traditional domain of historical study. The historian can deal directly with most outward manifestations of music-making—the distribution and continuity of its traditions and institutions, its materials, its monuments, its uses. He may note, for instance, that in the United States today music is close to a billion-dollar industry—an important factor in social organization and in cultural (including political and economic) expansion. He can make surveys, inventories, and samplings of the material produced and the number and kinds of people involved, the time spent, credit and prestige gained, and so forth. He may tie these observations in with others contributing to an understanding of historical processes in general. He may make comparative studies of the various arts, including music, as sociohistorical functions.

In this approach very valuable work has been done—and much remains to be done. Music tends to appear here as an element in culture which bears out or illustrates conclusions arrived at by general study. But in common with other widespread cultural activities, music must not only be fitted into the picture made by general study but must be examined as a possible contributor of additions to the general picture—expressions of cultural characteristics and values which, at least in part, may not be susceptible to treatment by the methods traditionally used in the building of the general picture. Such an examination requires consideration of the inner, technical operation of the various musics and the types of music idiom which crosscut them. And this clearly does not fall within the traditional domain of historical study.

Obviously, the historian cannot be a specialist in every technique within his total field. Trained as he is, primarily or exclusively in the art of language, he must as a rule depend, for full development of nonlinguistic sources in his study, upon completion of his task by specialists—in the case of music, by the musicologist, who alone, owing to his training in both the art of music and the art of language, must not only pass upon the data *qua* music but also must make presentation of music-technical processes as source material for historical study.

The inner, technical operation of the various musics and of their socially and historically determined music idioms has been considered the peculiar domain of musicology. Musicology is an ancient study. It has its mythological, ancient, medieval, Renaissance, and modern "periods." As a twentieth-century science and critique, it is, however, of comparatively recent growth. It is full fifty years behind parallel studies in the field of language. We have two types of musicologist: the historico-musicologist, who has been concerned almost exclusively with the history of European fine-art (written) music up to about 1900; and the comparative musicologist, who has been concerned almost entirely with non-European (chiefly unwritten) musics from about 1900 to the present day. There has been so much preliminary spade work to do and such small forces at work that the tying in of music historical studies with general historical studies—and especially with social and cultural historical work—has not been done.

We face a situation, therefore, in which there are very generally lacking: (1) a concept of the field of music as a whole; (2) a concept of music as a social and cultural function; (3) utilization by musicologists of current concepts of total culture; (4) understanding of the relations between written and unwritten, and between verbal and nonverbal source material.

If the outer relations of music with culture cannot adequately be studied by the historian without consideration of the inner, technical operations of the art of music, certainly the reverse holds true, viz., the inner, technical operations of the art of music cannot adequately be studied without consideration of the outer relations of music and the culture of which it is a part. Upon second thought, therefore, to lay the blame for the neglect of music sources by the historian at the door of the general historian would seem to be unfair. The general historian would seem to have done as much as, if not more than, has the musicologist to effect a *rapprochement* of musical and cultural studies.

Coming now to my second question—how are we to go about remedying the situation in which we find ourselves?—it would seem that alignment of the fields of music and culture must be approached from both sides. Gain will be measured, I would say, as much in terms of what the social historian can see in a music-continuum (once the musicologist makes an understandable presentation of it) as in terms of what the musicologist can see in social history (once the historian presents him with a general-culture continuum into which music can be fitted).

The task of the historian would seem to be to add his support to the importunities of those who urge the musicologist to fill in the gaps listed above under items (1), (2), and (3). This will not be easy, for the musicologist is, along with the professional musician and the layman in general, well accustomed to regarding music as a thing apart from, rather than bound in with the worlds of daily life and scholarship. This centuries-old trend became grossly exaggerated during the last hundred years or so, when large-scale music organization required the support of wealth and fashion and so came to emphasize the rare rather than the common, the difficult rather than the easy, the *recherché* rather than the ordinary. It was during this time that fine-art music became "good" music and other idioms either "bad" music or not music at all. Today, however, a fortuitous combination of hard knocks and golden opportunities is bringing many musicians and musicologists to a more appropriate sense of reality. But the social historian can still be of considerable help in persuading them that music exists in the here and now more than in some kind of "other world."

In respect to item (4) above, the two approaches of the musicologist and the historian have some things in common which should be spoken of here. For example, owing to the nature of technological development, both studies have been inclined to emphasize written sources. Writing itself—both in language and in music—being a prestige, or elite profession, has inevitably attained more prestige by writing up prestige material. Or, when in a tight place, it has conferred prestige upon material not quite up to scratch—as when a fine-art composer utilizes a folk song by "slicking it down" sufficiently to pass in polite society. Surviving records of what men have seen and heard, thought, felt and done in the past have been—to extents we never can absolutely fix—reconstructions, representations. Printing has extended the scope of this procedure, but has not altered the fact that the hand-wrought transcription constitutes for later study not so often a primary as a secondary type of source material.

Now at last, through direct sound and sight-recording, unwritten and nonverbal sources can not only be represented but in a measure *re*-presented. The written document, the written score, the graphic design or modeled artifact, and the literary account of such must still, I presume, constitute the main skeleton of the corpus into which the selective judgment, imagination, and literary skill of the historian may breathe a species of renewed life. But in the phonograph and the photograph, and still more the sound film, there lie not only checks upon these traditional media, but in addition a wealth of new materials which prior to the twentieth century were totally inaccessible as sources of history—and in a primary rather than a secondary form.

It is obviously too soon adequately to evaluate this wealth. That it may afford more than a little embodiment and no little animation to the skeleton of written sources seems certain. That it may modify and even drastically revise conclusions arrived at by purely written techniques is possible. The devising of a number of new techniques and the revision of some old ones are probably in order.

I must hasten to add: the trend of social and cultural studies to include unwritten and nonverbal sources and techniques presents problems of method not within my competence to discuss. But the parallel expansion of musicological sources and techniques which must be made in order to effect contact with these new methods of cultural studies is very much within my field. In handling this problem with my musicological colleagues, I have urged that the alignment of music-historical and general historical fields may perhaps best be sought in respect to contemporary rather than past history. For it is only from our times on that these new tools and techniques are available. I have proposed, therefore, in place of the single concern with inner, technical operations of music, a three-branched definition of the task of musicology, viz.: the presentation in language of an account (1) of the nature of music-technical processes, (2) of the relation between the universe of music and the universe of discourse, and (3) of the function of the total field of music in the total field of culture.

In the first, the intramusical view, the various sciences which touch upon music—*Hilfswissenschaften*—are subordinated to musicology. In the second, musicology coöperates upon equal footing with other language disciplines. In the third, the extramusical view, musicology becomes subordinated in turn, as a *Hilfswissenschaft,* to the complex of studies which makes up the study of culture. I am still hoping that this proposition will find more than merely scattered favor among my colleagues.

Among the hypothetical values to historical study, which might conceivably (after the preliminary spade work has been done) render inquiry into folk music as a source of social history worth while, first to be mentioned is the universality of the folk idiom. As the musical vernacular of the "common man," its study compensates in part for the still strong temptation to tread the primrose path of prestige and great-man theories. It constitutes the first-hand approach to music materials, through which the other idioms can be seen in a truer perspective. It brings into the picture a new quantitative criterion to offset traditional overemphasis upon qualitative criteria that have so long dominated the field.

Second, is the anonymity of folk idiom—and with it the feeling that one is dealing directly with a socially molded thing, with a deep-set cultural function expressing not so much the varieties of individual experience as the norms of social experience.

Third, the forms of folk idiom do not show rapidly changing fashions, as do those of fine and popular idioms. Consequently, its content-type may, it would seem, be to express not so much the transitory as the more enduring characteristics of a culture.

Fourth, employment of an oral, not a written tradition, means that the content of the folk idiom comes straight to us without the intervening censor of sophisticated handling.

Fifth, as a means of cultural expression and communication, the folk idiom is nearer, more familiar to and hence more within the grasp of the historian's readers, and perhaps (if he will be frank) of the average student of history himself, than is fine-art music.

Sixth, it is more of a piece with other materials handled by the social historian.

Seventh, emphasis upon folk idiom, as upon popular and primitive idioms, will tend to break down barriers set up by the theory of the "other-worldliness" of music.

Lastly, I may say that the non-fine-art idioms constitute the field into which the normal expansion of both comparative and historico-musicology seems likely to take place. The social historian may expect aid from the musicologist at an earlier date in these than in the fine-art field.

Folk-music idiom would seem, therefore, to be the field in which the various parties in the complex I have been discussing, anthropologists, historians, and musicologists, can get together most easily —the field in which the new techniques of sound and sight-recording can be developed to advantage, and in which materials can be gathered for the filling in of the main gaps caused by overreliance upon written sources.

I have painted an enthusiastic picture of the possibilities, because I have a hunch that something can be done with them. But do not let me imply that these possibilities can be realized overnight. As a musician I cannot escape personal bias in favor of the thought, so long entertained by many great teachers of mankind, that music has power to salve many of the ills of the world; that though it be prostituted to violence, fraud, and special interest, though it may serve as a dissipation or a drug as easily as a discipline, once it is freed of dominance by language its normal function is to harmonize where language makes conflict and to reconcile where language contradicts. But I am quite aware that after a perfunctory acknowledgment, the vast majority of scholars proceed in complete disregard of such pious sentiments. I do not blame them. Until music can gain for itself or have gained for it more exact objective appraisal, these sentiments must remain worth little more, in our predominantly verbal universe, than the breath which expresses them.

The crux of the problem we are discussing here is the fact that history employs one art—language—music, another. Both arts communicate content. What language says of music, what music says of itself, and what each says of man, his social organization and his cultural growth may be identical, similar, or different. We have no means of telling. We may feel reasonably certain that the content fields of the arts of music and language touch or even to some extent overlap. In some respects they may be commensurable. But on the whole, I feel, the content fields and the social functions of the two arts are complementary and compensatory, rather than correspondent. In our exploration of folk music as a source of social history, therefore, we should not look for any such fantastic result as ability to express in language the content of music. We may draw conclusions from observed uses of music. We may try to translate, as it were, from one art to another—provided, of course, we are comparatively equally skilled in the techniques of both. But beyond this we cannot seem to go.

Because language can do no more than this, there has been a tendency in social and historical studies to exclude music as a determining factor in cultural dynamics. Music, as "unmethodical thought," reflected but did not mold the world of men and things. The limitations of the art of language provide, obviously, no valid ground for excluding consideration of music as a creative factor in cultural growth, and hence in history. Indeed, as the development of modern scientific method proves, it is by the recognition of the limitations of purely verbal processes and by the emphasis upon objective observation and experiment that twentieth century thought has come to be what it is.

The same humility before the object of study which has distinguished the great sciences can and should be invoked in the handling of music, all the more because language is the dominating art in world culture. This holds, I would say, as well for the musicologist who looks outward from his own domain into the vastly larger one of social and cultural studies, as for the social historian who looks inward upon a "dark spot" which may be larger and more important than traditional practice has believed it to be.

In closing, please let me state the hope that the same breadth of view which includes this topic in a discussion of materials for historians will some day be shown by musicologists.

DOCUMENTARY PHOTOGRAPHS

Roy E. Stryker and Paul H. Johnstone

ALTHOUGH it is now a full century since Daguerre published his discovery of a method of sensitizing plates with iodine, the potentialities of photography as a means of preserving and of presenting social data are only beginning to be widely recognized. It has been technically possible for three-quarters of a century to produce good pictures under conditions favoring slow plates and cumbrous paraphernalia. And even early in this period there were high attainments in posed portrait photography and in photography of a self-conscious esthetic kind, working within a tradition borrowed from the older and formal graphic arts. But with the exception of a few cameras clicking in the wilderness, there was for a long time no perception of the possibilities of photographic documentation of living history.

Some of the more notable of these exceptions should be mentioned. Best known among the earliest ones, perhaps, is Mathew B. Brady. His Civil War photographs convey graphic impressions of important scenes and incidents with a vividness that could never be attained by verbal description alone. There were several other photographers whose work during the Civil War and after has documentary value. Many of them went into the Far West and did some very interesting exploration photography. There was Alexander Gardner, who made some Civil War pictures, but did his best work in the years following, making a photographic documentation of the construction of the Union Pacific Railroad. William H. Jackson, who was with the Department of the Interior for many years, began during the same period an excellent collection of Western pictures that is still in the possession of the government. Early in the twentieth century, in the years before the first World War, Lewis Hine made a fine photographic record of child labor, and of immigrants and slum conditions in New York City.

There should be mention, too, of the work of two Frenchmen. Charles Marville, in the mid-nineteenth century, took pictures of some of the condemned sections of Paris before they were destroyed

1. LOWER WHARF, YORKTOWN, VIRGINIA, 1862

(United States Signal Corps photo by Mathew B. Brady)

2. AERIAL SURVEY, KANKAKEE COUNTY, ILLINOIS

This is a type of photography that has been made possible by recent technological developments. (*Agricultural Adjustment Administration, United States Department of Agriculture*)

3. MEETING OF FARM SECURITY ADMINISTRATION REHABILITATION CLIENTS

The purpose of the meeting was to work out farm and home plans with the aid of the Farm Security Administration county supervisor and home supervisor in York, Nebraska, October, 1938. (*Farm Security Administration photo by Vachon*)

4. INTERIOR OF GENERAL STORE IN MOUNDVILLE, ALABAMA JULY, 1936

(*Farm Security Administration photo by Evans*)

5. MICHIGAN IRON MINER'S HOME

Part of living room in home of a former iron miner in Mansfield, Michigan, May, 1937. (*Farm Security Administration photo by Lee*)

6. SHARECROPPER FAMILY

Negro mother of sharecropper family teaching her children alphabet and numbers in their home near Transylvania, Louisiana, January, 1939. (*Farm Security Administration photo by Lee*)

7. ITALIAN IMMIGRANT MOTHER AND CHILD AT ELLIS ISLAND

The photographer was informed that 12,000 immigrants arrived the day in 1905 that this picture was made. (*Lewis W. Hine*)

8. GRAVEYARD AND STEEL MILL IN BETHLEHEM, PENNSYLVANIA
NOVEMBER, 1935
(Farm Security Administration photo by Evans)

9. ST. ANTHONY'S SOUP KITCHEN IN HOBOKEN, NEW JERSEY, 1940

St. Anthony's soup kitchen tries to feed the mouths that Hoboken overlooks. Each morning at 9 a.m. a long line of men assembles. They eat there: the little room is jammed. Then, on throughout the day, men and women and children come singly carrying baskets; they are given food—as much as the Sisters can supply—for their families. They get bread, vegetables, perhaps some cake. No questions are asked; the faces answer everything. Sister Eugenia estimates that 250 applicants appear daily, many in behalf of whole families. In winter the figure goes up.

The soup kitchen is supported by the Sisters' efforts. They hold card parties to raise funds, knit prizes themselves. Stores donate bread. Some of the men who come are idle seamen with no beds of their own. But the bulk are Hoboken natives who either can't get relief or don't get enough. The kitchen is open every day for men who have no place to eat; the family allotments are given on Monday, Wednesday and Friday. Sister Eugenia says: "We do what we can; we wish we could do more." In addition to the soup kitchen, people also get aid from local Catholic churches.

to make way for the modern improvements undertaken under Napoleon III. Later, around the end of the century, Eugène Atget turned his camera on many intimate and revealing scenes of Paris and Parisian life.

In spite of the notable achievements of a few individuals in the field of documentary photography, the prestige of galleries and salons, the preference of photographic magazines, the acclaim of critics and judges, and even the predilections of most of those technically most competent continued to favor the self-conscious estheticism of the tradition inherited from the graphic arts. This is, to an unfortunate degree, still true. A survey of the photographic magazines in this country for the last thirty years discloses surprisingly little change in the type of photographs reproduced; the 1,500 prints selected to be hung in the Grand Central Gallery in New York at the International Photographic Show in 1938 might very well have come from a camera club of a quarter of a century ago.

Meanwhile, however, there have been developments in the journalistic field that, with the aid of certain important improvements in equipment, accessories, and means of reproduction, have provided the occasion for the rise of a new and dynamic school of photography as much or more concerned with social substance than with mere composition and technique for their own sake. The development of methods for reproducing the photograph in newspapers was, of course, of crucial primary importance to the growth of commercial photography. On March 4, 1880, the *New York Daily Graphic* printed what was probably the first half tone ever published, following a method first evolved by Frederick E. Ives in 1878 and later perfected by Stephen H. Hargan. It was not until January 21, 1897, however, when the *New York Tribune* published a front page photograph of the newly elected senator from New York, that the half-tone illustration became an established feature of American journalism. The use of photography in journalism gradually increased thereafter. Perhaps the most outstanding developments in photographic reproduction and presentation were the development of the rotogravure page by the *New York Times* during the first World War, the increased use of photography during the 1920's by a great many slick paper publications, and the first use of the wire-photo in 1935. At the same time many improvements were being made that converted the camera itself into an instrument of much greater flexibility. Faster films, more perfectly synchronized flashlight equipment, cameras more durable and portable made it possible to take excellent pictures under physical conditions that would previously have been completely forbidding. Most recently, the use of the miniature camera, with fast lens and fine-grain film, has given rise to the vogue for unposed, slice-of-life, and so-called "candid camera" pictures. All these have had their influence upon the development of documentary photography as it exists today.

Documentary photography has vast and as yet unrealized potentialities for recording as well as for presenting data that should be of vital interest to social scientists and historians. There is a great, and for the most part unused treasure of social documentation in the photographic morgues and files of newspapers, picture magazines, and syndicates. There are literally millions of negatives in the possession of such private organizations as these. Many government agencies have smaller collections that are of important documentary value. The Farm Security Administration, of the United States Department of Agriculture, has 40,000 negatives that depict the farming practices, the ways of living, and the people themselves in a great variety of type-of-farming and rural cultural areas spread over the whole United States.

Within the peculiar field to which it is adapted, photography is a more direct and powerful means of communication than verbal communication can ordinarily hope to be. The photograph cannot ordinarily stand by itself, but there are certain things that the photograph, set in a context that the historian or social scientist can supply, can communicate better than words alone. The historian of the French Revolution would be more sure of his material if the *cahiers* had been accompanied by documenting photographs, or if Arthur Young in his travels through France had been equipped with a Speed Graphic to illustrate graphically his verbal descriptions. Suppose the conventional drawings of "a typical manor" in medieval history texts might be replaced by a few good photographs of real, individual manor houses and villages and lands. Samuel Pepys's description of London life during the Restoration is among the most vivid and intimate to which historians have access; yet that description would undoubtedly be much more vivid and real if Pepys had carried with him through the streets of Restoration London a miniature camera with F.2 lens and synchronized flash-bulb equipment. Let anyone who doubts the potentialities of photography on this score go through the pages of almost any social history, counting the adjectives and the descriptive passages that constitute an attempt by the indirection of verbal symbols to evoke graphic images that photography can supply directly and much more accurately.

There are, of course, drawings and paintings of contemporary events and personages from many periods and cultures; but graphic art has so regularly been subject to artistic conventions that such drawings are more valuable to us as an indication of the prevailing esthetic code and the subjective qualities of the individual artist than as a direct social record. Graphic documentation by the formal arts has presented a hundred figures of the glittering upper crust in glaring spotlight, while the millions lingered in outer darkness. Such preoccupation with those who have so frequently been assumed to be the elite does not conform either to modern trends in historiography or to the preoccupations of the more modern social sciences, that have seemed to find in the mass of people, as well as in those at the top, social material important enough to record and analyze.

Photography can, of course, be perverted to serve almost any end, just as history can. For the moment that a photographer selects a subject, he is working upon the basis of a bias that is parallel to the bias expressed by an historian when he selects his subject, his angle of approach, or his materials. But photography can easily reach the vast number of human beings whose lives ordinarily are unrecorded, either in literary sources or in formal graphic sources. For photography is inexpensive, as painting or drawing never could be; and documentary photography has, in fact, already split off from the esthetic domination that has generally ruled the expensive and formal graphic arts.

Documentary photography is a new means with which the historian can capture important but fugitive items in the social scene. But if photography is to serve this purpose best, it must have not only the recognition, but the actual aid of the historian. For a great deal of the material that has been accumulated for strictly contemporary purposes is not accompanied by the kind of identification—easy to supply now, but later impossible—that would be most valuable to the future historian; many significant items are overlooked; and, above all, the collections are in many cases so vast, so full of inconsequential material, and for historical purposes so unordered that they will be difficult and tedious to use. Historians and social scientists could contribute much by coöperating in the selection of materials and in the making of shooting scripts, intended specifically as historical records, as well as in supplying verbal documentation to accompany the pictures when they are printed. This kind of coöperation between the photographer and the historian today would give the social historian of tomorrow a photographic record that would be concentrated and orderly, and accompanied by the additional information necessary to give the photographs accurate meaning.

Until recently there has been ample excuse for the neglect of photographic raw materials. With the exception of a few collections, such as the Brady collection, there has been little that the social historian could use. But within the last decade new equipment and new materials, hardly dreamed of even at the turn of the century, have stimulated a crop of new photographers. And a valuable and exciting product is coming from their cameras—potent raw material from which to compound new histories and make old ones more vivid. In photography the historian has, if he will accept it, a new edge to his tool. A young generation, right on his heels, is being conditioned by the picture magazine, the rotogravure, the news reel. On all sides there is a growing dependence upon this powerful and stimulating medium of expression. The historian really has no choice but to accept it.

The photographs which follow illustrate some of the types of documentation which photographs can provide. The physical details of material culture are, of course, the easiest and most obvious items susceptible of visual documentation. Such details are to be noted in each of the pictures included,—the ordnance, shipping, and clothing revealed in picture No. 1; interior decorative details of pictures Nos. 5 and 6; the consumer goods displayed in No. 4, housing and factory construction shown in No. 8. Incidental information that would escape ordinary record is often contained in these material details. The calendars in pictures No. 4 and No. 6, the religious motto in No. 5 allow one to glimpse the business and religious life of the time.

Clues to social organization and institutional relationships are also to be found, even in as limited a collection as is here included. Every culture puts its stamp upon the terrain and creates its own landscape.[1] The Middle Western rural landscape shown in picture No. 2 reveals the independent farmstead, squared fields and highways, with the type of economic and social organization implicit therein. Its significance as a cultural record may be realized by considering what this landscape would look like if the agrarian culture of the Middle West were organized on the basis of the type of peasant village which characterizes Central Europe, or on the type of land-holding which has imposed its pattern upon the landscape of the lower St. Lawrence Valley.

Set alongside of picture No. 2 with its revelation of the independent family farm, picture No. 3 becomes an eloquent historical document, for it reveals farmers with this cultural background now making a group approach to their farming problems. Picture No. 8 speaks volumes about the unplanned growth of an industrial city, although the dramatic composition of the photograph makes it an example of a type that is interpretative as well as documentary.

The full documentary value of such pictures as Nos. 5 and 6 depends on some knowledge of the representativeness of the examples. If photographic records are to prove of maximum value to the historian, their identification should be not only as precise and complete as possible but should give such supplementary information as will provide a basis for interpretation. If the photographer were familiar with the community in which No. 5 was found, he could indicate whether this home represented the prevailing style of lower middle class interior, whether it was a relic of a former period, or merely a reflection of eccentricity in taste. Similarly, the photographer of No. 6, familiar with the Negro sharecroppers of the cotton area, could note whether this was one of the better or poorer houses, and one of the more or less enterprising of families. In the case of such a picture as No. 3, the information as to the representative character of the illustration would ordinarily be available to the historian in the files of the Farm Security Administration.

The importance of knowing the representativeness of photographs used for documentation (as indeed of all fragmentary records) is well illustrated by the pictures of "Middletown homes"

[1] See Nikolaus Creutzburg, *Kultur im Spiegel der Landschaft*, Leipsig, 1930.

which appeared in *Life* magazine at the time of the publication of *Middletown in Transition* by Robert and Helen Lynd.[2] The four homes selected were those of the leading manufacturer, the mayor, a WPA worker with a family of nine and an interest in philosophy, and a resident of shacktown. This collection could easily mislead an historian if he did not have access to the fact that the town was mainly composed of homes entirely unrepresented in this sample, those of industrial workers and lower middle class artisans, tradesmen, and clerical workers, or that the average size of WPA families was, say, 4.5 rather than 9, and that even among the social and economic class represented by the mayor, the fact that his wife was a collector of old glass made the pictured interior unique rather than representative.

Documentary photographs, further, can interpret the human, and particularly the inarticulate, elements. Volumes on immigration do not tell the human story that can be read in No. 7. A succession of such, rather than only one of the 12,000 that waited their turn behind the Ellis Island grill that day, would convey what words could barely hope to achieve. In this picture are reflected the order, the security, the sense of status, and the personal relationship which characterize the peasant culture from which this immigrant has come. In juxtaposition with the Ellis Island grill, it vividly poses the acute problem of cultural transition which the process of immigration involves. Pictures 8 and 9, showing two aspects of the urban industrial milieu of which the immigrant from a peasant culture has become a part, carry the study on with a social documentation which has an insistence for the historian that no verbal document can carry. The text which accompanies No. 9 adds the factual data which, in combination with the picture, produce a significant social document.

[2] II (May 10, 1937), 15–25.

DIALECT AREAS, SETTLEMENT AREAS, AND CULTURE AREAS IN THE UNITED STATES

HANS KURATH

THE LAST two decades have witnessed notable progress in dealing with the English spoken in the United States. The vague generalizations regarding sectional differences in our speech, and the even vaguer generalizations concerning the relation of American English to British English are uttered with less assurance now that the facts of American usage of the present and of the past are being scientifically recorded in the field and gathered from printed and written sources and presented to scholars for interpretation. One may hope that before long—in two or three decades—we shall have a realistic account of the state of our language and its genesis, as one phase of our social and cultural history.

Moreover, the work of the linguists has reached a stage that permits one to anticipate results that will have a significance extending far beyond the strictly linguistic field. The student of local, regional, and national culture; of folk ways in matters of food, shelter for man and beast, implements, social customs, and amusements; of folklore such as beliefs, sayings, songs, and tales; and of regional literature and art will find a useful and ready ally in the linguist and profit from his findings and his method of procedure. And since our national culture has its foundation in regional cultures, just as our national language rests upon our regional forms of speech, historians and linguists will work hand in hand also in problems of national scope.

Henry L. Mencken was the first to call attention in a forceful manner to the fact that American English can be understood only if one relates it to the population history and the cultural history of the United States.[1] His interest was focused primarily on vocabulary, where the connection between language and history is the most obvious. In 1925 George P. Krapp[2] applied this point of

1 Henry L. Mencken, *The American Language,* New York, 1919. 4th ed., corrected, enlarged, and rewritten, 1936.

2 George P. Krapp, *The English Language in America,* 2 vols., New York, 1925.

view not only to vocabulary but also to pronunciation, drawing his material largely from early New England town records and diaries, in which unconventional spellings betraying local and regional pronunciations abound, and from dialect writers like James Russell Lowell [3] and A. B. Longstreet [4] and from early American lexicographers and grammarians like Noah Webster [5] and J. E. Worcester.[6] An attempt to relate regional differences in American pronunciation to the history of settlement and the English provenience of the settlers and to delimit the major dialect regions was made by the present writer in 1928.[7]

All these efforts were doomed to fall short of the mark for lack of accurate factual information, but they gave impetus to research in a field that is of the greatest importance and interest not only to students of our language, but to scholars engaged in the investigation of other phases of our social and cultural history and to the layman as well.

The great task of gathering systematically the facts essential for a scientific account, descriptive and historical, of our language was begun in 1925. *The Dictionary of American English,* compiled and edited at the University of Chicago, undertakes to record the vocabulary and the grammatical forms of the written language from earliest colonial days to 1900.[8] The dictionary is a mine of information for the historian as well as the linguist, especially because the first occurrence of words in print or writing is scrupulously noted. A glance at such entries as the following should convince any student of American cultural, social, and political history of the great importance of this undertaking: *frontier town* (1654–), *frontier* (1700–), *Americanize* (1797–), *alien* (1781–), *abolition* (1787–), *abolitionist* (1834–), *backwoods* (1742–), *backwoodsman* (1784–), *buckshot* (1775–), *bundling* (1781–), *ark* (flat-

[3] *The Biglow Papers,* Cambridge, 1848. [4] *Georgia Scenes,* Augusta, 1835.

[5] *Compendious Dictionary of the English Language,* New Haven, 1806; *American Dictionary of the English Language,* New York, 1828.

[6] *Comprehensive Pronouncing and Explanatory Dictionary of the English Language,* Boston, 1830.

[7] "The Origin of the Dialectal Differences in Spoken American English," *Modern Philology,* XXV (1928), 385–95; *American Pronunciation,* Society for Pure English, Tract No. 30, Oxford, 1928.

[8] Sir William A. Craigie and James R. Hulbert, *A Dictionary of American English on Historical Principles,* Chicago, 1936–. "A" to "Gold Region," 1140 pp., have been published to date. A statement concerning the scope and the character of the dictionary will be found in the prefaces in Volume I.

bottomed boat, 1759–1855), *Conestoga wagon* (1808–), *cache* (1805–), *butte* (1805–), *bayou* (1818–), *Bowie knife* (1836–), *adobe* (1843–), *applejack* (1816–), *apple butter* (1819–), *apple bee* (1827–), *camp meeting* (1803–), *anxious seat* (1835–), *commuter* (1865–), *alumna* (1882–), *coeducation* (1852–), *bootlegger* (1889–), *Anti-saloon League* (1892–), *boll weevil* (1903–).

Many of these terms were doubtless current before they appeared in print or writing, especially those denoting homely things and institutions, so that their first appearance in writing indicates the time when the thing or institution they denote became common or attracted attention, rather than the date of origin. The instances cited in the dictionary also often provide a clue to the section in which they first were current or to which they are confined.

A record of the spoken language of all levels of society in all parts of the country is the object of the *Linguistic Atlas of the United States and Canada,* a research project sponsored by the American Council of Learned Societies, for which preparations began in 1929.[9] Up to the present moment, field work has been completed in New England (213 communities) and the greater part of the South Atlantic States from Maryland to Georgia (about 200 communities), and field recording is now in progress in Pennsylvania (about 75 communities). It is hoped that the Middle Atlantic States can be surveyed within five more years, so that we shall soon have an accurate record of the spoken language of all classes in the entire area settled by 1800.[10] The first of the three volumes of the New England section of the *Atlas* was published in 1939.[11] The number of points investigated is sufficiently large to permit of establishing the dialect areas and their relation to settlement areas, trade areas, and culture areas.[12]

Before entering upon a discussion of the significance of the *Linguistic Atlas* for the student of American society, it seems desir-

[9] Hans Kurath, *Report of the Conferences on a Linguistic Atlas of the United States and Canada,* Linguistic Society of America, Bulletin No. 4, 1929.

[10] Surveys of the Great Lakes Basin and the Ohio River Valley, and of Louisiana and Texas are now in progress by scholars collaborating with the Atlas staff.

[11] Hans Kurath and others, *Linguistic Atlas of New England,* 242 maps, Providence, 1939. Also *Handbook of the Linguistic Geography of New England,* Providence, 1939.

[12] The method of selecting communities and informants is described in Chap. II of the *Handbook,* and the dialect features investigated are given in Chap. V.

able to say a few words about the nature of language and its function in society, in order to dispel misconceptions propagated by our schools and by writers whose evangelical zeal for improving our language is second only to their ignorance of American usage.

Speech is a form of social behavior. In human society speech is universal and all-important. The cohesion of groups, the functioning of individuals as a group, the spreading of attitudes, of opinions, of ideas from person to person, from group to group, and from nation to nation are largely mediated through speech or the visual representation of speech, the written language.

In intimate groups such as the family, the village, the neighborhood, and the city, communication is largely by word of mouth (i. e., speech); among larger groups, such as nations, predominantly through the writing of speech (i. e., the written or printed language).

For the sake of easy and accurate communication, the speech habits of a group tend to be uniform. The more intimate and frequent the contacts between the individuals of a group, the more alike their speech. However, complete uniformity is never attained in speech, any more than in other social habits or conventional activities. New words, constructions, and pronunciation are constantly introduced by individuals and spread only gradually to other members of the group (if they spread at all), and old speech forms are abandoned sooner by some than by others.

Social and regional separation of varying degrees results in social and regional dialects, i. e., sets of socially or regionally restricted forms of speech. The looser the net of communication, the greater the differences in speech will be with the passing of time, as between social sets in one community or region, or as between regions.

When several types of speech are introduced into one community, as was the case a hundred or a thousand times over in colonial America and again during the westward movement, the speech differences in the newly created community are more or less leveled out in the course of two or three generations, and a new blend, relatively as uniform as the speech of any older community, arises. The contributions to this new dialect of the several elements that entered into it can be determined if the "mother dialects" are known, though the precise manner of survival of any

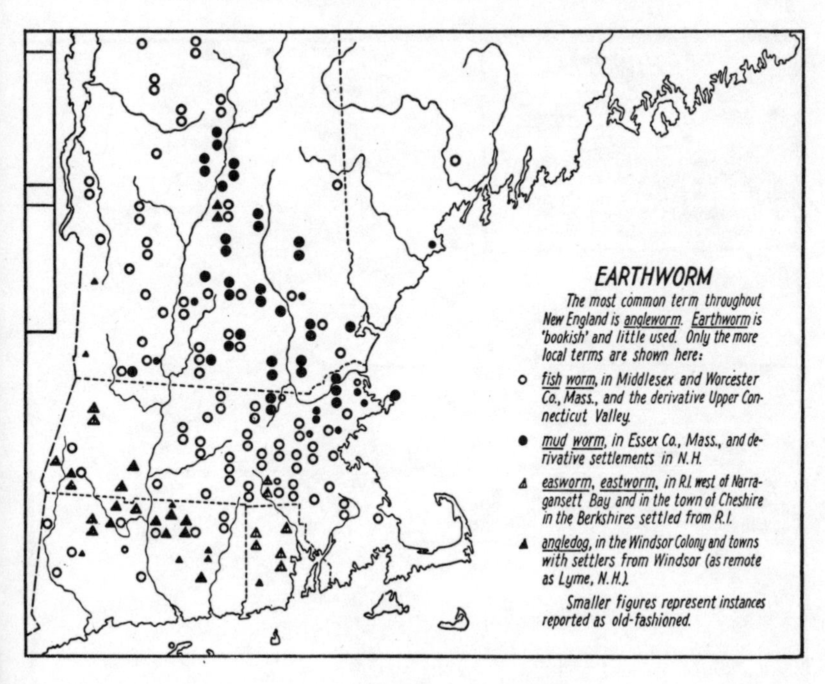

CHART 1

given speech form may be difficult to determine. The number of persons speaking each of the dialects brought into the new settlement and their relative social prominence in the community, as well as their common written language, are determining factors.

Turning to the American scene, we observe that during colonial times, in a largely agricultural population, the geographic range of the individuals and of the communities—towns, hundreds, and even the seaports and the "cities in the wilderness"—was greatly restricted, and hence the dialect areas created in the course of several generations were small. The great diversity of speech on the Atlantic seaboard from the Penobscot to the Savannah is a direct result of these early conditions. Not only are the major areas—Eastern New England, the Middle Atlantic Slope, and the South Atlantic Seaboard—clearly defined in their local speech forms; even smaller areas, such as the Merrimack Valley, Narragansett Bay, Long Island Sound, eastern Maryland, the Virginia Tidewater and Piedmont, and the Charleston area—all early settlement

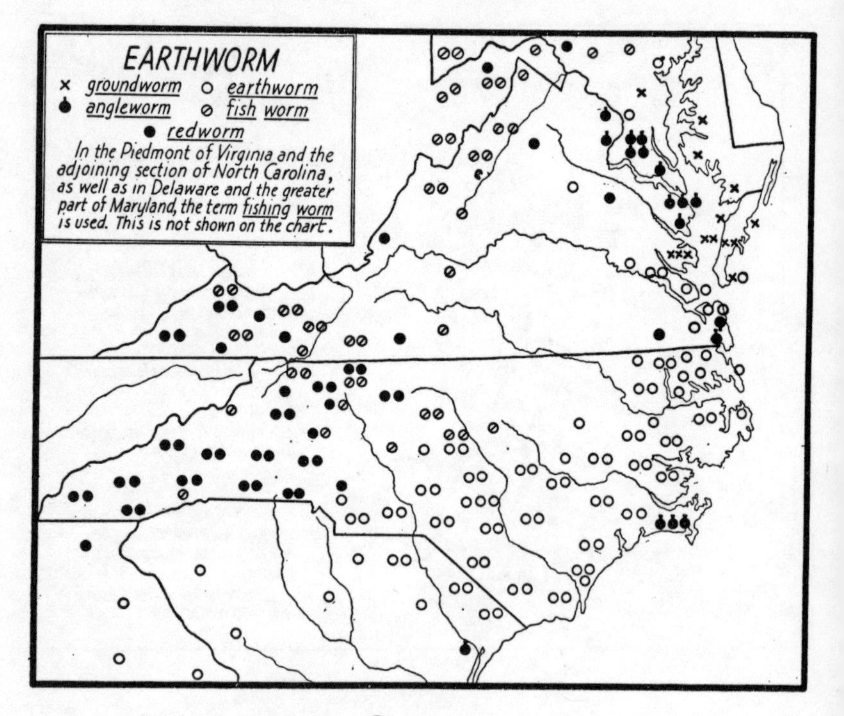

CHART 2

or trade areas—have preserved in a measure distinctive dialect features to this day, despite the leveling effect of better communication during the last century. Charts 1, 2, and 3 serve to illustrate this fact.[13]

The distribution of other speech forms reflects the major settlement areas, such as eastern New England, the lower Connecticut Valley, Virginia east of the Blue Ridge, the Charleston area, and the Appalachians.

All of New England east of a line following roughly the crest of the Green Mountains southward into the Berkshires, then eastward into Worcester County, Massachusetts, and then southward through the hills of western Worcester County and of Tolland County, Connecticut, to the mouth of the Connecticut River, was occupied in the main by gradual expansion inland from the coastal

[13] Other illustrations are given in H. Kurath, *Handbook of the Linguistic Geography of New England,* charts 18–23, pp. 35–38.

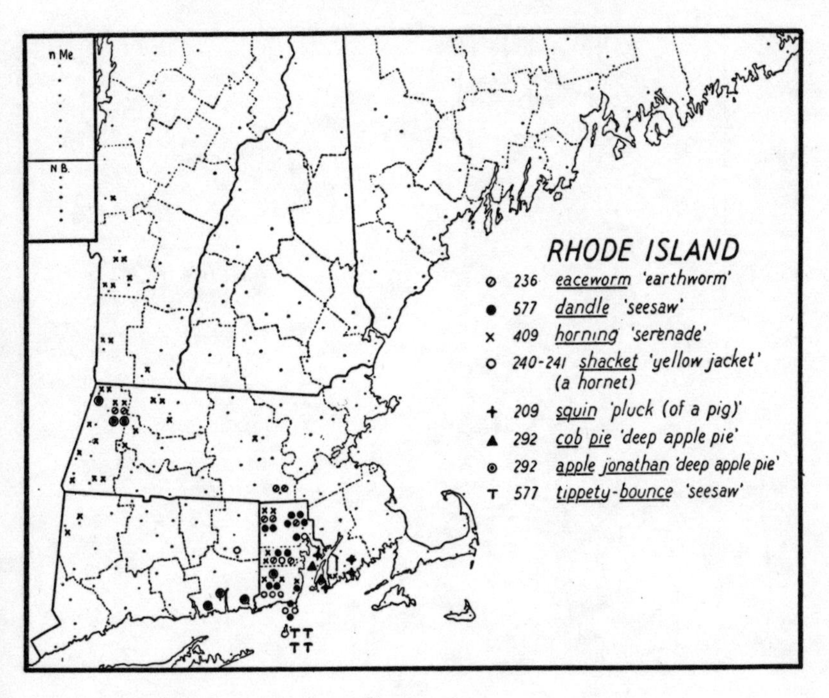

CHART 3

settlements of New London, Narragansett Bay, Plymouth, Massachusetts Bay, New Hampshire, and Casco Bay.[14]

During a century of slow growth, contacts between these coastal settlements had brought about more or less uniform usage in certain features of speech, which were then carried inland. The settlements on the lower Connecticut River and on Long Island Sound west of the river also had attained uniformity on certain points before western Connecticut, the Housatonic Valley in Massachusetts, and western Vermont were taken up by descendants of these early settlers. The "seam" between these two major settlement areas in New England is paralleled to this day by many word boundaries, some of which are shown on Chart 4.[15] Some features of pronunciation show a similar regionalism.[16] The two major dialect areas of New England are thus the direct result of their

[14] See Marcus L. Hansen, in *Handbook of the Linguistic Geography of New England,* pp. 62–93; also Plate I in the back of that book.

[15] From the *Handbook,* p. 29.

[16] *Handbook,* pp. 30 and 34 (Chart 16).

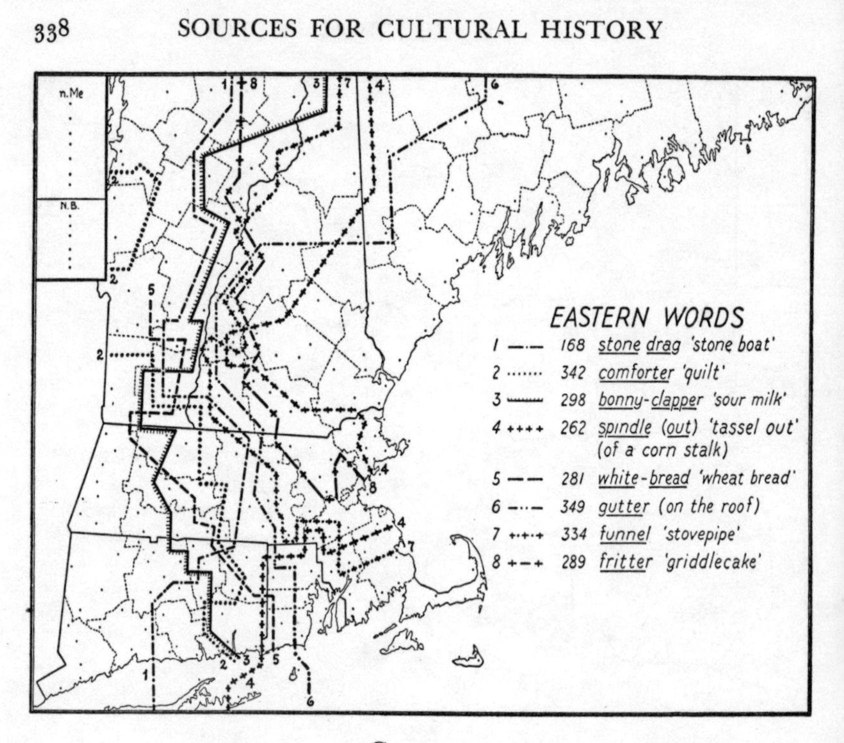

CHART 4

settlement history. The orientation of eastern New England in cultural matters, itself at least in part determined by family connections "back east" as well as by trade connections, has doubtless helped to preserve this dialect boundary.

The correspondence of present dialect boundaries with settlement boundaries is even more striking in Virginia. Between the Potomac and the Roanoke, the Blue Ridge separates the area settled by gradual expansion from the early centers on Chesapeake Bay and from the Pennsylvania settlements in the Shenandoah Valley and the Appalachians, and this physical barrier has helped to keep the two areas distinct in speech. The boundary between "coastal speech" and "mountain speech" is not as clearly defined in North Carolina, where the Pennsylvania Scots and Germans swept down into the Piedmont, but it is there. The flaring of the dialect lines in the south-central part of the state points to an extensive interpenetration of coastal and mountain elements in the population, perhaps also to a spreading of speech forms down the Cape Fear River from the population centers of the Piedmont.

Chart 5 illustrates the dialect situation created by the settlement. In the coastal settlements of Virginia and North Carolina (also of South Carolina and Georgia), farmers get their cows from the pasture by calling *co-wench! co-wee;* the near horse is called the *line horse, wheel horse,* or *nigh horse;* the bolster lies *jam across* or *slam across* the bed; one gets up at *quarter of* seven; and a child born out of wedlock is an *oatfield colt.* In the Appalachians, the Blue Ridge, and the western Piedmont of North Carolina, *sook cow!* is the cow call; the near horse is the *lead horse, saddle horse,* or *near horse;* the bolster lies *plum across* the bed; one gets up at *quarter till* seven; and the *oatfield colt* becomes a *woods colt.* The fact that the South Atlantic states have remained largely agricultural, with the population rooted to the soil until recent times, has doubtless helped to preserve sharper dialect boundaries here than one encounters in New England.

The rapid western expansion of the population between 1790 and 1840 from the Green Mountains and the Appalachians to the Mississippi Valley resulted in the creation of much more extensive dialect areas than one finds on the Atlantic Slope. By inference from what is known about these westward migrations and from our observations concerning the correspondences on the Atlantic Slope between settlement areas and speech areas, one expects to find three major dialect areas separated by lines, or bundles of lines, showing an east-west trend: (1) a Northern Area in which the characteristics of the speech of western New England predominate;[17] (2) a Southern Area, including the Gulf States and the lower Mississippi Valley (the cotton belt and the tobacco lands, probably as far north as western Kentucky), in which Tidewater and Piedmont characteristics predominate; and (3) a Middle Area comprising the Appalachians and the Ohio River Valley. Here Appalachian and Pennsylvania dialect features must be common, but "Southern" islands, such as the Blue Grass region of Kentucky, and some "Northern" islands, such as Marietta, are imbedded in it.

[17] Eastern New England's population was absorbed into an expanding overseas and coastwise trade and into rapidly developing industrial enterprises.

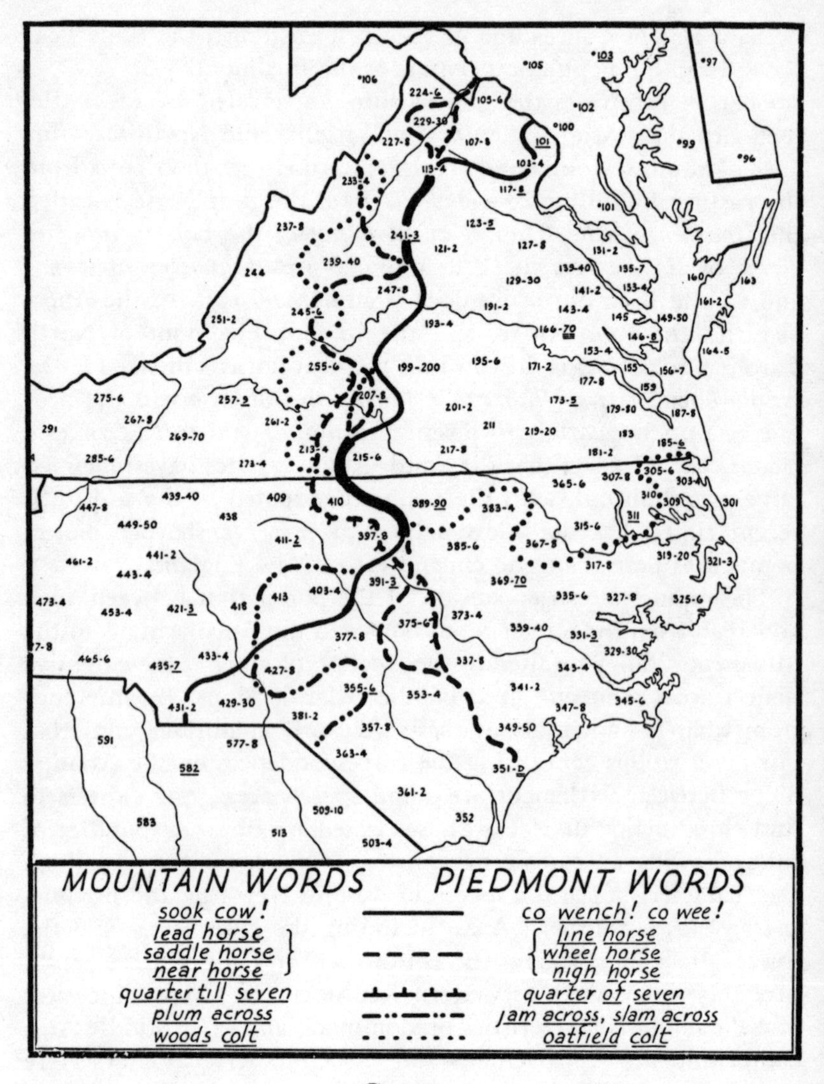

CHART 5

Little accurate and definitely localized linguistic material is available as yet for this trans-Appalachian area. However, the survey of the Great Lakes area and the Ohio Valley, recently begun at the University of Michigan under the direction of Albert H. Marckwardt, will soon enable us to draw the linguistic boundary

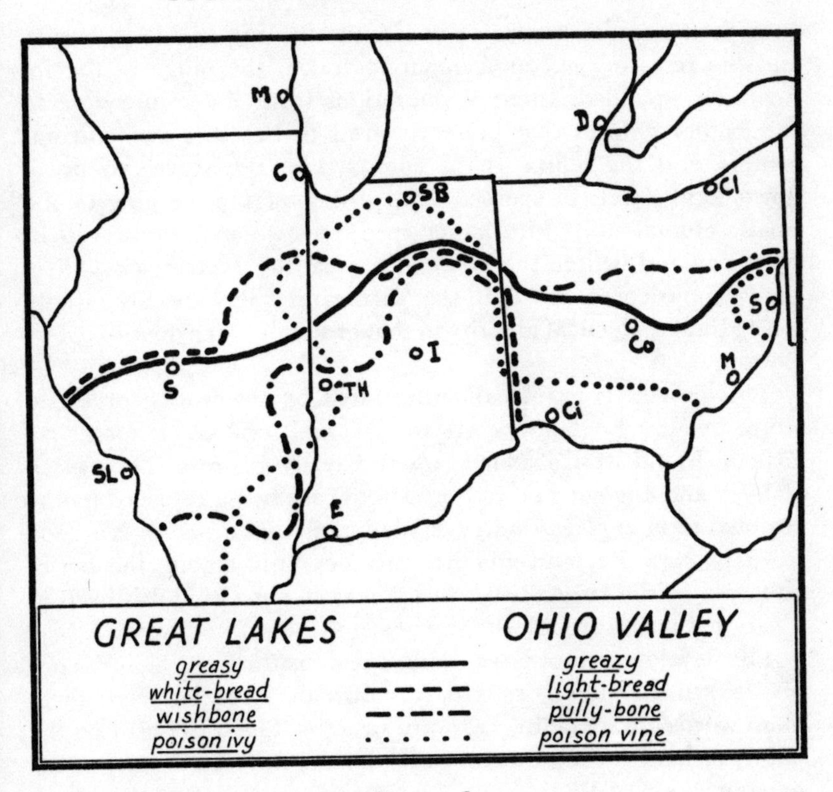

CHART 6

between the Northern and the Middle area. A sample of what we may expect to find has been put at my disposal by Mr. Marckwardt. In Chart 6 are presented the northernmost boundaries of *light-bread* in the sense of wheat bread, of *pully-bone,* of *poison vine,* and of the pronunciation of *greasy* to rhyme with *easy.* The corresponding Northern words are *white-bread, wishbone, poison ivy,* and the Northern *greasy* has the *s* sound of *geese.* These lines reflect the northern boundary of the settlements made from the Ohio Valley, whatever the ultimate provenience of the settlers may have been.

The flaring of the lines in Ohio and in Illinois shows that Northern forms are spreading southward from the great population centers in the northern parts of these states, while in Indiana the cultural center of Indianapolis is retarding the retreat.

With the improvement of roads, the coming of the railroads, and the resulting encouragement to travel, the range of the individual expanded. Internal migrations from the countryside to the factory villages that presently grew to be cities and cultural centers, and the reflux to the countryside, also served to break down local habits of speech. This process of the merging of the small colonial units into larger speech areas can be observed in New England, where the Casco Bay area, the Merrimack Valley, the Plymouth area, and even the Narragansett Bay area are rapidly losing their dialectical identity in that of a major area dominated by Boston.

This process is graphically illustrated by the words for earthworm in New England, where the colonial local terms *eaceworm* (Rhode Island west of Narragansett Bay), *mudworm* (Merrimack Valley), and *angledog* (Windsor Colony) are being replaced by the regional term *angleworm* in everyday speech. *Earthworm* is a book word in New England and has currency only among the better educated in the larger cities, but it may in time establish itself as a national term through the influence of the printed word.

The development of larger dialect regions through the influence of a cultural center is strikingly shown in Virginia. Here Piedmont words are spreading eastward into the Tidewater area on the points of land jutting out into Chesapeake Bay, northward to the neighborhood of Washington, D. C., and southward to the North Carolina line, where they are usually arrested. The present spread of a number of these words is shown in Chart 7. Expressions like *snake feeder* (dragon fly) and *red-worm* (earthworm) have retreated into the Blue Ridge and the Appalachians south of the James River, and the Tidewater words *mosquito hawk* (dragon fly) and *press peach* (clingstone peach) appear now only on the points of land in Chesapeake Bay and on the Eastern Shore. All these phenomena show that the Virginia Piedmont is a well-defined culture area, from which powerful influences radiate.

Much of the leveling of dialect differences is, however, to be attributed to schools and the printed word rather than the direct influence of cultural centers such as Boston. This infiltration of literary forms of speech through schools and through reading is reflected in a characteristic distribution pattern. "New" words or pronunciations appear side by side with "old" ones everywhere—

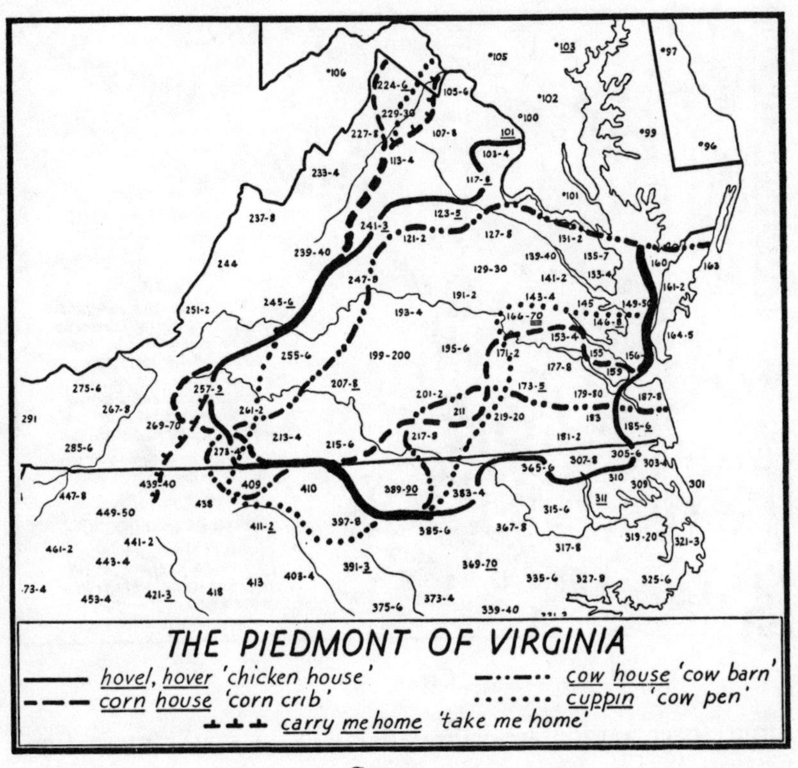

CHART 7

though not in the same proportion. In New England the new forms are more common in the larger population centers on the lower Connecticut River and around Boston than in the rural areas to the north. Characteristic examples of this type are the literary word *funnel* (for pouring liquids), which is replacing the regional New England word *tunnel,* and the standard pronunciation of the word *yolk* to rhyme with *yoke,* which is crowding out the older local pronunciations *yelk* and *yolk* (with the *l* sounded), as shown in Chart 8.[18]

The areal spread of dialect forms across old settlement boundaries from culturally or economically important centers is another interesting phenomenon that has been graphically illustrated in New England, where Hudson Valley words like *stoop* (a porch, of Dutch origin) and *pot cheese* (cottage cheese) are now current, the

[18] From *Handbook,* p. 27.

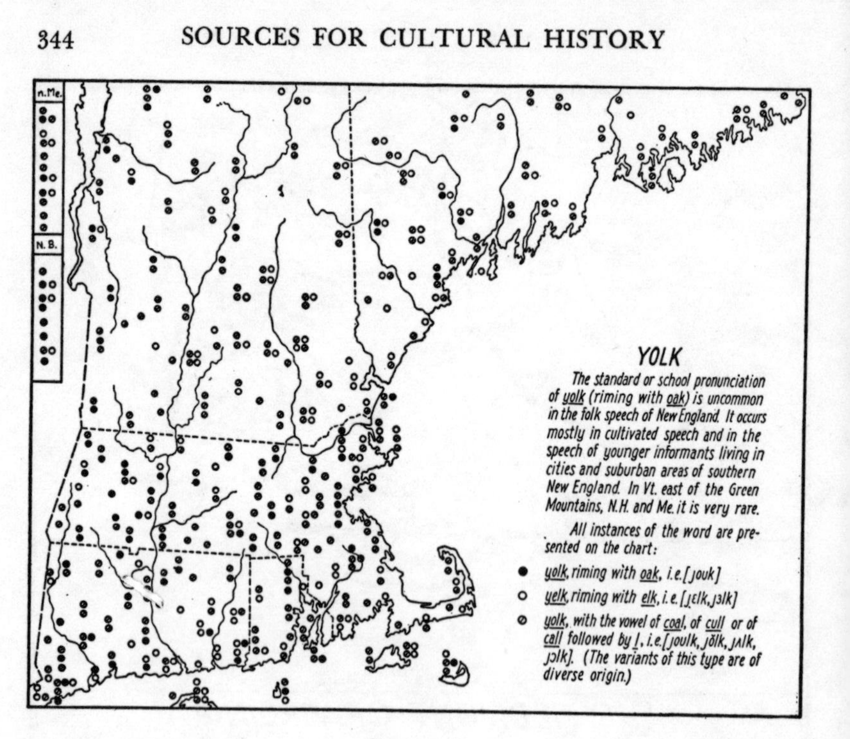

CHART 8

former over a wide area, the latter only in southwestern Connecticut.[19]

In this paper an attempt has been made to show that the geographic variations in American English are the result of the history of the settlement and of the influence of trade areas and culture areas on the speech of the American people. The illustrations given can easily be multiplied by drawing on the rich collections of definitely localized facts of usage in the *Linguistic Atlas.* The determination of the relation of dialect areas to settlement areas, trade areas, and culture areas has been made possible through the work of F. J. Turner and his school of historians and by the recent work of historians and geographers, incorporated in the great *Atlas of the Historical Geography of the United States.*[20] The growing interest in population history and in social and cultural history on the part of historians, geographers, and sociologists will doubt-

[19] See *Handbook,* p. 31 (Chart 10).

[20] Charles O. Paullin and John K. Wright, *Atlas of the Historical Geography of the United States,* Washington and New York, 1932.

less enable us before long to clear up further the interrelations between the linguistic history of our nation and other phases of its history. It is especially important that the relation of the shifting boundaries of trade areas and culture areas to settlement areas be investigated more thoroughly than hitherto, for the gradual submerging of the smaller settlement areas in larger trade and culture areas is the process that leads from strictly local cultures to regional cultures and ultimately to a national culture. To the solution of this problem, the linguist can certainly make a major contribution, since he can demonstrate in great detail the spreading of speech forms—words, idioms, grammatical forms, and pronunciations—from village to village across old settlement boundaries; for instance, from the settlements on the western part of Long Island Sound to Narragansett Bay and beyond, from the Boston area to the cities of Springfield and Hartford on the lower Connecticut River, from the Virginia Piedmont into the Shenandoah Valley and up the James River beyond the Blue Ridge, and from the population centers of northern Illinois and Ohio southward into the Ohio River settlements. This spreading is an eloquent symptom of the influence radiating from cultural centers.

The regionalism that is so clearly reflected in speech inevitably appears also in other cultural phenomena such as folk ways and folklore. It is to be anticipated that students of these subjects will receive as much help from linguistic research in this country as did the folklorists in Germany and the Scandinavian countries, where the geographic point of view has been so fruitfully applied.

In conclusion it should be pointed out that the study of the linguistic history of the non-English elements in our population, which has barely begun, can be of great significance in the investigation of the cultural contribution of these elements to our regional and national culture. Bilingualism, the transition in the course of several generations from the language of their European homes to English, and the survival of non-English features in their speech are phenomena parallel to biculturism, the transition from the traditional European culture to the culture of the new environment, and the survival of European traits in the culture of these groups. Here, as elsewhere, the linguist, who has the advantage of dealing with specific and easily observable facts in accordance with a well-established technique, is in a position to be a successful pioneer.

LATIN LITERATURE AS A SOURCE FOR THE STUDY OF MEDIEVAL CULTURE

CORNELIA C. COULTER

A SURVEY of the Latin literature of the Middle Ages as a source for the study of history brings both interesting and significant results; it reveals a vast body of material, and at the same time it shows the definite limitations of such material as a basis for historical knowledge. Of the writing in Latin that has come down to us from the Middle Ages the great bulk was produced by the clergy, and by far the largest part of this writing is on religious themes. This preponderance of the religious over the secular is of course partly due to the accident of survival, and here ecclesiastical literature had a great advantage over secular; members of the clergy possessed facilities for recording and preserving their thoughts which were not available to the laity, so that the chances of survival of a doctrinal treatise, as against those of a popular tale or song, were about 100 to one. Therefore, when we attempt to use Latin literature as an index to the history and culture of the Middle Ages, we must remember that in the main it reflects the interests and the point of view of the most highly educated class of the period, the clergy, and that it cannot give us a complete picture of the less educated and the less articulate groups of society.

Yet even this predominantly religious literature, with its mass of theological treatises, sermons, biblical commentaries, and essays on church management, still allows some glimpses into the life of everyday folk. Cyprian prefaces his treatise on martyrdom (*De exhortatione martyrii*) with a letter in which the soldier of Christ is represented as preparing for the spiritual conflict, exercising in the camp of the heavenly host, and equipping himself against the darts and shafts of the devil—a conception based on passages in the New Testament, but worked out with details that mirror life in the Roman army in the third century after Christ.[1] Jerome's letter to Laeta about the training of her little daughter for a holy

[1] In Migne, *Patrologia latina*, IV, 677–80.

life calls up a picture of the child playing with wooden or ivory blocks in the shape of letters of the alphabet or struggling to draw their outlines with a stilus on a tablet of wax; and his warnings against rouge and red dye for the hair, necklaces of gold, and pearls and masses of jewels for the head make us see by contrast the worldly young woman who had not had the advantage of his counsel.[2] The histories of Gregory, Bishop of Tours, of the Venerable Bede, and of Paul, the Deacon, contain a fair amount of folk material: the story of a candle left beside a cask of oil in a storeroom, that set fire to all Paris and thereby fulfilled the dream of a certain woman in the city three nights before; [3] the legends of Caedmon's gift of song and of Brother Drythelm, who would stand in an icy stream in midwinter, and to sympathetic inquiries would answer simply, "I've seen it colder"; [4] the grim jest of Alboin, king of the Langobardi, who invited his wife to drink from a cup made of her father's skull, and so roused her to plot his own murder.[5]

As time goes on, the secular element increases in quantity and importance. Chronicles are written in Germany, France, and England, including such material as local legends, national customs, student life at Oxford and Paris, and details of the Crusades. Collections of stories are made—by the clergy, to be sure, but with a large folk element in their content, and with the folk definitely in mind as an audience: marvelous tales from the East; garbled accounts of Greek mythological figures like Io and Oedipus; beast fables, with a moral attached; anecdotes of kings and princesses and peasants, of quarrelsome and unfaithful wives; of the way the devil conducted himself in an encounter with a woman, a schoolboy, or a hermit.[6]

The poetry of the early Middle Ages reflects the religious interest of the times in hymns for morning and evening or for the different seasons of the church year, paraphrases of Old and New Testament stories, and lives of saints and martyrs. But mingled with these are

[2] *Epistula* 107, 4–5 (Migne, *Patrologia latina,* XXII, 871–72).

[3] Gregory of Tours, *Historia Francorum,* ed. by R. Poupardin (Paris, 1913), VIII, 33.

[4] Bede, *Historia ecclesiastica gentis anglorum,* ed. by Charles Plummer (Oxford, 1896), IV, 22; V, 12.

[5] Paulus Diaconus, *Historia Langobardorum,* ed. by Georg Waitz (Hannover, 1878), II, 28.

[6] For examples of these themes, see Charles H. Beeson, *A Primer of Medieval Latin* (Chicago, 1925), pp. 35–107; Karl P. Harrington, *Medieval Latin* (Boston, 1925), pp. 417–28, 433–46.

occasional bits of verse that show an interest in current events, in personal relationships, and in the world of nature. Venantius Fortunatus writes graceful verses to accompany gifts of flowers or chestnuts to his patroness Radegunda, thanks her and her sister for the eggs and plums that they have sent him, or tells them how, at the end of a feast, the wine so went to his head that he could not control either pen or fingers.[7] Walahfrid Strabo tells of reclaiming wild ground to make a garden, and of the growth of medicinal herbs and fragrant blossoms by which he was rewarded.[8] One ninth-century writer describes Ireland as a land flowing with milk and honey; another sings the praises of "Roma nobilis"; still another prays for help in the defense of Modena.[9] Fables feature the lion, the calf and the stork, the gout and the flea.[10] And in the eleventh and twelfth centuries the Wandering Scholars are responsible for large numbers of drinking songs, love songs, poems on the seasons, riddles, and narrative verse, both serious and humorous.[11] An occasional addition in the margin of a manuscript or at the end of a long text reveals the writer's feelings—the physical discomfort of cramped hand and aching back; the joy that he experiences at the completion of his task, like that of a sailor making port after a long and weary voyage.[12]

Aside from the content of both prose and verse, the form of the Latin literature of the Middle Ages gives a clue to the culture and interests of the writers. The language is a continuation of the popular speech of classical times, as we find it in the familiar letters of Cicero and his friends, in folk sayings preserved by Varro and snatches of popular song quoted by Suetonius, and in tombstone inscriptions put up by humble folk all over the Roman world. This Latin is far simpler in structure than the Latin of Cicero's orations or the *Aeneid;* much more given to rhyme and assonance and play on words; rich in superlatives, in intensive adverbs, and diminutives; and sprinkled with slang and with words borrowed from the

[7] Venantius Fortunatus, *Miscellanea,* VIII, 8; XI, 13, 20, 23 (in Harrington, *Mediaeval Latin,* pp. 57–59).

[8] Extracts in Harrington, *Mediaeval Latin,* pp. 142–43; and in *The Oxford Book of Mediaeval Verse,* ed. by Stephen Gaselee (Oxford, 1928), No. 28.

[9] *The Oxford Book of Mediaeval Latin Verse,* Nos. 24, 34, 36.

[10] *The Oxford Book of Mediaeval Latin Verse,* No. 59; Harrington, *Mediaeval Latin,* p. 127.

[11] Cf. especially the collections under the names of *The Cambridge Songs,* ed. by Karl Breul, Cambridge, 1915; and *Carmina Burana,* ed. by Max Manitius, Jena, 1927.

[12] One such subscription is printed in Beeson, *A Primer of Medieval Latin,* p. 322.

Greek. All these features of style come out in the Latin of the early Middle Ages. The Spanish nun who made a pilgrimage to the Holy Land in the fourth century [13] frames her sentences with the same untutored simplicity as the freedmen of Petronius, and, like them, she adds emphatic adverbs to intensify her meaning and uses Greek words for certain common things. A twelve-page treatise of Jerome yields an average of between one and two diminutives to the page; [14] and the last sixty lines of a sixth-century poem on the creation contain six different superlatives.[15]

In poetry, too, although the formal meters like the hexameter continue to be used, the great mass of verse composition is done in two meters which were much closer in their rhythm to everyday speech: a short iambic and a long trochaic line. The iambic meter had been used by Plautus, with the ends of the phrases sometimes marked by rhyme or assonance.[16] It is found in fragments of Petronius, quoted by the grammarians,[17] and in the four-line poem addressed by the Emperor Hadrian to his soul; [18] and we hear it sounding in the fuller organ-strains of the great hymns of Hilary and Ambrose.[19]

The trochaic meter, too, had been used by Plautus, in a long swinging line that lent itself readily to humorous effects.[20] It was shouted by Caesar's soldiers in the ribald songs intended to ward off the jealousy of the gods from the conqueror; [21] and in the second century after Christ an unknown writer rang the changes on it in the lovely *Pervigilium veneris.*[22] The Christian poet Venantius For-

[13] *Peregrinatio ad loca sancta,* formerly ascribed to Saint Silvia, now generally assigned to Aetheria, ed. by Wilhelm Heraeus, Heidelberg, 1908.

[14] *De perpetua virginitate B. Mariae* (Migne, *Patrologia latina,* XXIII, 193–216).

[15] *The Oxford Book of Mediaeval Latin Verse,* No. 20.

[16] Technically, the meter of the medieval poets is dimeter, consisting of two measures, or four feet, whereas Plautus uses an eight-foot line called octonarius; but the long line of Plautus normally divides into two phrases of two measures each, and the close connection between the two types of iambic meter is clear from the fact that in several passages a series of octonarii is followed by a dimeter, or vice versa (*Menaechmi,* lines 995–1005; *Mercator,* lines 135–40; *Mostellaria,* lines 130–32; *Rudens,* lines 938–44).

[17] E. g., *Grammatici latini,* ed. by Heinrich Keil (Leipzig, 1857–80), I, 518; VI, 138. It is also found in a short poem quoted by Aulus Gellius, *Noctes Atticae,* XIX, 11, said to have been composed by a gifted young friend of Gellius.

[18] *The Oxford Book of Latin Verse,* ed. by H. W. Garrod (Oxford, 1912), No. 287.

[19] E. g., *Latin Hymns,* ed. by William A. Merrill (Boston, 1917), pp. 1–6.

[20] E. g., *Amphitruo,* lines 1009–14. This line, like the iambis octonarius, tends to break up into two phrases. In the later medieval period these two parts were treated as separate units and combined into a great variety of stanza forms.

[21] Suetonius, *Julius,* 51.

[22] *The Oxford Book of Latin Verse,* No. 320.

tunatus uses this meter with exquisite effect in a hymn on the Holy Cross, which shows a similarity to the popular Latin verse of an earlier day not only in the basic form of the meter but in details such as alliteration and the repetition of forms of the same word in emphatic positions, with the verse accent and the word accent coinciding.[23]

By the eleventh century verse forms have undergone considerable change. Iambic dimeter and trochaic septenarius continue to be the favorite meters, but word accent has gradually displaced quantity as the basis for verse composition, and rhyme, which had occurred in the earliest hymns as a sporadic and half-accidental phenomenon, has become more and more essential, so that definite stanza forms appear, based on these two features. This rhymed accentual verse of the medieval church became perhaps the most delicate instrument ever discovered for the expression of human emotion—the infinite sorrow and longing of the soul, its infinite tenderness.[24] Hymns of this type are taken over into medieval Latin drama, and very much accentuate the moving effect of such plays as the *Visitatio sepulchri,* performed by the monks of Saint-Benoît-sur-Loire.[25]

Secular lyrics of the eleventh and twelfth centuries use the verse technique developed in the composition of hymns, but tend to be written in shorter lines, with a predominating trochaic rhythm. A new meter, called the "goliardic," appears and is used repeatedly in the lyrics of the Wandering Scholars, of which the drinking song taken from the "Confession" of the Arch-Poet is the most familiar example:

> Meum est propositum in taberna mori.
> ['Tis my purpose fixed to die in a public tavern.][26]

Our study of all these verse forms is at present seriously handicapped by our very fragmentary knowledge of the music. Hymn tunes and musical settings for certain parts of the church service have come down to our own day, in some cases appearing with very

[23] Merrill, *Latin Hymns,* pp. 18–19. Note especially the alliteration of lines 23–24, and compare the repetition in these lines with that in Plautus, *Amphitruo,* lines 1009–14, and in the refrain of the *Pervigilium Veneris.*

[24] E. g., Merrill, *Latin Hymns,* pp. 38–40, 49–51; *The Oxford Book of Mediaeval Latin Verse,* No. 62.

[25] For the text, see Karl Young, *The Drama of the Medieval Church* (Oxford, 1933), I, 393–97.

[26] *The Oxford Book of Mediaeval Latin Verse,* No. 66, lines 41 ff.

little change in the service of the Roman Catholic Church or the Church of England hymnal. The text of many of the liturgical plays is accompanied in the manuscripts by symbols indicating the melody to which the words were to be sung; but most of these symbols are still waiting to be translated into modern notation and to be interpreted by the only medium that really gives a correct impression of the music—the human voice. In the case of the secular songs, far less has survived. Some of the elaborate stanza forms in varying meters suggest composition for already existing melodies or dance tunes; [27] but these tunes, alas! have perished. The melody called "Puella turbata" ("The Maiden in Distress"), which was used in the church service, must have been attached originally to a popular song; [28] and the meter and the tune of six lines near the close of the *Visitatio sepulchri* suggest kinship with songs of the Wandering Scholars; [29] but in both cases we can merely hazard a guess as to the popular words which were sung to these tunes.

Clearly, then, Latin literature of the Middle Ages, voluminous as it is, cannot give a complete picture of the period. It enables us to follow medieval religious thought in great detail, but pays comparatively little attention to the popular and the secular. Nevertheless, when read with a seeing eye and a hearing ear, it does reveal something of the activities and interests of the common people. There is room for still more study, especially in the writings of obscure authors; there should be more complete editions of texts, including some that have heretofore been considered relatively unimportant, such as fragments of verse and marginal notes; and, in particular, a great deal more work should be done on the music.

[27] Cf. F. J. E. Raby, *A History of Secular Latin Poetry in the Middle Ages* (Oxford, 1934), II, 333, n. 3.

[28] *Hymns Ancient and Modern,* Historical edition (London, 1909), p. 449.

[29] Text in Young, *The Drama of the Mediaeval Church,* I, 393–97; music in E. de Coussemaker, *Drames liturgiques du moyen âge* (Rennes, 1860), pp. 178–87. The passage begins *Resurrexit hodie.*

INDEX

Abrams, Charles, quoted, 180
Adams, John, 172
Agriculture, coöperative movement, 76; decreased employment capacity, 297; in Balkan peasant family, 106-8; under Russian collectivism, 133-39; under Russian mir, 125-32
Alexander, Franz, 48-57
Allen, G. C., quoted, 243
Allport, Floyd, 179
Ambivalence, 36
American Council of Learned Societies, 333
American English, 331 ff.; cultural significance of non-English words, 345
American Hellenic Educational Progressive Association (Ahepa), 65, 66
American Historical Association, 6; statement of Program Committee, quoted, 15
Americanization, process, 65; techniques of study, 77; two-way adjustment, 74
American Protective Association, 79, 81
American Telephone and Telegraph Company, 171, 176
Ancestor worship, 114, 119, 123
Anderson, Eugene N., 15
Anderson, H. H., 41
Anglo-Saxon tradition, 70, 87
Anthropology, concept of culture, 10, 20-33; social, definition, 20; statistical approach, 26
Aristotle, 204, 208, 213
Arkwright, Richard, 140, 141
Army, Dutch, 186
Army, French, 185
Army, German: as cultural institution, 94, 182; common soldier, 183-85, 191, 195; length of service, 192; management, 183; officer personnel, 188-92, 195; pay, 194
Army, Prussian, 187-90
Articulate groups, 8, 62; *see also* Dominant groups
Assimilation, 74, 78-82, 86
Atget, Eugène, 325
Atlas of the Historical Geography of the United States, 344
Authoritarianism, effect of control on dominated groups, 40-44

Balkans, zadruga, 95-108
Bankers Trust Company, 173
Baron, Hans, quoted, 209
Beard, Charles A., *Economic Interpretation of the Constitution,* 4; quoted, 6, 37, 47, 176
Beckwith, Martha Warren, quoted, 313
Bede, The Venerable, 347
Behavior, diversification in urban conditions, 239; effect of industrial city on standards, 231 ff.; expression of human needs, 22; formed by social structure, 30; historical and psychological aspects, 34 ff.; in industrial city, 238-41; shaped by urban forces, 241
Behavior pattern, 31, 69, 230, 278
Bestor, Arthur E., 254-59
Biggerstaff, Knight, 109-24
Billington, Ray Allen, 78-82, 86
Biological needs, 20-22
Bismarck, Otto Eduard Leopold, Prince von, 190, 192
Black Death, 291, 292, 293
Boatright, Mody C., *Tall Tales from Texas,* 312
Boston, cultural flowering, 264-67
Botkin, B. A., 308-15
Bourgeois tradition, 72
Boyce, Gray C., 202-11
Brady, Mathew B., 324
Brinton, Crane, *The Anatomy of Revolution,* 45
Brooks, Van Wyck, 260, 261
Bullock, C. J., 175
Burke, Kenneth, quoted, 37
Burns, Robert, 311
Business regulation, 165

Calvinism, 257, 264, 267, 270
Catholic church, effect on American culture, 72; music, 351
Chambers Edinburgh Journal, excerpt, 140
Channing, Edward Tyrrel, 268
Character, formed by treatment during infancy, 30; relation to social structure, 32
China, democratization of social structure, 247; impact of Western ideas on, 120-24; modernization, 243-51

Chinese large-family, administrative functions, 116-20; clan-village, 113; history, 109; land tenure, 111, 112; marriage customs, 110, 119, 123; reasons for breakdown, 120-24; relation to small family, 110; structure, 111-14
City, milieu for immigrant adaptation, 67-69; position in American culture, 68; *see also* Industrial city; Manchester
Class, beginnings of, 24; in industrial city, 145, 231; in Japan and China, 244; in New England, 262; in Russia, 130, 131, 134
Classics, effect on theology, 210; folk material in, 348; use by twelfth-century authors, 205-9
Cobbett, William, 157, 159
Cobden, Richard, 151, 155; quoted, 146
Cochran, Thomas C., 168-81
Collectivization, 132-39
Colm, Gerhard, "The Corporation and the Rise of National Socialism," quoted, 165
Comic strip, 311
Communities, Chinese, 113, 114; company-dominated, 178; effect on inhabitants, 278; industrial, 140-45; Russian peasant, 125 ff.; study of, 284-85; zadrugal, 97 ff.
Company-dominated town, 178
Confucius, 109
Congregationalism, 262, 267, 270
Connecticut, science and reform in, 267-70
Conscience, 56-57
Coöperative movement, 76, 85
Corporation, administration, 174; as cultural institution, 94, 162; competition with state, 164-67, 175; dual character, 172-74; effect on individualist standards, 178-80; factor in modern history, 162-67; material for study, 169-71; nonbusiness, 177, 181; social history in United States, 168-81; topics for study, 174-81
Cotton industry, 140-42
Coulter, Cornelia C., 346-57
Court Leet, 149, 150
Cultural centers, influence on dialect areas, 341-45
Cultural change: dynamics of, 13, 225-70; industrial city a factor in, 228-42; processes, 225-27, 244, 245, 249
Cultural groups, 24 ff., 62 ff., 75, 83
Cultural institutions: corporation, factor in modern history, 94, 162-67, in United States, 168-81; family, 93, in Balkans, 95-108, in China, 109-24, in Russia, 125-39; German army, 94, 182-96; industrial city, 93, 140-61, 228-42; measure of importance of, 162
Culture, conditions for flowering, 258; contrast between Chinese and Japanese, 243-51; definitions, 10, 22, 25, 229; dynamics of change in, 13, 225, 226; effect of conquest on, 27; preservation of Chinese, 117; processes for maintaining, 29; psychological function, 31; relation of articulate and inarticulate groups to, 8; role of ideas in, 199-201; sociological role, 32; sources for study, *see* Cultural history
Culture, American: Anglo-Saxon basis, 70, 87; composite of contemporary cultures, 89; flowering of New England, 252-70; nationalistic impulse in, 253; nationality groups, 74-89
Curti, Merle, 259-64
Cyprian, Saint, *De exhortatione martyrii*, 346
Czechs in United States, 304

Daguerre, Louis, 324
Dana, James Dwight, 270
Danes in United States, 76, 85
Danielian, N. R., *A.T.&T.*, 171, 176
Davie, Maurice R., 74-78, 86, 89
Davison, Henry Pomeroy, 173
Democracy, 40-44; lack of democratic practice under, 41
Demography, 287-307
Detroiser, Rowland, 148, 159
Dewey, John, 213
Dialect areas, 331-45; breaking down, 342-44; charted, 335-44
Dictionary of American English, 332
Division of labor, 22-24, 184; in Chinese large-family, 116; in factory work, 158; in industrial city, 231; in zadruga, 98, 108
Doherty, John, 157, 159
Dominant groups, 8, 28, 61
Donald Duck, 311
Dooley, Mr., *see* Dunne, Finley Peter
Drew, Daniel, 178
Dunne, Finley Peter (Mr. Dooley), quoted, 3, 71

Education, in industrial city, 154, 156, 241; process of, 29; relation to democracy, 43; relation to flowering of New

England, 261, 262; relation to German army, 191
Emerson, Ralph Waldo, 254-58, 268; *The American Scholar,* 253; "Historic Notes," 255, 257; "Prudence," quoted, 256
Emigration, effect on Balkan peasant family, 107; on Chinese large-family, 121
Engels, Friedrich, 184
English in United States, 76
Ethos, definition, 25; relations of, among disparate groups, 26, 27, 28, 32
Evans, W. D., 146

Factory discipline, 147 ff.
Factory system, 141, 147 ff.
Family, Balkan communal-joint (zadruga), 95-108; Chinese peasant, 109-24; controls replaced by factory discipline, 147; in agrarian culture, 93; Russian peasant, 125-39
Filial piety, 115, 119
Finns in United States, 62
Folk, the, 308
Folk idiom, reflection of culture, 320
Folk literature, 311
Folklore, definition, 308; relation to social history, 308-15; techniques for preserving, 314; types, 310-14
Folk music, relation to social history, 316-23; techniques for preserving, 319
Folkways, interaction, 75; in Latin literature, 346-51; language, *see* Dialect areas
Ford Motor Company, 172
French Canadians in United States, 64
French in United States, 88
Freud, Sigmund, 55
Frontier, 67
Frontier hypothesis, Turner, 304-6
Frustration, 37-40

Gabriel, Ralph H., 252
Gardner, Alexander, 324
Gaskell, P., 148, 153
German army of Second Reich, *see* Army, German
Germans in United States, 65, 70, 72, 81, 86, 304
Germany, struggle between corporation and state, 164, 165
Gestalt psychology, 12
Gibbon, Edward, 3, 4, 6
Goldenweiser, A. A., quoted, 230
Goliardi, 203, 348, 350, 351
Gorer, Geoffrey, 20-33
Gould, Jay, 178
Government, by families in China, 116, 117, 123; of Manchester, 149-52; relation to corporation, 164-67
Greeks in United States, 65, 88
Green, Constance McLaughlin, 275-86
Gregory, bishop of Tours, 347

Hale, Edward Everett, quoted, 268
Hargan, Stephen H., 325
Harvard College, 265, 268, 270
Hawthorne, Nathaniel, 254
Heckscher, W. S., quoted, 207, 208
Heywood, Benjamin, 153, 154
Hine, Lewis, 324
Historian, concern with functional relationships, 11; cultural approach as technique, 10-15; need for new intellectual tools, 6, 9, 14; presentation determined by social outlook, 4-6; scientific attitude, 3-5
History, changes affecting writing of, 3-8; cultural approach, 10-16; economic, 276; interpretation of, 52-57; interrelations with psychology, 34-46, 48-57; medieval intellectual, 202-11; "new," 6-8; written records, 5
  History, local: as material for culture study, 275-86; inadequacy of chronicles, 279; sources, 281-83; techniques for selection, 284-85; for writing, 280, 284
  History, sources of cultural: dialect areas, 331-45; documentary photography, 324-30; folklore, 308-15; folk music, 316-23; Latin literature, 346-51; local history, 275-86; population data, 287-307
Hitler, Adolf, 43; *Mein Kampf,* quoted, 195
Holmes, Oliver Wendell (justice), 214
Holmes, Oliver Wendell (poet), 266, 268
Hsiao-ching (*Classic of Filial Piety*), 110
Hu Shih, 243-51
Human nature, 35, 36, 54 ff.

Ideas, cultural role, 199-222
Immigrant, contribution to American life, 75, 79-82, 86; impact of city life on, 67-71; significance of background, 84-86; *see also* Nationality groups
Immigrant-American societies, 82
Inarticulate groups, importance of culture, 8, 62; lack of data on, 277
Individualism, in China, 122, 123; in Russia, 130, 131; in the industrial city, 239
Industrial capitalists, 149, 160, 165

Industrial city, as cultural institution, 93; as social milieu, 231-33; center of cultural change, 228-42; effect of technology on, 235-38; factors in cultural development, 233-40; impact on national culture, 161; regimentation, 158; *see also* Manchester
Industrial culture, 72, 73, 231
Industrial discipline, 147, 158, 164
Industrialization, in China, 121; in Japan, 246; of Manchester, 140 ff.; of Russian agriculture, 93, 136
Industrial revolution, factor in flowering of New England, 254; factory town the outgrowth of, 140
Industrial workers, characteristics, 145-49, 231; condition, 148; political activity, 159; status, 233, 234
Instincts, 35
Institutions, *see* Cultural institutions
Intelligence tests, 43
Irish in United States, 64, 65, 72, 79, 88
Italians in United States, 63, 64, 69, 72, 88; letter from political group, quoted, 70
Ives, Frederick E., 325

Jackson, William H., 324
Japan, acceptance of new ideas, 250; militarism, 246, 250; modernization, 243-51
Jazz, 311
Jerome, Saint, 346, 349
Jews in United States, 68, 304
Johnstone, Paul H., 324-30
Junkers, 187

Kansas, population movements, 301-4, 305
Kantorowicz, Hermann, quoted, 203
Keller, Charles R., 267-70
Kirkland, Edward C., 252-54
Know-Nothing party, 79, 81
Kolkhoz, 133-39; artel form of organization, 137-39; effect of tractor on, 136, 137; relation to government, 135, 136; relation to peasants, 133-35, 137
Korson, George, *Minstrels of the Mine Patch,* 313
Krapp, George P., 331
Krazy Kat, 311
Ku Klux Klan, 81
Kurath, Hans, 331-45

Labor legislation, 147
Labor market, 146, 147, 148
Labor unions, *see* Trade unions
Labor unit: family, 95 ff.; peasant worker, 133; factory hand, 148
Laissez-faire, 165
Lamont, Thomas William, quoted, 173
Land tenure: by Chinese family, 111, 112; collectivization, 132-39; in zadrugas, 100-108; under Russian mir, 126-31
Landry, B., 205-7
Landwehr, 188, 189
Language, nature and function, 334
Large-family, *see* Chinese large-family
Latin literature, reflects cultural changes, 348-51; source for social history, 346-51; verse forms, 349
Le Conte, Joseph, quoted, 46
Lederer, Emil, and Lederer-Seidler, Emy, *Japan in Transition,* 243; quoted, 246
Leidy, Joseph, 266
Lenin, Nicolai, 130, 137
Lerner, Max, quoted, 202, 211
Lewin, Kurt, 40, 44
Liberalism, based on belief in intelligence, 213-15, 217, 220; definition, 212; economic, 220-22, 233-35; historic position of, 212-22; prospects, 218-22; recognition of social function of state, 217; role of government, 215-17
Li-chi (*Book of Rites*), 110
Linguistic Atlas of the United States and Canada, 333, 344
Linton, R., 30
Lippmann, Walter, 217; quoted, 234
Littell's Living Age, excerpt, 144, 160
Liverpool and Manchester Railway, 142, 156
Locke, John, 213
Longfellow, Henry Wadsworth, 253, 266
Longstreet, Augustus Baldwin, 332
Lorimer, Frank, 287-90
Lowell, James Russell, 268, 332
Lowie, Robert H., quoted, 232
Lynd, Robert S., *Knowledge for What?,* 46

Macaulay, Thomas Babington, 3, 4, 6
Machiavelli, Niccolò di Bernardo, 213
MacWilliams, David, 159
Madison, James, 172
Malin, James C., 300-307
Malinowski, B., 25
Malthus, Thomas Robert, 287
Management, corporation, 163, 166; military, 183 ff.
Manchester, description in 1850, 144; ed-

ucational institutions, 154, 156; first industrial city, 140-61; growth, 140-45; political institutions, 159-61; press, 157; recreations, 155; religious activity, 155; slums, 146, 148, 152, 153; social institutions, 152-54; social structure, 145, 146, 148 ff.; struggle for municipal control, 149-54, 159-61
Manchester Guardian, quoted, 151, 157, 228
Manchester Guide, excerpt, 143
Marckwardt, Albert H., 340
Marshall, Leon S., 140-61
Marville, Charles, 324
Marx, Karl, 6, 55, 184
Masses, distribution of intelligence, 42; effect of urban association on, 238-41; industrial, 73, 228; lack of social information on, 8; origin of, 159; reëducation of, 241; study of, 241, 274, 277
Medieval Latin, structure, 348; verse meter, 347, 350
Melting pot, 63, 79
Mencius, 109
Mencken, H. L., 331
Mexicans in United States, 64, 65, 70
Mickey Mouse, 311
Middle Ages, absorption of ideas of antiquity, 204-11; Latin literature, 346-51; literacy among laity, 203; population data, 291-93; secular thought, 202 ff.
Middle West Utilities Company, 169, 180
Migration, age of participants, 305; corporations a factor in, 180; during depression, 306; economic factors in, 296-99; in Kansas, 301-4, 305; in Middle Ages, 293; in New South, 295
Mir, Russian, 125-32; administrative functions, 127, 128; characteristics, 125-27; control over households, 128-30; land tenure, 126-31; liquidation, 132; relation to government, 128, 131; role in revolution, 130-32
Moltke, Helmuth Karl Bernhard, Count von, 190, 192; quoted, 191
Moseley, Philip E., 95-108
Motivations, 36, 56
Murray, Margaret, 28
Music, complementary to language, 322; distinction between fine-art and other, 318; folk, 316-23
Musicology, 317 ff.

Nationality groups in United States, 62 ff.; assimilation, 74-82; cultural contribution, 78-82; in agriculture, 304; interrelationships, 67-73; shaping industrial culture, 72, 73; transitional character of culture, 82-84, 87-89; Czechs, 304; Danes, 76, 85; English, 76; Finns, 62; French, 88; French Canadians, 64; Germans, 65, 70, 72, 81, 86, 304; Greeks, 65, 88; Irish, 64, 65, 72, 79, 88; Italians, 63, 64, 69, 72, 88; Jews, 68, 304; Mexicans, 64, 65, 70; Negroes, 65, 304, 311; Norwegians, 83, 85, 88; Pennsylvania Dutch, 62; Poles, 63, 64, 65, 72, 88; Portuguese, 64, 88; Scandinavians, 70, 85, 304; Spanish, 62, 70; Syrians, 88; Welsh, 76
Negroes in United States, 65, 304, 311
New Economic Policy (NEP), 131
New England, flowering of, 252-70; characteristics of leaders, 259-64; cultural unity, 254-59; in Boston, 264-67; in Connecticut, 267-70; religious background, 259, 260, 262-65; scope, 265-67; social and intellectual unrest, 255-57; social-economic background, 253, 261-64
Nondominant groups, lack of data on, 28, 277; significance in culture, 26-28, 61 ff.; source of new industrial culture, 70-73
Nordau, Max, quoted, 53, 54
Nordström, J., 207
Norwegian-American Historical Association, 82, 84
Norwegians in United States, 83, 85, 88

Ogden, James, quoted, 146
Oman, Sir Charles, quoted, 203
Ornitz, Samuel, *Haunch, Paunch, and Jowl,* 71
Oviatt, F. C., quoted, 177

Panofsky, Erwin, 207, 208
Pareto, Vilfredo, *Mind and Society,* 6
Parker, Theodore, 254
Paul the Deacon, 347
Peel, Sir Robert, 141, 143
Pennsylvania Dutch, 62
People's Journal (Manchester), excerpt, 158
Phillips, Ulrich B., quoted, 285
Photography, documentary, 324-30; development of, 324-26; illustrations of use, 328-30; in the press, 325; material, 324, 326; superiority over drawings, 327
Poles in United States, 63, 64, 65, 72, 88
Political Register (Manchester), 157

Politics, position under liberalism, 219
Poor Man's Advocate (Manchester), 157
Population data, 287-307; sources, 292, 300; techniques of handling, 289
Population Index, 290
Population movement, *see* Migrations
Porter, Kenneth W., "Trends in American Business Biography," quoted, 168
Portuguese in United States, 64, 88
Press, photography in, 325
Propaganda, 38, 238
Property, in Chinese family, 111, 112; in industrial city, 239; in zadruga, 100-106; socialization of concept, 239; under Russian kolkhoz, 136; under Russian mir, 125, 126, 129, 131
Protestantism, 71
Psychology, confusion of national and individual, 49; interpretation of historical events, 48-57; interrelations with history, 34-47; of democracy, 40-44; of development of responsibility, 44; of social change, 45-47; of war and peace, 37-39
Pujo Committee, 174
Puritans, influence on New England flowering, 260, 262-65

Qualey, Carlton C., 82-84, 88

Radcliffe-Brown, A. R., 25
Railroads, 142, 156, 172, 253, 254
Ranke, Leopold von, 3
Rationalization, 50; by historians, 52-55; universal need for, 54-57
Raushenbush, Stephen, 162-67
Raymond, Daniel, 172
Religion, Catholic in United States, 72; effect on cultural pattern, 71; in China, 114, 115; in New England, 257, 259, 262, 265, 267, 268, 269, 270; in relation to population trend, 291; medieval, 203-10; Protestant in United States, 71
Revolution, 45, 46; *see also* Industrial revolution
Róheim, G., 30
Roucek, Joseph S., 86-89
Rourke, Constance, quoted, 314
Royse, M. W., 86-89
Russell, Josiah C., 291-93
Russia, peasant family, 125-39

Sabine, George H., 212-22
Sandburg, Carl, *Abraham Lincoln, The Prairie Years,* 308; *The American Songbag,* 308; *The People, Yes,* quoted, 308
Sansom, G. B., quoted, 250
Scandinavians in United States, 70, 85, 304
Schramm, Percy Ernst, 207, 208
Science, in Connecticut, 270; in Middle Ages, 204, 210
Scientific attitude, 3-6, 7
Seeger, Charles, 316-23
Self-justification, 54-56
Shakespeare, William, 311
Sheridan, J. B., quoted, 175
Shryock, Richard H., 264-67
Silliman, Benjamin, 269, 270
Social change: cultural approach for study, 13; goal, 46; obscurity of causes, 8; psychology and history in study of, 45-47; *see also* Cultural change
Social Democratic party, 191
Social milieu, 145, 200, 232, 233
Social status, 30, 72, 233
Social structure: device for maintaining culture, 30, 31; restraints and gratifications under, 32
Societies, character differentiated by cultures, 29; traits in common, 22
Society, criteria of, 21; definition, 32; divergent groups in, 27; economic stratification in, 64, 134; synchronic and diachronic views, 26, 28; viewed by anthropologist, 20-33
Society for the Psychological Study of Social Issues, 45
South, population movements in, 294-99
Southern Pacific Railroad, 172
Spanish in United States, 62, 70
Spengler, Oswald, *Decline of the West,* 6
Stakhanovist speed-up, 134
Stalin, Joseph, 136; quoted, 137
State, competition with corporation, 164-67; social function, 217
Steffens, Lincoln, *Autobiography,* 71
Stolypin laws, 131, 132
Stratification, economic, 64, 134
Stryker, Roy E., 324-30
Stumm-Halberg, Carl, Freiherr von, quoted, 194
Sumner, William Graham, 25
Syncretism, 75-78
Syrians in United States, 88

Taylor, John Edward, 157
Taylor, William Cooke, *The Natural History of Society,* 228
Technology, basis of social change, 246; influence on cultural forms, 236-38
Totalitarianism, 162

Thomas, W. I., and Znaniecki, F., *The Polish Peasant in Europe and America,* quoted, 88
Thoreau, Henry David, 254, 256, 268
Tractor, factor in collectivization, 136
Trade unions, 146, 157, 158, 159, 180
Tradition, disintegration in urban life, 238; role in Japan, 245 ff.; role in New England "flowering," 258, 264; rural aspect of American, 68; *see also* Culture
Transcendentalism, 259, 263
Tuckerman, Joseph, 263
Turner, Frederick Jackson, 344; "The Significance of the Frontier in American History," 235; quoted, 236
Turner, Ralph E., 228-42
Turner frontier hypothesis, 235, 279, 304, 305, 306

Uniformity, product of urban life, 239
Unitarianism, 253, 254, 259, 262, 268
United States: adaptation of immigrant to tradition, 68-70; conditions determining group relationships, 66-68; contemporary culture, 89; corporation in, 168-81; cultural debt to foreign-born, 75, 79-82; cultural groups in, 62-73; cultural tradition, 69-72; dialect areas, 331-45; ethnic group consciousness in, 63-66; history-writing from "Plymouth Rock" view, 87, 88; industrial culture, 72; local history, 275-86; nationality groups in, 74-89
United States Department of Agriculture, Farm Security Administration, 326
Urban association, 238-40
Urban milieu, impact of, 156 ff.
Utopias, 255, 259

Vagts, Alfred, 182-96
Vance, Rupert B., 294-99
Vaughan, Robert, 228, 229
Veblen, Thorstein, 23, 178
Volin, Lazar, 125-39

Wandering scholars, 203, 348, 350, 351
War, organization of national economy for, 184; psychological interpretation of, 37-40, 49; relation of army to, 182
Ware, Caroline F., 3-16, 62-73, 86-89
Warner, W. L., *Yankee City,* 27
Watson, Goodwin, 34-46
Webster, Noah, 332
Wehrwirtschaft, 184, 196
Welsh in United States, 76
Winther, Oscar Osburn, 84-86
Women, factory employment of, 148; position in Chinese family, 110, 119, 123; rights in zadruga, 100, 103, 104
Worcester, Joseph Emerson, 332
Works Progress Administration, Federal Writers' Project, 80, 87; Historical Records Survey, 281, 282, 285
Written records, inadequacy, 5, 8-9, 279

Yale College, 268, 270

Zadruga, characteristics, 99-108; communal system, 99 ff.; division of labor, 98, 108; effect of emigration on, 107; factors in break-down, 100, 101, 106-8; history, 95; in Albania, 107, 108; in Bosnia, 96, 100; in Bulgaria, 103; in Croatia, 96, 98, 99, 100-101, 102, 103, 107; in Dalmatia, 107; in Herzegovina, 100; in Montenegro, 108; in Rumania, 98; in Slavonia, 101, 104; land tenure, 100-108; personal income, 104, 105; small-family, 99-101; study of, 98; women's property rights, 100, 103, 104; types, 97 ff.
Znaniecki, F., *see* Thomas and Znaniecki

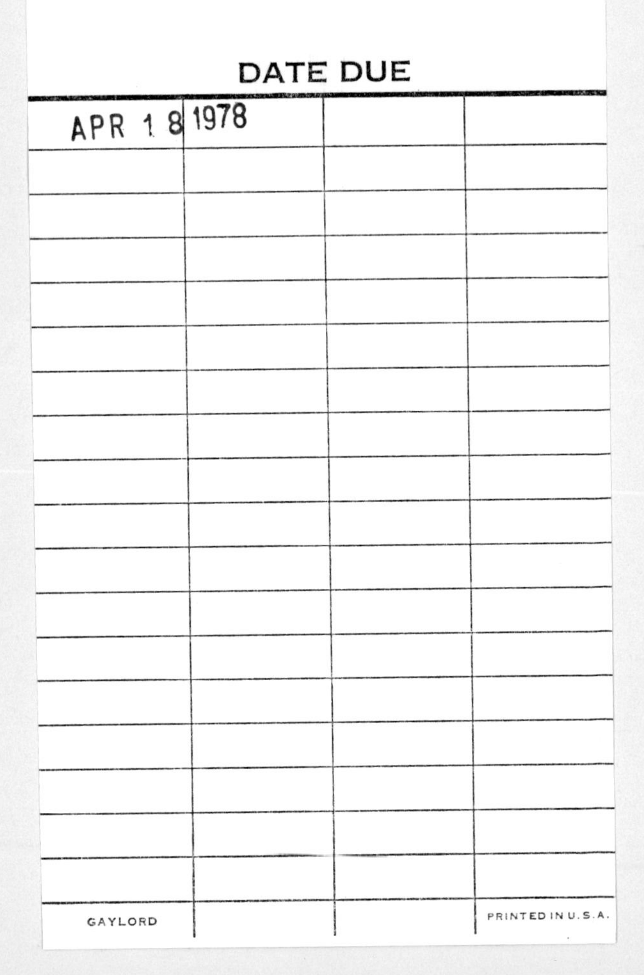

DATE DUE

APR 1 8 1978			